D1138013

CHRISTIAN POLITICAL ETHICS

THE ETHIKON SERIES IN COMPARATIVE ETHICS

—————————————— *Editorial Board* ——————————————

Carole Pateman,
Series Editor

Brian Barry   Sohail H. Hashmi   Philip Valera
Robert P. George   Will Kymlicka   Michael Walzer
                           David Miller

The Ethikon Series publishes studies on ethical issues of current importance. By bringing scholars representing a diversity of moral viewpoints into structured dialogue, the series aims to broaden the scope of ethical discourse and to identify commonalities and differences between alternative views.

TITLES IN THE SERIES

Brian Barry and Robert E. Goodin, eds.
*Free Movement: Ethical Issues in the Transnational Migration
of People and Money*

Chris Brown, ed.
Political Restructuring in Europe: Ethical Perspectives

Terry Nardin, ed.
The Ethics of War and Peace: Religious and Secular Perspectives

David R. Mapel and Terry Nardin, eds.
International Society: Diverse Ethical Perspectives

David Miller and Sohail H. Hashmi, eds.
Boundaries and Justice: Diverse Ethical Perspectives

Simone Chambers and Will Kymlicka, eds.
Alternative Conceptions of Civil Society

Nancy L. Rosenblum and Robert Post, eds.
Civil Society and Government

Sohail Hashmi, ed., Foreword by Jack Miles
Islamic Political Ethics: Civil Society, Pluralism, and Conflict

Richard Madsen and Tracy B. Strong, eds.
The Many and the One: Ethical Pluralism in the Modern World

Margaret Moore and Allen Buchanan, eds.
States, Nations, and Borders: The Ethics of Making Boundaries

CHRISTIAN POLITICAL ETHICS

EDITED BY

John A. Coleman, S.J.

PRINCETON UNIVERSITY PRESS   PRINCETON AND OXFORD

Copyright © 2008 by Princeton University Press

Published by Princeton University Press, 41 William Street, Princeton,
New Jersey 08540

In the United Kingdom: Princeton University Press, 3 Market Place,
Woodstock, Oxfordshire OX20 1SY

Library of Congress Cataloging-in-Publication Data
Christian political ethics / edited by John Coleman.
    p. cm. – (The Ethikon series in comparative ethics)
  Includes bibliographical references and index.
    ISBN 978-0-691-13140-5 (hardcover : alk. paper) – ISBN 978-0-691-13481-9 (pbk. : alk.
paper) 1. Christianity and politics. 2. Christian ethics. 3. Political ethics. I. Coleman,
John Aloysius, 1937–
  BR115.P7C37955 2007
  241'.62—dc22   2007012801

British Library Cataloging-in-Publication Data is available

This book has been composed in Palatino

Printed on acid-free paper. ∞

press.princeton.edu

Printed in the United States of America

10 9 8 7 6 5 4 3 2 1

Contents

PART IV: INTERNATIONAL SOCIETY

PART V: WAR AND PEACE

Preface _____

JOHN A. COLEMAN, S.J.

A lurking ambiguity lies just under the surface of the foundational texts of the New Testament about state, citizenship, and society. On the one hand, two key texts, Romans 13:1–7 and I Peter 2:13–14, insist that Christians should be "good citizens" within the Roman Empire. These texts serve, perhaps, as apologies from Christians to the surrounding, not necessarily benignly intentioned, pagan society, assuring it of Christian cooperative benevolence. The I Peter text states: "For the Lord's sake accept the authority of every human institution, whether of the emperor as supreme, or of governors, as sent by him to punish those who do wrong and to praise those who do right." Romans 13:1 asserts that the authority of government comes directly from God: "Obey the government, for God is the one who has put it there. There is no government anywhere that God has not placed in power." Elements of the same positive attitude toward the state and government can be found in the enigmatic and terse response of Jesus in Mark 12:13–17 about paying taxes to Caesar: "The things of Caesar give back to Caesar and the things of God to God." Clearly, the "things of Caesar" have some rightful autonomy, legitimacy, role in God's design—even if not under any tutorial sway from Christians. Just as clearly, there are "things of God" that escape the jurisdiction of Caesar.[1]

A very different attitude toward the Roman empire can be found in the Book of Revelation. A local official, it seems, in Western Asia Minor was promoting the cult of the emperor Domitian and of the goddess Roma (Rev. 13:1–18). A severe crisis of conscience broke out among the early Christians of Western Asia Minor when faced with the demand that they cooperate with this effort. So the writer of Revelation argues that Christians may not participate in this imperial cult, and in Revelation 17, John, the Seer, presents a particularly lurid description of the emperor as a beast and the goddess Roma as a prostitute. In Revelation the potential compatibility of the things of Caesar and the things of God is scrutinized and is found limping. Non cooperation and even resistance is urged. Finally, Acts 5:29 ("We ought to obey God rather than men") seems to authorize, sometimes, religious civil disobedience, although this authorization remains, probably, circumscribed and hedged. Thus, the foundational texts of the New Testament suggest, sometimes, cooperation and support of the state whose authority comes from God. Christians are called to be dutiful and good citizens. Other texts mandate possible clashes between the Christian moral conscience and the state (when the state commands things clearly against the commands of God). Revelation, it appears, allows resistance to the state. The early church claims an arena/domain that does not belong to the state: "the things of God."

We find the same ambiguity in the writings of the early Patristic period. Some writers adduce evidence of a kind of *semina verbi*, the seeds of the Word of God, already present in the pagan society, culture, and state. They denominate some pagans, especially those who lived before the birth of Christ, such as Socrates, as examples of an *anima naturalitur Christiana*—a soul who is connaturally (although unconsciously) Christian—one who acts with Christian virtues, perhaps even under the impulse of unconscious grace. This stance allows, again, cooperation, discernment, and joint action by Christians with non-Christians for the common good. On the other hand, some of the Patristic writings label, as Augustine did, the pagan virtues as, in reality, splendid vices. Tertullian could gasp, rhetorically: "What does Jerusalem have to do with Athens?"

These foundational texts and their alternative stances toward state and secular or pagan society recur and run their course throughout Christian history. So, too, do the three varied, ideal-typical, responses—repetitiously returning throughout Christian history—of Christians to issues of state and culture, limned by Troeltsch in his magisterial *The Social Teaching of the Christian Churches*. Troeltsch posits a threefold historical Christian orienting response to culture and the state: church, sect, mysticism. The Church orientation certainly involves, minimally, that Christians will cooperate with others for the common good of the society and state and that they will be dutiful citizens. It generally incorporates some notion of a natural law. After Constantine, the church orientation sometimes even came to mean a formative role of the Christian church to put its stamp of morality on society and the state. The sectarian response listens more keenly to the contrarian texts of the New Testament: to Revelations and Acts. It primarily bears witness, often as a counter-cultural witness. It nurtures a certain distrust and wariness about the state and the secular. The sect jealously guards its "things of God" from being contaminated by the "things of Caesar." Finally, Troeltsch's category of mysticism points to a kind of individualism, the soul's cleaving to the eternal and to God, little preoccupied with the fleeting vagaries of state and society. Every soul, whatever its historical context or conditioning, is equally close to or equidistant from God.[2]

In a sense, the essays in this volume reprise this trajectory of Christian reflection on state and society. Some of the chapters (Banner, Coleman, Stackhouse, Miller, Biggar, Finnis, Boyle) are closer to Troeltsch's church model; some (Koontz and Cartwright) to the sect model; and at least one, David Little's chapter on "Conscientious Individualism," has some affinities with the individual mystical mode of Troeltsch. With one exception, the chapters in this book were originally written for publication in earlier volumes of the Ethikon series, where they appeared alongside a rich variety of other perspectives (Islamic, Jewish, liberal, feminist, critical theory, Confucian, international law, natural law, and realism). The chapters here were written for volumes that explored the ethics of war and peace; international society; boundaries and justice; alternative conceptions of civil society; the relation of civil society and government; and the social management of ethical pluralism. A strikingly large number of the essays in this volume (ten of the thirteen) are, in fact, paired, and were originally already in close dialogue with one another.

Thus, these essays tend to mask a much richer dialogue by Christians with interlocutors of other ethical traditions. Such dialogue between Christian ethicists and moral thinkers from other religious or secular traditions is nothing new in Christian political ethics. It dates from the earliest Patristic period. Christians have usually held some variant of a doctrine of "human reason" that functions, alongside the divine commands of the Bible, as a source of human action, reflection, and discernment. There exists a long-standing Christian trope of the two books, the Bible and the "book" of nature, as sources for revelation and religious wisdom. Perhaps less obvious in the ethical dialogue as it appears, partially disguised, here is the way some important elements of secular thought had, originally, a religious or Christian provenance. Jeremy Waldron has recently argued, forcefully, that the secular legacy of John Locke on notions of equality depends on a very specific Christian warrant.[3] He reminds us of Locke's own awareness of this provenance of portions of the secular from originally Christian political thought: "Many are beholden to revelation who do not acknowledge it."[4]

Two seminal insights impel Christians to engage in political ethics. On the one hand, the utter sovereignty of God—that he is Lord—means that no human enterprise or arena escapes God's scrutiny, judgment, presence, providence, concern. Christians do not think that there are any authentically human acts (other than automatic responses) that do not also have moral implications. To carve out a domain of life that remains totally free of religious reflection and influence strikes Christians as a kind of practical atheism or idolatry, as if, for example, God could be called Lord of the Universe, yet be precluded from any mingling

with the economy, the state, or international law. Christians feel compelled to ask themselves: What is God doing and enabling in our concrete institutions, history, worlds? Christians, then, try to cooperate
with and sustain or further what they discern God is calling and enabling them to achieve in history, society, and the worlds of work.

On the other hand, as Max Stackhouse ably puts it: "Christianity is
driven into engagement with culture since it does not claim that its
sources contain all that is necessary to form the laws of society." Christianity has resources to bring to issues of economics, politics, culture,
and society, but it is not omni-competent or infallible. Christianity remains still a learning as well as a teaching body. Christian political
ethics contains a quasi-missionary or voluntarist impulse: the desire to
influence society in the direction of Christian virtues and institutions
compatible with Christian values. It also must exercise a necessary humility. Christians can and do learn from the secular, which, in their
view, is never totally morally neutral or simply secular. Fundamental
respect for persons as made in the image of God entails, as Little and
Skillen argue in their essays in this volume, respect for conscience. Conscientious differences confront Christians with the brute fact of ethical
pluralism.

A full-fledged Christian political ethics would treat of state and society; international law and international relations; the economy; ecology; the reality of marriage and family; medical issues of health, life,
and death; and questions of war and peace. It would state and defend,
theologically, principles of ethics; draw upon virtue theory to talk about
the virtues needed for a common life; and display a systematic reflection on how to apply principles and virtues to concrete, even hard,
cases (casuistry). Willy-nilly, Christians will address the family, politics,
culture, and the economy—the four principalities and powers Stackhouse evokes as Eros, Mars, the Muses, and Mammon in his chapter on
national civil societies in this volume. Most of the above issues are at
least touched upon in this book. The main subsections of the book are
"State and Civil Society," "Boundaries and Justice," "Pluralism," "International Society," and "War and Peace." The section on "State and
Civil Society" focuses on divergent Christian views of both state and
society—the remit and limits of each. Three essays address, in comple-
mentary but differing ways, the realities of state and civil society.
Michael Banner gives us an overview of both Catholic and Protestant
views of civil society, and at least alludes to Orthodox views. He masterfully limns for us the Augustinian, Aquinas, and Reformed positions. John Coleman presents a portrait of social Catholicism's vision of
state and civil society, and Max Stackhouse responds to Coleman's
essay by highlighting what he sees as the virtues in the Calvinist Reformed federal theology and its vision of spheres of creation.

In "Boundaries and Justice," Richard Miller and Nigel Biggar explore two visions of penultimate loyalty to one's own state and society: patriotism and civic loyalties. Both authors struggle with the value of limited loyalties, the tensions in Christianity between the legitimacy of nurturing a sense of place (the incarnational dimension), and the greater cosmopolitan thrust toward a Catholic universe (in the Greek sense of *Katholikos*, i.e., worldwide loyalties). Miller captures one pole in this tension between rootedness in place and cosmopolitanism: "Borders ask us to privilege local solidarities, but Christian *agape*, exemplified by Jesus's teaching and example, is altruistic and cosmopolitan." Borders should not trump hospitality and a wider love of neighbor. In the process of addressing boundaries in his chapter, Miller opens up larger issues touching on ownership and distribution of property, an option for the poor and ecological stewardship. Biggar nuances the position: "It is natural that individuals should feel special affection for, and loyalty toward, those communities that have cared for them and given them so much that is beneficial." In the end, believing in the incarnation, Christians affirm, claims Biggar, that "although transcending time and space, God is not alien to them. In this case what is transcended is not repudiated and may be inhabited."

The third section of the book, "Pluralism," contains two chapters. David Little and James Skillen spar on the issue of Christian acceptance, in principle, of pluralism. Both agree that Christians must honor and respect an honest, even if erroneous, conscience. This honor and respect has ramifications for law and a society tolerant of mores that diverge from the Christian vision. Both Little and Skillen, however, reject any species of relativism. In a sense, Little, who draws on a strand of natural law to mount his argument, also engages in casuistry, that is, the art of applying principles deftly, but with a systematic acumen, to concrete cases. Like the classical casuist, Little presents us with generalized—but not exceptionless—presumptive rules: "Reasons justifying policies that impinge closely on concerns protected by fundamental moral prohibitions have a much-reduced margin for error." Little's essay is a supple presentation of the Christian account of and concern for conscience. He evokes four cognitive standards to bring to the formation and adjudication of cases of conscience: (1) reviewing and consistently accounting for one's own basic commitments as they relate to the case at hand; (2) giving proper consideration to a fundamental universal moral law that underlies all consciences; (3) pursuing, evaluating, and applying all relevant factual data pertinent to the cases, and (4) clarifying all motives, flattering and unflattering, that might influence the verdict or its implementation.[5]

Skillen presses whether Little's account of the fundamental universal moral law might remain too general and too abstract and fail to encompass as much as should be included. Skillen also contests the appeal to conscience alone to generate the criterion by which to distinguish church from state, or family from state, or business from state. We need more than just conscience (even one rightly formed and conforming to the dictates of the natural law), Skillen argues, to demarcate the plurality of competencies and jurisdictions among institutional spheres. Both Little and Skillen, then, apply their account of a Christian acceptance of a diverse and plural world (but one that eschews relativism) to concrete moral dilemmas: suicide, for example, or the extension of civil liberties (including marriage rights) to homosexuals.

Globalization presents new challenges to Christian political ethics, although both Protestant and Catholic voices have been long actively engaged with questions of international law and relations. In the fourth section of the book, "International Society," Max Stackhouse evokes a vision of an international civil society, "global in scope, supporting a comprehensive vision of justice and developing a moral and spiritual network of trusting relations." Stackhouse argues that such an international global civil society may preserve us from some of the imperialism, ethnocentrism, and exploitation of crass nationalisms. Stackhouse transposes to global society his "spheres of creation" vision presented in the earlier chapter on national civil societies. John Coleman is less sanguine than Stackhouse about the extent and beneficence of nascent global civil society, but more hopeful about a global governance. Again appealing to social Catholicism, Coleman probes the new questions raised to it by the nascent phenomena of globalization. Both authors touch base with issues of international law (also broached earlier in Miller's essay on boundaries).

Because I am writing this preface in a time of a deeply contested war, I found the essays on war and peace challenging, compelling, and instructive. In the fifth section, "War and Peace," John Finnis explores classic just war theory and its permutations, which led to a limitation of justified reasons for war to legitimate defense. Joseph Boyle lifts up the argument why a state cannot easily engage in a justified war of punishment rather than mere defense: it serves as both judge and implicated party. Boyle reminds us that war is a paradigm case of coercive violence with variations (civil war, police action, humanitarian intervention, domestic policing) that raise questions quite similar to those which arise from the theory of just war. Boyle also champions the possibility of conscientious objection to wars (even just wars). Just war theory, by the nature of the case, takes the ethicist back to casuistry: how to apply principles to relevantly similar or cognate cases and how cases illuminate and even reshape the principles. Thus, the case of modern war restricts the classic just cause arguments for war.

Theodore Koontz and Michael Cartwright postulate that the kinds of questions we permit to guide our thinking about war and peace shape the resources upon which we can draw. Pacifists, nonviolent resisters, and those who advocate for abolition of war often have different notions about power and truth and the efficacy of nonviolent means than do just warriors or those who adhere to *realpolitik*. It makes a difference, too, if just warriors and pacifists dialogue about common assumptions as well as their disagreements. Both strands of ethical tradition envision true peace. Both are aware of a sinful world. Koontz contends that we need to pay more attention to building the peace than to asking when we may go to war. But just warriors, too, know of alternatives to war and a vision of an ultimately more peaceful world. The end of war—if it can ever be tolerated—is the establishment of peace. The U.S. Catholic Bishops' Letter on Peace, using just war reasoning, conspicuously contains a long section on the international order and alternatives to war.[6] Opponents of just war theory, however, remain very skeptical about the possibility of moral restraint in warfare, once it has begun. In an age that seems destined to fight—in some form—a long drawn-out "war against terror," the four essays in this section of the book are timely and topical.

These chapters show a coherence and a set of related themes about Christian responsibilities and citizenship; about civil disobedience; about the moral values brought to complex issues of international law and a globalizing society; about the perennial resort to coercive force to solve intractable violences. This collection also displays the inherent pluralism within the Christian tradition itself: Calvinist, Catholic, Anabaptist. As there are varieties of Christian pacifism, so there are varieties of Christian just war theories. All of the essays in this volume argue to the abiding relevance of Christian political ethics to issues of policy and political adjudication. They seek to confront and reshape novel situations, drawing on the traditions that have shaped Christianity. These essays attempt to take their Christian political ethics outside of the churches or ecclesial academies to engage the issues and forge more reasonable and humane solutions to world problems, much as do those who are more secular in their orientation.

An earlier volume in the Ethikon series, *Islamic Political Ethics: Civil Society, Pluralism, and Conflict*, culled the previously published essays about Islam in the Ethikon series and found that they made an important independent contribution as a collection. The editor presumes the same is true of the Christian essays now collected from the various Ethikon volumes. In the end, the reader jumping in *in medias res* will find herself grappling with the kinds of questions that engage the struggle for a humane civil life and society.

The trustees of the Ethikon Institute join with Philip Valera, president, Carole Pateman, series editor, and the volume editor in thanking
all who contributed to the development of this book. In addition to the
authors and the original volume editors, special thanks are due to the
Ahmanson Foundation, The Pew Charitable Trusts, the Sidney Stern
Memorial Trust, the Doheny Foundation, the Carnegie Council on
Ethics and International Affairs, and Joan Palevsky for their generous
support of the various Ethikon dialogue projects from which these essays and other books emerged. Finally, we wish to express our thanks
to Ian Malcolm, our editor at Princeton University Press, for his valuable guidance and support.

Information on Sources

Chapter 1 was first published in *Alternative Conceptions of Civil Society*, ed.
Simone Chambers and Will Kymlicka (Princeton: Princeton University
Press, 2002), 113–30.

Chapters 2 and 3 were first published in *Civil Society and Government*, ed.
Nancy L. Rosenblum and Robert Post (Princeton: Princeton University
Press, 2002), 223–64.

Chapters 4 and 5 were first published in *Boundaries and Justice*, ed. David
Miller and Sohail H. Hashmi (Princeton: Princeton University Press, 2001),
15–54.

Chapters 6 and 7 were originally published in *The Many and the One*, ed.
Richard Madsen and Tracy B. Strong (Princeton: Princeton University
Press, 2003), 229–68.

Chapter 8 was originally published in *International Society*, ed. David R. Mapel
and Terry Nardin (Princeton: Princeton University Press, 1998), 201–14.

Chapters 10, 11, 12, and 13 were originally published in *The Ethics of War and
Peace*, ed. Terry Nardin (Princeton: Princeton University Press, 1996), 15–53
and 169–213.

Notes

1. John Donahue, S.J., and Daniel J. Harrington, S.J., *The Gospel of Mark* (Collegeville, Minn.: Liturgical Press, 2002), 343–48, treats Mark 12:13–17 on the
temple tax and compares it to Romans 13:1–7, I Peter 2:13–14, and Revelation 17.
2. Ernst Troeltsch, *The Social Teaching of the Christian Churches*, trans. Olive
Wyon, 2 vols. (New York: Macmillan, 1931).

3. Jeremy Waldron, *God, Locke and Equality: Christian Foundations in Locke's Political Thought* (New York: Cambridge University Press, 2002).

4. Cited in Jon Tasioulas's review of Waldron, *God, Locke and Equality*, in *The Times Literary Supplement*, Nov. 12, 2004, p. 17.

5. For classical understandings of casuistry and attempts at modern retrievals of it, cf. Albert Jonsen and Stephen Toulmin, *The Abuse of Casuistry: A History of Moral Reasoning* (Berkeley: University of California Press, 1988); and Richard Miller, *Casuistry and Modern Ethics* (Chicago: University of Chicago Press, 1996).

6. "The Challenge of Peace: God's Promise and Our Response," 1983 Pastoral Letter of the United States Bishops' Conference, in David O'Brien and Thomas Shannon, eds., *Catholic Social Thought: The Documentary Heritage* (Maryknoll, N.Y.: Orbis Press, 1992). This document (nos. 200–273, pp. 535–51) presents detailed suggestions about specific steps to reduce the danger of war (including the resort to nonviolent alternatives) and shaping an international order to guarantee a more peaceful world.

Part I _____

STATE AND CIVIL SOCIETY

1

Christianity and Civil Society

MICHAEL BANNER

IN ITS CONTEMPORARY USAGE the term *civil society* typically refers to the totality of structured associations, relationships, and forms of cooperation between persons that exist in the realm between the family and the state. Where such patterns of association, cooperation, and structured relationships are thought to be weak or inconsequential, as in the corporatist East of yesteryear (where individuals are said to have related chiefly to the State) or as in the capitalist and individualistic West (where personal relationships may arguably occur only within the family, and perhaps not even there), it has become commonplace to lament the nonexistence of civil society. Christianity, it is usually supposed, will be prominent among the mourners on whichever side of the globe the wake is observed.

I shall suggest in this chapter, however, that the relationship of Christian thought to the question of civil society is a matter of some complexity. This complexity is not a matter of the simple muddle that occurs where the ambiguities of the term *civil society* are not recognized and addressed, but has to do with the history and variety of Christian social thought. Obviously enough, the tradition of Christian thought about society and community predates questions concerning the existence, character, and qualities of civil society, without thereby having nothing to say in answer to them. Thus, though one might, in delineating a Christian conception of civil society, chart only the reactions of Christian thought to the rise of civil society under the patronage of modern liberalism, the intellectual roots of any such reactions would not necessarily emerge clearly into view, and thus the reactions might seem somewhat thinner than they really is. Such an approach might also conceal the stimulus that Christianity itself gave to the emergence of civil society in its modern form. The tradition of Christian social thought is, however, not just lengthy but also varied. Even if its different strands possess, naturally, a certain family resemblance, it is not monolithic. There is, then, nothing that can be identified as the Christian answer to the question of civil society. Rather, there is a tradition of social thought that, in its different versions, is relevant to the questions posed by the modern debate about the existence, character, and qualities of civil society.

In the light of these considerations, this chapter approaches the task of answering some of these questions by attempting to outline particular and important moments in this tradition, taking as a point of departure Augustine's understanding of the two cities, which, as I shall point out, is questioned in different ways by Thomas and Calvin, and reconceived by Luther. In turn, the Lutheran reconception of the Augustinian approach is, it will be noted, criticized in the work of such figures as Bonhoeffer and Barth, while the Thomist tradition is developed in the social teaching of the Roman Magisterium. Attention will be drawn to the implications of these different approaches for contemporary questions regarding civil society, though the survey can, at best, be illustrative and not exhaustive.

Ingredients

The question "Who or what does civil society include?" has been posed from within the Christian tradition as a question, in effect, about where and in what form society is instantiated. And one influential answer from within the Christian tradition to that question is, in brief, "the church," since outside that community, social relations, public or private in modern terms, lack characteristics or qualities essential to them. Though this Augustinian answer was highly influential, it was in turn, however, as we must presently indicate, contested or reconceived, giving rise to different answers, or at least different emphases, in Christian thinking about the nature of human community.

Crucial to the thought of the New Testament in general, and the thought of Paul in particular, is the contrast underlying Paul's exhortation to the Romans: "Do not be conformed to this world, but be transformed by the renewal of your mind."[1] The character and significance of this contrast must, however, be properly understood. Wolin gets it right when, having cited this verse, he comments:

> This attitude must not be understood as mere alienation or the expression of an unfulfilled need to belong. Nor is it to be accounted for in terms of the stark contrasts that Christians drew between eternal and temporal goods, between the life of the spirit held out by the Gospel and the life of the flesh symbolized by political and social relationships. What is fundamental to an understanding of the entire range of [early] Christian political attitudes was that they issued from a group that regarded itself as already in a society, one of far greater purity and higher purpose: "a chosen generation, a royal priesthood, an holy nation, a peculiar people."[2]

Wolin is also right to observe of a much-used and misused text that "the critical significance of the Pauline teaching [in Rom. 13] was that it brought the political order within the divine economy and thereby compelled its confrontation by Christians."[3]

Given such roots, it is hardly surprising that a dominant strand in the Christian tradition has thought about society by means of a contrast between two kingdoms, realms, or—as in the locus classicus of Christian social thought, Augustine's *City of God*—between two cities. According to Augustine,

> although there are many great peoples throughout the world, living under different customs in religion and morality and distinguished by a complex variety of languages, arms and dress, it is still true that there have come into being only two main divisions, as we may call them, in human society: and we are justified in following the lead of our Scriptures and calling them two cities.[4]

What is here characterized as a division *within* society is for Augustine in another sense, however, a division *between* societies, only one of which properly deserves the name. That this is a division between societies is the force of the use of the word *city* to mark the two divisions, since, employed where in Greek one might read *polis*, the word serves to indicate all-encompassing communities. The two cities, that is to say—the city of God (sometimes the heavenly city) and the earthly city—are to be understood as two polities, "two political entities coexistent in one space and time," "distinct social entities, each with its principle . . . and each with its political expression, Roman empire and church."[5] But these distinct "social entities," in virtue of their different origins, histories, and ends, are to be contrasted more starkly still; for if we quibbled with the notion that the division between the two cities was one within society, and noted that it is actually a division between societies, we must also reckon with the fact that one of these is for Augustine the form, here on earth, of the one true society, whereas the other is a society only in a superficial sense. How so?

"The two cities," says Augustine, "were created by two kinds of love: the earthly city was created by self-love reaching the point of contempt for God, the Heavenly City by the love of God carried as far as contempt of self."[6] Now the difference in ends or objects of love creates two quite different cities: "The citizens of each of these [two cities] desire their own kind of peace, and when they achieve their aim, this is the peace in which they live."[7] The heavenly city, united in love of God, enjoys a peace that "is a perfectly ordered and perfectly harmonious fellowship in the enjoyment of God and mutual fellowship in God."[8] The earthly city also desires peace, but its peace is of a different kind.

The citizens of the earthly city, in a prideful love of self over love of God, have each rejected the rule of God and chosen in preference a self-rule as intolerant of any other rule as it is of God's; for "pride is a perverted imitation of God . . . [that] hates a fellowship of equality under God, and seeks to impose its own dominion on fellow men, in place of God's rule. This means that it hates the just peace of God, and loves its own peace of injustice."[9] The love of self becomes, then, that *libido dominandi*, or lust for domination, that has driven the Roman Empire. Peace is achieved through the imposition of one's own will by the exercise of force, and is at once costly in its creation,[10] unjust in its character,[11] and unstable in its existence.[12] This is not to say that there is no difference between the Roman Empire and a band of brigands, to refer to Augustine's infamous jibe,[13] but it is to say that the peace of all other societies is different in kind from the just and certain peace of the true society found in the city of God, represented here on earth in the church, which is the city of God "on pilgrimage."[14]

The implications of Augustine's thought for the question of where, and in what form, society is instantiated are brought out in Joan Lockwood O'Donovan's summary of his argument:

> Augustine's polarising of the two cities . . . radically questioned the sense in which the social relations belonging to the *sacculum*, the passing order of the world, could be thought to comprise a society, a unity in plurality or harmonised totality. For on his view the secular *res publica* is not a true community knit together by charity and consensus in right—that is present only where faith in Christ and obedience to His law of love bind persons together—but a fragile and shifting convergence of human wills with respect to limited categories of earthly goods in a sea of moral disorder, of personal and group hostilities.[15]

Society, properly so called, exists in the city of God, and not in the earthly city. And so too civil society—for if the grounds for a stable structure of association and cooperation are certainly lacking for the whole, they are finally lacking for simple human associations as such.

The claim that society, properly understood, exists in the church is lost, however, if the theme of the "two cities" as Augustine develops it is transposed by an interpretation of the two cities as two spheres, a move associated with Lutheranism (if not quite so certainly with Luther).[16] Such a move dissolves the tension between the differently characterized cities by construing their relationship in terms of a functional division concerning, say, the worldly and the spiritual, or outer and inner. With the imagery thus construed, it becomes possible for the church to understand itself as an instance of civil society, rather than as its locus. But this is just what is prohibited in Augustine's thought, in which the two cities are not related spatially, to use Bonhoeffer's term,[17] but temporally or eschatologically; that is to say, the cities do not rule *over* different *spheres,* but rather, ruling over the same spheres, rule *in* different, albeit overlapping, *times.*[18] Just because of this overlap, the city of God must seek its distinctive peace amid the earthly peace and will make use of it as it makes use of earthly things in general (and thus has grounds for distinguishing between the different forms of the earthly city insofar as they do or do not prove useful to its purpose). But this overlap does not license the granting of autonomy, if one may put it so, to the earthly city. Coming at the point from the other side, one can agree with Markus when he observes that according to the Augustinian picture, "there was no need for Christians to be set apart sociologically, as a community separated from the 'world,' . . . uncontaminated by it and visibly 'over against the world.' On the contrary: the Christian community was, quite simply, the world redeemed and reconciled."[19] Monasticism (at least in its distinctly Augustinian theory in the *Rule of St. Benedict,* if not in its later, less-Augustinian practice) maintains this insight, presupposing not an autonomy of spheres (and thus, in our terms, that there are versions of society), but rather that the monastery, which was first of all a lay movement, displays the secular (i.e., temporal) form of society, of which the earthly city is but a sorry caricature.

If Luther subtly reconceives the Augustinian picture, Thomas and Calvin offer more straightforward challenges to it, while Orthodoxy developed independent of it, though struggling with essentially the same issues and problems. Although Augustine was writing at a time when Christianity had become the official and favored religion of the Empire, it was chiefly in Byzantium that the "conversion of the state" led to a radical questioning of the contrast between civil church and uncivil society, to put it in modern terms, that belongs to early Christian thought. This conversion did not unsettle Augustine's picture: the earthly city had not become the city of God "merely because the kings serve it [i.e., the church], wherein lies greater and more perilous temptations."[20] In the East this sense of danger or tension was not always maintained, even if the charge of "caesaropapism" (i.e., the subordination of the church to political rule) risks ignoring some of the subtleties involved, or at least the predominantly pragmatic character of the handling of these issues. It does, however, indicate the danger to which Orthodoxy has seemed especially prone, at least to Western eyes; that is, of having a "charismatic understanding of the state" that "lacked political realism,"[21] and that thus too readily assumed the possibility of Christian society outside the immediate life of the church. Arguably Eastern monasticism, like its Western counterpart, preserved a rather different perspective.[22]

In the West, "the alternative theological answers . . . to the Augustinian problematic of secular society are," to cite Joan Lockwood O'Donovan again, "the Thomistic-Aristotelian rejection of it and the Calvinist-Puritan conversion of it."[23] She continues:

> Under Aristotelian influence St. Thomas exchanged the Augustinian conception of a conflictual and disjunctive social order for a more organically harmonious one. His minimising of the spiritual distance between the traditionally "pre-lapsarian" institutions such as marriage and family and the post-lapsarian institutions such as private property and political rule enabled him to weave social life into a unified moral texture. He viewed sinful society as retaining the inherent harmony of a hierarchy of natural ends and functions, each part having its appointed place within the teleological whole. With no disjunctive division between different communities, especially between political and non-political communities, all together constituted a real social totality, a common will directed toward a common good.

For Calvin the handling of Augustine was different:

> Unlike St. Thomas, Calvin's response to the Augustinian problematic of secular society was a reorientation rather than a displacement of it. For Calvin the disorder of sinful social relations could not be mitigated by an appeal to a natural social teleology, but required a different conception of order: a more exclusively political/juridical one based immediately on God's providential rule over sinful humanity and elaborated in the (largely Old Testament) ideas of divine-human covenant, divine commandment and divinely established offices. The unity of civil as well as of ecclesiastical society depended on their institutional structuring by God's commandments that defined the rights and duties of every social "office" as a vehicle of His revealed law in the creation and redemption of the world.

Society

According to the tradition that flows from Augustine, then, civil society as genuine society—that is, even minimally, as a stable structure of association and cooperation between persons—exists in the city of God, or in the church that is, here and now, its imperfect token. In contrast with this society, all other associations are radically defective. But what makes the church, or the city of God, itself a society and not a simple aggregate?

It might be supposed that this is not a problem, or not a very severe problem, within the Augustinian framework, simply because in identifying the church as society we avoid the issue that must arise for those who think of society as variously realized and manifested and thus as having parts. This supposition would, however, be mistaken for two reasons. In the first place, even of the church it can be asked what unites its members. Furthermore, and in the second place, in stressing that talk of "two cities" does not presuppose a division of spheres—that is, to repeat Markus's formulation of Augustine's viewpoint, that "the Christian community was, quite simply, the world redeemed and reconciled"—attention is drawn to the fact that the life of the church might be expected itself to be differentiated, since it will comprise more than those functions that might be attributed to a church by a contemporary sociologist. Thus Bonhoeffer, for example, to be regarded as a modern exponent of this tradition, thinks of the Christian life as structured according to "divine mandates," including labor (or culture), marriage, and government, and the first of these may involve patterns and instances of association and cooperation that will raise a question as to the coordination or unity of what is in another sense a single society.

In his dispute with the Donatists, Augustine came to stress order, sacraments, and doctrine, and most importantly baptism, as what renders real within the church the rule of Christ, and thus unites the church as one body. This rule of Christ within the life of the church in, or rather as, the world brings unity to this differentiated society as each of its members uses everything for the sake of a higher end, namely, God.

For the Thomist tradition, which thinks of society as existing outside the church in virtue of the claims made upon human life by its natural ends, it is the common good that serves to unite its parts. The classical organic image of society thus maintains its naturalistic quality, with a special emphasis, however, on the need for the head to identify the common good and coordinate its pursuit.[24] The sense in which the unity of society is an achievement is heightened in Calvin's conception. Order for Calvin, as Wolin points out, "required a constant exercise of power,"[25] though here the instrument of its realization is not a single head, but a wider structure of institutions and offices. This structuring of Christian society, giving participation a more crucial role than any direct and individual rule, whether in matters civil or more narrowly ecclesiastical, was to have significant consequences for the growth and development of civil society in the particular sense in which that term is now most often used. It was in the Calvinist congregations of New England that there developed a practice of association, cooperation, and self-government that was determined to protect the social space thus revealed, occupied, and mapped out against encroachment by the state. This space is, of course, the space of civil society as it is classically conceived, and its imagining has roots, as we shall have cause to note again, in Reformation thought and perhaps even further back in the Christian tradition.

Values

Though Thomas and Augustine may have looked for society in different places, and expected it to be sustained in different ways, there was
no difference between them in believing that the good or value of such
society (within the church in Augustine's account, or outside it in
Thomas's) lies precisely in its sociality, since it is in sociality that the
human good is realized.

Augustine had been tempted to represent the good life as a neo-
Platonic quest with contemplation at its core. As he distanced himself
from these philosophic roots, however, he came to stress the thoroughly
social character of human life. Thus, though the earthly city is contrasted with the city of God, the contrast is not between the sociality of
one and the asociality of the other, but rather between the doubtful
sociality of one and the true sociality of the other, a sociality with a horizontal as well as a vertical dimension. The heavenly city, we will recall,
united in love of God, enjoys a peace that "is a perfectly ordered and
perfectly harmonious fellowship in the enjoyment of God and *mutual
fellowship in God.*"

Thomas's grounding in Aristotle required a move in the other direction, so to speak: not in explicit recognition of the value of society, but
rather a modest qualification of the assumption in its favor. (Thus in his
commentary on the *Politics,* in glossing Aristotle's reflection on the
"monstrous," we might say "inhuman," condition of those deprived of
society and isolated from political life, Thomas, as D'Entrèves puts it,
"finds it necessary to make an express reservation with regard to ascet-
icism, in favour of the idea of a higher degree of perfection to be at-
tained by retiring from the world rather than by participating in it. But
he is at pains to emphasize the exceptional character of a life of this
kind, and the necessity, for the attainment of such an ideal, of more than
human capacities."[26]) But however that may be, the essential agreement
between Thomas and Augustine is evidenced in the former employing
the latter's argument in justifying or explaining the prohibition of incest.
According to Thomas, an end of marriage is "the binding together of
mankind and the extension of friendship: for a husband regards his
wife's kindred as his own. Hence it would be prejudicial to this extension of friendship if a man could take a woman of his kindred to wife
since no new friendship would accrue to anyone from such a marriage.
Wherefore, according to human law and the ordinances of the Church,
several degrees of consanguinity are debarred from marriage."[27] Here
he simply repeats the reasoning of Augustine when he explains why,
apart from in the first generations, men were forbidden to take their
sisters as wives: "The aim was that one man should not combine many

relationships in his one self, but that those connections should be separated and spread among individuals, and that in this way they should
help to bind social life more effectively by involving in their plurality a
plurality of persons."[28] (What is striking here is that the freedom of
marriage, which the church vigorously maintained in other ways, gives
way before the good of the extension of sociality.)

The good of sociality is, then, a presupposition of both these streams
of thought within the Christian tradition. And, according to Leo XIII in
Rerum Novarum, it is the fact that this is a good that explains the existence of civil society in the modern sense, as well as in its older sense:
"Just as man is led by [a] natural propensity to associate with others in
a political society, so also he finds it advantageous to join with his fel-
lows in other kinds of societies, which though small and not independent are nonetheless true societies."[29] Thus "the natural sociability of
men" is held to be the principle from which both the state and private
associations are born and the good that they serve, and this prior
grounding of both determines the relationship between them: "It is by
virtue of the law of nature that men may enter into private societies and
it is for the defence of that law, not its destruction, that the state comes
into being."[30]

In the Thomist tradition, however, this "natural propensity" to association in society and societies has been understood as more than a
tendency to mere association. Rather, it is a tendency to association in
societies that presuppose and foster that community of purpose, interest, and sympathy that is expressed by the notion of solidarity. It is on
the basis of such anthropological presuppositions that modern Roman
Catholic social thought from *Rerum Novarum* on (through, for example,
Pius XI's *Quadragesimo Anno* and down to John Paul II's *Laborem Exer-
cens*) has offered a critique of liberalism and socialism that both, though
in different ways, deny the naturalness of human solidarity. Free-market
liberalism is thought to conceive of humanity as made up of competitive individuals lacking a common good distinct from the aggregate of
individual preferences. Socialism seems no less to doubt the naturalness of social solidarity, albeit that the conflictual character of society is
a matter of class, rather than individual, interests and is, furthermore,
not intrinsic, but is historically conditioned and contingent.

The recent *Catechism* of the Roman Catholic church extends this
analysis somewhat by finding what we might think of as a hierarchy of
values in society, each serving the human good. In the first place the
Catechism offers what seems like a pragmatic reason for "socialization"
(meaning here "the creation of voluntary associations and institutions . . .
'on both national and international levels, which relate to economic and
social goals, to cultural and recreational activities, to sport, to various

professions, and to political affairs'"[31]), namely, that it "expresses the natural tendency for human beings to associate with one another for the sake of attaining objectives that exceed individual capacities."[32] In the second place, however, in mentioning again humankind's natural sociability and thus entertaining the thought that human society is an end in itself, it goes on to connect "socialization" with a further good:

> The human person needs to live in society. Society is not for him an extraneous addition but a requirement of his nature. Through the exchange with others, mutual service and dialogue with his brethren, man develops his potential; he thus responds to his vocation.[33]

Elsewhere it is said that the "vocation of man" is "made up of divine charity and human solidarity,"[34] just because "the human person is . . . ordered to God" as well as to others.[35] The *Catechism* notes in addition, however, that "[a]ll men are called to the same end: God himself" and that "there is a certain resemblance between the union of the divine persons and the fraternity that men are to establish among themselves in truth and love."[36]

The further good that might be found in human society in virtue of this "resemblance" has been more central to Protestant thought that, if it affirms the "natural sociability" of human kind, does so not on the basis of supposed knowledge of the natural law, but more definitely on the basis of a theological anthropology. For Karl Barth, for example, that "the humanity of man consists in the determination of his being as a being with the other" is a counterpart of the prior fact of humankind's calling to be the covenant-partner of God.[37] Thus here the value that might be attributed to civil society is found not only in its satisfying human sociability or solidarity as such, but in the fact of this human sociability and solidarity being a likeness of, and a preparation for, the sociability and solidarity of the life of God, into which humans are called. The value of civil society is for this tradition, then, firmly eschatological, so we might say.

Risks

In recent Roman Catholic teaching the risks associated with civil society are the risks associated with society itself, namely, that higher levels of association will tend to deprive lower levels of association and individuals of their proper responsibilities. According to Pius XI in *Quadragesimo Anno*:

> Just as it is gravely wrong to take from individuals what they can accomplish by their own initiative and industry and give it to the community, so also it is

an injustice and at the same time a grave evil and disturbance of right order to assign to a greater and higher association what lesser and subordinate organizations can do. For every social activity ought of its very nature to furnish help to the members of the body social, and never destroy and absorb them.[38]

This wrong is to be prevented by respect for the principle of subsidiarity (a term first employed in Pius's encyclical, though plainly the idea is much older). This principle, which functions as a balance to the emphasis on the common good that had been central to *Rerum Novarum*, states that

a community of a higher order should not interfere in the internal life of a community of a lower order, depriving the latter of its functions, but rather should support it in case of need and help to co-ordinate its activity with the activities of the rest of society, always with a view to the common good.[39]

The *Catechism* offers a theological rationale for this principle, which protects civil society against the state, but also individuals against civil society:

God has not willed to reserve to himself all exercise of power. He entrusts to every creature the functions it is capable of performing, according to the capacities of its own nature. This mode of governance ought to be followed in social life. The way God acts in governing the world, which bears witness to such great regard for human freedom, should inspire the wisdom of those who govern human communities. They should behave as ministers of divine providence.[40]

Thus behaving, those with authority will acknowledge the existence of lower authorities and the rights of the individual, a theme that has been increasingly important in Roman Catholic social thought of the last fifty years and that features prominently in the *Catechism*, even though there is some evidence (in *Evangelium Vitae*, for example) of a growing sense of the need to bring some order and discipline to a mode of discourse that has given us rights to abortion, to die, and so on.

The Augustinian tradition, as we have seen, was suspicious of the exercise of power because of the fundamental corruption of the human will. Societies and associations, at whatever level, may provide occasions for domination and oppression. (Liberation theology is, in a sense, an heir to this tradition and has sought to supplement and strengthen it by learning from the Marxist critique of society and civil society. The complaint against it from some of its critics, however, has been that it has not related what it has learned from Marx to the major themes of Christian doctrine, but rather has allowed the latter to be replaced by, or wholly subordinated to, other categories and concepts.) The Augustinian tradition has addressed and characterized the risks that societies pose, however, not by the formulation of an abstract principle, such as the principle of subsidiarity, nor necessarily by an elaboration of an account of human rights. Apart from anything else, to have taken this route might appear to treat the two brackets, so to speak, of the modern discussion of civil society (namely, the state and the individual in his or her privacy) as themselves autonomous and beyond criticism, when against the command of God they can possess no such autonomy. The command of God is in principle, in a manner of speaking, totalitarian, as the monastic rules we have already referred to presuppose in opening the whole of the life of ruled (monks) and ruler (abbot) to the Rule.

If, however, there is a suspicion of the principle of subsidiarity and rights, it is plain enough that the totalitarian character of the rule of God itself provides a basis for a critique of all social institutions and associations, a point that was formulated with a certain clarity and force in the *Barmen Declaration* of 1934. This document can be seen as a protest at the tendency of Lutheranism, having converted Augustine's two cities into two spheres, to accord a certain independence to the state and civil society as concerned with the outer and not the inner life, which is the concern of the church. In Luther's most important treatment of this matter, the distinction is used to "safeguard religion against the unwelcome attentions of ungodly princes,"[41] and thus (by the way and to mention another occasion when Christian thought is found at the origins of civil society) provides arguments that would later be taken over almost *tout court* by advocates of religious toleration.[42] But the distinction of spheres seemed also to deny to the church, in principle, the right to offer a critique of action in the public realm, even when that action involved, as here, the determination of the limits and character of society by myths of *Volk*, blood, and soil. Against such a distinction the *Barmen Declaration* asserts that "Jesus Christ is . . . God's vigorous announcement of his claim upon our whole life" and that "through him there comes to us joyful liberation from the godless ties of this world," and rejects "the false doctrine that there could be areas of our life in which we would belong not to Jesus Christ but to other lords, areas in which we would not need justification and sanctification through him."[43] As Torrance comments: "[T]o confess the Lordship of Christ over all areas of life (intellectual and cultural, ecclesial and civil) means that, in the light of the Gospel, we are unconditionally obliged to be true to and obedient to the One who is in his person God's Word to humankind. Culture, therefore, may neither determine the sphere of the Gospel nor relativise its imperatives but, conversely, culture and society require to be perceived, interpreted and evaluated critically in the light of the Gospel."[44] (This point will be important in relation to the issue of freedom, treated below.)

If the Protestant tradition has had cause to recapture a sense of its critical responsibility toward society, civil or otherwise, the Roman tradition, which has perhaps never lost this sense, has had cause to consider whether its own hierarchies, structures, and government are themselves in need of critical examination in the light of the principles of subsidiarity and a proper respect for the individual that have been used to examine secular society. Since Vatican II, at least, there has been a wide recognition that if society and civil society pose certain risks to the individual, so too may certain understandings of the church and of its "Magisterium" (i.e., teaching office and authority).[45] The disputes within Roman Catholicism concerning the bearers of this authority and its scope point to the fact that the principle of subsidiarity is not so much a rule by which precise boundaries can be determined, as a general caution against interventions from above except as a last resort.

Responsibility

We have already seen how the principle of subsidiarity focuses the question as to who is to do what in civil society. According to this norm, responsibility is to remain at the lowest level from state to individual, provided that its remaining there is compatible with the common good. This serves, subject to interpretation and judgment, to attribute responsibilities to individuals, families, local communities and associations, and so on, to vindicate them in their different roles and, against certain understandings of its duties, to restrain the state. Of course the interpretation of this principle is a matter of contention, as we have noted, and no more so, perhaps, than in relation to the discussion of the market that stimulated the encyclicals that first brought the theme of subsidiarity to attention. While a libertarian approach is likely to think that responsibility for human well-being lies with the individual pursuing his or her interests in the marketplace, on certain interpretations of the principle of subsidiarity and on certain understandings of the common good, this responsibility does not lie at this level alone but is shared with others, including the state.

Within Protestant thought the question of responsibilities is handled in effect by means of a theme already mentioned, namely, that of the so-called mandates or orders of creation. Reflection on this theme is an attempt to elaborate an ethic that takes seriously the fact, as Brunner puts it, that

> [t]he world, that which is not "I," is not something material, needing to be shaped and moulded by us. To think it is betrays an impertinent, arrogant habit of mind springing from the delusion that man is a god. The world is not a shapeless mass of matter, it is not a chaos which we have to reduce to form and order. It was formed long ago: it is given to us in a rich variety of form. In its *form* the will of God is stamped upon that which exists. We ought to understand this existing shape or order as the expression of the Divine Will. . . . We are to range ourselves within this order.[46]

According to Brunner, the order we are called to respect does not consist only in "our natural existence, but also . . . [in] our historical existence." Thus, when he claims that "[r]everence for the Creator, whose work, in spite of all human perversion, is the one existing reality, demands as our first reaction obedience to the existing order, and grateful acceptance of the goodness of the Creator in the orders, through which alone He makes it possible for us to serve our neighbour, and, indeed, to live at all,"[47] he means by the "orders" something more than the mere biological givens of human existence. He means, in fact, "those existing facts of human corporate life which lie at the root of all historical life as unalterable presuppositions, which, although their historical forms may vary, are unalterable in their fundamental structure, and, at the same time, relate and unite men to one another in a definite way."[48] Brunner names five such orders: the family, the state, culture, the church, and the economic order, and concludes that "the Command of God comes to us related to these orders of reality . . . [and] can be perceived in and through them."[49]

Brunner's handling of this theme was the cause of considerable controversy; Barth (sharply and with some imprecision) and Bonhoeffer (sympathetically and with more care) took exception to it.[50] The details of this controversy need not trouble us, since what is important to note here is that in seeking to handle the theme better, Brunner's critics share the underlying conviction that provides the basis of his concern, namely, that the created order possesses a good that makes a moral demand on us and on our ordering of social life. This has the implication for Bonhoeffer that even if government is itself, or has, a mandate, "[i]t is not creative. It preserves what has already been created, maintaining it in the order which is assigned to it through the task which is imposed by God. It protects it by making law to consist in the acknowledgement of the divine mandates and by securing respect for this law by the force of the sword. Thus [for example] the governing authority is not the performer but the witness and guarantor of marriage."[51]

The seeming specificity of the principle of subsidiarity may be lacking, and the need to develop a fuller account of the parts of society and their relationship may be obvious, but what is also evident is that the Protestant treatment of the ethics of creation leads to a belief in a differentiated society, with various responsibilities lying with different forms of social life that extend from the individual to the state.

Freedom

Again, the principle of subsidiarity, which has already been stated, provides a way of approaching the question of the appropriate balance between individual autonomy and the organizations and associations of society. It is plain here, however, that the interpretation of its precise requirements is a matter of some difficulty, as is evident when the *Catechism* asserts that the "right to the exercise of freedom . . . must be recognised and protected by civil authority within the limits of the common good and public order."[52] What is equally plain is that the freedom which is here in question is a freedom within or under the moral law, and not the absolute freedom of those versions of liberalism that the affirmation of solidarity was meant to preclude. According to *Evangelium Vitae:*

> When freedom, out of a desire to emancipate itself from all forms of tradition and authority, shuts out even the most obvious evidence of an objective and universal truth, which is the foundation of personal and social life, then the person ends up by no longer taking as the sole and indisputable point of reference for his own choices the truth about good and evil, but only his subjective and changeable opinion or, indeed, his selfish interest and whim. This view of freedom leads to a distortion of life in society. If the promotion of the self is understood in terms of absolute autonomy, people inevitably reach the point of rejecting one another. Everyone else is considered an enemy from whom one has to defend oneself. Thus society becomes a mass of individuals placed side by side, but without any mutual bonds.[53]

It is this notion of freedom, according to the encyclical, that "exalts the isolated individual in an absolute way, and gives no place to solidarity," which lies at the root of "the contradiction between the solemn affirmation of human rights and their tragic denial in practice" in abortion and euthanasia.

For O'Donovan, the modern liberalism with which Christianity may need to contend has its beginning in the church's assertion of what he terms "evangelical liberty," "which is to say, the freedom freely to obey Christ."[54] The assertion of this freedom could not but have consequences for society: "The voice of a prophetic church in its midst, which speaks with divine authority, loosens the hold of existing authorities and evokes the prospect of liberty"[55]—for here the freedom of the individual against certain authorities is a presupposition of the assertion of the existence of yet higher authorities to which these others must themselves submit. Thus,

> [f]reedom ... is not conceived primarily as an assertion of *individuality*, whether positively, in terms of individual creativity and impulse, or negatively, in terms of "rights," which is to say immunities from harm. It is a social reality, a new disposition of society around its supreme Lord which sets it loose from its traditional lords. Yet individual liberty is not far away. For the implication of this new social reality is that the individual can no longer simply be carried within the social setting to which she or he was born; for that setting is under challenge from the new social centre. This requires she give herself to the service of the Lord within the new society, in defiance, if need be, of the old lords and societies that claim her. She emerges in differentiation from her family, tribe and nation, making decisions of discipleship which were not given her from within them.[56]

In the early period it was perhaps the practice of avowed virginity that was the most marked sign of this freedom of decision and differentiation against authorities for the sake of a yet higher authority. But in relation to all earthly societies, the exercise of freedom thus conceived remains vital to Christian self-understanding, just because the ordered and differentiated society of the city that God intends is not to be identified with the imperfect societies of other cities that recognize other authorities or none.

Further Reading

Aquinas: Selected Political Writings. Edited by A. P. D'Entrèves (Oxford: Blackwell, 1959).
Augustine. *City of God.* Translated by H. Bettenson (Harmondsworth: Penguin, 1972), esp. bk. 19.
Barmen Declaration. Translated by D. S. Bax. *Journal of Theology for Southern Africa* 47 (1984).
D. Bonhoeffer. *Ethics.* Edited by E. Bethge, translated by N. H. Smith (London: SCM, 1955).
Catechism of the Catholic Church (London: Chapman, 1994).
Martin Luther and John Calvin. *On Secular Authority.* Edited and translated by H. Höpfl (Cambridge: Cambridge University Press, 1991).
The Rule of St. Benedict. Translated by J. McCann (London: Sheed and Ward, 1976).

Notes

1. Rom. 12:2 (in the Revised Standard Version).
2. S. S. Wolin, *Politics and Vision: Continuity and Innovation in Western Political Thought* (Boston: Little, Brown, 1960), 99, citing I Pet. 2, 9.
3. Ibid. 98.
4. Augustine *City of God*, trans. H. Bettenson (Harmondsworth: Penguin, 1972), 14.1.
5. O. M. T. O'Donovan, *The Desire of the Nations* (Cambridge: Cambridge University Press, 1996), 83 and 203.
6. Ibid. 14.28.
7. Ibid. 14.1.
8. Ibid. 19.13.
9. Ibid. 19.12.
10. Of the imperial peace, Augustine exclaims (*City of God* 19.7): "Think of the cost of this achievement! Consider the scale of those wars with all that slaughter of human beings, all the human blood that was shed!"
11. The prime mark of this injustice is the existence of slavery. According to Augustine (*City of God* 19.15), the proper relationship between human beings is "prescribed by the order of nature, and it is in this situation that God created man. For he says, 'Let him have lordship over the fish of the sea, the birds of the sky . . . and all the reptiles that crawl on the earth.' He did not wish the rational being, made in his own image, to have dominion over any but irrational creatures, not man over man, but man over beasts. Hence the first just men were set up as shepherds of flocks, rather than as kings of men."
12. In the midst of a melancholy review of the woes of life produced by division and conflict within house, city, world, and even within that "angelic fellowship" posited by "those philosophers" who insist that "the gods are our friends," Augustine notes (*City of God* 19.5) that the peace of the earthly city is "a doubtful good, since we do not know the hearts of those with whom we wish to maintain peace, and even if we could know them today, we should not know what they might be like tomorrow."
13. "Remove justice," writes Augustine (*City of God* 4.4), "and what are kingdoms but gangs of criminals on a large scale? . . . For it was a witty and a truthful rejoinder which was given by a captured pirate to Alexander the Great. The king asked the fellow, 'What is your idea, in infesting this sea?' And the pirate answered, with uninhibited insolence, 'The same as yours, in infesting the earth! But because I do it with a tiny craft, I'm called a pirate: because you have a mighty navy, you're called an emperor.'"
14. Augustine *City of God* 15.21.
15. J. L. O'Donovan, "Société," in *Dictionnaire critique de théologie*, ed. J-Y. Lacoste (Paris: Presse Universitaires de France, 1998). For a fuller account and discussion of Augustine's argument, see O. M. T. O'Donovan, "Augustine's *City of God* XIX and Western Political Thought," *Dionysius* 40 (1987): 89–110.
16. For Luther's most important grappling with the issues, see *On Secular Authority*, ed. and trans. H. Höpfl (Cambridge: Cambridge University Press, 1991).

17. D. Bonhoeffer, *Ethics*, ed. E. Bethge, trans. N. H. Smith (London: SCM, 1995), 178: "God and the world are thus at one in Christ in a way which means that although the Church and the world are different from each other, yet there cannot be a static spatial borderline between them."

18. The city of God is a "city whose kingdom will be eternal" (*City of God* 15.8), whereas the earthly city persists only until the day "when all human lordship and power is annihilated and God is all in all" (*City of God* 19.15).

19. R. A. Markus, *Saeculum: History and Society in the Theology of St. Augustine* (Cambridge: Cambridge University Press, 1970), 167.

20. Cited in O'Donovan, *The Desire of the Nations*, 197.

21. J. Meyendorff, *Byzantine Theology: Historical Trends and Doctrinal Themes* (Oxford: Mowbray's, 1975), 216.

22. See G. Florovsky, "Antinomies of Christian History: Empire and Desert," in his *Christianity and Culture* (Belmont, Mass.: Nordland, 1974), 67–100.

23. O'Donovan, "Société."

24. In, for example, "On Princely Government" (*De Regimine Principum*), having rehearsed arguments that demonstrate that "the fellowship of society" is "natural and necessary to man," Thomas continues: "It follows with equal necessity that there must be some principle of government within the society. For if a great number of people were to live, each intent upon his own interests, such a community would surely disintegrate unless there were one of its number to have a care for the common good: just as the body of a man or of any other animal would disintegrate were there not in the body itself a single and controlling force, sustaining the general vitality of all the members. As Solomon tells us (Prov xi, 14): 'Where there is no ruler the people shall be scattered.' This conclusion is quite reasonable; for the particular interest and the common good are not identical." See *Aquinas: Selected Political Writings*, ed. A. P. D'Entrèves (Oxford: Blackwell, 1959), 3.

25. Wolin, *Politics and Vision*, 171.

26. D'Entrèves, *Aquinas: Selected Political Writings*, xvii; citing *Commentary on the Politics* 1.1: "If any man should be such that he is not a political being by nature, he is either wicked—as when this happens through the corruption of human nature—or he is better than man—in that he has a nature more perfect than that of other men in general, so that he is able to be sufficient to himself without the society of men, as were John the Baptist and St Anthony the hermit."

27. Aquinas, *Supplement to the Summa Theologiae*, trans. Fathers of the English Dominican Province (London: Burns Oates, 1920), 54.3.

28. Augustine *City of God* 15.16.

29. Leo XIII, *Rerum Novarum*, trans. Catholic Truth Society (London: CTS, 1983), par. 37.

30. Leo XIII, *Rerum Novarum*, par. 38.

31. *Catechism of the Catholic Church* (London: Chapman, 1994), para. 1882, citing *Mater et Magistra* 60.

32. Ibid., para. 1882.

33. Ibid., para. 1879.

34. Ibid., para. 1699.

35. Ibid., para. 1711.

36. Ibid., para. 1878.

37. K. Barth, *Church Dogmatics*, III/2, ed. G. Bromiley and T. F. Torrance, trans. H. Knight et al. (Edinburgh: T. and T. Clark, 1960), 243.

38. Cited in "Subsidiarity, Principle of," in *The New Dictionary of Catholic Social Thought*, ed. J. A. Dwyer and E. L. Montgomery (Collegeville, Minn.: Liturgical Press, 1994).

39. *Catechism*, para. 1183, citing *Centesimus Annus*.

40. *Catechism*, para. 1184.

41. H. Höpfl, editor's introduction to Luther, *On Secular Authority*, xiii.

42. Ibid., xi.

43. *Barmen Declaration*, trans. D. S. Bax, *Journal of Theology for Southern Africa* 47 (1984): 1.1.

44. A. J. Torrance, introductory essay to *Christ, Justice, and Peace*, by E. Jüngel (Edinburgh: T. and T. Clark, 1992), xii.

45. For a treatment of subsidiarity in relation to the teaching authority of the church and for further references, see J. Mahoney, *The Making of Moral Theology* (Oxford: Oxford University Press, 1987), 169–74.

46. E. Brunner, *The Divine Imperative*, trans. O. Wyon (London: Lutterworth Press, 1937), 124–25.

47. Ibid., 214.

48. Ibid., 210.

49. Ibid., 93.

50. For Barth see especially "Nein" in E. Brunner and K. Barth, *Natural Theology*, trans. P. Fraenkel (London: Centenary Press, 1946), 65–128; and for Bonhoeffer, see *Ethics*, especially the section entitled "The Last Things and the Things before the Last."

51. Bonhoeffer, *Ethics*, 182.

52. *Catechism*, para. 1738.

53. John Paul II, *Evangelium Vitae*, English trans. (London: Catholic Truth Society, 1995), paras. 19 and 20.

54. O'Donovan, *The Desire of the Nations*, 255.

55. Ibid., 252.

56. Ibid., 254.

2

A Limited State and a Vibrant Society

CHRISTIANITY AND CIVIL SOCIETY

JOHN A. COLEMAN, S.J.

IT WOULD BE foolhardy indeed, and risk a superficial mere "skimming view," to attempt, in the small compass of one essay, any comprehensive or encyclopedic overview on the topic of Christianity's position on the state and civil society. The competing *Staatslehren* (where there even is one!) of different Christian theological "families," such as Catholics, Calvinists, Lutherans, Anabaptists, and the Orthodox, do not fully agree or even always converge on their doctrines of the state and society.[1] To avoid this trap of even trying to achieve a fully rounded summary of the varying positions, I will focus primarily on the tradition I know best: the social teaching of Catholicism.

Yet I will also raise up the Reformed tradition's theory about the "spheres of creation" as a useful conversation partner and, at times, perhaps a corrective to the Catholic theory of subsidiarity and the common good. These two seem to be, on balance, the two major traditions in contention among most Christian authors who engage in social theology about state and society. Some authors, such as Don Browning, see a certain complementarity and convergence between these two traditions.[2] Recent Catholic social thought explicitly evokes the "covenantal" aspect that lies behind the theory of spheres of creation.[3] Others, such as Max Stackhouse, suggest deeper abiding tensions between the two.[4]

Before we move to look more closely at social Catholicism and a comparison with the Calvinist tradition of spheres of creation, however, we need to avert several special difficulties in treating a long spiritual/theological/historical/cultural tradition such as Christianity. Christianity shares with other world-religious traditions, such as Hinduism, Confucianism, and Judaism, an existence of thousand of years and an embodiment in quite diverse epochs and cultures. Some of these normative texts clearly are anchored in premodern understanding. In some places, the Christians have been in ascendancy; in other places, in a minority. In still other places, they have suffered persecution and oppression. Naturally, Christianity's attitude toward the state has varied depending on whether it has been in or out of power. It is very difficult to capture the religious traditions in any simple ahistorical ideal type.

Moreover, we need to attend to three other aspects when treating Christianity's conceptions of civil society and the state. (1) Christianity complicates the comparative project by introducing, inevitably, a third term to the equation: *the church*, civil society, and the state. As we will see, the church does not usually think of itself as just one other free association within civil society, totally equivalent to the other free associations. (2) Christianity has been in a—often centuries long—contact and dialogue with many other ethical traditions: natural law, liberalism, and, more recently, feminism. (3) Christianity in recent decades has absorbed new and important experiences about the relevance of civil society that reshape its classic doctrines.

Church, State, and Civil Society

One obvious place to look for a sense of the Christian range of positions on state government and civil society is to inspect the varying doctrines concerning church-state relation.[5] Although the church in no way exhausts civil society, it tends to belong in that realm rather than the state.[6] Even those Christians who held (or those few who continue to hold) some variant of a position supporting a state-sponsored church would still generally appeal also to a version of a doctrine of the "freedom" of the church from too much governmental control or entanglement.

The freedoms of civil society (the freedoms of speech, association, etc.), as they arose in the West at least, derive ultimately from a Christian provenance, rooted in an assertion of the liberty of the church (*libertas ecclesiae*). Ernst Troeltsch argued as much when he contended that the early church, in demanding to be conceived of as a separate sphere whose authority was derivative from God and conscience before God and not from the state, made its main contribution to social theory to anchor a *novum* in history: "free spaces" in society that did not derive their legitimacy directly from the state.[7]

The Christian churches have often claimed this "free space" not just for the church but for families as well. Both classic Catholicism and Protestantism saw the family as an "autonomous sphere of creation" whose authority derived directly from God and not through the mediation of the state, civil society, or even the church. Hence, the family is also, while within civil society, not on an even par with other associations of civil society. Its derivative theological authority is stronger than the authority of the other associations. Frequently, a theological position on the "freedom of the church" will closely mirror a larger position on civil society, as in arguments that contend that the church itself flourishes best and most freely in societies that, more generally, allow free markets and freedom of speech, assembly, petition, and mobility.[8] But if the church is conceived of as *in* and, perhaps, as an essential anchor of civil society, most Christian theorists—at least with anything approaching a somewhat robust ecclesiology (i.e., the doctrine of the church)—see the church as also somehow a species apart from the other free associations of civil society. Its authority derives from God and not from the state or the associational nexus of civil society. The church is *in* but not really fully *of* civil society. Few Christian theologians or churches want to assimilate the church entirely under the rubric of broader secular accounts for civil society, even if the church is seen as appropriately located in civil society and, thus, free from direct state governance or ordering.

Christianity and the Other Traditions

Throughout its history, Christianity has almost never existed (in fact or in its own theory) as a hermetically sealed-off religious enclave, untouched by or unrelated to other religious voices or more "secular" social movements.[9] Early Christian thinkers engaged in a dialogue with and selective absorption of elements from Stoicism and the civic republican tradition of Rome, especially as found in Cicero. Both the notion of a common good and an appeal to a natural law, found in a number of Christian doctrinal families (but especially strongly within Catholicism), derive originally from these pre-Christian traditions. Saint Ambrose wrote his own Christian analogue to Cicero's Stoic *De officiis*.[10] Augustine appropriated his central notions about the justice that could be found in a this-worldly republic from Cicero's *De re publica* (arguing, of course, that, because it lacked real justice, there never really was a Roman republic).[11]

In Augustine and, later, Aquinas and in some seventeenth century Reformed thinkers, such as Justus Lipsius and Samuel Pufendorf, we find a strong convergence with elements of the natural law and virtue traditions of the Roman Stoics.[12] David Burrell has argued that there was even a vigorous interreligious conversation (often focused on questions of state and society)—at least among the intellectuals in the three traditions—among Judaism, Islam, and Christianity in the Middle Ages.[13] Aquinas, in the *Summa Contra Gentiles* at any event, shows a strong acquaintance with the thought of Maimonides and of the Islamic Aristotelians.

In a similar way, Protestantism (relatively early) and Catholicism (strongly in the twentieth century but already incipiently in the nineteenth in representative figures such as Lamennais and de Montelbert in France and Bishop von Ketteler in Germany) have long wrestled with the challenges and experience of liberalism and, later, socialism.[14] From John Locke onward, Christianity has been in partial contestation, argument, and—once again—selective appropriation and transformation of elements from the liberal and the liberal-egalitarian traditions. Since World War II, social Catholicism has both incorporated and transmuted elements from the rights and democracy language of liberalism and addressed critical theory.[15] Moreover, both the Protestant and the Catholic traditions have, more recently, engaged in dialogue with (including selective retrieval, appropriation, transformation, and/or rejection of) feminist theory.[16] Contemporary Catholic natural law arguments, to cite another example, seem as akin, in places, to more modern variants of natural law as to medieval accounts, based on a now-rejected teleology.[17]

It would be a serious mistake, then, to take the classic periods of medieval or counter-Reformation Catholicism and Reformation Protestantism and reify them as if they have not continued as living and growing traditions. In that sense, Christianity has long since been in dialogue with modernity and with other influential moral traditions. As a result, some of what now seems typically Protestant or Catholic (at least in their more liberal variants) stems from that engaged argument and appropriation.

Christianity, Civil Society, and Recent Societal Upheavals

In 1989, Pope John Paul II (long before the theme became recherché) sponsored a high-level symposium at the Vatican on the topic of civil society. Luminaries such as Leszek Kolokowski, Adam Michnik, and Jürgen Habermas had the pope's attentive ear for three days of dialogue on that topics. At the time William Safire, the *New York Times* columnist, stated that this symposium was little noted in the press yet might be one of the most important events of the year. Clearly, in his social encyclical issued in 1991, *Centesimus Annus*, the pope echoed many of the themes of a market and civil society, what the pope praises as "a society of free work, of enterprise and of participation."[18] In a similar way, the World Council of Churches has been conducting, for many years now and at different locales, regular sophisticated colloquiums on civil society. The term *civil society*, usually traced to Hegel, may postdate medieval or counter-Reformation Catholicism and Reformation Protestantism, but both of these two traditions claim to find traces of it in their own traditions.

Moreover, the churches have struggled firsthand with the reality of civil society (or its foreclosure) in the post–World War II periods and again in the late 1960s through 1989. The churches were faced with the dilemmas of being situated in authoritarian dictatorships or totalitarian regimes that restricted not only the liberty of the churches but more fundamental human liberties. Often, in places such as Chile, Poland, and Brazil and in Hungary and East Germany, the churches (predominantly Protestant in East Germany and Catholic in Chile, Poland, and Brazil) served as the only institutional carriers of (or protective umbrella for) any oppositional civil society. A rich comparative sociological literature exists that documents the Christian churches' role as midwives to a reborn (or firstborn in some cases) civil society in the transition from dictatorships.[19] Solidarity in Poland and the transitions to democracy from dictatorship in Spain, the Philippines, Chile, and Brazil all attest to the church's role in these laboratories in the construction of civil society. To be sure, a more cynical reading of a recent Catholic championing of civil society might wonder how deep are the roots of this newfound turn to civil society in a church that, even into the 1950s, could support a fusion of church and state in Salazar's Portugal and Franco's Spain. Others suspect a more Machiavellian motive in the Catholic support of civil society movements as a covert and merely tactical support for the interests of the church. Postcommunist Poland might be an instructive case here, where some factions of the church hierarchy seem to have reverted to elements of a confessional state. Still, these elements in Poland are deeply contested by intellectual Catholics and, precisely, on a Catholic theoretical basis, grounded in the teaching of Vatican II. Adam Michnik, the dissident Polish former communist, at least gives some credibility to the perduring sincerity of the Catholic turn toward civil society.

In the nature of the case, this essay is mainly theoretical, engaging in a comparative analysis of alternative visions and traditions of conceiving civil society and the state. But it would be a serious mistake to think for one moment that Christian thinking on civil society and the state has been spun only from some theoretical or doctrinal weave of classic texts. Fifty years of intense experience of dissent from totalitarian regimes and of ongoing coalitions with more secular dissidents in various societies have engraved on Christianity's recent memory the wisdom of guaranteeing a separately institutionalized, quasi-autonomous realm of civil society as a "free public space." It would take another and differing essay, of course, to detail the cases that have fed into this experience of the churches in helping to forge civil society, but the reader is warned not to see the theory sketched as coming only from revelation, the Bible, or dogma.

But this is not to say that theology has not had an independent role to play in mediating the varying Christian positions on church, state, and civil society. It will help to sketch at least some of the fundamental theological questions that will determine the differing Christian positions on these three concepts.

Theological Background Questions Shaping Christian Theories of Church, State, and Society

A number of theological questions lurk behind divergent Protestant and Catholic views on church, state, and civil society. Any easy correlation between and among these competing Christian positions is difficult. I rehearse several of these key theological topics here less to argue for any substantive position on any one question than to indicate the extreme difficulty in forging any unitary Christian or even Protestant position on state and civil society. Presumably, both Catholics and Protestants will have to parse carefully through these questions to reach any fully argued position on church, society, and state. Among these theological issues are:

1. What is the nature of the church or the religious people? Is it a merely voluntary association of persons (among, perhaps, many such associations, even if united for religious purposes)? Does the church therefore see itself as subject to the self-same limits and rules as any other voluntary association in society? Or does the church, rather, represent a juridical and ordered institution ordained by God? If the latter, its claimed authority will always be potentially in conflict with the authorities of the state or civil society. The query whether to obey the laws of God or of the state haunts Christian history. The church will rarely see itself as *merely* another unit within civil society. Behind this question of ecclesiology lies a second: Who speaks for the church on public issues in society and with what intrinsic religious warrant?[20]

2. What is the nature of the state? To what degree is it primarily the result of sin? To what degree is it ordained by God even from the beginning? The Reformers, steeped in a reading of Augustine, generally followed him in seeing the state as a result of sin rather than an originary intention of God for creation. Sociality for Augustine was prelapsarian. The state was not. Yet even in a postlapsarian epoch, this postulated priority of sociality over the state need not necessarily lead to any special privileging of civil society over the state. Sin may require instead a powerful constraining state. Thomas Aquinas

(and his followers, even among Protestants) tended more broadly to accept the need for an indispensable coordinating authority of the state among plural actors, even had Adam never fallen.[21]

Are there permanent or accidental aspects of the state (war-making, coercion, office-holding, oath-taking) inconsistent with Christian discipleship? How does the church handle such religious conflict? (e.g., by demanding from its members conscientious objection against serving in armies or police forces? By refusing to allow them to take oaths in law trials?) To what extent (if at all) can the state be perfected to serve more closely the purpose of the kingdom of God?[22]

3. These last sets of questions relate to the underlying Christian doctrines of creation, sin, and redemption/sanctification. Those Protestant Christians (e.g., Wesleyans) and Catholics who have a stronger teaching on the actual transformative power of sanctification might foresee more positive possibilities ingredient in the state than those who think that sin perdures strongly (perhaps even *just* as strongly, even if not "imputed" to the believer because of "justification" through the merits of Christ) even after redemption. And when might this process of redemption/sanctification (extending even to the social order) begin? Postmillennialists (such as, for example, those who espoused the social gospel tradition in America) may be more likely to see the possibility of a gradual social perfection accruing in and through state and society (a "social salvation" to counteract social sin) than premillennialists, who expect a catastrophic declension in societal morals and order before the second coming of Christ.[23]

Whatever their position on the relation between sin and redemption, most Protestants nurture a relatively strong sense of sin, such that they foster limited expectations of what a state or society can achieve.[24] Following Augustine, they see even the "best-case scenario" as a kind of "rough justice," in sharp tension with Christian normative ideals of community, virtue, and neighbor love. Moreover, their sense of sin tempers any inflated enthusiasm for governmental or societal exercises of power. Neither the state nor civil society is *privileged* as a locale somehow less sinless. As Reinhold Niebuhr, a major modern retriever of political Augustinianism, argued, we need a check-and-balancing of powers in society in order to hold any power center in check against its *expected* sinful aggrandizements.[25]

4. To what degree must the church or the people of God be independent of the state? Is there a gradation in forms of church-state relationship, some more in accord with Christian concerns than others? Does the independence of the church and state deny all relationship between the two? Is God sovereign over the state also? If so, in what forms does this sovereignty of God over the state manifest itself? Traditionally, the Anabaptist view, for example, expects little convergence between church and state or church and "secular"

civil society. It calls for a countercultural witnessing more than for direct efforts to sustain, nurture, or transform the commonly social.[26]

Catholicism and Calvinism, however, are more open to a true transformative power of Christian input on the state and society. Calvinism, because of Calvin's more positive "third use of the law" (to direct people toward righteousness, as opposed to Luther's two, solely negative, uses of the law: to convict the sinner and to coerce wrongdoers), has a broader sense than Lutheranism or the Anabaptist tradition of openness to a sense of a kind of natural-law structuring of the social and what Calvin called natural "equity."[27] The Calvinist doctrine of spheres of creation and the cognate, but distinct, Calvinist federal tradition in theology and politics come closer to that "world transforming" impetus in Christianity similar to that found in some strands of post-Vatican II social Catholicism.[28]

5. What obligations toward the state have the church and Christians as citizens with dual loyalties? To what extent should the church support the aims of government? Is patriotism a Christian virtue? If so, on what grounds and with what limits?[29]

6. To what extent is state sovereignty (if there is legitimately any such thing) limited by a broader global sense of what Catholics, as members of a worldwide communion of Christians, would call an "international or global" common good, which would relativize somewhat any state or national civil society?[30]

7. With what means and under what conditions may Christians oppose a tyrannical or unjust government? Theological traditions among Protestants differ on the question of the legitimacy of revolution or organized protest against unjust laws. Luther was intransigent in demanding continuing submission to unjust rulers as a kind of worthy punishment of the subjects' general sinfulness. The Reformed tradition (and Catholicism) is clearer about the legitimacy of resistance to tyrannical government as a corrective to unjust law and in pointing to an *orderly* resistance to unjust government through recourse to the rank of the magistrates in the civil service of government.[31]

8. How virtuous can a government be? How does Christianity enhance this virtue? If little in the way of virtue is to be expected in governments, is civil society a more privileged locale for the exercise and nurturance of a virtuous citizenry? What are the roles of order, peace, justice, welfare, and the care for societal freedom as part of God's intentions for creation (or for redemption)?[32]

Thomas Sanders, from whom this list of theological topoi is mainly derived, contends that very few of these questions have attracted the sustained attention of Protestant-wide bodies, with the exception of religious liberty, the nature of the church, and the *religious* base for social and political responsibility.[33] John C. Bennett has claimed that "there is no one Protestant doctrine concerning church-state relations."[34]

The Catholic Theory of Church-State

Nor (given the range of theological questions we saw above) should we expect that there would be only *one* Catholic position on church-state questions. Writing at the time of the Vatican Council II debates on the Declaration on Religious Liberty (*Dignitatis Humanae*), John Courtney Murray could distinguish five different positions in the Council debates in the *aula*.[35] One was the older Catholic view that "error" had no rights, that only the one who is in the truth, therefore only the Catholic, has an intrinsic and natural right to religious freedom. Moreover, this reactionary stance claimed for the Catholic Church a preeminent juridical position *within* the state apparatus as something demanded by faith and reason. As the nearly unanimous vote in favor of the Declaration on Religious Freedom at the Council showed, this position was held by a decidedly minuscule minority. Those rearguard Catholics who may continue to hold it lack articulate spokesmen or suasive argument and would seem to be ruled out by the authoritative character of the conciliar document. Yet, clearly, variants of the older Catholic integralism (i.e., the claim for a church hegemony over the morality of state and society when Catholics are a majority) continue to exist among extreme traditionalist Catholics.[36]

Among those who did support a declaration on religious freedom at the Council, some pleaded for a merely practical document, a declaration of pastoral policy rather than a statement of theological principle. They were countered by the argument that this might seem to be the work of opportunists, a dubious—you will excuse my embarrassment at the consecrated term—jesuitical act of mental reservation.

Still others wanted to ground the declaration upon the indubitable Catholic principles of the freedom of the act of faith and the freedom of conscience (and a concomitant duty to follow a sincere, even if erroneous, conscience). To say "error" has no rights is a category mistake. Only persons have rights. Their human dignity demands respect for their deepest self-definition as religious and the integrity of their conscience. Atheists, too, have this same religious liberty. But proponents of the final declaration contended that this tack alone would not eventuate in a rationally justified stance in favor of religious expression *in the public order*. The subjective rights of conscience could still be countered in public by the claimed objective claims for truth.

Significantly, Murray's case for religious freedom of both persons and ecclesial groups is very closely linked to and dependent upon a corollary Catholic argument for civil society and its mediating structures. At crucial points, Murray's argument for religious liberty subsumes a case for subsidiarity and the common good as crucial middle terms in his argument. The Catholic case for religious freedom Murray contended, is tied to the Catholic understanding of a limited government and the proper sway (and autonomy) of the free spaces in civil society. To this I will return shortly.

After the Council, the final two seriously competing Catholic theological positions on religious liberty remained Murray's and a second position, largely that of French theologians who want to root religious freedom *entirely* in theological grounds (e.g., the freedom of the act of faith; the rights of personal and collective conscience). Murray countered by arguing that the ultimate case for religious liberty must rest on a complex, religio-political-moral-juridical structure of argument that appeals simultaneously to the exigencies of human nature and the learning experiences (including experiences of constitutional structures) of history. As Yale theologian George Lindbeck has remarked about similar Protestant moves to substantiate religious liberty purely on particularist Christian theological premises: "There is no way one can show, on these grounds alone, why responsible persons who are not Christian should grant religious liberty to all. Moreover, a purely theological argument for religious liberty does not lend itself to civil discussion in a broader secular context."[37]

Murray wanted the Vatican II document to include a clear statement about the *juridical* need to enshrine religious liberty as a *civil* right in a constitutional government of limited powers. The Declaration on Religious Liberty did, in fact, follow Murray on this point.[38] Murray—and the documents of the Vatican Council—was clear, however, that the Council was not, in their declaration of religious liberty, arguing for some "privatization" of religion or separation of church from *society*. This represents a not-trivial point.

For Murray saw *Dignitatis Humanae* as a forerunner for the final document of the Council, *Gaudium et Spes* (the Church in the Modern World). By setting the church free to pursue, vigorously, its social ministry *in civil society*, the Declaration on Religious Liberty set a tone for that final document. As Murray notes, "*Gaudium et Spes* is clear that the church's ministry is religious, not political in nature; yet the animating religious vision of the Gospel has substantial political potential."[39] The general thrust of the postconciliar Catholic social thought has been to fight vigorously against narrow "church" conceptions of the religious task and the pervasive privatization of religion. It champions what José Casanova calls a new form of "public religion in the modern world," in a civil society that is not seen as some neutral private sphere, but rather as one in alignment with the state.[40]

The key issue here, it seems to me, is the extent to which an understanding of separation of church and state promotes or restricts the church's role as a mediating structure *in civil society*. What scope, beyond worship and catechesis within the sacristy, is allowed to the church for action in education, welfare, health, the media, and the world of work and economics? The strategy and style for church influence upon the tenor of culture and societal life has changed dramatically in the post-Vatican II era, with the church's adoption of a new posture of dialogue and pluralist participation in society. But there is no evidence that its ambitions toward having some legitimate access and voice and influence upon the quality and morality of public life have in any way diminished. Social Catholicism contests a view that would set up some putatively neutral "technical rationality" in the economy and technology as absolutely free from any deeper moral assessments. In this point, post-Vatican II social Catholicism is actually closer to critical theory in places than to classic liberalism.

The Link Between Catholicism's Sense of Its Own Mission and Its Theory of State and Society

To understand the church's shift to an admittedly new position on religious liberty, it is essential to turn to a classic Catholic distinction between state and civil society. I want to develop this distinction because it bears out my contention that the Catholic structure for the argument for religious liberty is simultaneously a strong case for civil society and its mediating institutions.

The state's true care for religion, Murray argued, is restricted to its care for the freedom of religion. Its care consists in the state's recognition of the church's claim, under the rubric of *libertas ecclesiae*, for immunity in the juridical order in matters touching religion (free exercise and no establishment). Murray and the Vatican document on religious liberty shifted the burden of a *public* role for religion from the state—which in Murray's view, in any event, is simply incompetent to make *any* judgments about religious truth whatsoever—to the wider society, the people acting through their voluntary mediating structures and corporate groups. No one should be coerced into religious behavior, since "[t]he truth cannot impose itself except by virtue of its own truth, as it makes its entrance into the mind at once quietly and with power."[41]

But neither should others be restrained from a public expression of religion in civil society or in the context of the national life.

The freedom asserted in *Dignitatis Humanae* as a limit on state power, however, is much more than the freedom of the church or of individual religious consciences. The document signals as well the rightful freedom of mediating corporate groups. Indeed, it envisions as normative neither the confessional state nor the laicist secular state, but the limited constitutional state. There is a juridical as well as moral and theological premise to *Dignitatis Humanae*: "The demand is also made that constitutional limits should be set to the powers of government in order that there may be no encroachment on the rightful freedom of the person *and of associations*."[42]

State Versus Society

In its classic distinction between state and civil society, Catholic social thought contains a strong animus against the view that the public sphere is synonymous with the government or the formal polity of the society.[43] It does not want, however, to relegate civil society to the purely *private* sphere. Here, I would argue, social Catholicism, like feminism and critical theory in their own contexts, *contests* elements of modernity, but now within an acceptance of a differentiation that is not a premodern organicism. Some would restrict the church's public role to a mere undergirding for reciprocity, duty, and responsibility generally and would eschew, as inappropriate, any religious advocacy on specific policy issues.

José Casanova, drawing mainly on modern Catholic case studies, has argued, to the contrary, that there *is* a proper role for public religion in modernity. Casanova notes that from the normative perspective of modernity, religion may enter the public sphere and assume a public form only if it accepts the sanctity of the principle of freedom of conscience. It can also do so only if it *does* accept some legitimate differentiation of spheres in modern society (but differentiation need not mean total autonomy).

But once that sanctity of conscience and the rightful quasi-autonomy of secular spheres are acknowledged, Casanova argues, modernity's often unthinking privatization of religion can be legitimately contested in at least three instances:

1. "When religion enters the public sphere to protect not only its own freedom of religion but all modern freedoms and rights and the very right of a democratic civil society to exist against an absolutist, authoritarian state." The very active role of the Catholic Church in the processes of democratization in

Spain, Poland, and Brazil and the role of the Lutheran and Reformed Churches in East Germany in similar processes serve as illustrations of this first case.[44] In these test cases, religious historic carriers of freedom almost alone continued to be capable of sustaining and protecting the modern freedoms and rights in authoritarian regimes.

2. "When religion enters the public sphere to question and contest the absolutized lawful autonomy of the secular spheres and their claims to be organized in accordance with principles of functional differentiation *without regard to extraneous ethical or moral considerations*" (emphasis mine). The Pastoral Letters of the U.S. Catholic Bishops questioning the "morality" of the state's nuclear policies and of the lack of "justice" in the inhuman consequences ingredient in certain elements of a capitalist economic system that tends to absolutize rights to private property and claims to be totally self-regulating by unchecked market forces, are examples of this second—note modern, not premodern—contestation in public by religion. As the American bishops state forcefully in their letter on the American economy, their desire is to open a wider public deliberation, not to impose their own solutions.[45]

3. "When religion enters the public sphere to protect the traditional life-world from administrative or juridical state penetration, and in the process opens up issues of norm and will formation to the public and collective self-reflection of modern discursive ethics." This represents Casanova's third case of a justified public resort by religion in the modern world.[46] Casanova mentions here the societal debates about abortion by religious groups, but other examples might include public debates about capital punishment, euthanasia, genetic engineering, and the like. What is key here is that religion only challenges in civil society and public deliberation and does not impose by recourse to state power.

Just as feminists and some critical theorists are calling for a reopening of what seemed a settled set of boundaries about public-private, so a public version of Christian religion *within civil society* contests views of the privatization of religion that make religion irrelevant or assume that it is somehow "in bad taste" to expose one's religiosity publicly.[47]

Seyla Benhabib takes on the liberal model of "public dialogue" with its "neutrality" rule about any public discussion of "human goods," as opposed to procedures. This rule imposes, according to Benhabib, "conversational restraints" that function as "gag rules." Entire ranges of matters get excluded from public deliberation—from the private economy to the realm of norm formation. As Benhabib notes: "The model of a public dialogue based on conversational restraint is not neutral, in that it presupposes a moral and political epistemology; this in turn justifies an implicit separation between the public and private of such a kind as leads to the silencing of the concerns of excluded groups." It also glosses over and ignores the extent to which the political order inevitably involves contestation and struggle. "All struggles against oppression in the modern world begin by redefining what had previously been considered 'private,' non-public and non-political issues as matters of public concern, as issues of justice, as sites of power which need discursive legitimation."[48]

Casanova captures well the contestation quality of the new forms of *modern*—not premodern—public religion (of which social Catholicism is one prominent case) that have emerged since the 1980s around the world:

> What is at issue is the need to recognize that the boundaries themselves are and need to be open to contestation, redefinition, renegotiation, and discursive legitimation. According to Benhabib, "If the agenda of the conversation is radically open, if participants can bring any and all matters under critical scrutiny and reflexive questioning, then there is no way to *predefine* the nature of the issues discussed as being ones of justice or the good life itself prior to the conversation. This should include all boundaries: private and public; moral and legal, justice and the good life, religious and secular." . . . What I call the 'deprivatization' of modern religion is the process whereby religion abandons its assigned place in the private sphere and enters the undifferentiated sphere of civil society to take part in the ongoing process of contestation, discursive legitimation and redrawing of the boundaries.[49]

This is not to say that all forms of public religion—or all forms of public Catholicism, for that matter—are good either in themselves or for the body politic. It is to say that social Catholics will and do contest liberal theories that claim that the state must be neutral in respect to all definitions of the human good. It is to say that social Catholicism (and other forms of public religion in the modern world) gives rise to protest movements against claims about the "inevitability and benign invisible hand" of the globalization process, against the arms race, against ecological destruction, against the despoilment of native peoples, against social engineering schemes affecting families. This is much more than some simple generic undergirding by religion of societal norms of reciprocity, duty, and responsibility.

To be sure, world Catholic social movements are not of a piece. Neoconservative Catholics such as Michael Novak and Richard Neuhaus contest parts of the thrust ingredient in the post-Vatican II social Catholicism.[50] In places, some Catholic movements remain integralist. Yet a pattern has emerged worldwide, ranging from the defense of Indian rights by the Canadian Catholic Church; the land commissions in Brazil and elsewhere in Latin America to protect the people from the expropriation of their lands by economic forces claiming to represent "modernization"; the American bishops' yearly support for economic development in inner cities; the human rights commissions in many countries mainly staffed by church people.[51] At least in its official documents and in its proposed church-world strategy—if not always in its empirical behavior—the general thrust of postconciliar Catholic thought has been to oppose narrow "churchy" conceptions of the religious task and the pervasive privatization of religion.

The justification for this deprivatization of religion in Catholicism can appeal to two signal warrants (among many!). In 1971, the Synod of World Bishops claimed that "[a]ction on behalf of justice and participation in the transformation of the world fully appear to us as *a constitutive dimension of the preaching of the gospel*, or, in other words, of the church's mission for the redemption of the human race and its liberation from every oppressive situation."[52] The very document on religious liberty that accepts the modern differentiation of church and state is unyielding about the *public* scope for religion *within civil society*: "It comes within the meaning of religious freedom that religious bodies should not be prohibited from freely undertaking to show the special value of their doctrine in what concerns the organization of society and the inspiration *of the whole of human activity*. Finally, the social nature of the human and the very nature of religion afford the foundation of the human right to hold meetings and to establish educational, cultural, charitable and social organizations, under the impulse of their own religious sense."[53]

Clearly, this is not John Rawls's or Bruce Ackerman's program for neutrality about public goods.[54] If classic liberals and even some modern liberal egalitarians might feel uncomfortable with this new form of modern public religion, they might take some comfort in the Catholic insistence on a variant of a limited state. Catholic social thought does not assume that everything public must ipso facto be governmental. In distinguishing between state and society it also distinguishes between the public order entrusted to the state—an order of unity, coercion, and necessity, an order that includes essential elements of the common good through the state's coordinating and regulative activities, crucial for distributive justice, which cannot be guaranteed only by the free market or free rational choice mechanisms—and the elements of the common good that are entrusted to the whole society, a zone of comparative freedom and pluralism.

Catholic social thought is pluralistic in its insistence on the limited service character of the state. The state exists as an instrument to promote justice and liberty. The ends of the public order entrusted primarily or essentially to the state's nurturance of the common good are fourfold: public peace, public morality (based on civil practices and truths), welfare and justice, and the freedom of the people. As Murray puts it, "[T]he democratic state serves both the ends of the human person (in itself and its natural forms of social life) and also the ends of justice. As the servant of those ends, it has only relative value."[55] If the state is both subject to and the servant of the common good, it "is not the sole judge of what is or is not the common good." Moreover, "in consequence of the distinction between society and state, not every element of the common good is instantly committed to the state." On the contrary, "government submits itself to judgment by the truth of society; it is not itself a judge of the truth of society."[56]

Perhaps the clearest and most developed statement of this Catholic distinction between state and society is found in Jacques Maritain's now-classic book *Man and the State*. Maritain ascribes to the state an instrumental, service character that is a part—the topmost part and agency, to be sure—of the whole society, which he calls "the body politic." The state is the part that specializes in the interest of the whole! Its authority is derivative. It exists not by its own right and for its own sake, but only in virtue and to the extent of the requirements of the common good.

At least two corporate units in society, the family and the church, have rights and freedoms fully anterior to the state. Other corporate units—voluntary associations such as universities, labor unions, agencies in the public interest—stake out a zone of free sociality in society. The right to voluntary association is based on the social nature of the human person whose sociality is not exhausted by citizenship in the state. Maritain asserts that "the state is inferior to the body politic as a whole and is at the service of the body politic as a whole."[57] He denies that the state, as such, is a subject of rights or is the head of the body politic. It serves a purely instrumental role in the service of the people, the proper subject of rights. Note how in this view, civil society—what Maritain calls "the body politic"—is not merely a residual category or some sphere of privacy. The Catholic limited state contains more communitarian impulses and assumes that the state does have a proper, if limited, role in ensuring the common good. Its overlap with the liberal constitutional state is real but imperfect. Catholic notions of the common good make some liberals nervous. The common good assumes the possibility of some substantive set of public goods not totally subordinated to the purely procedural notion of the right. In Catholic theory, a societal common good must be achieved by the processes of deliberative democracy, never imposed by the church.[58]

Subsidiarity

Maritain argues that mediating structures should be as autonomous as possible because family, economic, cultural, educational, and religious life matter as much as does political life to the very existence and prosperity of the body politic. Normally, the principle of subsidiarity should govern the relation between state and mediating structures "since in political society authority comes from below through the people. It is normal that the whole dynamism of authority in the body politic should be made up of particular and partial authorities rising in tiers above one another to the top authority of the state."[59]

Subsidiarity began life as an esoteric Catholic term, first coined in 1931 by Pius XI in his encyclical *Quadragesimo Anno*, although the principle to which it points has long existed in democratic social theory and is found in social Catholicism at least from the time of Charles Montelembert in the first half of the nineteenth century.[60] It also presently serves, along with the common good—largely because of the intervention of the Catholic socialist Jacques Delors, who served as European Commission president in the early 1990s—as one of the two major policy aims of the European Economic Community.

Subsidiarity is a derivative rule of the state-society distinction. Its purpose is to delineate both the moral right and the moral limitations of state interventions in cultural, social, and economic affairs. Its formulation reads: "It is a fundamental principle *of social philosophy* . . . that one should not withdraw from individuals and commit to the community what they can accomplish by their own enterprise and industry. So, too, it is an injustice and at the same time a grave evil and disturbance of right order to transfer to the larger and higher collectivity functions which can be performed and provided by the lesser and subordinate bodies. Inasmuch as every social activity should, by its very nature, prove a help to members of the body social, it should never destroy or absorb them."[61]

Subsidiarity rests entirely on secular warrant. It is in no sense a religious maxim, nor does it find direct warrant in the Bible. It grew out of reflection on social experience, not revelation. Catholic social thought looks to it as a congealment of historic wisdom about the arrangement of social orders. It is a presumptive rule about where real vitality exists in society. Clearly, as *Quadragesimo Anno* realized and *Mater et Magistra* made very clear, the state can and must intervene for public welfare when intermediate associations are deficient. As *Quadragesimo Anno* puts it, the state legitimately acts to "encourage, stimulate, regulate, supplement and complement" the action of intermediate groups.[62] But the presumption is that such intervention, while justified in the name of the common good, should never "destroy or absorb" the lesser or intermediate bodies. In point of fact, the principle of subsidiarity is simply a Catholic version of the theory of democratic pluralism to be found, in more secular guise, in Tocqueville, Durkheim, and, more recently, Michael Walzer.[63]

The "secular" warrants for subsidiarity are many. Thus, E. F. Schumacher, in invoking it, explicitly contends that the principle is a rule for efficiency, the best way to increase both productivity and participant sat-isfaction.[64] H. A. Rommen insists on intermediate structures as a fountain of creativity and experiment: "The state is not creative but individual persons in their free associations and their group life are creative."[65]

Maritain's argument for subsidiarity is redolent of Emile Durkheim's communication theory of government in *Professional Ethics and Civic Morals*, where Durkheim pleads for intermediate associations because the state is too abstract and distant. As Maritain puts it, "To become a boss or a manager in business or industry or a patron of art or a leading spirit in the affairs of culture, science and philosophy is against the nature of such an impersonal topmost agency, abstract so to speak and separated from the moving particularities, mutual tensions, risks and dynamism of concrete social existence."[66]

The principle of subsidiarity is not writ large on the fabric of the uni-verse because it is a distilled wisdom, an empirical generalization from experience and a maxim for ordering a sane society rather than an ontological principle or a phenomenological description of how states always or actually operate. It would take another essay to discuss ef-forts to enforce subsidiarity *within* the church, where the legitimacy of the principle has been acknowledged at the highest levels but, in prac-tice, frequently discounted.[67] Clearly, tension remains between Catholic ecclesiology, which continues to see the church in hierarchical-organi-cist terms, and the Catholic theory of the good "secular" society, which is no longer seen as organicist and where egalitarian and not hierarchi-cal norms prevail—just as it would take another essay to assess contes-tations by Catholic feminists of continuing patriarchal elements *within* the church.

The principle of subsidiarity is of renewed interest today precisely because of some new threats to the voluntary society. The first is the ex-tensive growth of the regulatory state, which will not be easily disman-tled for romantic visions of some simpler society. The second stems from the fact that increased government regulation and intervention is coupled with the growth of "professional monopolies." Detailed regu-lations, certification, and preconditions imposed upon the service sec-tor of society, coupled with an expansion of market metaphors, lead to fears they are pricing voluntary agencies out of the market in health and, increasingly, in welfare.[68] Alternately, they may be turning the nonprofit voluntary sector into a mirror of the logic of the market and the logic of the state.[69]

Catholic social thought links subsidiarity to two other principles: solidarity and the common good. "No bigger than necessary" has a corollary—as big as necessary, however, to achieve the common good. Especially when faced with the behemoth of economic concentration

and power, Catholic social thought allows and expects the state to re-
tain certain regulatory powers for the protection of the common good.
It has never held that that government is best which governs least. The
state does have some indispensable roles to play in furthering the common good.

Subsidiarity may sound like a mere bromide, but it has some bite in
actual policy debates. Take, for example, welfare reform, with which
Catholic voices (e.g., Catholic Charities U.S.A., the United States Catholic
Conference) have strongly engaged. Catholics opposed schemes such
as Texas's complete privatization of the administration of welfare by
total outsourcing and turning its administration over to the for-profit
Lockheed Martin. This move denies a legitimate and necessary role for
the state in overseeing care for the common good. On the other hand,
Catholics have also supported some outsourcing and rejected government monopoly over deliverance of welfare services by appealing to
subsidiarity. The government, in this view, must provide a *fair* framework, but agencies of civil society should be engaged in the actual
deliverance of welfare. Cynics may simply dismiss this as a species of
protection for Catholic institutional interest, but it is remarkable just
how consistent Catholic social policy on welfare has been on these
points since the mid-1930s.[70]

The Economy and the Common Good

Social Catholicism tends to fear the totalitarianism of the market as
much as that of the overregulatory state. Catholic human rights theory
includes *social* as well as *civil* rights.[71] Social Catholicism assumes a
priority to meeting basic needs in determining the direction of the economy. It justifies even some cases of nationalization of property, if necessary to counteract monopoly, and champions worker codetermination
schemes in industry.[72] The tradition is best described as social democratic in its thrust. It accepts a market economy without buying into a
myth of a totally self-regulating market. The market may be part of civil
society, but it is an unequal and hegemonic part. Left to its own devices,
it undermines the very mutuality, loyalty, and commitments that make
for good civil society. So Catholic social thought demands that the economy must recognize needs and be participatory and ecologically sustainable as well as productive. The economy is for being and not just
having. There must be fair sharing.[73]

Again, one of the major Catholic complaints about the 1996 Welfare
Reform package was that it scouted any independent claim to justice
based on human need. Catholics applauded the work rules in as
much as access to work is seen as a deeply central element in what the

American bishops have called justice as participation in the economy.[74] But work rules alone—a merit-based source for justice in distribution— do not sufficiently acknowledge the claims of need.

The connection between the Catholic case for religious liberty and its wider theory of state and society should by now be clear. The freedom of the church that the church calls for must be such as not penalize or impede its freedom to pursue its religious mission, as it understands it, in society. But the church's self-understanding in terms of its mission to society rests on particularist theological warrant. We cannot expect that self-understanding to become public property enshrined in law. The church can garner public support for the freedom it demands for itself in fidelity to gospel warrant only if it states its case *simultaneously* on secular warrant. Social Catholicism is notoriously bilingual. It appeals both to gospel images and to what John Rawls has called "public reason."[75]

The secular warrant for the argument for the kind of relation to society the church seeks is the argument for mediating structures as a key element in public policy. As John Courtney Murray clearly saw, the freedom of the church is inextricably linked to other civil freedoms: "The personal and corporate free exercise of religion as a human and civil right is evidently cognate with other more general human and civil rights—with the freedom of corporate bodies and institutions within society, based on the principle of subsidiary functions; with the general freedom for peaceful purposes, based on the social nature of man; with the general freedom of speech and of the press based on the nature of political society."[76]

The Subsidiarity and the "Spheres of Creation" Tradition

It may be useful to compare this Catholic variant to other theological families. Anabaptists accept the zone of civil life as the sphere of spontaneity and creativity but limit the state severely. As one statement from an Anabaptist position puts it, "[T]he real dynamic of society does not lie in the state; state action is obviated when subordinate groups, like the church, effectively deal with education, health, relief and social security. Christians should not rely too much on the state and thus become completely obligated to it."[77] Clearly in this tradition, there is no sense of the state's role in furthering the common good.

One Calvinist variant of "spheres of creation" was very instrumental in carving out the kind of subsidiarity state in the Netherlands. The *Gereformeeden* conclude to something akin to subsidiarity in their slogan, "Sovereignty in our own circle." *Gereformeeden* control over their own mediating structures serves as a crucial check on idolatrous claims of state sovereignty, even when the state provides subsidy.[78] But the permeability of the boundaries between state and the other spheres, while not ruled out in exceptional cases, is less clear than in Catholicism. There is a weaker sense that the state, as such, has any legitimate roles to play in securing the common good.[79] At times, the "sovereign spheres" are given such autonomy that it is unclear (1) what to do if they fail to achieve the goods that are entrusted to their scope; and (2) how to adjudicate conflicts between the spheres that constitute civil society among themselves or with the state.[80] Moreover, authors differ strongly on how many spheres of creation there are. The answers range from three (e.g., the state, family, church) to as many as seven or more.[81] The more the range of such orders and spheres, the broader and more sophisticated the possibilities for a rounded and interesting notion of civil society. Much of the Christian Right in America, by restricting themselves exclusively to church and family, make it impossible to really conceive of a civil society. Finally, absent some sense of a "natural law" or "public reason" to ground outreach beyond revelation to fellow citizens, this account of "spheres of creation" is often not very bilingual. It relies on biblical warrants alone.

Closest to the Catholic vision of the common good, solidarity and subsidiarity, it seems to me, is the Calvinist federal tradition of covenantal theology. As one treatise puts it, society is built up from the bottommost units of the family and associational life into towns, cities, and provinces, and, finally, a federal commonwealth. "In each case, a covenant creates the more comprehensive level of political order. But the more inclusive entity does not negate the significance, participation, and consent of the covenanted groups that comprise it. Each level retains its importance and its integrity as an operative community with appropriate governmental functions."[82] Federal theology seems to envision something akin not only to subsidiarity, but to a needed role of the most inclusive unit (presumably the state) to act for the commonweal. But here, unlike Maritain's notion of civil society as an encompassing concept, the body politic, the concept of civil society seems to be atomized into leveled and compartmentalized units. Their relation is mainly to the topmost unit or the next encompassing level. No full-blown theory of solidarity and the common good unites the levels to each other.

Boundaries, Needs, and Liabilities

In the Catholic theory of civil society and the state, subsidiarity (freedom, spontaneity, creativity, grass-roots consensus, the anchoring of a sense of belonging) sets *presumptive* boundaries to the limited state.

But the boundaries can be permeable because subsidiarity is juxta-posed to solidarity and the common good. Against views that would judge civil society always good and the state presumptively bad and suspect, or the state as expendable and civil society sufficient, or, finally, views of an omnicompetent state, social Catholicism sees the state as structurally and permanently necessary to secure the common good. It knows, as a recent document, *A Call to Civil Society*, puts it, that there can be a bad civil society![83]

It is more difficult for me to find a similar presumptive rule to adju-dicate the permeability of boundaries between the state and the other spheres in the "spheres of creation" doctrine. How do these spheres interact among themselves (church, family, economy, universities, pri-vate associations, lower levels of civic life, etc.), and in what sense do they serve "public" functions that enjoin some version of state regulation, supplementation, complementarity, and nourishment? The "sovereignty" or "autonomy" of the spheres is clearly stated. Their interdependence and cohesion is not well explicated.

In any event, as David Martin argues, "Christianity creates counter-cultures *above* and below the unity of the natural society."[84] The state it-self, whatever the empirical vigor and counterbalance of civil society, is held to a higher law: justice, respect for human dignity, and the com-mon good. It is also limited by legitimate loyalties not just to the "little platoons" of civil society, but to an interdependent "objective" common good in global society.

In the tradition I have been expounding, civil society needs the state for those public goods the state alone can provide or guarantee: the coordination of order, a structure of civility and peace among pluralist visions of the good, the regulation of welfare and justice, the forging of a "common civic faith and purpose" that cross-cuts any one particular-ist tradition.[85] Notoriously, the mechanisms of civil society (remaining voluntary, dispersed, conflictual, and following a kind of free-choice market mechanism) cannot, of themselves, guarantee the fulfillment of fundamental human needs (the "social" rights) or fair distributive justice.

In turn, as the subsidiarity literature insists, civil society offers a zone of freedom, spontaneity, creativity, a grass-roots anchoring of "belong-ing." It remains the primary locale for the anchoring of virtue. In point of fact, moral traditions are strongly rooted in the religious institutions and the neutral state cannot easily promulgate a unitary theory of virtue.[86] The face-to-face seedbed of mutuality, trust (what Jacques Maritain once referred to as "civic friendship") is inculcated primarily in civil society.[87] Yet the necessary morality of both the economy (keep contracts, pay fair wages, etc.) and the state (pay taxes, vote, be responsible and informed as a citizen) depend on this prior vivid experience of reciprocity, duty, responsibility, and solidarity.[88]

The major liabilities the state poses to civil society occur when it sacrifices subsidiarity to centralizing efficiency or turns the "common good" into a mere interest-balancing. The state that knows it is partially entrusted with the common good can also forget that it does not have a monopoly on its definition. It can also substitute the morality aimed at abstract others (e.g., law and market) for any attention to the need for a more richly textured experiential seedbed for mutuality, reciprocity, and social trust.

In turn, civil society may become enthralled to one sector of it: the economy. This in turn can dictate what counts as state action for the public good. As *A Call to Civil Society* well puts it: "Business, labor and economic institutions do not exist apart from the rest of civil society. That the economy is part of civil society demonstrates that it is part of our moral order as well—not some extrinsic force and certainly not an end in itself but rather a major reflection of our judgments about the conditions for human flourishing and the larger meanings of our common life."[89] Civil society can try to substitute its often chaotic voluntarism and its ideals of freedom for the need for coordinating and regulating activities by the state. It can substitute particular interest for the common good. Not in my neighborhood, after all, is a kind of call from the zone of civil society! There seems no one magic abstract rule to control these liabilities. Vigilance and citizen participation to monitor not only the state but the economy and the other institutions of civil society seem necessary.

Citizenship

Christians see the authority of the state as God-derived. Hence, they tend to see the duties of citizenship as incumbent on them. In point of fact, at least in America, those who are church members do tend to vote more often, be engaged more in voluntarism in civil society, and give more money to charity and philanthropy.[90] Indeed, more than other forms of voluntary civil associations (again in America), churches seem to add to elements of the democratic potential to society.[91]

Christian theorists have sometimes complained of the leveling character of citizenship ideals, their being tied too closely to purely procedural norms and their introduction of relativistic notions of morality or truth into the common life (perhaps, even, their claim to permit, for the sake of common life or peaceful consensus, behavior the disciple judges repugnant and seriously sinful). The rules of the game of citizenship substitute a realm of public opinion for an arena of substantive truth. Some disciples see and decry this citizen arena as purely a "naked public square."[92]

Theorists of citizenship, for their part, have not lacked legitimate complaints about the deleterious intrusion of an ideal of Christian discipleship into the commonwealth of citizens. The brutal and passionate wars of religion, to be sure, spawned the Enlightenment ideals of secular reason and religious tolerance.

The litany of complaints against the intrusion of discipleship into citizenship reaches back to Roman times. A typical rebuke—voiced strongly by Rousseau—is that the Christian ideal of a universal solidarity undercuts urgent commitment to *this* particular nationally defined sovereignty and general will.

Other complaints of citizens to the disciples have noted the otherworldliness of the Christian ideal, its lack of seriousness about the historically contingent. The Marxists, for their part, talk of the ideological misuses of religion to compensate for the suffering of the poor or to legitimate the wealth of the dominant. A final rebuke notes the way Romans 13:1–7 has often been interpreted to legitimate a mere dutiful citizenship, a mere passive obedience, rather than that more active, critical engagement of citizen-politicians so eloquently espoused by Michael Walzer. As Walzer contends, "[T]he citizen/voter is crucial to the survival of democratic politics; but the citizen/politician is crucial to its liveliness and integrity."[93] The empirical evidence cited at the beginning of this section does not seem to bear out claims that Christians are less active citizens than others; *e contrario.*

Many disciples conflate their ideals of discipleship and citizenship. At times this can inject a hypermoralism into citizenship life. Citizens are not called to be saints. As Michael Walzer once noted about citizenship, "[T]he standards are not all that high; we are required to be brethren and citizens, not saints and heroes." At least one strand in Christian thinking, however—that of the Thomists—will not allow a conflation of law and morality as if they were, at all points, the same. Thomas insisted that not all acts of vice are to be forbidden by human law, nor are all acts of virtue to be enjoined by it, but only what, given the moral development and customs of a particular society, is reasonably possible in order to promote the common good.[94]

The law that regulates citizenship duties must be moral, but it does not enshrine all of the moral. The morality of citizenship in this Thomistic sense would seem to agree with Walzer that the citizenship ideal does not have to look to saints and heroes. In an intriguing throwaway line in his book of essays, *Citizenship Today*, D. W. Brogan claims that "a Christian citizen has more duties than and different from those that the state defines and demands."[95] Brogan feels Christians are always minimally called to the duties and demands the state legitimately defines. But they must go beyond that humane minimum to try to inject some wider ideal of neighbor-love into the social fabric. Christian ideals might add to the wider repertoire of citizenship such notions as a countercultural vision of a more ideal community and of forgiveness. Christians may feel called to add a note of self-sacrificing *agape* to the justice ideals of citizenship. But this is supererogation, not the content of the citizenship ideal itself. By its nature, modern citizenship must be an *equal* citizenship, held commonly by believers and nonbelievers.

Groups and Individuals

Social Catholicism champions the right to association as rooted in the radical sociality of humans. It does not have any firm rules about when government should interact with individuals mainly through communal associations. Rhetorically, the tradition, in its official statements, strongly endorses a right to one's culture (especially for ethnic or enclave people in a wider pluralist society) and to one's language. But beyond this rhetorical evocation of the right (which would seem to demand communal associations to keep the language and culture alive in a situation when a people is a minority), no firm rules about how to deal with the situations where communal right are denied have been proposed.[96]

Conflict

Christians have shown a certain allergy toward the idea of social conflict. Social Catholicism, in earlier periods, held to an overly organicist and unitary vision of social life. This has been more recently displaced by a greater openness to struggle and some forms of social conflict. Donal Dorr, for example, has traced the calls for the poor "to struggle" and to join other societal groups in the "struggle for justice" in recent documents of social Catholicism.[97] One virtue of the Reformed tradition's view of society is that it has a less organicist heritage. Social Catholicism can learn from that, although, as Dorr notes, it has already in liberation and political theology and in recent documents shed that earlier organicist bias. And Protestant thought—as Robert Bellah has recently argued—lacking a stronger communitarian bias when voluntarism blots out older and richer notions of the covenant, does tend to undercut any sense of a "possibly" common good.[98]

Clearly, with its sense of a higher law to civil law (even if the authority of those who propagate civil law comes ultimately also from God),

Christianity knows and has embodied civil disobedience. As the Book of Acts puts it, the apostles said to the authorities, "We must obey God and not the laws of men" (Acts 4:19). Christian theories of a justified revolution tend to follow the rules for a just war. It must be a last resort. There must be a reasonable chance of success in achieving a just new society. The means used must be proportionate and protect innocent life. The end must be the restoration of civil peace. Presumption always lies against any resort to violence. The more mild conflictual forms of social protest, struggle or civil disobedience, exact a less heavy calculus. They can more easily be countenanced or even mandated, especially if nonviolent. Here again, however, the rule seems to read that the act of conflict or disobedience will not undermine respect for law and rightful governmental authority. Ultimately, such acts envision a return to a civil conversation about the goods to be pursued in common.[99]

In the end, however, as Paul Ricoeur has argued, there is a kind of *aporia* in the relationship of citizenship and discipleship:

> It is not responsible (and is even impossible) to deduce a politics from a theology. This is so because every political involvement grows out of a truly secular set of information, a situational arena which proffers a limited field of possible actions and available means, and a more or less risk-taking option, a gamble, among these possibilities.[100]

Politics remains more art than science, an art, moreover, exercised in a world not yet fully redeemed and transformed by grace, in that paradoxical arena that mingles coercion with rationality and justice. The disciple neither knows better than the unbeliever nor necessarily loves more that truly political common good which might be both genuinely possible and enhance justice and the common life.

Notes

1. Many American evangelicals simply lack anything like a coherent *Staatslehre*. But see two more thoughtful recent attempts at one in Charles Colson, *Kingdoms in Conflict* (New York: William Murrow, 1987); and Michael Cromartie, ed., *Disciples and Democracy* (Grand Rapids, Mich.: William Eerdmans, 1994).

2. Don Browning et al., *From Culture Wars to Common Ground* (Louisville, Ky.: Westminster/John Knox, 1997), 243–44.

3. For an appeal to covenant language to root Catholic social teaching, see "Economic Justice for All" (the U.S. Bishops on the Economy), in *Catholic Social Thought: The Documentary Heritage*, ed. David O'Brien and Thomas Shannon (Maryknoll, N. Y.: Orbis, 1992), 586–88.

4. Max Stackhouse, "Theology and the Global Powers: Revising Our Vision of Civil Society" (paper represented at a conference on Religion, Social Capital, and Democracy, Calvin College, October 16–17, 1998), 11–12.

5. Thomas Sanders, *Protestant Concepts of Church and State* (New York: Holt, Rinehart and Winston, 1964); and John Bennett, *Christians and the State* (New York: Charles Scribner's Sons, 1958).

6. See José Casanova, *Public Religions in the Modern World* (Chicago: University of Chicago Press, 1994), 40–66.

7. Ernst Troeltsch, *The Social Teaching of the Christian Churches*, vol. 1, trans. Olive Wyon (New York: Harper and Row, 1960).

8. One argument for this is found in Michael Novak, *The Spirit of Democratic Capitalism*, 2nd ed. (Lanham, Md.: Madison Books, 1991).

9. Beware, however, of calling anything truly "secular" before the eighteenth century. Plato, Aristotle, the Stoics, and John Locke are not secular.

10. Roy Defarri, ed., *Saint Ambrose: Theological and Dogmatic Works* (Washington, D.C.: Catholic University Press, 1963); Marcus Tullius Cicero, *On Duties*, ed. M. T. Griffin and E. M. Atkins (New York: Cambridge University Press, 1991).

11. Augustine, *The City of God*, ed. D. B. Zema and Gerald Walsh (New York: Fathers of the Church, 1950), 19.21.

12. Samuel Pufendorf, *De Jure Naturae* (London: Oxford University Press, 1934); Justus Lipsius, *Justi Lipsii de Cruce Libri Tres* (Amsterdam: Andreae Frisii, 1670).

13. David Burrell, *Freedom and Creation in Three Traditions* (Notre Dame, Ind.: University of Notre Dame Press, 1993); *Knowing the Unknowable God: Ibn-Sina, Maimonides, Aquinas* (Notre Dame, Ind.: University of Notre Dame Press, 1986).

14. Thomas Bokenkotter, *Church and Revolution: Catholics in the Struggle for Democracy and Social Justice* (New York: Doubleday Image, 1998), 39–173. For an overview of Christianity and socialism, Denis Janz, *World Christianity and Marxism* (New York: Oxford University Press, 1998).

15. For Catholic rights theory, David Hollenbach, *Claims in Conflict: Retrieving and Renewing the Catholic Human Rights Tradition* (New York: Paulist Press, 1979); R. Bruce Douglas and David Hollenbach, eds., *Catholicism and Liberalism* (New York: Cambridge University Press, 1994); for contemporary Catholic dialogue with critical theory see J. B. Metz and Jean Pierre Jossua, eds., *Christianity and Socialism* (New York: Seabury Press, 1977); and J. B. Metz, *Faith in History and Society* (New York: Seabury Press, 1980).

16. For Catholic feminist theoretical voices see Elizabeth Schussler-Fiorenza, *Bread, Not Stone* (Boston: Beacon Press, 1985); *Discipleship of Equals: A Critical Feminist Ekklesia-logy of Liberation* (New York: Crossroad, 1993); Rosemary R. Reuther, *Sexism and God Talk: Toward a Feminist Theology* (Boston: Beacon Press, 1983); for a representative Protestant view of feminism, cf. Letty Russel and J. Shannon Clarkson, eds., *Dictonary of Feminist Theologies* (Louisville, Ky.: Westminster/John Knox Press, 1996).

17. Robert George, ed., *Natural Law Theory* (New York: Oxford University Press, 1992); John Finnis, *Natural Law and Natural Rights* (New York: Oxford University Press, 1980). But see the more theological account of natural law in Jean Porter, *Natural and Divine Law* (Grand Rapids, Mich.: William Eerdmans Co., 1999).

18. *Centesimus Annus*, in O'Brien and Shannon, *Catholic Social Thought*, 465.

19. Michael Fleet and Brian Smith, *The Catholic Church and Democracy in Chile and Peru* (Notre Dame, Ind.: University of Notre Dame Press, 1997); Scott Mainwaring, *The Catholic Church and Politics in Brazil* (Stanford, Calif.: Stanford University Press, 1986); Jeffrey Klaiber, *The Church, Dictatorships, and Democracy in Latin America* (Maryknoll, N.Y.: Orbis, 1998); for a Protestant perspective, Guillermo Cook, *The Expectation of the Poor* (Maryknoll, N.Y.: Orbis Press, 1986). See also the many entries on East German churches in the English-based periodical *Religion in Communist Lands.*

20. The "Who speaks for the church?" question is raised on the Protestant side by Paul Ramsey, *Who Speaks for the Church?* (Nashville, Tenn.: Abingdon, 1967); a Catholic position is found in J. Bryan Hehir, "The Right and Competence of the Church," in *One Hundred Years of Catholic Social Thought*, ed. John Coleman (Maryknoll, N.Y.: Orbis, 1991), 55–71.

21. The classic case for governmental authority, absent sin, is Yves Simon, *A General Theory of Authority* (Notre Dame, Ind.: University of Notre Dame Press, 1962).

22. For a more optimistic view of the state and society's relation to the kingdom of God, Jon Sobrino, *Christology at the Crossroads* (Maryknoll, N.Y.: Orbis Press, 1978).

23. Walter Rauschenbush, *A Theology of the Social Gospel* (New York: Abingdon, 1945). Rauschenbush spoke of "social salvation." For premillennial views, Michael Lienesh, *Redeeming America: Piety and Politics in the New Christian Right* (Chapel Hill: University of North Carolina Press, 1993).

24. For a profound sensibility to sin by a Catholic writer, Bertrand de Jouvenal, *On Power* (Boston: Beacon Press, 1968).

25. Reinhold Niebuhr, *Moral Man and Immoral Society* (New York: Charles Scribner's Sons, 1960); Reinhold Niebuhr, *Christianity and Power Politics* (Hamden, Conn.: Archon Books, 1969).

26. For another Anabaptist view, Stanley Hauerwas and William Willison, *Resident Aliens: Life in the Christian Colony* (Nashville, Tenn.: Abingdon, 1989).

27. Allen Verhey, "Natural Law in Aquinas and Calvin," in *God and the Good*, ed. Clifton Orlebeke and Lewis Smedes (Grand Rapids, Mich.: William Eerdmans, 1975), 80–92.

28. For an argument that post-Vatican II Catholicism has its own world-transforming analogue to the Protestant ethic, see Ivan Vallier, *Catholicism, Social Control, and Modernization* (Englewood Cliffs, N.J.: Prentice-Hall, 1970), 148–61. This world-transforming strand in social Catholicism can be seen in recent Catholic social encyclicals and the rise of liberation theology.

29. I treat many of these issues in John Coleman, "The Two Pedagogies: Discipleship and Citizenship," in *Education for Discipleship and Citizenship*, ed. Mary Boys (New York: Pilgrim Press, 1989), 35–75.

30. Jacques Maritain, *Man and the State* (Chicago: University of Chicago Press, 1951), 53, denies sovereignty to the state.

31. Philippe Duplessis Morney's *Vinciciae Contra Tyranos*, published in 1579, treats of a just revolution. Charles McCoy and J. Wayne Baker, *Fountainhead*

of Federalism: Heinrich Bullinger and the Covenantal Tradition (Louisville Ky.: Westminster/John Knox, 1991), 47–50; for Aquinas on the right to oppose tyranny, Summa Theologiae II-II, q. 42, 2 ad 3.

32. This list of the ends of government is found in John Courtney Murray, We Hold These Truths (New York: Sheed and Ward, 1960).

33. Sanders, Protestant Concepts of Church and State, 279.

34. Bennett, Christians and the State, 205.

35. John Courtney Murray, "Religious Freedom," in Freedom and Man, ed. John C. Murray (New York: P. J. Kenedy and Sons, 1965).

36. John Coleman, "Catholic Integralism as a Fundamentalism," in Fundamentalism in Comparative Perspective, ed. Lawrence Kaplan (Amherst: University of Massachusetts Press, 1992), 74–95.

37. George Lindbeck, "Critical Reflections," in Religious Freedom, ed. Walter Burghardt (New York: Paulist Press, 1977), 54.

38. The call for a juridical guarantee for religious freedom as a civil right is in The Declaration on Religious Liberty, no. 6. The text is found in David O'Brien and Thomas Shannon, eds., Renewing the Face of the Earth: Catholic Documents on Peace, Justice, and Liberation (Garden City, N.Y.: Doubleday, 1972), 291–306.

39. John Courtney Murray, "The Issue of Church and State at Vatican Council II," Theological Studies 27 (March 1966): 599–600.

40. Casanova, Public Religions.

41. Declaration on Religious Liberty, no. 1.

42. Ibid., no. 6.

43. See Jean Bethke Elshtain, "Relationship of Public to Private," in The New Dictionary of Catholic Social Thought, ed. Judith Dwyer (Collegeville, Minn.: Liturgical Press, 1994), 796.

44. Casanova, Public Religions, 57–58, for these three conditions for a modern, public religion.

45. U.S. Catholic Bishops, "Economic Justice for All," in O'Brien and Shannon, Catholic Social Thought, 604, for a call for a "common deliberation" about economic policies.

46. Casanova, Public Religions, 58.

47. For any public expression of religion as a form of bad taste, see Richard Rorty, "Religion as Conversation Stopper," Common Knowledge 3, no. 1 (1994): 1–2.

48. Seyla Benhabib, "Models of Public Space: Hannah Arendt, the Liberal Tradition, and Jürgen Habermas," in Habermas and the Public Sphere, ed. Craig Calhoun (Cambridge, Mass.: MIT Press, 1991), 82.

49. Casanova, Public Religions, 65.

50. Cf. Richard Neuhaus's monthly comments in his journal, First Things. Michael Novak authored his own lay commission's neoconservative counterargument to the 1985 Bishops' Pastoral on Economic Justice.

51. For the Canadian Bishops on Indian Rights, cf. "Northern Development: At What Cost?" in Do Justice: The Social Teaching of the Canadian Catholic Bishops, ed. E. F. Sheridan (Sherbrooke, Quebec: Editions Paulines, 1987), 275–86. For human rights commissions in Chile, see Brian Smith, The Church and Politics in Chile (Princeton: Princeton University Press, 1982), 318–27.

52. "Justice in the World," in O'Brien and Shannon, *Catholic Social Thought*, 289.

53. *Declaration on Religious Liberty*, in O'Brien and Shannon, *Renewing the Face of the Earth*.

54. John Rawls, *Political Liberalism* (New York: Columbia University Press, 1993); Bruce Ackerman, *Social Justice in the Liberal State* (New Haven: Yale University Press, 1980). Rawls and Ackerman see a problem of basing human or basic citizenship rights on a religious foundation that is not shared. In their view, human rights are too important to be held hostage to foundational arguments.

55. Murray, *We Hold These Truths*, 308.

56. John Courtney Murray, S.J., *The Problem of Religious Freedom* (Westminster, Md.: Newman Press, 1965), 42.

57. Maritain, *Man and the State*, 13.

58. Not all liberals privilege the right always over the good. William Galston, for example, allows a place for some nonprocedural goods in *Liberal Purposes: Goods, Virtues and Diversity in the Liberal State* (New York: Cambridge University Press, 1991). Nor do all Catholics agree that the state has a role in defining and enacting the common good. Alisdair MacIntyre argues that the common good must be entirely defined in civil society, not by the state, in his chapter "The Political and Social Structures of the Common Good," in *Dependent Rational Animals* (Chicago: Open Court, 1999), 129–54.

59. Maritain, *Man and the State*, 11

60. For Montelembert's championing of subsidiarity in the 1840s see Bokenkotter, *Church and Revolution*, 52–55.

61. In O'Brien and Shannon, *Renewing the Face of the Earth*, 62.

62. Ibid.

63. Cf. Michael Walzer, "The Problem of Citizenship," in *Obligations: Essays in Disobedience, War, and Citizenship* (Cambridge, Mass.: Harvard University Press, 1970), 203–28.

64. E. F. Schumacher, *Small Is Beautiful* (New York: Harper and Row, 1973). Schumacher, as a Catholic, was familiar with subsidiarity.

65. H. A. Rommen, *The State in Catholic Thought* (St. Louis: B. Herder and Co., 1945), 253.

66. Maritain, *Man and the State*, 21; Emile Durkheim, *Professional Ethics and Civil Morals* (London: Routledge and Kegan Paul, 1957), 73ff.

67. Cf. John Coleman, "Not Democracy but Democratization," in *A Democratic Catholic Church*, ed. Eugene Bianchi and Rosemary Reuther (New York: Crossroad, 1992), 226–47.

68. Catholic Charities U.S.A. agencies must now compete with for-profit companies such as Lockheed Martin for welfare caseload outsourcing in welfare-to-work programs. William Ryan, "The New Landscape for Nonprofits," *Harvard Business Journal* (January–February, 1999), 127–36, contends that the competitive entrance of for-profits into welfare deliverance will erode commitments to community development initiatives among nonprofits.

69. The merger of nonprofit hospital systems has made of them giant bureaucracies driven by the bottom lines of the requirements of the law and the market.

70. For Catholic policy voices in the welfare reform debate appealing to sub-sidiarity and the common good, Thomas Massaro, *Catholic Social Teaching and U.S. Welfare Reform* (Collegeville, Minn.: Liturgical Press, 1998); U.S. Catholic Conference Administrative Board, "Moral Principles and Policy Priorities on Welfare Reform," *Origins* 24, no. 41 (March 30, 1995): 674–78. For a consistent double appeal to subsidiarity yet a legitimate governmental role for the common good in Catholic welfare policy, see Dorothy Brown and Elizabeth McKeown, *The Poor Belong to Us: Catholic Charities and American Welfare* (Cambridge, Mass.: Harvard University Press, 1997); John A. Coleman, "American Religion and Policy Advocacy: Catholic Charities U.S.A. and Welfare Reform," *Journal of Policy History* 13, no. 1 (January 2001): 73–108.

71. Hollenbach, *Claims in Conflict*.

72. For an argument to nationalize property if necessary to bring about true competition against monopoly, see *Quadragesimo Anno*, no. 42, in O'Brien and Shannon, *Catholic Social Thought*, 67.

73. Philip Land, "The Earth Is the Lord's: Thoughts on the Economic Order," in *Above Every Name: The Lordship of Christ and Social Systems*, ed. Thomas Clarke (New York: Paulist Press, 1980).

74. For justice as participation in the economy, David Hollenbach, *Justice, Peace, and Human Rights* (New York: Crossroad, 1988), 71–83.

75. Rawls, *Political Liberalism*, 11–15; Don Browning, *From Culture Wars to Common Ground*, 243, attributes this Catholic bilingualism (rooted, in part, in natural law) to the Catholic ease in addressing public issues in society and rooting their case (for their own church public) in the Bible *and* in secular warrant (for the broader public). He contrasts this to the difficulty of elements of the New Christian Right to disentangle their "civil" from "sacred biblical" discourse.

76. Murray, *The Problem of Religious Freedom*, 26–27.

77. Cited in Sanders, *Protestant Concepts of Church and State*, 107.

78. For subsidy politics in the Netherlands: Arend Lijhart, *The Politics of Accommodation* (Berkeley and Los Angeles: University of California Press, 1968); John A. Coleman, *The Evolution of Dutch Catholicism* (Berkeley and Los Angeles: University of California Press, 1978), 58–87.

79. Abraham Kuyper, *Calvinism* (New York: Fleming and Revell Co., 1890) seems to allow some governmental intrusion on the separate spheres in strong emergency situations. But it is quite abnormal.

80. Browning, *From Culture Wars to Common Ground*, 77, seems to argue that the assumption is that the divine will wants the diverse spheres of creation to be unified. But the mechanism for doing so—short of God's will and action—is left hanging.

81. Stackhouse, "Theology and Global Powers," lists four orders of creation. Evangelicals who are part of James Dobson's Focus on the Family network mention only three: state, church, and family. Kuyper, *Calvinism*, seems to have envisioned seven.

82. McCoy and Baker, *Fountainhead of Federalism*, 58.

83. The Council on Civil Society, *A Call to Civil Society* (New York: Institute for American Values, 1998), 14. The Council is a joint effort of Catholic, mainline Protestant, Evangelical, Jewish, and secular voices.

84. David Martin, *Dilemmas of Contemporary Religion* (Oxford: Basil Blackwell, 1978), 37.

85. For the need for a nontheologically based "public philosophy," see Council on Civil Society, *A Call to Civil Society*, 12.

86. Ibid., 8.

87. Jacques Maritain, *Christianity and Democracy* (New York: Charles Scribner's Sons, 1944), 50–51.

88. For this argument that the "abstract moralities" of law and economy need face-to-face anchoring of mutuality and trust in civil society, Allan Wolfe, *Whose Keeper?* (Berkeley and Los Angeles: University of California Press, 1989).

89. Council on Civil Society, *A Call to Civil Society*, 11.

90. For the involvement of church members in civic participation: John Wilson and Thomas Jonaoski, "A Contribution of Religion to Volunteer Work," *Sociology of Religion* 56, no. 2 (Summer 1995): 325–38; Robert Wuthnow, Virginia Hodkinson, et al., *Faith and Philanthropy in America* (San Francisco: Jossey Bass, 1990).

91. Sydney Verba, Kay Schlozman, and Henry Brady, *Voice and Equality* (Cambridge, Mass.: Harvard University Press, 1995), gives the evidence of the democratic potential in church membership.

92. Richard Neuhaus, *The Naked Public Square* (Grand Rapids, Mich.: William Eerdmans, 1984).

93. Michael Walzer, *Spheres of Justice* (New York: Basic Books, 1983), 308.

94. *Summa Theologiae* I-II q. 96 aa. 2, 3.

95. D. W. Brogan, *Citizenship Today* (New York: Macmillan, 1963), 103.

96. The Canadian Catholic philosopher Charles Taylor takes up this Catholic theme of linguistic and cultural rights and applies it to policy in his essay "The Politics of Recognition," in *Multiculturalism*, ed. Charles Taylor (Princeton: Princeton University Press, 1994).

97. Donal Dorr, *Option for the Poor: A Hundred Years of Catholic Social Teaching* (Maryknoll, N.Y.: Orbis, 1992), 288–316.

98. Robert Bellah, "Flaws in the Protestant Cultural Code: Some Religious Sources of America's Problems," *America* (July 21–August 6, 1999), 9–14.

99. For the metaphor of civic conversation as a ground for civility, see the chapters "Creeds at War Intelligibly" and "The Origins and Authority of Public Consensus," in Murray, *We Hold These Truths*, 102–39.

100. Paul Ricoeur, *Politick en Gelof: Essays van Paul Ricoeur*, ed. Ad Peperzak (Utrecht: Ambo, 1968), 87. I do not have French originals that appeared in *Esprit* available to me. I argue that "the moral concept of citizenship in a religiously pluralistic world will have to be based on a wider notion than discipleship— probably, at root, in a non-theological understanding of the rights and duties of membership in the commonwealth or the tradition of civic republican virtue." "The Two Pedagogies," 37.

3

Christianity, Civil Society, and the State

A PROTESTANT RESPONSE

MAX L. STACKHOUSE

I AM DELIGHTED to have a chance to respond formally to John Coleman, for I have done so often in my mind and too seldom in person. He is one of the most important Christian thinkers in the area of social thought. Obviously a deeply committed Roman Catholic, he is also one who has taken some pains to study major strands of Protestant thought, just as many Protestants who are committed still to motifs from the Reformation have tried to sympathetically reengage the Roman Catholic tradition since Vatican II. However, I engage his chapter as one who is convinced that the view he takes as his counterfoil, the "Reformed tradition's theory about the 'spheres of creation,'" offers an even more convincing account of the nature of civil society and politics, and what they demand of us, than does even his most agreeable kind of Roman Catholicism. I say this with full awareness that with the election of Popes John XXIII and John Paul II, some major reconvergences of the whole tradition are apparent. It is all the more important, thus, that we all discuss how we both may become more catholic and more reformed, and how we can marshal the deeper unities and common resources of our faith to benefit civil society, political life, and humanity generally. After all, the destiny of the West—both internally and in its external impact—will be substantially shaped by the practical consequences of the interaction of religion and society, for many of the core structures of the West are founded on theological presuppositions, even if these assumptions are overlaid by non-, post-, or even antireligious constructs. If we do not understand this, we will not understand civilization or be able to shape its structures and dynamics at the deeper levels.

Coleman and I agree that there are many strands in the Christian reading of social/political matters that offer persistent minority reports, but that two main streams of the tradition generated the most articulate frameworks to deal with the analysis and guidance of the complex social systems in which we live. This is so because these two streams have already deeply stamped our institutional forms and our habits of mind, and because these two streams see it as part of the duty of the faithful ever and again to influence and repeatedly reform the recalcitrant aspects both of the human soul and of the social and political environments of the common life for the well-being of all. These traditions have thus developed distinctive models of society as a part of their "public theology." One of these may be called the "hierarchical-subsidiarity" view, most fully articulated by the Roman Catholic tradition, but held by others as well,[1] and the other the "federal-covenantal" view, most fully articulated by the Reformed tradition, but also held by others.[2]

These two positions share more than they dispute, at many levels. Both oppose those secular understandings of human existence wherein legitimate social life consists only of voluntary agreements constructed by autonomous individuals on the basis of rationally calculated marginal utility. They also oppose those pagan views that see persons as little more than a manifestation of some collective spirit or interest. The one view denies the ethical sociality of humans; the other obscures the moral dignity of the human person, including the capacity to transcend collective consciousness. The rejection of these two ideologies entails also suspicion of the "two agent" theory of some social contract theory—the view that the private individual (who may or may not have religious preferences, familial connections, and cultural or commercial interests—all of which are voluntary and private matters) and the public state are the only two decisive forces in human affairs, and that each must support and sustain the other.[3]

Still, significant differences remain, and it may help clarify matters to identify the points of divergence as they bear on our questions. The fundamental differences, I think, were artfully stated by F. W. Dillistone almost a half century ago. He recognized, as did Ernst Troeltsch before him, an intimate relationship between theology, ecclesiology, and social philosophy. In *The Structure of the Divine Society* he compared two models. The hierarchical-subsidiary model presumes a naturally differentiated, complex "body" ordered by means of a dual internal hierarchical structure, one spiritual and internal, one material and external, that aids the many parts or "organs" of the whole in fulfilling their innate tendency to actualize virtue and the common good. In contrast, the federal-covenantal view is a "pluralist" model in which religious and other institutions in society—familial, cultural, economic, educational, medical, and the like, including political ones—are conceived as a matrix of potentially networked associations, each held together by bonds of a set of pledged agreements that, while each would pursue the purposes to which it is distinctively called, all would be governed by commonly debated but also commonly accepted principles of right and wrong.[4] Both of these views avoid the perils of libertine individualism and political totalitarianism, and both support the view that between the person and the collective are the decisive "organs" or institutions of the civil society. The difference is this: One view sees these as comprehended by a natural moral solidarity made effective by compassionate but magisterial leadership that seeks to guide the whole to fulfill innate good ends. The other view sees various spheres of life, each populated by associative "artifacts," each constructed on the basis of a common discernment of need and a calling to fulfill that need, a recognition of a pluralism of institutions with possibly conflicting ends, and an ongoing critical analysis of our interpretations of transcendent principles of right that may be used to assess the presumption of innate tendencies to virtue, magisterial leadership, and any singular view of the common good.

The reason that we need to debate, and not simply ignore, such remaining divergences is that many believers share something of what might be called a cybernetic theory of society.[5] That is, while we acknowledge the tremendous power of multiple material forces, from evolutionary psychology to material interests, in shaping who we are and how we live in complex relationships, we hold that religious and social convictions, as relatively low-energy systems, are able both to interpret with remarkable accuracy the nature of those systems *and* to substantially guide their functioning—at least when there is an appropriate linkage between the ideas and the social systems of life.[6] However much we are formed by the high-energy systems of our chemistry and our instincts, our social and historical contexts, or the ways in which we find ourselves embedded in communities or traditions, we are not simply nature's effect, society's puppets, or an ensemble of our communities of origin. We have some capacity to exercise freedom precisely as we resist, affirm, interpret, or creatively reconstruct the decisive, if lower-energy, possibilities these provide. This is especially important for societies shaped by Christian (and, to a degree, Muslim or Buddhist) frames of reference, for these are "converting" religious traditions that have had enormous influences in changing cultures.[7]

The higher-energy systems to which I refer are, at the first level, family, politics, culture, and economy. I say "at the first level" for these are the social "spheres" or "sectors" found in every viable society—an observation that gave rise to the view that they were part of "nature" or "creation." They are present (in various forms) in all societies because the inevitable energies of Eros, Mars, the Muses, and Mammon must be structured in order to aid and not harm social life.

Thus every society will have a family structure, an institution for controlling violence, a cultural system, and an economic order.[8] They, and various other "spheres" of civil society, such as those of the professions—for example, education, law, medicine, and technology (engineering, architecture, and the like)—are found in complex form only in quite developed societies. These spheres, together with religion and the primary spheres, constitute civil society in contemporary civilizations, and may well be implicit in the practices of all societies. The relationships between what I here call "spheres," each of which pursues its own virtues and ends, are ordered both by the more general functional requirements of society at large and by a conviction that all are governed by a moral order that transcends the society—indeed, that has divine roots.[9] I take this to be a matter on which Professor Coleman and I agree, although we are both aware that some dispute it. If this is so, it implies that the kind of religion linked into these systems is fateful for the form of civil society, and thus also for the state as the political instrument, and is not the author or master either of the civil society or of the religious loyalties and commitments at its core. A politically or nationally or class- or gender- or aesthetically focused religion, for example, will bend the whole social system in particular directions, as would, say, a wisdom- or healing- or law- or technique-oriented one. Thus, getting religion as right as we can, establishing its own integrity, and getting it properly linked into these other social realities is both extremely subtle and quite decisive.

It does seem that some objections can be raised about the hierarchical-subsidiarity view. It may indeed be based on three debatable assumptions that shape both how reality is perceived and a sense of what we ought to do about it. These three beliefs are: that society has, or should become, a kind of "solidarity" marked by a kind of political sovereignty, that this whole has or should have a cohesive or unified inner disposition, and that both its exterior unity and its interior orientation should be sustained by an inevitable and necessary hierarchy that both represents the whole and serves it. Thus, all parts of the society should seek the "common good," and the virtuous person will act sacrificially for the well-being of this whole.[10] Coleman appears to agree with many other contributors to the current debates on civil society, that it is essentially about a "community" that has both civil and political aspects, and that the former, if vital, best serves the latter. However, his accent on the doctrine of subsidiarity, like the accent on "democratic participation" in less overtly theological views, puts the priority on "lower-level" forms of community and association, and demands a kind of "servant leadership" for their sake of those who have higher authority.

The questions that can be raised about this view are whether "solidarity," demanding a hierarchy of leadership that comprehends particular social political units, should be the case, and whether that whole involves the coincidence of civil society, moral order, and political sovereignty. Even if we recognize that we live in a universe, and thus in something of a wholistic system, the way of thinking about the whole may be conceived in a quite alternative manner—one fateful for our views of civil society and political life. It seems plausible, for instance, that society is constituted by a series of pluralistic sectors, spheres, and specific institutional relations, some "natural" in the sense that they are functionally prerequisite for a society to exist at all, some "historical" in the sense that they are constructed at specific times and places to fulfill useful roles in civilization for a time, and some "religious" in that they point to metaphysical and moral forces that are both transnatural and transhistorical. At none of these levels is it at all clear that they do or must coincide with political boundaries.

On the contrary, it is quite likely that several of these spill over national, social, and religious borders in ways that no political or national spiritual authority can, or should be able to, control—a fact that, if true, would make solidarity quite dubious as a value. People from these various areas of the common life may form overtly political associations, called factions, advocacy groups, community organizations, coalitions, lobbying networks, or even parties, with links to people in other places and with various religious convictions, to construct or deconstruct political regimes, to bend or block political policies toward what they care about in civil society and around the world. Wherever these are vibrant, we can be assured that civil society is well developed. Their vitality, however, may also indicate that civil society is being experienced as under threat and that leaders are mobilizing resources from sources near and far to provide the means to meet the threat. Civil society may also be alive and well when people feel no need to participate in these because they are involved in other cooperative activities, both at home and with links around the world, that seem more fateful for personal or social well-being. In short, the more active people are in civil society, the less interested they may be in politics. Many do not think that politics is, or should be, all that important for what is really going on in life. When this happens, politics is, in one sense, simply restored to its place as one among several spheres of civil society, no more determinative for the whole than economics and education, art and technology, family life, culture, law, and religion.[11]

The very multiplicity of the areas of human action suggests not a common, organic whole, but a pluralism of spheres and sectors in which humans live. Let us consider, for example, the significance of how daily newspapers and weekly magazines are organized—national politics and international affairs, economics and business, science, health and technology, sports, arts and entertainment, education, religion, hobbies and human interest, and so forth. Or consider the various course listings in any one of the social science departments in the university: psychology, which deals with intra- and interpersonal relationships; economics, which deals with commercial and financial relationships; political science, which deals with power and policy relationships; anthropology, which deals with cultural and customary relationships; sociology, which deals with the interaction of systems and the attitudes toward them. Or the main divisions of law: constitutional law, business law, criminal law, family law, international law, patents, tax law, and the like. I mention these to suggest that society is not a solidary unit coincidental with a religious culture and a polity; rather, civil societies are a complex set of spheres and sectors, populated by a host of "principalities and powers, authorities and dominions," to use New Testament images, constantly changing and variously arranged according to shifting historical developments and dynamic spiritual and moral influences.

Contemporary society, particularly, is a clustered network of institutions, each having its own pyramid of inner organization with its own moral and spiritual purpose, each negotiating its way through a welter of interactions. This has become more and more dramatic in our increasingly global society, where most of the spheres, sectors, areas of interest and engagement, or religions, and most of the institutions within them, have become voluntary and have escaped the control of any singular unified political or priestly control.

In brief, a massive pluralism of goods and a welter of rights in complex interaction, not solidaristic unity or hierarchic order, is the shape of society. In this context, the more complex the society becomes and the more global it is in reach, the more politics becomes but one subordinate cluster of institutions necessarily accountable to a much larger whole, and every hierarchy will be downsized in its functional utility and impact.

It is doubtful that nation-states will cease to be; but it is likely that they will become parts of larger federations of various kinds, frequently serving nonpolitical ends. In that context, the principle of "subsidiarity" becomes (as Coleman argues) even more important, especially as a reminder that higher levels of authority in each area must not only define and repeatedly refine the coordinating principles, purposes, and values of that area of life, but must help its members negotiate the complex relationships with other spheres, sectors, and areas. Neither they nor any single religion, however, will comprehend the whole, although it is the special task of religion to point to what does. That keeps society open. If we forget this, civilization and civility shrivel.[12]

In such a context, the definition of what constitutes the common good is and must be highly provisional, for what we hold to be "common" is often much too tied to the nationalistic definition of the whole, and thus our view of what is "good" may prematurely close off options that are better kept open. It is better to suggest that each area of human life is to be covenantally ordered internally, and related by federal agreements to other areas under a common discernment of the universal moral order that governs the world. What often passes for the "common good," in this view, is neither common enough nor good enough to meet that test. This suggests that our discernment of what is common and good is basically to be guided by the awareness of what is universally right. Thus, characteristically, in the Reformed (as well as the Jewish) traditions the Ten Commandments are taken as a revealed witness to what is right and wrong, and ideas such as "self-evident truths" (as in Locke), "the categorical imperative" (as in Kant), and "universal human rights" (the United Nations Declaration) are taken as "the law written on the heart" (to echo Paul).[13] These are the foundations of a free, morally ordered society, definitive for what we can accept as common and good because they are equally true everywhere and practically useful to all people in all circumstances of life with their many aims and ends.[14]

Obviously, this view questions the virtue of solidarity, especially as it has developed in modern social Catholicism. If solidarity means obeying the command to love the neighbor, to overcome enmity or need, and to form bonds of both faith and service by constructing new organizations in civil society that manifest the right, then the term may be embraced. But if it means a demanded loyalty to prescribed beliefs, a required obedience to culturally and socially (or even biologically) preprogrammed ends, or an expected moral identification with our class or race or nation or religious community of origin, it will have to be seen, as Augustine saw the virtue of the Stoics, as "splendid vice." That is because it too often prevents us from being converted to a higher vision—especially to what some of us call "the Kingdom of God" or "the New Jerusalem," that cosmopolitan community of grace and compassion beyond every social group and historical achievement in church or society. Under the plumb line of this standard, we see ourselves in multiple alliances to fulfill our several vocations in the various spheres, sectors, and areas of life, the comprehensive integration of which is not realized in a church or a state. This would entail a fresh view of responsible citizenship in a global civil society, a new, indirect relationship of person and state, and a wider vision of the catholicity of the churches and the ecumenicity of the great world faiths.

This would, at best, take the form of federal-covenantal renewal in the midst of nature and history, guided by a public theology that points toward that universal righteousness that is likely to be realized only in another life. In this view, civil society, with all its associations, is to serve an end other than its own, or the state's, fulfillment, and we make a tragic error if we reverse these priorities.

Notes

1. The concept of "subsidiarity" was apparently first used in church polity in opposition to the proposed declaration on papal infallibility by Bishop Dupanloup of France in the debates of Vatican I. He and others argued that higher authorities (in the church) were to be auxiliary to, furnishing aid and support for, local and regional bodies, not ruling over them as a secular power might. As is well known, the opposition failed and infallibility was affirmed, accepted also by this bishop. However, the concept of "servant leadership" expressed something integral to the whole tradition, and the term "subsidiarity" gradually became accepted as a way of stating that the higher authorities must serve the lower, and local, needs when the latter are incapable of solving a particular problem. This idea was applied, eventually as a statement of a social-ethical ideal in both church doctrine and political life, in a way that both affirmed and qualified notions of local and regional integrity in church and society. It is of considerable importance that it has become a dominant category of the European Union as a way of relating transnational to national authority.

2. This point is made, if somewhat polemically, by James Hastings Nichols, *Democracy and the Churches* (Philadelphia: Westminster Press, 1951); more recently by William J. Everett, *God's Federal Republic* (New York: Paulist Press, 1988); and most masterfully by Daniel Elazar, *The Covenant Tradition in Politics*, 4 vols. (Piscataway, N.J.: Transaction Publishers, 1995–98).

3. This I take to be the Bentham/Mill tendency on one side, the Hobbes/Rousseau tendency on the other. I have traced the devastating impact of these utilitarian and contractual views, as they became established in public policy, on religion, family life, and civil society in *Covenant and Commitments* (Louisville, Ky.: Westminster Press, 1997), esp. chap. 4.

4. F. W. Dillistone, *The Structure of the Divine Society* (London: Lutherworth Press; Philadelphia: Westminster Press, 1951). Similar points were made by Ernst Troeltsch, whom Coleman cites, in *The Social Teaching of the Christian Churches* (1911, German; New York: Harper and Bros., 1931).

5. I take this insight to be a continuing contribution by Talcott Parsons to social theory. See, e.g., *Societies* (Englewood Cliffs, N.J.: Prentice-Hall, 1966), esp. chap. 2.

6. I am convinced that the modern concept of civil society derives from the awareness of freedom from nature's dictates, from the conventions of society, and from the demands of political rulers, given with a notion of a relationship to God—which also required covenantal participation in "nonnatural consociations." This idea was articulated for modernity in a fresh way by Johannes Althusius, *Politics*, abridged and translated by F. S. Carney, with a preface by C. J. Friedrich (Boston: Beacon Press, 1964). The relationship of "grace" and "natural law" in these relations, however, has a deeper root, as recently argued

in Michael Cromartie, ed., *A Preserving Grace: Protestants, Catholics, and Natural Law* (Grand Rapids, Mich.: Eerdmans Publishers, 1987). For an influential view that acknowledges the historic role of religion but doubts the ongoing capability of faith or church to generate a viable civil society, see Adam Seligman, *The Idea of Civil Society* (New York: Free Press, 1992).

7. This is a major theme of the volume edited by John Witte and R. C. Martin, *Sharing the Book: Religious Perspectives on the Rights and Wrongs of Proselytism* (Maryknoll, N.Y.: Orbis Books, 1999), which includes my article, written with Deirdre Hainsworth, "Deciding for God: The Right to Convert in Protestant Perspectives," 201–30.

8. These are the four I treat in my address, "Theology and the Global Powers: Revising Our Vision of Civil Society," to which Coleman refers in his chapter (e.g., n. 4). It is my contention that the medieval concept of the three natural "estates," which are reflected in Lutheran (and, in some texts, Calvinist) ideas of the "Orders of Creation" (family, religion, and regime), omit the economy (previously seen as a natural function of the household, with it governed by the regime) as an independent arena of human action. Thus, I spoke of the construction of the corporation as a new institutional matrix for economic life—a major force in civil society, not fully acknowledged as such by many contemporary observers. The term "sphere" is drawn from an influential post-Enlightenment Calvinist perspective, made famous by Abraham Kuyper's *Calvinism* (New York: Revell, 1899), reprinted often as *Lectures on Calvinism* by Eerdmans Publishers. This term corresponds to the "department of life," frequently used by his friends Ernst Troeltsch and Max Weber, and to what later theologians such as Karl Barth and Dietrich Bonhoeffer call "Orders of Preservation" or "Mandates." The latter terms, as I have tried to show in several places, involve both "natural communities" and socially constructed institutions such as universities, hospitals, advocacy organizations, and television stations. These vary in their number and relationship (to each other and to the "primary orders") according to material conditions, historical developments, and spiritual-moral influences.

9. This is one of the main insights of Emil Brunner in his Gifford Lectures after World War II. See his *Christianity and Civilisation* (New York: Charles Scribner's Sons, 1948); and it is a central point of my *Creeds, Society, and Human Rights: A Study in Three Cultures* (Grand Rapids, Mich.: Eerdmans Publishers, 1985), as we faced both the Soviet system and the decolonialized countries in a new way. "Civil society" will be differently arranged not only modestly in a Reformed as compared to a Catholic setting, but more dramatically in a Hindu, Muslim, Marxist, or Confucian one. Each will assign a different role to politics and have a distinct view of the duties and rights of citizens. But an absence, repression, or marginalization of a theological view is devastating.

10. The predominant form of this pattern is very old, and is stated in a famous letter of Pope Gelasius in 494. It is claimed that there are two powers in society, the spiritual and the temporal, the latter to be subsidiary to the former. Much non-Roman teaching has a similar pattern, conceiving "society" as a single body and having twin authority structures, one spiritual and one political. This is true not only in Lutheran lands, where the contrast of Law and Gospel

emphasized the distinction between outer and inner, but also in all those countries influenced by the Caesaro-Papist traditions of Eastern Orthodoxy, by Erastian doctrines as in Anglicanism, and by the several continental lands effected by the Peace of Westphalia. In the latter cases, temporal authority is held to be the guardian of the spiritual, with the spiritual responsible for the moral texture of society. These all have coincidental boundaries that comprehend religious and political authorities, and see civil society as subject to both. The rise of the secular nation-state has often been seen to be the more radical subordination and privatization of religion, as political authority took responsibility for civil society. This latter view is now increasingly under question, a fact that accounts for the renewed interest in both the models under discussion here. See, e.g., José Casanova, *Public Religions in the Modern World* (Chicago: University of Chicago Press, 1994).

11. It is surely the case that human societies need governments and hierarchies of various kinds for particular purposes; but only in some periods do they become the comprehending institutions many claim them to be. We have known for centuries that the form they take can be, and is, shaped by complex social dynamics, by human decisions, and by perceptions of what is ultimately the holy, righteous, and virtuous life—at least since Samuel debated with God the issue of whether to anoint kings in ancient Israel, since Plato and Aristotle debated the ideal forms of governance, since the *Arthashastra* presented a model of "good" (as opposed to evil or bad) rule by a maharaja, and since Confucius instructed his students on the virtuous form of society and polity.

12. This is a critical insight of both David Landes's massive *The Wealth and Poverty of Nations* (New York: Norton, 1998); and of Daniel Elazar's summary volume of his four-volume study *Covenant and Civil Society*. It is also a significant theme in Francis Fukuyama's twin volumes, *The End of History and the Last Man* (New York: Free Press, 1992) and *Trust: The Social Virtues and the Creation of Prosperity* (New York: Free Press, 1995). These authors suggest, from rather different standpoints, that economic and moral issues are more comprehensible than political ones and that when political or familial orders attempt to comprehend the whole, they tend to limit the vitality of civil society.

13. The firm support of human rights by Catholic and Protestant leaders, especially since World War II, is a key point of convergence.

14. An artful perspective on this vision can be found in Wilhelm Roepke, *The Moral Foundations of Civil Society* (New Brunswick, N.J.: Transaction Press, 1996); or in the older J.F.A. Taylor, *The Masks of Society: An Inquiry into the Covenants of Civilization* (New York: Appleton-Crofts, 1966).

Part II _____

BOUNDARIES AND JUSTICE

4

Christian Attitudes toward Boundaries

METAPHYSICAL AND GEOGRAPHICAL

RICHARD B. MILLER

CHRISTIANS began to think systematically about the ethics of land, territory, and boundaries within a specific set of historical circumstances. European claims to dominion in the New World during the sixteenth and seventeenth centuries generated a new range of questions in moral theology for Catholics and Protestants alike, theology developed most notably by Cajetan, Vitoria, Soto, Suarez, Molina, Las Casas, Gentili, and Grotius. Yet these authors did not generate normative principles for addressing questions of dominion and boundaries *de novo*; they drew on a tradition of categories, distinctions, and concrete practices that give substance to the Christian imagination regarding political and social issues.

Here I want to identify elements of that tradition, focusing on broad themes and distinctions that frame much of what Western Christians have presupposed in various discussions of boundaries, ownership, distribution, diversity, mobility, and autonomy during the early modern and modern periods. We will see that Christianity asserts the priority of metaphysical boundaries over geographical ones. Central to this priority is the belief that God is the highest good, a source of love and order in this-worldly affairs, requiring loyalty that transcends the divisions of political life. Moreover, although some Christians articulate a clear rationale for boundaries, dominion, and regional loyalties, such a rationale stands in tension with obligations to love the neighbor, near or distant, irrespective of political affiliation. Whether (or how) Christians are to reconcile their duties to others, given the importance and corrigibility of borders, remains a contested issue in the tradition today.

With these thoughts in mind, I will pursue three goals in this chapter, which is largely descriptive and analytic: first, to represent Western Christianity's various responses to the issues before us in this essay; second, to call attention to tensions within those responses; third, to identify how some Christians have sought to resolve those tensions by specifying the practical requirements of duties to their neighbors.

In this last capacity I will discuss how Christian social critics have de-fined the scope and weight of their obligations to others as these duties connect with cases of individual or collective conscience.[1]

Boundaries

How Christians assess territorial boundaries is largely a function of how they conceive the boundary that distinguishes creation from its Creator. Ethical and political questions are framed by an understanding of the relationship between an unchanging God and the changing, finite, natural order. Traditionally, God and creation have been under-stood as ontologically different, constituting separate orders of being. Christians believe that God is the source and sustainer of natural life, and this belief leads to important ethical and psychological conse-quences. Individuals who trespass the boundary separating finite from infinite being, extending themselves beyond human limitations, are judged as guilty of the most fundamental wrongdoing, the sin of pride. Accordingly, the religious and ethical life must be shaped by the virtue of humility, in which the believer gratefully acknowledges her depend-ence on God for life and salvation.[2] Boundaries are important because they define an order of being and value, along with corresponding attitudes that should structure the Christian's life.

Marking off the boundary that distinguishes God from creation, of course, does not say much about how Christians are to understand re-gional or other boundaries that provide the specific contours of social life. In general, one measure of an individual's relationship with God is how she relates to her neighbor. Love of God and love of neighbor, while distinct, are not irrelevant to or independent of each other. Main-stream Christianity typically believes that failure to love God properly, a life that lacks the grace necessary for *humilitas*, will generate disor-dered relationships with one's neighbors—relationships affected by *libido dominandi*.[3] Those who deify their own needs and desires are prone to violate the boundaries that require Christians to respect the needs and desires of fellow creatures. Ignoring one set of boundaries leads prideful humanity to ignore other limits as well; a wrongly or-dered moral psychology is illusory and dangerous. Conversely, honor-ing one's limits before God ought to produce a corresponding set of behavioral limits with respect to oneself and the created order. For Christians, matters of political ethics are informed by considerations of moral and religious psychology. In personal and political affairs, the Christian life is marked by an understanding of finite freedom, of bounded love.

Various subtraditions within Christianity have sought to specify in greater detail how individuals are to understand the patterns and processes of the created order, the laws of nature that ought to give direction to individual and collective decision-making about this-worldly affairs. God is not only the source and sustainer of natural life; the deity also has ordered creation according to principles that are discernible to human reason and that stand apart from positive law or social convention. Principal among such natural law tenets is the claim that individuals have an innate tendency to develop a common life, that membership in community is a natural human good.[4]

Such natural tendencies nonetheless rely on various customs, which serve instrumentally to facilitate the terms of social cooperation, among other goods. On this basis, Christians can sanction geographical boundaries, for such conventions are necessary to mark off one human precinct from another. Territories have their own identities and autonomous jurisdictions; they provide useful ways for human groups to establish their own habits, loyalties, and practices for common living. As a natural fact, human beings seem to need a sense of place.

How Christians are to view territorial boundaries is a function, then, of how their affections or loves are ordered, and how individuals make practical arrangements in their natural quest for a common life. These ideas derive, respectively, from Augustine and Aquinas, and they inform much of what Christians say about social and political conventions like geographical boundaries. Moreover, when considered together, these ideas frame the ethics of borders in Christianity, for they alert us to a tension between duties to near and distant neighbors. Natural law considerations lend credence to the notion that borders help to fulfill basic human goods, which, as a practical matter, involve regional loyalties and fellow-feeling. For this reason, at various times Christians have affirmed the importance of location and particularity: the feudal kingdom, Calvin's Geneva, the New England commonwealth, and the national or ethnic church are familiar examples. At the same time, Christianity requires an indiscriminate, unconditional love of others, irrespective of political, social, or national affiliation. Borders ask us to privilege local solidarities, but Christian *agape*, exemplified by Jesus's teaching and example, is altruistic and cosmopolitan.[5]

Given these competing demands between the natural law and the law of love, various theologians have sought to define an "order of charity," a hierarchy of loves and loyalties required by the complex relationships of everyday life.[6] All else being equal, may I love my wife more than my mother-in-law? My son more than my nephew? Fellow educators more than affluent stockbrokers? The living more than the dead? These questions are a function of how our loves are constrained by nature and circumstance, requiring us to define our responsibilities toward others. But Christian thinkers differ widely over whether such a ranking is permissible, and, if so, how individuals should concretely order their loyalties.[7] To many Christians, allowing believers to develop a hierarchy of responsibilities accedes too much to everyday custom, thereby dulling the edge of Christianity's capacity for social criticism, its radical message of selfless, indiscriminate love.

However such debates are sorted out, metaphysical boundaries in Christianity do not directly inform the ethics and politics of geographical borders. That is because, in Christianity, political developments are conceived as part of an order that is present but passing away. Christian thinking about the ethics and politics of boundaries takes into account not only the difference between the Creator and creation, but also the difference between time and eternity. The Kingdom of God— communion with God and the saints—is relevant to life in this world in that it represents an ideal of friendship and equality, but it is an object of hope, never to be identified with any specific political or social arrangement.[8] Christians believe themselves to be on a pilgrimage in this life, and no temporal reality is to be elevated to the status of an unchanging good.[9]

This distinction between eternity and time has clear implications for Christian politics and ethics, especially among those who wish to preserve Christianity's radical message, for it suggests that borders are ephemeral phenomena, and that regional loyalty might weaken the demands of neighbor-love. Conventions that encourage us to localize our commitments may also encourage us to find eternal satisfaction in temporal activities, thereby generating disordered attachments toward the passing realities of political and social life.[10]

Boundaries in Christianity, then, help define a hierarchy that distinguishes between absolute and relative goods. God, the eternal, unchanging good, is the only object of unqualified loyalty. All other relations are to be framed by an understanding of how temporal, created reality relies upon and remains subordinate to the immutable good.[11] Those who order their lives by these distinctions understand (1) the duty to respect the boundaries that distinguish natural life with its intrinsic integrities, and (2) the mandate of universal love and unconditional solidarity. Christians traditionally embrace the second of these two claims, and sometimes the first as well. In any event, the extent to which territorial boundaries have a place in Christian politics and ethics is a function of whether borders can function within an overarching theocentric cosmology.

Within this cosmology, Christians typically view regional boundaries as one feature of life in the Earthly City, complete with local loves and what Augustine calls a "shadowy peace." The goods associated with civic life have a real but relative status, and boundaries may find sanction in Christian belief insofar as they contribute to these lesser goods. Like political authority, coercion, and (for some Christians) war, territorial boundaries function as an instrumental good. So long as they are not used to the disadvantage of others, boundaries may enable groups to coordinate their political and social arrangements toward a common good, one that is bound together by temporal attachments and practical needs. But these needs are relative and provisional, enjoyed by Christians as fugitive goods when compared to the hopes and ideals represented by the Kingdom of God.

Ownership and Distribution

In Christianity questions of ownership and distribution of land and resources are informed by a special concern for the poor. In the Gospel of Mark readers are told that, in response to a man who asked how to attain eternal life, Jesus says, "Go, sell what you have, and give to the poor, and you will have treasure in heaven" (Mark 10:21). The Great Judgment in the Gospel of Matthew describes Jesus as saying: "Truly, I say to you, as you did it for the least of these my brethren, you did it to me" (Matt. 25:40). The Gospel of Luke adds,

> Blessed are you poor, for yours is the kingdom of heaven.
> Blessed are you that hunger now, for you shall be satisfied. . . .
> But woe to you that are rich, for you have received your consolation.
> Woe to you that are full now, for you shall hunger.
>
> (Luke 6:20–25, 24–25)

On these grounds Christians are sometimes suspicious of worldly goods and attend carefully to substantive issues of distributive justice.

Moreover, questions of ownership are framed by the boundary that separates Creator and creation, eternity and time, as well as by the patterns and processes that provide integrity and direction to the created order. That means that Christians often approach matters of ownership according to two general requirements: (1) to have rightly ordered loves, in which relative goods are loved relatively, and absolute goods are loved absolutely, and (2) to make practical arrangements that enable individuals to flourish according to their natural tendencies and endowments. As a result, Christians possess distinct and, at times, competing orientations for addressing issues of ownership: love of God and the neighbor in need, on the one hand, and considerations derived from the law of nature, on the other.

Attention to rightly ordered loves, as I have suggested, focuses attention on matters of moral psychology. How, Christians often ask, should individuals attach themselves to the material world? How should the will be ordered? What priorities ought to shape the religious and moral life? This attention to rightly ordered loves has traditionally implied a set of limits for ownership, and such limits typically have been understood in light of the common goods of creation. Many Christians believe that the goods of creation are given by God to be enjoyed by all (see Lev. 25). In early Christian times this conviction meant that, ideally, no one was to be left wanting or denied resources that are basic to human life and well-being. One measure of rightly ordered attachments is the extent to which an individual succeeds in putting private property to good use, given the requirements of living in community. In this respect, Christians from the earliest times distinguished their beliefs from the Roman view of absolute ownership, which imposed no limits on the right to private property.

Belief that the goods of creation are to be held in common led to two specific approaches toward property in relation to the poor in early Christianity. The first, recorded in the Book of Acts, is one of communal sharing. We are told that first-generation Christians in Jerusalem "sold their possessions and goods and distributed them to all, as any had need" (Acts 2:45). But early Christians did not create a communistic commune. Peter tells Ananias that he is not obligated to sell his property, and having sold it he still has the proceeds at his disposal (Acts 5:4). Among the Jerusalem Christians, the overriding principle was that "no one said that the things which he possessed were his own, but they had everything in common" (Acts 4:32). How material goods were actually shared depended on the needs of some and the free generosity of others.

The second approach, based on the writings of Paul, requires almsgiving. Here the idea is that the blessings given to some oblige them to assist others who are not well-off, that private property is to be voluntarily redistributed. Paul instructs the church in Corinth to contribute liberally to him so that he may distribute funds to needy Christians in Jerusalem (I Cor. 16:1–4). Macedonian Christians have contributed generously, he observes, and he urges those in Corinth to give similarly: "Each one must do as he has made up his mind, not reluctantly or under compulsion, for God loves a cheerful giver" (I Cor. 9:7).

In either case, the idea is that private property is not an absolute good, that there are limits to property as a value and source of satisfaction. For early Christians, the needs of fellow believers defined those limits in practical, tangible ways. The goal, as Paul describes it, is to produce equality within the community, so that "your abundance at the present time should supply their want, so that their abundance may supply your want. . . . As it is written, 'He who gathered much had nothing over, and he who gathered little had no lack'" (II Cor. 18:13–15). For other Christians, the central question surrounding private ownership was one of degree or, more accurately, proportionality. Clement of Alexandria (c. 150–215), for example, argues that accumulating wealth is not intrinsically evil, for the test of virtue is whether material possessions are the center of value. Clement thus understands Jesus's instruction to "go, sell what you have, and give to the poor" (Mark 10:21) as a command to renounce materialistic passions, not material wealth per se. Indeed, individuals who are relatively impoverished may be guilty of avarice; the question is not *whether* but *how* one relates oneself to property and dominion. So Clement writes, "A poor and destitute man may be found intoxicated with lusts; and a man rich in worldly goods temperate, poor in indulgences, trustworthy, intelligent, pure, chastened."[12] Here the issue of ownership is framed not so much by the needs of others, but according to the character of the owner. Much of Christianity has taken this route, focusing on the dispositions involved in owning property. Virtue and vice pertain not to redistributive principles or the neighbor in need, but to self-referring properties, the internal ordering of the soul. Accumulated property is dangerous not because it contributes to an unjust or uncharitable economic order, but because it draws the soul away from the love of God.

Yet even this emphasis on character and virtue implies limits, a social mortgage on private property. Clement argues that the most virtuous way to relate to one's possessions is to give them away, that ownership beyond sufficiency is contrary to the natural, created order. All humanity is meant to live in harmony; failure to share is inhuman. Indeed, if Christianity required material renunciation, Clement observes, then it would be impossible to exercise Christian charity to the poor. "How could one give food to the hungry, and drink to the thirsty, clothe the naked, and shelter the houseless," he asks, "if each man first divested himself of all these [material] things?"[13] Virtue requires not the wholesale rejection of property, but temperance and generosity. Possessions are provided by God "for the use of men; and they lie to our hand, and are put under our power, as material and instruments which are for good use to those who know the instrument."[14]

Subsequent to these developments, responses to questions about love, virtue, and material attachment took more radical shape, interpreting Jesus's instruction to renounce worldly goods in literal rather than figurative terms.[15] In the fourth century of the common era, Christian monks fled in desperation and social protest to the deserts of Egypt. Followers of Antony and Pachomius, two central figures of

Egyptian monasticism, held that faith and private ownership were incompatible.[16] Those who followed the tradition of Antony followed an ascetic ideal of absolute poverty, living in the desert with only the barest essentials. The chief idea was that, to be authentic, spiritual detachment from worldly goods must be incarnated in tangible, material ways. Poverty to the point of deprivation was a virtue; love of God involved radical self-denial.[17]

Those who followed the example of Pachomius socialized rather than renounced the institution of property. Pachomius's rules for cenobitic monasticism included common possession of all goods. As Justo L. González writes, "In this rule, all things were to be held in common, not only in the sense that they must be at the disposal of the needy in the community, but even more in the sense that no one would be able to dispose of them."[18] The goal of communal monasticism was not to abandon property, but to put a high regard on communal life, including partnership in owning material goods.

Thomas Aquinas's (1227–74) treatment of ownership and theft develops with characteristic clarity the limited right of private property. In the *Summa Theologiae*, Aquinas argues that it is natural for humans to possess external things as regards their use. "Man has a natural dominion over external things," he claims, "because, by his reason and will, he is able to use them for his own profit, as they were made on his account: for the imperfect is always for the sake of the perfect."[19] Private property is necessary, Aquinas adds, because individuals are likelier to care for things when they own them privately rather than collectively. Moreover, as a practical matter there are fewer occasions of disorder and strife when property is privately owned.[20] For Aquinas, the more radical route of selling one's property and giving to the poor is a counsel, not a precept, optional rather than required, and incumbent only on those Christians with a special calling.[21]

But dominion and ownership are not absolute rights for Christians who possess property, as Aquinas argues in his discussion of the Sixth (or Seventh) Commandment, "Thou shalt not steal." Among other reasons, theft is wrong because it is "contrary to justice, which is a matter of giving each person his due."[22] Yet for Aquinas the prohibition against taking property does not hold universally; there are some impoverished individuals who have no alternative but to take another's possessions. About such circumstances, Aquinas writes, "Everything is in common. Therefore a person who takes somebody else's property which necessity has made common again so far as he is concerned does not commit theft."[23] The notion of "theft" implies circumstances of moderate provision; in those circumstances, it is possible to justify the institution of private property. But such a justification is relative to circumstances that are not applicable to those who suffer from extreme deprivation. Indeed, to take property that necessity has rendered "common" is to acquire one's just due. Private ownership of external goods may be conducive to order and peace, but such goods should also be used "as common, so that one is ready to communicate them to others in their need."[24]

By the Middle Ages, then, the limited right of private property and the criterion of right use were recognizable features of Christianity. These concepts became mainstays in Christian thought and practice during the early modern period, providing a platform from which to develop arguments about the connection between rightful ownership, territories, and access to natural and human resources. In the sixteenth century, the issue of private property in relation to territories and boundaries generated cases for practical deliberation when questions arose about the right of Spanish conquerors to the land and territory of indigenous Americans.[25] However, in this context traditional ideas were designed more to protect individuals from encroachment than to require individuals or groups to share in common goods. Francisco Vitoria (c. 1483–1546) argues that many Spanish claims to dominion were false pretexts to acquisition—that alleged heresy, sin, irrationality, or madness on the part of native Americans were all insufficient bases for acquiring their land. Dominion is granted by God and cannot be denied for these reasons. Addressing his views directly to Charles V, Vitoria held that territorial dominion is only a temporal, natural good, distinct from supernatural matters of faith, religion, and salvation. Amerindians have dominion owing to the natural fact that they inhabit their land and "have judgment like other men." Vitoria writes:

> This is self-evident because they have some order in their affairs: they have properly organized cities, proper marriages, magistrates and overlords, laws, industries, and commerce, all of which require the use of reason. They likewise have a form of religion, and they correctly apprehend things which are evident to other men, which indicates the use of reason. Furthermore, "God and nature never fail in the things necessary" for the majority of the species, and the chief attribute of man is reason.[26]

Natural reason is the great leveler, putting indigenous Americans morally and politically on a par with the Spanish invaders.

Complicating this line of argument, Vitoria adds that the Spanish have a natural right to seek conversions, that "Christians have the right to preach and announce the Gospel in the lands of the barbarians."[27] In his mind, this right can be inferred from the natural law, because "brotherly correction is as much part of natural law as brotherly love."[28] This right likewise permits the Spaniards to use force to defend themselves if they are attacked by native Americans or to protect Christian converts if they are attacked by others who reject Christian teaching.[29] Although Vitoria claims that Amerindians have the right to their land, he acknowledges limits to that right: They may not obstruct Christian evangelization. Truth has rights, and native Americans' right of dominion may not bar Spaniards from exercising their rights of evangelization, free passage, and self-defense. The indigenous population is thus bound by the natural law to allow the Spaniards to travel, teach, and preach. However, Amerindians are not obligated to accept Christian tenets, and war cannot be used against them to force conversions.[30] The main point here is that natural rights and the natural law allow for both dominion and the freedom of religious preaching; the latter might at times limit the former. In Vitoria's mind, this tension is not between revelation and reason, or religion and natural law; it is a tension within the natural law itself. In this way, Vitoria crafts a basis on natural law grounds for using force to protect some religious interests—so long as the use of force is subsumed by the justice of self-protection.

Owing to the work of Vitoria and others, the idea that lacking religious orthodoxy is a sufficient condition for forfeiting rights to dominion has disappeared in the modern period. But the idea that private ownership and dominion are limited rights has survived. This fact is especially apparent in the tradition of papal encyclicals, beginning with Leo XIII's *Rerum Novarum* (1891) and continuing throughout the twentieth century, a tradition that emphasizes universal human rights and the dignity of all persons as images of God.[31]

Witness as one example the writings of Paul VI. Drawing on the principle of the universal purpose of created things and the commandment to love the neighbor, Paul VI writes that "private property does not constitute for anyone an absolute and unconditioned right."[32] When others lack what is necessary for basic well-being, "no one is justified in keeping for his exclusive use what he does not need."[33] But Paul VI does not repeat the early Christian notion that excess property should be voluntarily relinquished. Rather, coercion may be used in some circumstances: "If certain landed estates impede the general prosperity because they are extensive, unused or poorly used, or because they bring hardship to peoples or are detrimental to the interest of the country, the common good sometimes demands their expropriation."[34] Echoing the views of Aquinas, Paul VI suggests that the needs of humanity outweigh the rights of dominion when these two claims conflict and that, as a matter of justice, one may take possession without consent of the owner. Moreover, for Paul VI the problem has less to do with how materialism might corrupt the virtue of the wealthy than with how the disparity of resources has produced inequitable economic arrangements worldwide.

Two features of Paul VI's statements stand out. First, the right of expropriation does not permit individuals to secure basic provisions vis-à-vis a common set of goods, whatever Paul VI might say about the universal purpose of created goods. Rather, he argues that those in need have claims only to goods that others have in surplus: Excessive goods become "common" for those in dire need.

Second, Paul VI's permission of expropriation is confined to participants who are active in the internal affairs of a nation-state. One nation is not permitted to intervene to produce equitable arrangements in another sovereign state's domestic affairs. Relations between states must be regulated by the principle of solidarity with the needy, but coercion is not an appropriate method to acquire territory or other possessions. Rather, he suggests, boundaries remain sacrosanct, allowing for only noncoercive measures to satisfy competing goods. In particular, states should turn to the redistributive and relief efforts of international agencies that rely on a World Fund. Such a fund would use money otherwise spent on military arms, and its aim would be "to relieve the most destitute of this world."[35] Echoing the views of the early church, Paul VI sketches a vision of international sharing, in which the needs of some are met by the voluntary generosity of others.

Liberation theologians—Christians informed by Marxist analysis—typically insist upon a "preferential option for the poor," adding that mainstream Christian approaches to territory and ownership wrongly proceed by criticizing the institution of surplus wealth rather than poverty.[36] In liberation theology, issues of land and territory include two items typically ignored in standard Christian accounts: first, a critical discussion of the modes by which property has been *acquired* (rather than how it should be redistributed); second, an insistence that discussions of redistribution operate within a liberation rather than a developmental paradigm. Developmentalism, liberationists allege, presumes a situation in which Latin American countries remain dependent on and subservient to the capitalist enterprises of First World nations and corporations. As Gustavo Gutiérrez (1928–) remarks, satisfactory assessment of land and boundaries will not occur until social analysis is framed by the ideal of liberation, focusing on "the aspirations of oppressed peoples and economic classes," and emphasizing "the conflictual aspect of the economic, social, and political process which puts them at odds with wealthy nations and oppressive classes."[37] Emphasis falls on sharing ownership of the means of production, recalling the tradition of collective ownership in early Christianity.[38]

For ecologically minded Christians, issues of territory and ownership call attention not only to duties to the disadvantaged, but also to responsibilities to the natural world itself. Typically such responsibilities are developed under the idea of stewardship. Briefly described, stewardship requires Christians to accept land and natural resources as a divine gift. The goods of creation are to be used with an eye to future generations and to the divine purposes of creation. Stewardship may thus require humans to subordinate their interests to the needs of the biosphere; nonhuman life imposes claims on human decision-making. Accordingly, landed property and natural resources are to be developed not only with human but also with wider natural needs in view—although Christian ethicists are often vague about what those natural purposes are.[39]

Diversity

Territorial boundaries serve an instrumental, functional role, marking off groups that seek practically to coordinate the terms of a common life. Such groups will doubtless be culturally, linguistically, and religiously different, developing codes and habits designed to make their common life more convenient.[40] Insofar as we understand such differences as a function of relative, fugitive goods, they may find sanction within Christian belief and practice. Having separate living spaces is a necessary condition for communities to develop their respective histories, customs, and identities.

Yet even if boundaries may serve some general human function, their exact lines are drawn in specific social and historical circumstances. Providing the social contours of civic life, boundaries are the fruits of contingency and political constraint, not lacking in self-interest. When seen as products of circumstance or accident, and when recognized as potential sources of division among humans, they appear arbitrary from a theological point of view.

One critical question for Christians is whether membership in and loyalty to such communities becomes a final object of value. Temporal communities demand commitment from their citizens; the danger of idolatry is not remote. And idolatry can bring intolerance toward differences, a sense of superiority toward members of other communities. (I will provide examples of such intolerance in Christianity below.) When regional boundaries contribute to overweening collective pride, they produce tendencies that have religious and ethical dimensions: self-righteousness, divisiveness, dogmatism, intolerance, inequality.

Within Christianity these dimensions have been subject to withering criticism, especially (but not only) from twentieth-century Protestants. H. Richard Niebuhr (1894–1962), to take a prominent example, protested against provincialism of all kinds—cultural, national, ethnic, and religious. Niebuhr articulated what Paul Tillich calls the "Protestant principle," a form of religious and social criticism that "contains the divine and human protest against any absolute claim made for a relative reality. . . . The Protestant principle is the judge of every religious and cultural reality, including the religion and culture which calls itself 'Protestant.'"[41]

In Niebuhr's mind, this principle has relevance to two problems. First is the replacement of a disinterested, nonpreferential perspective by partial loyalties and preferential loves. Boundaries that mark off different groups are problematic because they represent the sinful tendency to elevate the particular to the status of the universal. For Niebuhr, the remedy rests in the faith of "radical monotheism," faith in a transcendent object of loyalty that relativizes humanity's cultural and social achievements.[42] Radical monotheism demands a loyalty to "the universal commonwealth of Being," and particular loyalties have meaning only by virtue of their affirmation of and subordination to the "One beyond the many."[43]

Second is the tendency of religions to rationalize rather than criticize forms of provincialism. Drawing on the writings of Max Weber and Ernst Troeltsch, Niebuhr observes the tendency of religious movements, including Christianity, to be more affirmative than critical of cultural practices, especially religious nationalism and patriotic zeal.[44] Religions tend to accommodate themselves to local customs and then rationalize those customs in light of a higher principle. In Christianity, this tendency has led to fragmentation along social, racial, and class lines, in which the earlier unity of Christian belief has given way to a tragic series of internal divisions, all sanctioned by religious claims.[45]

For Niebuhr, the solution to the dangers of parochialism and fragmentation lies not in the Christian affirmation of political, class, or other divisions, but in solidarity with those who suffer innocently. Such solidarity is the distinctive response required by the cross, Niebuhr argues, a unique angle of vision implied by Christian faith and practice. Rather than celebrating the identities formed by boundaries and territories, it is incumbent upon Christians to join in common cause with those who are being crucified by power politics—children, the poor, the infirm, "the humble, little people who have had little to do with the framing of great policies."[46]

Diversity is tolerable, then, within limits established by a theocentric point of view. Individuals need recognizable practices and traditions according to which they interpret themselves and the world around them, and communities serve an important role insofar as they nurture a sense of identity and membership. But for Christians, human life is marked by sin, the temptation to privilege local loyalties and loves. Hence the need for a critical principle, one that scrutinizes local customs from the perspective of transcendence. Religious criticism thereby reveals a range of persons whose needs are the object of attention and care: the innocent victims of history and politics.

Mobility

"Amongst all nations it is considered inhuman to treat strangers and travelers badly without some special cause," Vitoria writes, "humane and dutiful to behave hospitably to strangers."[47] Boundaries that mark off territories have a real but relative value, given their instrumental status in a world marked by finitude and sin. As a general rule, the value of borders and territory should not trump the (stronger) value of hospitality to strangers when those strangers pose no danger to the community.

Mobility across borders involves at least two cases: (1) travel and (2) immigration with subsequent application for membership. Travel is the easier case: Within Christianity, one test of the relativity of boundaries would be the extent to which they are permeable. In the beginning of the world, Vitoria argues, all things were held in common, and "everyone was allowed to visit and travel through any land he wished." Such rights are not eliminated by the institution of property; free human intercourse, itself a natural good, should not be impeded by the rulers of local jurisdictions.[48] Assuming that strangers impose no great hardship on a community, allowing them to enter and exit would seem "humane and dutiful."

To the more difficult question of immigration and membership, Christians (to the best of my knowledge) have not given much systematic thought.[49] At a minimum, however, the Christian imagination is informed by two duties: the obligation to protect the natural inclination for community and participation, and the commandment to love the neighbor, including enemies and strangers.

These two demands generate competing responsibilities, returning us to questions about near and distant neighbors, the order of charity. The need for community and identity would seem to allow for some restrictions across borders. To maintain a sense of "us," political communities must distinguish their members from "others," and such distinctions imply a form of discrimination. Moreover, the formation and continuation of communal identity presupposes that citizens are trained in civic practices, complete with rituals, the recollection of history, and the transmission of local customs in schools and popular culture. For such civil formation to be effective, communities need a relatively stable population, not one that is in flux and flow. For these (and perhaps other) reasons, the requirements of a common life involve restricting the terms of membership.[50] Internal order and local flourishing require limited access; subsequent membership requires that emigrés acquire civic habits that bear the stamp of a community's history and self-understanding.[51]

But as Niebuhr's remarks make plain, Christian responsibilities go beyond near neighbors and civic membership to embrace all humankind, especially those in acute need. The requirement to love the neighbor indiscriminately would suggest duties that transcend borders. How these duties are fulfilled in tangible ways is difficult to specify, but the cosmopolitan aspects of Christianity imply that borders should be opened for those seeking refuge from political and economic oppression. Cosmopolitanism likewise alerts us to the unseemly events that often prompt mass migrations: tyranny, intolerance, famine, or lack of hope at home. For these reasons Christians have cause to consider issues of mobility in tandem with issues of diversity and distribution. Restricting mobility across boundaries can reinforce local prejudice and global economic disparities.

Migration across regional and other borders is also a reminder that our understanding of "near" and "distant" neighbors is subject to change over time. Boundaries are not insuperable barriers, and individuals who were once foreigners can become friends or fellow-citizens within a generation. In this vein, Karl Barth (1886–1968) writes of the fluidity of borders and the idea that groups are bound to absorb others or dissolve into new configurations. Barth observes: "Whole languages of what were once very vital peoples are now extinct, or can live on amongst other peoples only as 'dead' languages. No frontier, however 'natural,' has ever proved stable, nor has any history, however distinctive, been able to guarantee the continuance of a nation."[52] In Barth's mind, the duty of the Christian is to affirm her given language, locale, and history—but only provisionally. The overall impetus is universalist: "To unite loyalty towards those who are historically near with openness towards those who are historically distant."[53] Nations and groups come and go, Barth remarks, and thus "we must not confuse the contrast of near and distant neighbors with the creation of God and its immutable orders."[54]

Autonomy

Christians teach that freedom is found in faithful obedience to God— that true autonomy is actually "theonomy," living under the authority of God's gracious power.[55] Typically addressed to individual consciences, such ideas have also taken on militant political dimensions, leading Christians to expand the geographical region of God's sovereignty. Whether in the context of the medieval crusades, the suppression of minority sects, the encounter with the Amerindians, the wars of the continental Reformation, or the Puritan revolution, Christians have freely invoked religion to justify the use of force to protect if not expand their territorial boundaries. Such justifications, privileging God's law to any set of human conventions, pay little heed to territorial borders or local autonomy. Central to such appeals is the honor of God and the concomitant duty to defend God's justice in the face of alleged infidelity or heresy. Frequently Christians cite various depictions of God-as-warrior in the Hebrew Bible to support the idea that religion, war, and the violation of communal boundaries are compatible (see, e.g., Deut. 20).

Seeking to justify war as a religious crusade, Christians have argued that righteousness should be visible in personal and social institutions: The holy commonwealth tolerates no exceptions or impurity, and war may be an instrument to purge the world of idolatry. In a letter to Christian knights leaving for Jerusalem, for example, Bernard of Clairvaux (1090–1153) writes that "for our sins, the enemy of the Cross has begun to lift his sacrilegious head there, and to devastate with the sword that blessed land, the land of promise. Alas, if there be none to withstand him, he will soon invade the city of the living God, overturn the arsenal of our redemption, and defile the holy places which have been adorned by the blood of the immaculate lamb." Reminding knights that self-sacrifice for the crusade merits an indulgence, Bernard writes that God "puts himself in your debt so that, in return for your taking up arms in his cause, he can reward you with pardon for your sins and everlasting glory."[56]

In the sixteenth and seventeenth centuries, religious justifications for war were used on behalf of killing other Christians rather than "infidels." Advocates for holy war such as Henry Bullinger argued that religion justified war against heretics near and far, believing that God commanded such wars and fought alongside holy warriors.[57] For such Christians, the reign of God, while still a distant hope, must become more clearly manifest in political arrangements. In a holy war one could distinguish clearly between the just and the unjust, and the duty of the former is to enforce the justice of God. Catholics, too, embraced these views: William Cardinal Allen, a seventeenth-century English bishop exiled in Flanders, thought that the defense of Catholicism justified the use of force, and that Protestant rule was to be resisted under the authority of the pope.[58]

In these cases we see the importance of metaphysical boundaries to the exclusion of territorial ones: True Christian belief should be

defended as a visible sign of God's sovereignty, regardless of geographical or other borders. Reckoning the demands of justice in these religious
terms, Christians have actively intervened in the affairs of various religious and political communities, fighting under the banner of a holy
war ideology.

Yet this legacy is not the entire story of Christianity's relation to
power, territory, and communal autonomy. Dissident voices of various influence also secured a foothold in the tradition, offering clear
counterexamples or direct criticism of intervention and imperialism.

Prominent among the counterexamples are communities that often
suffered at the hands of Christian crusaders: members of various
Anabaptist groups who sought freedom (and refuge) in southern
Germany and, later, in the Netherlands. Not unlike holy warriors, these
Christians believe that righteousness should be manifest in this-worldly
affairs, that one duty of the Christian is to form a community that witnesses to the Gospel in word and deed. Adult baptism, symbolizing
freely chosen faith, marks one's visible entrance to the community, the
communion of saints. Discipline is handled not through physical punishment but through the instrument of the ban, the practice of shunning
backsliders whose actions merit censure. For these Christians, boundaries are important, but they are cultural and religious, not enforced by
the power of the magistrate, whose office Anabaptists are forbidden to
assume. Boundaries are marked by a common commitment to cross-
bearing, informed by a literal understanding of Jesus's command to
love the neighbor and to suffer voluntarily.[59]

In addition to counterexample, Christians developed strong arguments against European imperialism in the sixteenth and seventeenth
centuries. Prominent among such critics were Catholic and Protestant
writers who self-consciously removed religion as a cause for war.
Prompted by religious wars on the continent and in England, as well as
the colonial encounter with Amerindians, writers such as Vitoria, Suarez,
Gentili, and Grotius appealed to reason and the law of nature as the
sole basis for using force.[60] The effect was to reduce war to a political
rather than a theological enterprise.

But reducing the justification to natural reason did not eliminate justifications for intervention or elevate territorial borders to a sacrosanct
value, for war can be an instrument to secure justice for innocents at
risk, regardless of where they reside. Vitoria argues that war could be
waged to protect the innocent from human sacrifice or cannibalism,[61]
to secure free passage for trade and missionary activity, to protect
converts from persecution or repression in their own lands, and to
protect populations from tyranny.[62] Such uses of force are viewed
within the paradigm of the just war, which assigns natural rights to

individuals irrespective of their other cultural, political, or religious af-
filiations. Similarly, seventeenth-century Protestant writers provide ra-
tionales for using force to assist outsiders or foreigners. Alberico Gentili
(1552–1608) states that the natural law forbids going to war for
purposes of religion, but that the "union of the human race" places obligations on sovereigns to protect individuals in other lands from cannibalism, human sacrifice, and other violations of the natural law, and to
fight piracy on the seas. Hugo Grotius (1583–1645) justifies the use of
force to protect citizens that one's own sovereign may have subjugated;
and to assist allies, friends, and (where risks are not excessive) strangers
in need.[63]

In this regard the writings of sixteenth- and seventeenth-century
Christians provide the seeds for contemporary discussions of humanitarian intervention, which likewise emphasizes securing justice as a
natural right. But in the modern context, considerations of human rights
are complicated by the values of political sovereignty and territorial
borders, values that can also be derived from the natural law.

Political sovereignty is now a core principle in the international security system, designed to ensure collective autonomy by barring interference from outside powers. It is meant to enshrine a community's
independence from outside control—the right of a community to determine its own laws and the means of ordering its own domestic life. In
international law and political theory, regional boundaries imply (at the
least) a firm presumption against intervention, a strong moral barrier to
any state that wishes to meddle in another's jurisdiction.[64]

This right of self-rule is compatible with Christian natural law arguments regarding humanity's need for community. Individuals cannot
flourish without some measure of local control of and participation in a
collective existence. Groups thus need autonomy because the individuals that inhabit them need to be left alone to form a life together. Collective autonomy endeavors to secure individual autonomy, the experience
of freedom, self-determination, and human dignity.[65]

In this way communities' need for autonomy to protect individual
liberty and human dignity can provide a justification for territorial borders. Yet the importance of autonomy implies limits to that justification
as well, and such limits have received increasing emphasis in contemporary discussions of international affairs. When borders serve less to
protect individual dignity than to protect leaders or groups who violate
human rights, those borders forfeit their legitimacy. On this view, justifications of borders are connected to more fundamental principles. When
those principles are not served, autonomy, borders, and the presumption
against intervention become problematic.

The tension in natural law morality between the value of *sovereignty*
and the value of *human rights* has become acute in recent political

thought, especially (but not only) in Catholic ethics, requiring social critics to specify the range and weight of each value.[66] By way of example, consider the recent writings of the U.S. Catholic bishops. Developing a trajectory from the papal encyclical *Pacem in Terris* (1963),[67] and the bishops' pastoral letter. *The Challenge of Peace* (1983),[68] the U.S. Catholic Conference International Policy Committee affirms "the unity of the human family, the interdependence of peoples and the need for solidarity across national and regional boundaries."[69] Advances in technology, worldwide communications, and economic relations have brought people closer together. These changes in transnational dynamics call into doubt the idea of sovereignty and point to the positive moral responsibilities that derive from the values of human dignity and solidarity. The effect is to weaken the value of sovereignty and to connect its legitimacy to the condition that it satisfy natural law tenets.

More specifically, assigning a relative status to the values of sovereignty and political autonomy allows considerations of human rights to trump sovereignty in certain circumstances. According to the bishops, those circumstances include instances in which whole populations are threatened by slaughter, aggression, genocide, or anarchy; when starving children need to be fed; or when it is necessary to strengthen international law and the international community.[70] Summarizing contemporary Catholic social teaching, Kenneth R. Himes writes:

> Catholicism promotes . . . a call to transform, through a prudent strategy, the status quo. The aim is that a true world order be achieved. Such an order would not necessarily mean the withering away of the state, but it will demand that a reciprocal relation of rights and duties be created between states and citizens and between states and other states. If just relations are thereby developed, it may be the case that states will be able to claim sovereignty properly understood, but overbearing claims of absolute sovereignty cannot be admitted. *Stronger than the appeal of sovereignty are the human rights of persons and the obligations of solidarity.* . . . In such a perspective, humanitarian intervention arguably can be part of a sound strategy for achieving international order.[71]

In this way modern Catholic social teaching conceives the value of state sovereignty as derivative from and subordinate to the value of human rights. States that act to undermine the rights of their citizens, or that fail to provide minimum conditions of human well-being, weaken their claims to political legitimacy.

In such circumstances, the cosmopolitan demands of Christianity outweigh the protections normally granted to political autonomy: Nations may intervene on behalf of the innocent who are suffering from oppression or neglect. As the U.S. Catholic bishops remark, "The people of far-off lands are not abstract problems, but sisters and brothers. We are called to protect their lives, to preserve their dignity and to defend their rights."[72] Autonomy and borders are conceived as justified but limited. When dignity is respected only in the breach, outsiders may intervene to secure the protection of distant neighbors—innocent persons whose well-being is at risk.[73]

Conclusion

When considering ethical and political questions pertaining to boundaries, Christianity asserts the priority of the metaphysical over the geographical. This priority has theological and ethical dimensions. Theologically, it implies a hierarchy of being and value according to which God is to receive unconditional loyalty. All lesser loyalties are subordinate to a fundamental love of God, bound as they are by finitude and dependence upon the deity as the author of good. Ethically, this priority assigns at most a provisional and qualified value to regional boundaries, a value that is corrigible when measured against the requirements of universal neighbor-love. Given their instrumental status in a world marked by finitude, sin, and human suffering, boundaries are only a relative good.

In contemporary Christianity, this relativity is evident in recent discussions of property and sovereignty. Within borders, surplus property may be redistributed in dire circumstances of poverty and economic disparity, in which the land of the wealthy may be expropriated for the benefit of the needy. Outsiders are not granted rights of expropriation, but foreign political actors may intervene militarily to secure humanitarian provisions and relief.[74] In the first case borders are sacrosanct when measured against the needs of others; in the second case they are not. In either case regional boundaries are seen as enabling groups to secure a common life together. But when such conventions do more to obstruct than to facilitate well-being, they can give way to demands—pursued by different methods—of universal *agape* and/or human rights.

Notes

I completed a draft of this essay as a fellow in the Program in Ethics and the Professions at Harvard University, and am grateful for the support of its director, Dennis Thompson. I wish to thank Judith Granbois and David H. Smith for their critical comments.

1. For a discussion of this procedure, see Richard B. Miller, *Casuistry and Modern Ethics: A Poetics of Practical Reasoning* (Chicago: University of Chicago Press, 1996), 17–25; James F. Childress, "Moral Norms in Practical Ethical

Deliberation," in *Christian Ethics: Problems and Prospects*, ed. Lisa Sowle Cahill and James F. Childress (Cleveland, Ohio: Pilgrim Press, 1996), 196–217.

2. This view is classically set forth in Augustine, *Confessions*, trans., with an intro. by R. S. Pine-Coffin (New York: Penguin Books, 1961).

3. For a discussion, see John M. Rist, *Augustine: Ancient Thought Baptized* (Cambridge: Cambridge University Press, 1994), 214–25.

4. See Thomas Aquinas *Summa Theologiae* I-II q. 94 a. 2.

5. This is not to say that the languages of love in Christianity are all the same. There are appreciable differences between, e.g., the eudaimonism of charity in Augustine and the Kantian understanding of *agape* of Kierkegaard. For a discussion of the former, see John Burnaby, *Amor Dei* (London: Hodder and Stoughton, 1938); for a discussion of the latter, and an attempt to craft a normative understanding of Christian love on that basis, see Gene Outka, *Agape: An Ethical Analysis* (New Haven: Yale University Press, 1972).

6. See, e.g., Thomas Aquinas *Summa Theologiae* II-II q. 26.

7. In addition to the material cited from Aquinas in the previous note, see, e.g., Karl Barth, *Church Dogmatics*, III/4 (Edinburgh: T. & T. Clark, 1961), 285–323; Soren Kierkegaard, *Works of Love*, trans. Howard and Edna Hong, with a preface by R. Gregor Smith (New York: Harper and Row, 1962).

8. See, e.g., Reinhold Niebuhr, *An Interpretation of Christian Ethics* (New York: Harper and Row, 1935), chap. 4 and passim.

9. See, e.g., Augustine *Confessions* bks. 4, 11, and passim; Augustine *City of God*, trans. Henry Bettenson, with an intro. by David Knowles (New York: Penguin Books, 1972).

10. For a recent expression of this view, see Stanley Hauerwas, *Should War Be Eliminated? Philosophical and Theological Investigations* (Milwaukee, Wis.: Marquette University Press, 1984).

11. See, e.g., H. Richard Niebuhr, *Radical Monotheism and Western Culture, with Supplementary Essays* (New York: Harper and Row, 1943).

12. Clement of Alexandria, "Who is the Rich Man That Shall Be Saved?" in *The Ante-Nicene Fathers*, ed. Alexander Roberts and James Donaldson (Grand Rapids, Mich.: Wm. B. Eerdmans, 1980), 596.

13. Ibid., 594.

14. Ibid., 595.

15. The differences between the tradition of self-renunciation and the view of Clement of Alexandria exemplify the two-tiered ethic in Christianity, as discussed in Ernst Troeltsch, *The Social Teaching of the Christian Churches*, 2 vols., trans. Olive Wyon, with an intro. by H. Richard Niebuhr (Chicago: University of Chicago Press, 1976).

16. For a discussion, see Justo L. González, *Early Christian Ideas on the Origin, Significance, and Use of Money* (San Francisco: Harper & Row, 1990), 161–66.

17. Ibid., 163.

18. Ibid., 164.

19. Thomas Aquinas *Summa Theologiae* II-II q. 66 a. 1.

20. Ibid., a. 2.

21. Ibid. I-II q. 108 a. 4. The distinction has its origins in Ambrose: *De Officiis Ministrorum* III, iv.

22. Thomas Aquinas *Summa Theologiae* II-II q. 66 a. 5.

23. Ibid., a. 7.

24. Ibid., a. 2.

25. See Bernice Hamilton, *Political Thought in Sixteenth-Century Spain* (Oxford: Clarendon Press, 1963).

26. Francisco de Vitoria, *De Indis*, in *Political Writings*, ed. Anthony Pagden and Jeremy Lawrence (Cambridge: Cambridge University Press, 1991), 250.

27. Ibid., 284.

28. Ibid.

29. Ibid., 286.

30. Ibid., 285.

31. See David J. O'Brien and Thomas A. Shannon, eds., *Catholic Social Thought: The Documentary Heritage* (Maryknoll, N. Y.: Orbis Books, 1992). For an overview of the philosophy of human nature in the papal encyclical tradition, and the various developments within that philosophy, see Charles E. Curran, *Moral Theology: A Continuing Journey* (Notre Dame, Ind.: University of Notre Dame Press, 1982), chap. 8.

32. Paul VI, *Populorum Progressio (1967)*, in *Renewing the Earth: Catholic Documents on Peace, Justice and Liberation*, ed. David J. O'Brien and Thomas A. Shannon (Garden City, N. J.: Image Books, 1966), para. 23.

33. Ibid.

34. Ibid., para. 24.

35. Ibid., para. 51.

36. Gustavo Gutiérrez, *A Theology of Liberation*, trans. and ed. Caridad Inda and John Eagleson (Maryknoll, N. Y.: Orbis Books, 1973), 27 and passim.

37. Ibid., 36.

38. Ibid., 291–306.

39. For a fuller theological defense of these ideas, and a sustained critique of anthropocentric rather than biocentric approaches to moral value, see James M. Gustafson, *Ethics from a Theocentric Perspective*, 2 vols. (Chicago: University of Chicago Press, 1981–84).

40. See, e.g., Thomas Aquinas on the function of human law in relation to natural law, *Summa Theologiae* I-II q. 95.

41. Paul Tillich, *The Protestant Era* (Chicago: University of Chicago Press, 1948), 163.

42. See, e.g., Niebuhr, *Radical Monotheism and Western Culture*, 11, 24, 32, and passim.

43. Ibid.

44. H. Richard Niebuhr, *The Meaning of Revelation* (New York: Macmillan, 1941), 57, 59. The problem of religious nationalism was especially acute for German Protestants between the world wars. For a discussion, see Karl Barth, *Church Dogmatics*, III/4, 305–23.

45. H. Richard Niebuhr, *The Social Sources of Denominationalism* (Cleveland: Meridian Books, 1929).

46. H. Richard Niebuhr, "War as the Judgment of God," *Christian Century* 59 (May 3, 1942): 631. I discuss Niebuhr's views in *Interpretations of Conflict: Ethics,*

Pacifism, and the Just-War Tradition (Chicago: University of Chicago Press, 1991), chap. 6.

47. Vitoria *De Indis, in Political Writings*, 278.

48. Ibid.

49. Paul VI speaks of the right of immigration, but his remarks are confined to the case of guest workers. See *Populorum Progressio*, para. 17.

50. For an instructive discussion, see Michael Walzer, *Spheres of Justice: A Defense of Pluralism and Equality* (New York: Basic Books, 1983), chap. 2.

51. The importance of community might also imply a limited right of exit, although it would be difficult to imagine how any authentic community could coerce membership.

52. Barth, *Church Dogmatics*, III/4, 301.

53. Ibid., 297.

54. Ibid., 301.

55. See, e.g., Augustine, "On the Spirit and the Letter," in *Augustine: Later Works*, trans. with an introduction by John Burnaby (Philadelphia: Westminster Press, 1955), 193–250; Martin Luther, "The Freedom of the Christian," in *Luther's Works*, ed. John Dillenberger (New York: Doubleday, 1961), 42–85; Paul Tillich, *Love, Power, and Justice* (New York: Oxford University Press, 1954).

56. See Bernard of Clairvaux, "Letter 391," excerpted in *War and Christian Ethics*, ed. Arthur Holmes (Grand Rapids, Mich.: Baker Book House, 1975), 88–89.

57. For a discussion, see James Turner Johnson, *Ideology, Reason, and the Limitation of War: Religious and Secular Concepts, 1200–1740* (Princeton: Princeton University Press, 1975), 110–17.

58. Ibid., chap. 2.

59. See, e.g., Menno Simons, *Complete Writings* (Scottdale, Pa.: Herald Press, 1956).

60. For useful discussions of these authors, see Quentin Skinner, *The Foundations of Modern Political Thought*, vol. 2 (Cambridge: Cambridge University Press, 1978); LeRoy Walters, "Five Classic Just-War Theories: A Study in the Thought of Thomas Aquinas, Vitoria, Suarez, Gentili, and Grotius" (Ph.D. diss., Yale University, 1971).

61. See Vitoria, *On Dietary Laws*, in *Political Writings*, 225–26; Hamilton, *Political Thought in Sixteenth-Century Spain*, 127.

62. Vitoria, *De Indis*, in *Political Writings*, 278–90; for a fuller discussion of the Spanish Scholastics and other critics of a crusading mentality, see Hamilton, *Political Thought in Sixteenth-Century Spain*, chap. 6; Johnson, *Ideology, Reason, and the Limitation of War*, chap. 3.

63. See Alberico Gentili, *De Iure Belli Libri Tres*, vol. 2, trans. John C. Rolfe, with an intro. by Coleman Phillipson (Oxford: Clarendon Press, 1933), 41, 74, 123–24; Hugo Grotius, *Rights of War and Peace*, trans. A. C. Campbell, with an intro. by David Hill (Westport, Conn.: Hyperion, 1979), bk. 2, chap. 25.

64. For a discussion of cases in which those presumptions are overridden, see Michael Walzer, *Just and Unjust Wars: A Moral Argument with Historical Illustrations* (New York: Basic Books, 1977), chap. 6.

65. On these and other grounds, Christians have argued for the importance of the liberty of conscience, proceeding in quite the opposite direction of a crusade ideology. Since at least the time of Martin Luther (1483–1546), Christians have crafted a language that emphasizes the freedom of the Christian. This view underscores the fact that an individual's religious well-being is finally her own responsibility. Salvation cannot be left to institutional representatives or other third parties; in matters of faith, the relationship must be uncoerced and direct. Communities need autonomy in part to protect the freedom necessary for an individual's sincere relationship with God.

66. See n. 1 above.

67. John XXIII, *Pacem in Terris* (1963), in *Renewing the Earth: Catholic Documents on Peace, Justice and Liberation*, 124–70.

68. U.S. Catholic Bishops, *The Challenge of Peace: God's Promise and Our Response* (Washington, D.C.: United States Catholic Conference, 1983).

69. U.S. Catholic Conference International Policy Committee, "American Responsibilities in a Changing World," *Origins* 22 (October 29, 1992): 339. See also J. Bryan Hehir, "Just War Theory in a Post–Cold War Context," *Journal of Religious Ethics* 20 (Fall 1992): 237–57.

70. U.S. Catholic Conference International Policy Committee, "American Responsibilities in a Changing World," 339.

71. Kenneth R. Himes, "Catholic Social Thought and Humanitarian Intervention," in *Peacemaking: Moral and Policy Challenges for a New World*, ed. Gerald F. Powers, Drew Christiansen, S.J., and Robert T. Hennemeyer (Washington, D.C.: United States Catholic Conference, 1994), 223–24 (emphasis mine).

72. U.S. Catholic Conference International Policy Committee, "American Responsibilities in a Changing World," 341.

73. Drawing on the principle of *agape*, Paul Ramsey develops an ethics of the just war that potentially opens the door widely to intervention and the danger that states could use an imperialistic rationale to meddle in the affairs of other states. Ramsey was aware of this problem, and thus sought to include the values of international law and order in the calculus of political practical reasoning. See Paul Ramsey, *The Just War: Force and Political Responsibility* (New York: Charles Scribner's Sons, 1968). For subsequent discussions of humanitarian intervention in Christian ethics, see J. Bryan Hehir, "The Ethics of Intervention: United States Policy in Vietnam (1961–68)" (Ph.D. diss., Harvard University, 1976); U.S. Catholic Bishops, "The Harvest of Justice Is Sown in Peace," in Powers et al., *Peacemaking*, 313–46; Kenneth R. Himes, "The Morality of Humanitarian Intervention," *Theological Studies* 55 (March 1994): 82–105, and "Catholic Social Thought and Humanitarian Intervention," 215–28; Richard B. Miller, "Casuistry, Pacifism, and the Just-War Tradition in the Post–Cold War Era," in *Peacemaking*, 199–213; John Langan, "Justice or Peace? A Moral Assessment of Humanitarian Intervention in Bosnia," *America* 170 (February 12, 1994): 9–14; James Turner Johnson, "Humanitarian Intervention, Christian Ethical Reasoning, and the Just-War Idea," in *Sovereignty at the Crossroads? Morality and International Politics in the Post–Cold War Era*, ed. Luis E. Lugo (Lanham, Md.: Rowman and Littlefield, 1996), 127–43; Richard B. Miller, "Humanitarian Intervention,

Altruism, and the Limits of Casuistry," *Journal of Religious Ethics* 28 (Spring 2000): 3–35.

74. Christian pacifists might find this claim incongruous if they understand humanitarian interventions to be a form of war. But pacifists might consider such interventions comparable to police actions rather than war. Insofar as the paradigm of police action is acceptable to pacifists, actions thus conceived might be justifiable, at least in theory. I discuss this point in "Casuistry, Pacifism, and the Just-War Tradition in the Post–Cold War Era," 199–213.

5

The Value of Limited Loyalty

CHRISTIANITY, THE NATION, AND TERRITORIAL BOUNDARIES

NIGEL BIGGAR

SOME OF the more interesting things that Christianity has to say about territorial boundaries come by way of its views on the nation, national identity and loyalty, and nationalism. Historically, of course, Christianity—or, rather, Christians—have said different and sometimes quite contradictory things on these topics. Some have considered each nation to be specially ordained by the eternal God, while others have stressed the mutable historicality of national compositions and boundaries.[1] Some have virtually equated loyalty to the nation with loyalty to God, while others have regarded it as inimical to pacific, universalist Christian faith. As with any historically longstanding and geographically widespread tradition, Christianity is far less a single coherent system of thought than it is a set of debates, sustained over centuries, unified by reference to common authorities, but bringing into play many points of view. Strictly speaking, then, to "represent" what the tradition has to say on any given issue would involve the exhaustive and impartial presentation of a number of rival points of view—and this would certainly have the value of adding grist to the mill of discussion. Nevertheless, if we are actually going to enter a tradition of discussion, and not merely survey it from the vantage point of Olympian neutrality, we must venture judgments, preferring some arguments to others and giving reasons for these preferences; rather than merely represent what the tradition *says*, we must present what we think it *should say*. This is what I have chosen to do here. Therefore, what follows is not a representation of all that Christians have said about nations and national loyalty, and about their implications for territorial boundaries, but rather a presentation of what I think Christians should say about them.

This essay, then, is much narrower in focus than Richard Miller's panorama, and it presupposes most of what he has to say—especially about the limitations of the rights of ownership by obligations to the common good. My main quarrel with him is over his specification of the Christian understanding of love as properly "indiscriminate and unconditional" or "cosmopolitan," and over the view of national loyalty that follows from it. That is the major point of disagreement between us. The argument that gives rise to this disagreement now follows.

The Creatureliness of Human Being: Historicality, National Loyalty, and Diversity

Christians should base their view of the nation on their understanding of human being as creaturely. This involves distinguishing it sharply from the universal and eternal being of God and taking seriously its historicality—that is, its boundedness by time and space. Humans come into being and grow up in a particular time, and if not in one particular place and community then in a limited number of them. Human individuals are normally nurtured, inducted into social life, and encouraged in certain self-understandings by their family and by other institutions—educational, religious, recreational, economic, and political—that mediate the history and ethos of their local and national communities. It is natural, therefore, that individuals should feel special affection for, and loyalty toward, those communities that have cared for them and given them so much that is beneficial; and, since beneficiaries ought to be grateful to benefactors, it is right that they should.[2] We have yet to specify the forms that such affection and loyalty should and should not take; but that they should take some form is clear.

This affirmation of a certain kind of national loyalty in terms of the Christian concept of the creatureliness of human being might seem at first sight surprising. For does not Christianity teach that human beings should love one another indiscriminately and unconditionally; and does not this imply that they should transcend all particular "natural" loyalties to family, ethnic community, and nation? Certainly, this claim is made; but, in my opinion, it is made mistakenly.

I would agree that all humans share the common status of children of God, who are indebted for the gift of secular existence and who stand in need of the gifts of forgiveness and of eternal life. I would also agree that we are all made "in God's image" and are thereby dignified with responsibility to manage the rest of the created world,[3] and that each of us is the subject of a vocation to play a unique part in God's Grand Project of bringing the created world to fulfillment. It is true, then, that each of us owes a certain respect to any fellow human being to whom we are related; and in this age of global communications there are few, if any, humans to whom we are not related somehow. Nevertheless, this is not to say that we owe all other humans equal care. We may be responsible, but ours is a responsibility of creatures, not of gods. We are limited in awareness, in energy, and in time. We are able only to take care of some, not all; and there are some to whom we are more strongly obliged by ties of gratitude, or whom we are better placed to serve on account of shared language and culture or common citizenship.

However, it is often said—and Richard Miller says it[4]—that Christian love for others is properly indiscriminate and unconditional. This claim has two main grounds, one biblical and the other theological. The biblical ground comprises those passages in the New Testament where "natural" loyalty to family is severely downgraded. Among these are Gospel passages where Jesus is reported as saying that only those who hate their mothers and fathers can be his disciples,[5] that those who would follow him must "let the dead bury the dead,"[6] and that his "family" now consists of those who have joined him in his cause;[7] and also, by implication, those passages in the Epistles where St. Paul recommends virginity or celibacy as a higher good than marriage.[8]

The theological ground consists of the typically Protestant concept of God's love as showered graciously on every human regardless of his or her moral status—a concept that was most fully developed in the twentieth century by the Swedish Lutheran theologian, Anders Nygren. According to Nygren, God's love is utterly spontaneous and gratuitous; it is not attracted to the beloved by any of their qualities (how could it be, since those whom it loves are all sinners?), and it is in no sense beholden to them; it is simply and absolutely gracious.[9] As God loves us, so should we love our neighbors, with a pure altruism that entirely disregards their qualities. It is quite true that Nygren himself was not directly addressing the question of whether or not a certain local or national partiality in our affections and loyalties is justifiable, and that his focus was on the religious relationship between God and sinful creatures. Nevertheless, he made it quite clear that Christians are to mediate to their neighbors the same unconditional and indiscriminate love that God has shown them.[10]

What should we make of these biblical and theological grounds? Do they really imply that Christian love should be oblivious to local and national bonds? I think not. Certainly, the so-called hard sayings of Jesus imply that natural loyalties are subordinate to the requirements of loyalty to God, and that sometimes the latter might enjoin behavior that contradicts normal expressions of the former. But, given that Jesus is also reported as criticizing the Pharisees for proposing a piece of casuistry that effectively permits children to neglect the proper care of their elderly parents;[11] and given that—notwithstanding his affirmation and commendation of Gentiles[12]—he apparently maintained his identity as a Jew;[13] there is good reason not to take these "hard sayings" at face value, and to read them as hyperboles intending to relativize rather than repudiate natural loyalties. As for St. Paul, it is notable that, although he reckoned virginity and celibacy superior, he persisted in regarding marriage as a good. In other words, in spite of his urgent sense of the imminent "ending" or transformation of the world by God, and of how this revolution of the current order of things would severely strain marital and family ties, St. Paul never went as far as to say that investment in society through marriage and children should cease. What he thereby implies is that, although the arrival of the world-to-come will involve the transformation of this world and its natural social bonds, it will not involve their simple abolition.

Upon close inspection, then, the New Testament grounds for supposing Christian love to be properly unconditional and indiscriminate are not at all firm. That is even more so in the case of the theological ground. Certainly, if we take Jesus to be God incarnate, we can infer that the love of God for wayward human beings is gracious—that is, both compassionate and forgiving. It is compassionate in that it sympathizes with wrongdoers in their weakness and confusion and ignorance; and it is forgiving in that it is willing to set past injury aside and enter once again into a relationship of trust. But note how limited is the scope of this love: it operates only between an injured party and the one who has done the injury. It is a mode of love, but not the whole of it. Accordingly, it is unconditional and indiscriminate only in a very restricted sense. As compassion, its being proffered is not conditional upon the demonstration of repentance, and it is therefore made available indiscriminately to all sinners. As forgiveness, however, it is only offered in response to an expression of genuine repentance, and therefore only discriminately to penitent sinners.[14] Therefore, insofar as God's love manifested in Jesus is a model for human love, the specific ways in which it is unconditional and indiscriminate bear on how we should treat those who have wronged us; but they have no bearing at all on how we should distribute our limited emotional, physical, temporal, and material resources in caring for the millions of fellow humans who can now claim to be—more or less closely—our neighbors.

So far I have argued that considered reflection upon the Christian concept of the creatureliness of human being—and, specifically, upon the original dependence of any human individual on a historical community—should lead Christians to acknowledge the validity of natural loyalties to those communities (including the nation) into which one is born and in which one is brought up. Now I want to contend that it should also lead them to regard a diversity of ethnic communities, including nations, as a natural necessity that is also good.[15]

Human communities, being creaturely, can only exist in particular times and places, and different geographical locations and historical experiences are bound to generate diverse communities. Human

communities, being human, may well all share some common characteristics, but experience of different places and histories is bound to
generate differences in political constitutions, institutions, customs,
received wisdom, and outlook. As a natural necessity, such diversity
could be regarded simply as an unhappy feature of the human condition, providing as it does the occasion for incomprehension and conflict
between communities, and therefore one to be transcended as soon as
possible. But Christians, believing as they traditionally do in the unqualified goodness and wisdom of the divine Creator, should be dis-
inclined to regard anything natural—whether created or following
necessarily from it—as simply evil. Further, human experience con-
firms that diversity among peoples can be a source of value as well
as of conflict. As postmodernists never tire of reminding us, there is
beauty in difference. But to restrict this value simply to the aesthetic
dimension would be to trivialize many of the differences that concern
us here. For differences between constitutions, institutions, customs,
wisdom, or outlook, if taken seriously, should provoke not merely wonder but reflection. Such differences should move each community to
ask itself whether others do not order their social life better, or whether
their received wisdom should not correct, supplement, or complement
its own. The value of communal (and so national) difference here is not
just aesthetic, but intellectual and moral: it can enable human beings to
learn from each other better ways of serving and promoting the human
good. In other words, its justification is not just postmodernist, but
liberal.

This argument that a Christian vision of things should affirm national diversity is supported by history. For, according to Adrian Hastings, Christianity has been a vital factor in the historical development
of national diversity through its habit of communicating its message by
translating it into vernacular languages.[16] Since "a community . . . is
essentially a creation of human communication,"[17] and since the writing down of a language tends to increase linguistic uniformity,[18] the
movement of a vernacular from oral usage to the point where it is regularly employed for the production of a literature is a major cause of the
development of national identity.[19] Therefore, by translating the Bible
into vernacular languages, by developing vernacular liturgies and devotional literature, and by mediating these to the populace through an
educated parish clergy, the Christian Church played a major part in the
development of diverse nationalities.[20]

And there is good reason to suppose that this role has not simply
been the accidental effect of a particular missionary strategy. After all,
different missionary strategies are possible; and we must ask why
Christianity chose the one that it did. It could, like Islam, have chosen

to spread the Word by assimilation rather than translation. Muslims regard the Qur'an as divine in its Arabic, linguistic form as well as in its content, and the consequent cultural impact of Islam has been to Arabize, "to draw peoples into a single world community of language and government."[21] In contrast, Christians do not ascribe divinity to any particular language, and they thereby implicitly recognize that the Word of God is free to find (somewhat different) expression in every language.[22] Accordingly, in the New Testament story of the birth of the Christian Church on the day of Pentecost, the disciples of Jesus "were all filled with the Holy Spirit and began to speak in other tongues," so that the multiethnic crowd who heard them "were bewildered, because each one heard them speaking in his own language."[23] Whereas the story of the tower of Babel in the Hebrew Scriptures presents linguistic diversity as a degeneration (caused by God's punishment of sin) from an original state when "the whole earth had one language,"[24] here the Spirit of God is presented as graciously accommodating Godself to it. This divine self-accommodation implies a respect for and affirmation of the historicality, and therefore diversity, of creaturely human being. Such affirmation is also implicit in the orthodox Christian doctrine of the divine Incarnation, according to which God Almighty became human in Jesus of Nazareth, and in becoming human became historical—that is, a particular man living in a particular time and place. According to the Christian story, it is characteristic of God to be willing to meet human creatures in the midst of their historicality and diversity. Although transcending time and space, God is not alien to them; in this case what is transcended is not repudiated, and may be inhabited. The Christian theological affirmation of human diversity finds further confirmation in the orthodox doctrine of God as a trinity. In Christian eyes, as in Jewish and Muslim ones, God is certainly one, but the divine unity is not simple. God is more like a community than a monad splendid in isolation. The Origin and Basis of the created world, then, is a unity that contains rather than abolishes difference—a unity in diversity, not instead of it.

Thus far we have argued that, on the ground of its understanding of human being as creaturely, Christianity should affirm the special loyalty that grows naturally out of gratitude to a national community that has sustained and nurtured its members; and it should also affirm a diversity of national communities, partly because human diversity is natural to human (and divine) being, and partly because it is aesthetically, intellectually, and morally enriching. There is, however, another dimension to human creatureliness that should lead Christians to qualify their affirmation of national loyalty and diversity: namely, moral responsibility for the common good.

The Creatureliness of Human Being: Responsibility
   for the Common Good

As creatures, human beings are bound not only by time and space, but also by the requirements of the good that is proper to their created nature. Roughly speaking, service of the human good is what makes actions right, and failure of such service is what makes them wrong. This good is not just private, but common; the good of the human individual—and of each human community or nation—is bound up with the good of others, both human and nonhuman. Acting rightly is important, then, partly because it respects or promotes the good of others in ways they deserve, and partly because in so doing agents maintain or promote their own good—and thereby help to make themselves fit for eternal life.

So human creatures are bound by an obligation to serve the common human good; but being creatures, their powers of service are limited. No human effort, individual or collective, has the power to secure the maximal good of all human beings (including the dead as well as the living), far less of nonhuman ones as well. Each of us must choose to do what we can, and what we may, to advance *certain* dimensions of the good of *some*, trusting God to coordinate our little contributions and guide their unpredictable effects to the benefit of the common good of all. Among those whom we choose to help, it would be right for us to include our benefactors, for gratitude requires it. Thus the justification for special loyalties to such communities as one's family and nation.

But note: What one owes one's family or nation is not anything or everything, but specifically respect for and promotion of their good. Such loyalty, therefore, does not involve simply doing or giving whatever is demanded, whether by the state, the electoral majority, or even the people as a whole. Indeed, when what is demanded would appear to harm the community—for example, acquiescence in injustice perpetrated by the state against its own people or a foreign one, or by one section of the nation against another—genuine national loyalty requires that it be refused. True patriotism is not uncritical; and in extreme circumstances it might even involve participation in acts of treason—as it did in the case of Dietrich Bonhoeffer, whose love for Germany led him into conspiracy to kill Hitler.[25]

National loyalty, as Christians should conceive it, shows itself basically in reminding the nation that it is accountable to God, at least in the sense of being obliged by the good given or created in human nature. By thus distinguishing between its object and God, such loyalty distances itself from the Romantic nationalism that absolutizes and divinizes the Nation, making its unquestioning service the route to a quasi-immortality.[26]

It is true, of course, that the Christian Bible contains and gives prominence to the concept of a People chosen by God to be the medium of salvation to the world; and it is also true that particular "Christian" nations have periodically identified themselves as the Chosen People, thereby pretending to accrue to themselves and their imperialist, "civilizing" policies an exclusive divine authority. But it is fair to point out that the notion of the Chosen People as referring to a particular nation strictly belongs to the Old Testament, not the New; and that one of the main points on which early Christianity differentiated itself from Judaism was precisely its transnational character. Full participation in the Christian religion was no longer tied to worship in the temple at Jerusalem, and was as open to Gentiles as to Jews; for, as St. Paul famously put it, "there is neither Jew nor Greek . . . ; for you are all one in Christ Jesus."[27] In early, emergent Christianity, the "People of God" came to refer no longer to a particular nation (Israel), but to the universal Church. Certainly, there have been many times when the Church as an institution has become wedded to a particular ethnic culture or the instrument of a particular nation-state. There have been times when the Church's *relative and conditional* affirmation of a particular culture or nation has lost its vital qualifications. But, in light of what we have said above, we may judge that these are times when the Church has betrayed its identity and failed in its calling. They are times when it has failed to maintain the distinction ironically attested by the Nazi judge, who, before condemning Helmuth von Moltke to death, demanded of him, "From whom do you take your orders? From the Beyond or from Adolf Hitler?"[28] And they are times when it has failed to observe the original priority so succinctly affirmed in Sir Thomas More's declaration, moments before he was beheaded for refusing to endorse Henry VIII's assertion of royal supremacy over the English Church, that he would die "the King's good servant, but God's first."[29]

A properly Christian view, then, insists that every nation is equally accountable to God for its service of the human good. No nation may pretend to be God's Chosen People in the strong sense of being the sole and permanent representative and agent of His will on earth; no nation may claim such an identity with God. This relativization still permits each nation to consider itself chosen or called by God to contribute in its own peculiar way to the world's salvation; to play a special role—at once unique, essential, and limited—in promoting the universal human good. It allows members of a given nation to celebrate the achievements of the good that grace their own history and to take pride in the peculiar institutions and customs in which they have realized it. At the same time, it forces them to acknowledge that their nation's achievement is but one among many; and so to recognize, appreciate, and even learn from the distinctive contributions of others.

But more than this, each nation must realize not only that other nations too have made valuable contributions to the realization of the common good of all things, but also that the achievement of the good in one nation is actually bound up with its achievement elsewhere. National loyalty, therefore, is properly extrovert. As Karl Barth puts it:

> For when we speak of home, motherland, and people, it is a matter of outlook, background, and origin. We thus refer to the initiation and beginning of a movement. It is a matter of being faithful to this beginning. But this is possible only if we execute the movement, and not as we make the place where we begin it a prison and stronghold. The movement leads us relentlessly, however, from the narrower sphere to a wider, from our own people to other human peoples. . . . The one who is really in his own people, among those near to him, is always on the way to those more distant, to other peoples.[30]

The point here is not that we should grow *out of* national identity and loyalty and into a cosmopolitanism that, floating free of all particular attachments, lacks any real ones,[31] but rather that, in and through an ever-deepening care for the good of our own nation, we are drawn into caring for the good of foreigners. This point is poignantly captured by Yevgeni Yevtushenko in "Babii Yar," his poem about Russian anti-Semitism:

> Oh my Russian people!
> I know you are internationalists to the core.
> But those with unclean hands
> have often made a jingle of your purest name.
> I know the goodness of my land. . . .
> In my blood there is no Jewish blood.
> In their callous rage all anti-Semites
> must hate me now as a Jew.
> For that reason I am a true Russian.[32]

Notwithstanding the tensions that may arise between national loyalty and loyalties that are more extensive, there is nevertheless an essential connection between them.

Christianity, Nationality, and Borders

Christianity, then, should give qualified affirmation to national loyalty and the nation. Such affirmation means that it refuses to dismiss national identity and loyalty simply as false consciousness. It resists liberal cosmopolitanism and Marxist internationalism on the ground that human beings are not historically transcendent gods, but historically rooted and embedded creatures. Accordingly, it recognizes the need to restrict cross-border mobility. Borders exist primarily to define the territory within which a people is free to develop their own way of life as best they can. Unrestricted mobility would permit uncontrolled immigration that would naturally be experienced by natives as an invasion. Successful, peaceful immigration needs to be negotiated. Immigrants must demonstrate a willingness to respect native cultures and institutions, and to a certain extent abide by them. Natives must be given time to accommodate new residents and their foreignness.

Further, the affirmation of national identity means that the consensus that comprises the unity of a nation needs to be more than merely constitutional; it also needs to be cultural. This is partly because a particular constitution and its institutional components derive their particular meaning from the history of their development; and so to endorse a constitution involves understanding that history and owning its heroes. It is also partly because, while consensus over individual and group rights is necessary to prevent the outbreak of conflict, it cannot be secured or sustained without a cultural *engagement* between groups that goes beyond mere respect and achieves a measure of mutual appreciation.

On the other hand, Christianity's qualification of its affirmation of nations means that it is alert to their historical mutability. Although growing out of an extension of natural loyalties, particular nations are human constructions whose culture and ethnic composition are always changing.[33] National myths of racial or ethnic or cultural purity, therefore, are immediately suspect, in which case foreign ways and immigrants can be regarded not just as challenges or threats, but as resources.

The proper willingness of nations to incorporate foreigners—and elements of their foreignness—is bound to produce cultural diversity; but should this be allowed to include a diversity of religions? There are good Christian grounds for supposing that it should. Even if Christians believe that, in the end, they are more right than others (as others no doubt believe that they are more right than Christians), it does not follow from this that others are absolutely or radically wrong. Christians believe that the Spirit of the Christ-like God is universally present to all creatures; so they should expect that God is somewhat known beyond the reaches of the Christian Church. Add to this the Protestant doctrine of the Church as a body that is still *learning* to be faithful—as at once righteous and sinful—and Christians come to be seen as those who have yet more to learn, and who might conceivably do so from non-Christians. Then, combining these theological considerations with the empirical observation (and Christians should not be averse to learning from experience) that the modern era has demonstrated that religious uniformity is not necessary for there to be sufficient moral consensus to ensure social stability, we arrive at the conclusion that a nation should be willing to tolerate religious diversity within its borders.

There are various ways of doing this. The classic liberal way is to aspire to keep public institutions religiously neutral, and thereby accord each religion equal status in the eyes of the state. Alternatively, there may be a society where most members feel some affinity—whether spiritual or cultural—with the state religion, and where members of other religious communities would prefer a polity in which a religion other than their own had privileged public status, rather than a fully fledged liberal arrangement where religion is systematically relegated to the private world. Here religious diversity would coexist with religious establishment.[34]

Christianity's view of the nation implies that its borders should be patrolled so as to control immigration, but that they should be open to foreign immigrants on certain conditions, and therefore that they should contain cultural and religious diversity. The Christian view also implies that the autonomy a nation enjoys within its borders is not absolute. It does not have the right simply to do with its resources whatever it pleases, but only to manage them responsibly; and where it has resources surplus to its own needs, it has a duty to devote them to the good of others—by welcoming refugees, for example, or by donating aid to foreign countries.[35] This concept of a morally limited right to autonomy over material and social assets contradicts the libertarian view that one has an absolute right of disposal over whatever one has acquired legally; and it does so partly on the ground that all creaturely owners are also dependents and beneficiaries. How much we own is due to benefactions and good fortune as well as to skill and entrepreneurial flair. Even where our property was genuinely virgin when we first possessed it, the fact that we had the power to discover it will have owed something to what we had inherited, and ultimately to what our ancestors had been given and the good fortune that had attended the development of their resources. As we have received, so should we give. National sovereignty, then, is not absolute; its exercise is subject to the moral claims of the common good, and when it fails to acknowledge those claims, other nations might have the moral right to intervene—if the requirements of prudence can be met (for example, if it seems that an intervention is likely to achieve what it intends and to do so without risking an escalating conflagration).

In the Christian view that I am commending here, national borders should be conditionally open and they may be transgressed if national autonomy is being exercised irresponsibly. They may also be changed. Nations, as Christians should see them, are neither divine nor eternal, but human and historical. Investment in a nation is not—with all due respect to Fichte—the route to immortality; for that runs through service of the Creator and Sustainer of all things. As historical, nations are mutable. Therefore, the patriot should be willing to contemplate changes in his or her nation—whether in its constitution or even in its very definition—if that is what justice and prudence together require. It is not written in heaven that the United Kingdom should always encompass Scotland, nor the Canadian confederation Quebec, nor the Yugoslav federation Kosovo. Nor is it written that the United States of America must remain united, any more than it was written that the Soviet Union should. Christianity properly precludes a simply conservative view of a nation's internal or external territorial boundaries, and withholds its support from political movements dedicated to preserving those boundaries at all costs.

On the other hand, Christians should be wary of demands for border changes that issue from nationalist fervor fueled by dishonest myths that idealize one's own nation and demonize or scapegoat another, that picture one's own simply as innocent victim and the other's simply as malicious oppressor. The Christian doctrine of the universal presence of sin means that we may not fondly imagine that the line dividing virtue from vice runs with reassuring neatness between our own people on the virtuous side and another people on the vicious one. The line between virtue and vice runs right down the middle of each human community, as it runs through the heart of every individual. Accordingly, no human may stand to another simply as righteous to unrighteous, and the wronged party always shares enough in common with the wrongdoer to owe him some compassion. Nationalist myths that say otherwise tend to exaggerate the injustice suffered, demand a radical and revolutionary remedy, totally discount any moral claims that the "enemy" might have, and brook no compromise.

For an example, take Northern Ireland. It is true that Catholic nationalists there have been seriously oppressed by Protestant unionists, sometimes systematically; and it is therefore reasonable for Catholics to be less than fully confident in British government and to seek protection under the Irish state. One way of securing this would be for the border between Northern Ireland and the Irish Republic to be completely erased, for the former to be incorporated into a "united" Ireland, and for British jurisdiction in the island of Ireland to be removed once and for all. This is what Irish nationalists have traditionally demanded. The problem with this is that there is a substantial ethnic community in Northern Ireland whose national allegiance is strongly British, and who want to become subject to the Irish state about as much as nationalists want to remain subject to the British one. An alternative solution—and one embodied in the Good Friday Agreement reached between the British and Irish governments and the political parties in Northern Ireland in April 1998—is to "thin" the border without erasing it. This involves setting up certain institutions that transcend the borders between Britain and Ireland, on the one hand compromising the substance of British sovereignty over Northern Ireland, while on the other hand maintaining the province's formal constitutional status as part of the United Kingdom. This reassures nationalists by giving Dublin substantial influence over British government in Northern Ireland; and by creating bodies with specific areas of responsibility (for example, for tourism or agriculture), whose jurisdiction runs through the whole of the island of Ireland and is unhindered by the border. But it also reassures the unionists by maintaining the border, eliciting Dublin's formal recognition of it,[36] limiting the jurisdiction of the cross-border bodies to specific areas of economic activity, and thereby securing Northern Ireland's place in the United Kingdom. One threat to this happy compromise, however, could come from the refusal of nationalists to regard it as a permanent settlement and their insistence on viewing it as merely a step on the road to the ultimate goal of the political unification of the whole of the island of Ireland under an Irish state. Such an insistence would be fueled by a traditional resentment of all things British and unionist, one that is blind to the considerable progress in remedying the injustices suffered by Catholics that British governments are widely acknowledged to have made since the 1970s; and that doggedly refuses to acknowledge the right of unionists to maintain their British allegiance for ever.

A Christian vision of things, then, militates against the idealization of the self and the demonization of the other that stifles sympathy and leads a bitter, dogmatic nationalism to brook no compromise in its determination to erase a national boundary. For the same reasons, it also militates against a nationalism that refuses all compromise in its determination to erect a national boundary sufficient to establish political independence. Certainly, Christians should acknowledge the right of an ethnic group to flourish in its own peculiar way—subject, of course, to the requirements of justice and fairness. They should also acknowledge that such peculiar flourishing might need the protection and support of special laws, perhaps a measure of autonomy, and in extreme circumstances even independence. Why should they contemplate independence only in extreme circumstances? Because its achievement is bound to embody a degree of alienation between two peoples formerly united. It involves political divorce, with all the attendant danger of lingering resentment that divorce risks; so if it can be avoided, it should be. For sure, there may be good reasons why independence should be sought and granted. Maybe an ethnic group in a multi-ethnic state has been maltreated, severely and over a period of time; and maybe either the state shows no sign of remedying the abuse, or the injured people can no longer be reasonably expected to trust the state to do what it says it will. Here the pursuit of independence would be consonant with the pursuit of justice. But Christians, with their sensitivity to the creaturely interdependence of human individuals and communities, and with their conviction that the Origin and Basis of things comprises a unity-in-diversity rather than the isolated and alienated unity of absolute self-sufficiency, should be skeptical of cries for independence; and all the more so when these arise from within a culture where independence is something of a fetish and where its prevalent concept is adolescent rather than adult. They should interrogate the demand, asking whether it will bring real and substantial benefits to the people as a whole—and not just, say, provide the local political class with a bigger stage to strut upon.

Conclusion

This essay has brought Christian thinking to bear upon the nature and purposes of territorial boundaries primarily through the concept of human being as creaturely. According to this concept, each human individual is born into, brought up in, and given a grip on life by a particular set of communities, which nowadays almost invariably includes a national community. As creatures, human individuals and groups are also subject to the moral claims of the good given in human nature. Since one of these claims is that beneficiaries ought to be grateful to benefactors, those who have benefited from a nation's protection and nurture owe it a certain loyalty. But this loyalty does not involve the blind endorsement of whatever policies a nation's leadership deems to be in its interests. More precisely, it does not involve the adoption of a narrowly private understanding of those interests. As the good of the individual is bound up with the good of the community, so the good of any single national community is bound up with the common good of all nations. Foreigners should be regarded, then, not simply as aliens but as distant neighbors; and where one nation has charge of more than enough resources to meet its own needs, it should devote its surplus to the good of others.

This view of national loyalty and of the nation carries the following implications for our understanding of territorial boundaries. First, boundaries perform the legitimate function of defining that area of the earth's surface in which a nation has certain freedoms to build its own way of life—in which it enjoys a certain autonomy. These national borders also rightly serve as barriers, insofar as immigration needs to be controlled in order to prevent the destructive invasion of a nation's way of life. Nevertheless, in that the incorporation of foreigners can enhance and enrich a national community, and in that racial or ethnic or cultural or religious purity is a nationalist myth, the barriers should be opened to immigrants whose admission will not be invasive. It follows that national borders should contain cultural diversity—and, given certain views of the Holy Spirit and of the Christian Church, religious diversity too. Further, borders should not be regarded as immutable; for they are as changeable as national constitutions. But they should not be changed in response to the demands of dogmatic, self-righteous nationalism, or in pursuit of the fetish of independence, but only out of deference to the requirements of justice and prudence combined.

Notes

1. See Karl Barth's discussion of these matters and of the history of Protestant thought about them in *Church Dogmatics*, III/4 (Edinburgh: T. & T. Clark, 1961), 285–323.

2. This is true, notwithstanding the fact that communities sometimes let members down badly, in which case it would be reasonable for those members' loyalty to their community to be diminished in proportion to the gravity of its failure.

3. The seminal notion that humankind is made "in God's image" derives from one verse in the Book of Genesis: "Then God said, 'Let us make man in our image, after our likeness; and let them have dominion . . . over all the earth'" (1:26). In the history of Christian tradition this phrase has been interpreted in many different ways; but the interpretation that is closest to the text understands it in terms of the practice of kings in the ancient world of setting up statues of themselves in outlying provinces or having their image imprinted on coinage, in order to represent the presence of royal authority throughout their empire. To be made in God's image, then, is to be made a representative or vicegerent of God, charged with exercising dominion in God's name over the rest of creation. For a history of the exegesis of Genesis 1:26–27, see Claus Westermann, *Genesis 1–11: A Commentary*, trans. John J. Scullion, S.J. (London: SPCK, 1984), 147–55.

4. See Richard Miller in the preceding chapter under "Boundaries": "Christianity requires an indiscriminate, unconditional love of others, irrespective of political, social, or national affiliation. . . . Christian *agape*, exemplified by Jesus's teaching and example, is altruistic and cosmopolitan."

5. Matthew 10:37; Luke 14:26.

6. Matthew 8:22; Luke 9:60.

7. Matthew 12:46–50; Mark 3:31–35; Luke 8:19–21.

8. I Corinthians 7.

9. Anders Nygren, *Agape and Eros*, trans. Philip S. Watson (Chicago: University of Chicago Press, 1982), 75–81. Nygren uses the New Testament word *agape* to designate this radically altruistic kind of love, which he believes to be peculiarly Christian, and to differentiate it from the Greek concept of love as essentially self-serving *eros*. *Agape and Eros* was originally published in Swedish in 1930 (Part I) and 1938 (Part II).

10. Ibid., 733–37.

11. Mark 7:9–13.

12. Matthew 8:5–13; 15:21–28.

13. Matthew 15:24, 26; John 4:22.

14. In brief defense of this understanding of forgiveness, let me make two points, one biblical and one empirical. First, in Jesus's parable of the prodigal son, the heartfelt repentance of the son is already fully established *before* we learn of his father's eager forgiveness (Luke 15:11–32). Second, it is unloving and foolish to forgive those who have shown insufficient awareness of what they have done wrong, both because it forecloses their moral education and growth and because it makes it likely that they will injure again.

15. A nation is an ethnic community that enjoys or aspires to a measure of autonomy in the organization of its public life through institutions of its own—whether religious, educational, legal, or political (see David Miller, *On Nationality* [Oxford: Clarendon Press, 1995], esp. chap. 2, "National Identity"). A nation need not be "independent." Scotland, for example, has its own national church, and educational and legal systems—and since 1999 its own parliament; but so long as it remains an integral part of the United Kingdom, it will not be fully "independent."

16. Adrian Hastings, *The Construction of Nationhood: Ethnicity, Religion, and Nationalism* (Cambridge: Cambridge University Press, 1997).

17. Ibid., 20.

18. Ibid., 19ff.

19. Ibid., 12, 20, 31.

20. Ibid., 22, 24, 191–92.

21. Ibid., 201. This statement needs to be qualified in that the traditional dogma of the untranslatability of the Qur'an has come under question as Islam has established itself in non-Arabic cultures.

22. Protestant fundamentalists, who believe the Bible to be inspired by God in the sense of being divinely dictated, come closest among Christians to the traditional Muslim view of the Qur'an; but not even they insist that the Sacred Scriptures should be read publicly only in Hebrew or Greek.

23. Acts 2:4, 6.

24. Genesis 11:1–9.

25. For a fuller exploration of these themes in the light of Bonhoeffer's life and work, see Keith Clements, *True Patriotism: Love of Country in Dialogue with the Witness of Dietrich Bonhoeffer* (London: Collins, 1986).

26. One classic expression of this nationalism is Fichte's: "The noble-minded man's belief in the eternal continuance of his influence even on this earth is thus founded on the hope of the eternal continuance of the people from which he has developed, and on the characteristic of that people. . . . This characteristic is the eternal things to which he entrusts the eternity of himself and of his continuing influence, the eternal order of things in which he places his portion of eternity. . . . In order to save his nation he must be ready even to die that it may live, and that he may live in it the only life for which he has ever wished" (J. G. Fichte, *Addresses to the German Nation* [Chicago: Open Court Press, 1922], 135–36). Benedict Anderson specifies this view of the nation as a modern phenomenon, providing as it does a substitute for declining religious modes of thought (*Imagined Communities: Reflections on the Origin and Spread of Nationalism*, rev. ed. [London and New York: Verso, 1991], 11–12).

27. Galatians 3:28.

28. Helmuth James von Moltke, *Letters to Freya: A Witness against Hitler* (London: Collins Harvill, 1991), 409.

29. According to a contemporary report carried in the *Paris News Letter*. See Nicholas Harpsfield, *The life and death of Sir Thomas Moore, knight, sometymes Lord high Chancellor of England*, ed. E. V. Hitchcock and R. W. Chambers, Early English Text Society, Original Series no. 186 (London: Oxford University Press, 1932), Appendix III, 266: "Apres les exhorta, et supplia tres instamment qu'ils priassent Dieu pour le Roy, affin qu'il luy voulsist donner bon conseil, protestant qu'il mouroit son bon serviteur et de Dieu premierement."

30. Barth, *Church Dogmatics*, III/4, 293–94.

31. Barth is right to suggest that such cosmopolitanism is not only undesirable, but impossible: "The command of God certainly does not require any man to be a cosmopolitan, quite apart from the fact that none of us can really manage to be so" (ibid., 293). Here I differ from Miller (in the previous chapter, under "Mobility"), who understands Barth's "overall impetus" to be "universalist," and interprets him as granting national identity and loyalty only "provisional" affirmation.

32. Yevgeni Yevtushenko, "Babii Yar," in *The Collected Poems, 1952–90* (Edinburgh: Mainstream Publishing, 1991), 103–4. Babii Yar is the name of a ravine on the outskirts of Kiev where at least 100,000 Jews were massacred in 1941. The massacre was carried out by German troops, but not without the tacit approval of many local Ukrainians, who shared in the long Russian tradition of anti-Semitism.

33. Barth is admirably alert to this (*Church Dogmatics*, III/4, 300–302).

34. Whenever proposals are mooted to end the Church of England's privileged status as the state religion of England, Jewish and Muslim leaders regularly leap to its defense. For a Jewish example, see Jonathan Sacks, *The Persistence of Faith* (London: Weidenfeld, 1991), esp. 68; and for a Muslim example, see T. Modood, "Ethno-religious Minorities, Secularism and the British State," *British Political Quarterly* 65 (1994): 53–73.

35. See Miller's discussion of Thomas Aquinas's concept of private property in the preceding chapter, under "Ownership and Distribution."

36. As part of the agreement, the Irish government committed itself to hold a referendum on amending articles 2 and 3 of the Irish constitution, so as to relinquish the Irish state's claim to the territory of Northern Ireland. The referendum was subsequently held and the proposal to drop the articles was approved.

Part III ———————————————————

PLURALISM

6

Conscientious Individualism

A CHRISTIAN PERSPECTIVE ON ETHICAL PLURALISM

DAVID LITTLE

Terms of Reference

Ethical Pluralism

There are several conceptual ambiguities about the term "pluralism" that need to be clarified. According to the dictionary, it is both a descriptive term, "the quality or state of being plural," and a theoretical or normative term, "the doctrine that there are more than one or two kinds of being or independent centers of causation"; "opposed to *monism, or dualism.*"[1] Accordingly, the phrase "ethical pluralism" might designate the simple existence of a diversity or plurality of ethical positions, or it might refer to a doctrine holding that ethics, as the systematic evaluation of human action, is *in its nature* incapable of being reduced to one comprehensive theory (whether monistic or dualistic). Isaiah Berlin, for example, is reputed to have held such a view (although a recent biography raises doubts about the coherence and consistency of Berlin's position).[2]

In respect to the normative usage, it may be helpful to distinguish between a "strong" and a "weak" theory of ethical pluralism. A "strong" theory is the one just stated; it would be committed to opposing monistic or dualistic theories. A "weak" theory would on normative grounds make room, up to a point, for diverse ethical positions and propose procedures for "living with" or tolerating them, without necessarily rejecting a monistic (or dualistic) theory. In any case, the weak theory is the version we shall be assuming in what follows. Some form of monism, occasionally in combination with a weak theory of ethical pluralism, would seem to be most consonant with Christian assumptions about unitary divine authority.

Christian Perspective

Christianity obviously encompasses a huge and highly complex range of material bearing on our subject. There exists within the tradition a wide diversity of views regarding how much and what sort of allowance should be made for different ethical beliefs and practices. Although there are strong reasons in the tradition for favoring at least a weak theory of ethical pluralism, and though some range of ethical diversity is usually permitted, important differences remain concerning the extent and character of that range of "pluralism" within and among Roman Catholicism, Eastern Orthodoxy, Protestant Christianity in its profusion, and the proliferation of unconventional sectarian and breakaway groups that have attended the Christian movement from its beginnings. As is well known, the differences have often been accentuated in blood. In a short essay, we cannot begin to examine the whole range of diversity.

Instead, we take up but one part—more accurately, one strand of ideas—from this vast tradition, attempt briefly to explicate and synthesize it, and then try to apply it constructively to a number of specific challenges to pluralistic thinking (social regulation, citizenship, life-and-death decisions, etc.).

We refer to this strand of ideas as "conscientious individualism" and hold that it is, sociologically and historically at least, central to the Christian understanding of the place of human beings in the world. Furthermore, we suggest that the way this notion developed within the context of Christianity implies an interesting approach to the challenges of ethical pluralism.

The Christian Context of Conscientious Individualism

It is not surprising that the idea of conscience[3] as a "private moral monitor"—in Greek, *syneidesis*—found its way into the experience of the early Christian Church, and thereby into the New Testament, or that the idea became thereafter a central and abiding subject of cogitation and dispute in the history of Christian moral theology. The idea as we know it was originally a product of the special conditions in which the Christian Church itself was born, and partly for that reason it has occupied a central place in Christian life and thought ever since.

> [The concept of] conscience [as we know it] only came into its own in the Greek world after the collapse of the city-state. The close integration of politics with ethics . . . was no longer possible: there was no sufficiently close authority, external to the individual, effectively to direct conduct. Consequently, . . . [people] fell back . . . on [individual] conscience as the only authority.[4]

The concept, *syneidesis*, does not appear much, if at all, in Plato and Aristotle, or in the Greek Stoics; when it does it is usually devoid of moral content, and simply refers to self-consciousness.[5] Roman Stoics, like Cicero and Seneca, do invest the Latin equivalent, *conscientia*, with moral significance, although that is not the primary emphasis; in any case, they are part of the same general milieu in which early Christianity appeared. Individual conscience as a seat of religious and moral authority and deliberation is thus associated with a period of significant social disruption and change, involving the emergence of what social scientists call "crosscutting cleavages" or "plural identities." Under such conditions, civil, religious, familial, ethnic, and other institutions and authorities are differentiated from each other, sometimes quite abruptly. Consequently, the individual, located at the point of convergence and encounter among the distinct and often competing authorities, has to mediate and negotiate among them, heightening the demand for personal moral and religious innovation and responsibility. In other words, the idea of conscience, as the Christian tradition came to embody it, correlates importantly with "pluralism"—ethical and otherwise, at least in the *descriptive* sense mentioned earlier.

The differentiation of the civil and religious authorities had a particularly strong impact upon the rise of conscientious individualism. That is primarily because of the implied distancing, if not complete separation, of force and coercion, typically administered by the civil authority, from the religious sphere, and to a certain degree from the moral sphere. *Ecclesia*, the Greek word for church, itself means "called out," or "set apart," and in its earliest and most formative expression, the Christian movement "called out" new adherents by means of individual persuasion rather than by civil coercion or by appealing to ethnic or other forms of group identity.

To be sure, the religious and moral spheres on occasion eventually fell under the jurisdiction of an ecclesiastical authority, which typically assumed its own coercive techniques of discipline and organizational control. Sometimes these techniques, as is well known, came close to revoking altogether the critical distinction between church and state. Sometimes, too, Christianity did become entangled with ethnic and political identity. But the underlying constitutive assumption—*that membership in this new community must, in order to be valid, rest upon a personal and voluntary determination and commitment for which each individual is ultimately responsible*—continued to exert a profound influence on the tradition, even during its most repressive phases.

The concept of conscience was one of the key ways in which that influence was conveyed and maintained, and it came to have, in fact, quite revolutionary consequences. The central image, as formulated by St. Paul in his letter to the Romans and elaborated in his first letter to the Corinthians, is a *forensic* one. The conscience is an internalized public forum—a *forum internum*, as it came to be known. It is a kind of personalized, inner lawcourt and legislative assembly governing an individual's thoughts and actions, which is possessed, according to Paul, by all human beings, Jew and Gentile alike. When conscience is in session, individuals experience "conflicting thoughts," as Paul says, "that accuse or perhaps excuse them"; there is prosecution, defense, and a final judgment, all aimed at determining whether an individual in a given case has or has not broken the law that is written on every human heart.[6]

But the conscience, according to Paul, not only functions "judicially," in the sense of passing judgment on past actions,[7] as it was commonly understood to do in the period around the first century B.C.E. In Paul's hands it took on two new features: First, the conscience is seen to act "legislatively," in the sense of anticipating the future and deliberating about what ought to be thought and done before the fact;[8] second, it is understood, apparently for the first time, as capable of becoming, in Paul's words, "weak" and "defiled"—capable, that is, of being subject to error.[9] The idea that the conscience can be mistaken paved the way for a momentous development in the history of Christianity that contributed to the rise of religious liberty and, by implication, opened the door to certain versions of ethical pluralism. That was the formation of the doctrine of *erroneous conscience*, which over centuries of Christian reflection and dispute came to imply that an individual's conscientious beliefs, though in error, ought, under some conditions, nevertheless to be tolerated.

In the interest of brevity, I offer the following summary description of, and brief commentary upon, the idea of conscience as it has evolved in the Western Christian tradition. This summary is proposed as a synthesis and composite of several different variations, but it refers especially to the views of the medieval scholastics, St. Thomas, Calvin and his Puritan descendants, and, among them, particularly Roger Williams.[10]

Conscience is a "private monitor" or *forum internum*—a center or seat of authority and deliberation inherent in each individual that calls for special deference and protection from the *forum externum* (the civil authority). As such, conscience is an aspect of personal consciousness that is a partly passive, partly active private operation involving cognitive, volitional, and emotional or affective elements, and that is to a certain extent subject to error, and thus to revision. It is "private" both in the sense of being experienced inwardly, and of applying only to activities over which the owner of the conscience has responsibility. It is activated by a thought or an action (performed or contemplated) that poses a particular challenge or dilemma for personal moral, religious, or other fundamental commitments. The response includes a review of basic commitments as they bear on the circumstances of the particular challenge or dilemma, and is to be conducted in accord with certain standards of operation (the traditional "intellectual" and "moral virtues"). The purpose of the response, or "verdict," is to convict or to exonerate the owner of the conscience in affirming the thought or performing the action in question, with the purpose of prompting the owner to think or act (retrospectively or prospectively) in accord with the dictates of conscience.

The operations of the conscience are "partly passive" in two senses. First, the operations depend, ultimately, upon a "law written on the heart," as Paul puts it—that is, upon a prior objective "natural" moral law, common to all owners of conscience, regardless of cultural, religious, or social identity. This law includes principles of nonmaleficence, benevolence, fidelity, veracity, fairness, and the like. Even though the conscience actively seeks to apply these principles to concrete dilemmas, the general principles themselves are "given." Second, the "verdict" of conscience manifests itself in the form of emotional or affective feeling-states—for example, "pangs of conscience" for guilty thoughts or behavior—that are mostly beyond the control of the individual. (Where conscience acquits or vindicates, there results a "clear conscience," which is marked by the *absence* of the "pangs" or negative feeling-states.)

On the other hand, the operations of conscience are "partly active" in the sense that they require initiative and performance on the part of the owner in compliance with certain cognitive and volitional standards, standards that, taken together, define what it means to be "conscientious." The *cognitive* standards call for "scrupulousness" or rigor, impartiality, and honesty in several respects:

1. reviewing and consistently accounting for one's basic commitments as they relate to the case at hand;
2. giving proper consideration to a fundamental universal moral law that underlies all consciences;
3. pursuing, evaluating, and applying all relevant factual data pertinent to the case;
4. clarifying all motives, flattering and unflattering, that might influence the verdict or its implementation.

The *volitional* standards require that the owner of the conscience implement or "take action on" the appropriate dictate of conscience. In traditional terms, the "intellectual" and "moral" virtues (wisdom, knowledge, understanding, prudence, justice, temperance, and fortitude) characterize the normative expectations associated with the cognitive and volitional standards of conscience.

If all the standards of conscientiousness are satisfactorily complied with, and the "pangs" are absent, there exists a "good" or "clear" conscience. However, if one or another of the cognitive or volitional standards is violated, or if the "pangs" are absent when they shouldn't be, conscience may be said to be deficient in one way or another. The most serious of possible violations is in regard to the second of the cognitive standards listed. If there is evidence that someone has systematically disregarded or is indifferent to a primary moral principle such as nonmaleficence, that person's conscience would be described as "evil." If, on the other hand, one complies with the cognitive but not with the volitional requirements, one may be said to have a "weak" conscience.

Or, one might make "cognitive mistakes." One might in a given case ignore or overlook a principle or rule one had publicly advocated; one might mistakenly think that certain ideals or practices promote good when they do not; or one might ignore or mistake relevant factual material. Finally, one might reason fallaciously in connecting principles to facts. In such instances, there is said to exist an "erroneous conscience," a category of deficiency we introduced earlier. Regarding that category, the important question is, whether such errors are committed negligently or carelessly, or whether they are committed innocently and are thus "honest mistakes." If the errors are based on negligence and carelessness, they are culpable; if not, they are inculpable (sometimes called "invincible ignorance"), and are thus excused.

As we mentioned earlier, the idea of "erroneous conscience" (in its *inculpable* version) had a powerful impact on the evolution of religious pluralism, and also has, as we shall presently try to show, some interesting implications for ethical pluralism.

As to religious pluralism, even so fervent a uniformist as St. Thomas took a potentially liberal line. He held that certain non-Christians might reject Christian belief conscientiously and thus blamelessly and should therefore be allowed without external constraint to act on their consciences. "Belief in Christ," he wrote, "is something good, and necessary for salvation. But if one's reason presented it as something evil, one's will would be doing wrong in adopting it."[11]

St. Thomas appears to have appreciated variations in culture and upbringing that might account for the possibility of "honest" or "conscientious" rejection of Christian doctrine.[12] But he also invoked a second consideration related to our previous comments about individual responsibility and early Christianity:

> The argument is very simple. The act of faith is essentially a free act; without an interior, free choice of the will there is no valid act of faith at all. It is therefore not lawful to use compulsion in any way to force Jews or pagans to accept the Christian faith. With regard to making the initial act of faith, St. Thomas accepts St. Augustine's principle: "A person can do other things

against his will; but belief is possible only in one who is willing." A man may sign a contract, join a firing-squad, pronounce an oath of allegiance, without any interior consent; but unwilling belief is an impossibility. The only valid act of faith is that which proceeds from a free, interior choice. Therefore, no one is to be compelled to believed.[13]

There are two important implications. One is that there exists a *natural right* to conscience,[14] whereby the conscience is (up to a point) to be protected from coercive interference, whether by the state or other institutions, in order to permit the exercise of personal sovereignty in matters of religious belief. The basis for this judgment is not simply theological—"the only valid act of [Christian] faith is what proceeds from a free, interior choice"; it is also "natural"—"an unwilling belief [of any sort] is an impossibility." The second implication is the validity of religious pluralism based on the universal right of free conscience.

Now it is clear that however liberal these implications, St. Thomas and many followers of his era were reluctant to take the full consequences of this position. The same might be said of Protestant reformers like John Calvin, as well as of some of his seventeenth-century English and American spiritual descendants, such as William Perkins, Richard Baxter, William Ames, and John Cotton, all of whom devoted extensive attention to the conscience, and did so under the partial influence, at least, of Thomism.

The story of the liberalization of conscience in the Christian tradition is complicated. The basic question at issue was always, and remains, *where exactly to draw the limits of tolerable conscientious difference.* In the epic struggle between John Cotton and Roger Williams in seventeenth-century Massachusetts Bay, Cotton argued that because the only proper conscience is a religiously orthodox one, the state does an individual a favor by enforcing essential doctrine and practice. "The fundamentals [of the Christian religion] are so clear," he wrote, "that a man cannot but be convinced of them after two or three admonitions." If after that he still rejects them and is then punished, he is not punished for following his conscience, "but for sinning against [it]."[15] For Williams such thinking subverted the very idea of conscience and unduly inhibited its proper functions. He advocated much greater latitude for religious and moral diversity and suffered expulsion from the "Holy Community" in Massachusetts Bay for his trouble. In that way, he shared the fate of some early Christian sectarians, Reformation Anabaptists, and radical English Puritans, among others, who also paid a high price for challenging the restrictive views of orthodox church authorities.

The doctrine of the freedom or sovereignty of conscience that emerged at the hands of radical Puritans in England and America like

Roger Williams, and that had such an important influence on John
Locke, is a plausible, if controversial, extension of the notion of conscientious individualism nurtured within the Christian tradition.[16]

Roger Williams and the Freedom of Conscience:
Some Implications for Pluralism

Roger Williams was unquestionably a maverick. He spoke of a "restless
unsatisfiedness of my soul,"[17] which drove him from England to the
New World, and then from church to church, in a radical spiritual quest.
In reaction to what he believed were the perversions of Anglicanism,
he joined first the Separatist Puritans in Massachusetts Bay, then the
Baptists in Rhode Island, and finally withdrew altogether, believing
that "Christians had lost their church, and there was no present way to
recover it."[18]

But however perfectionist his view of the church, Williams was not
socially indifferent or altogether inept in his political dealings, as has
been claimed.[19] Having established the Providence township in 1640,
Williams became "chief officer," and later "president of Rhode Island,"
and in these ill-defined roles struggled indefatigably to mold the new
colony into a coherent, effective, and tolerant political community. He
eventually secured a liberal charter and occasionally conducted creative and humane negotiations with native Americans in the area, in
stark contrast to the predatory policies of most of his fellow Puritans of
the time. That he was not completely successful as a politician was
hardly his fault alone. He had to contend with a distracted British
Parliament, duplicitous and unreliable neighboring governments, and
local special interests that, under the circumstances, would have been
difficult for anyone to handle.[20]

Williams's position may be summarized as an effort to expand the
limits of religious pluralism on the basis of a radicalized version of the
doctrine of erroneous conscience. St. Thomas and the more conservative Calvinist Puritan thinkers interpreted the doctrine in a way that
sharply restricted the range of permissible religious and moral disagreement and deviation. But Williams, in the spirit of the radical Puri-
tanism of his time, began advocating, and, when he got the chance,
undertaking in practice, to liberate the conscience to an unheard-of
degree. True to his vision, and at huge personal cost, he managed to
establish "the first commonwealth in modern history to make religious
liberty . . . a cardinal principle of its corporate existence and to maintain
the separation of church and state on these grounds."[21]

Williams had his own strong, if deviant, Calvinist convictions. He
did not agree with the religious views of many of his contemporaries.

He had doubts about the American Indians or "pagans," as he called them, about the "Mohammedans," the "Papists," and many Protestants of his time, especially the Quakers. He frequently and fervently voiced his opinions regarding the errors of these groups. Nevertheless, to his way of thinking the groups were all made up of conscientious people who had *a right to their error*. "[C]onscience is found in all mankind, more or less [erroneously], in Jews, Turks, papists, Protestants, pagans, etc.," and it ought everywhere to be duly respected and granted its rightful freedom.[22]

In keeping with the tradition of Paul, Augustine, Thomas, Calvin, and various Calvinist Puritans, Williams builds his case on the distinction between the "inner forum" and the "outer forum," which are, as Calvin put it, "two worlds over which different kings and different laws have authority." For Williams, such is the contrast between the "laws of the spirit" and the "laws of the sword," and he exhibits the difference by showing (à la Augustine) the futility of confusing the weapons of enforcement peculiar to each sphere.

> [T]o take a stronghold, men bring cannons, . . . bullets, muskets, swords, pikes; and these to this end are weapons effectual and proportionable. On the other side, to batter down idolatry, false worship, heresy, schism, blindness, . . . it is vain, improper, and unsuitable to bring those weapons which are used by persecutors. . . . [A]gainst these spiritual strongholds in the souls of men, spiritual artillery and weapons are proper. . . . [Thus,] civil weapons are improper in this business, and never able to effect aught in the soul.[23]

In Williams's hands, the implications of the distinction between the "laws of the spirit" and the "laws of the sword," between a "religious" and a "civil-moral" sphere, were dramatic. It meant people might err religiously and nevertheless be capable of living as reasonably responsible members of the civil community—in Williams's words, as "peaceable and quiet subjects, loving and helpful neighbors, fair and just dealers, true and loyal to the civil government."[24] That is because there exists, he says, "a moral virtue, a moral fidelity, ability and honesty, which other men (beside Church-members) are, by good nature and education, by good laws and good examples, nourished and trained up in, so that civil places need not be monopolized into the hands of Church-members (who sometimes are not fitted for them), and all others deprived of their natural and civil rights and liberties."[25]

In other words, despite religious disagreement and diversity, people may nevertheless exhibit moral fidelity, ability, and honesty—may, that is, be *conscientious* citizens, neighbors, tradespeople, and civil officials. Such a doctrine threatened all forms of preferential rule, whether based on religion or gender. The Massachusetts Bay colony from which Williams was expelled assigned full citizenship rights only to orthodox church members in good standing. Williams dispensed with that arrangement and extended full rights of citizenship to all, regardless of religious belief or affiliation, to members of the wide variety of Protestant groups, Jews, and others, who were all welcomed to Rhode Island.

Massachusetts Bay, like other political systems of the time, discriminated on the basis of religion because it was assumed that the religiously unenlightened were spiritually and morally deficient, and ought therefore to depend on the superior wisdom of those considered enlightened. Only the orthodox had "mature" consciences; only they could be entrusted to make the right decisions and institute the correct policies in civil and religious affairs. Williams completely rejected such theories. In civil matters, for example, *all* the people, "naturally considered," are "the sovereign original and foundation" of the state, who through a process of "consenting and agreeing," ought to enjoy the right "to see [the state] do her duty, to correct her, to redress, reform, establish, etc."[26] This is an expanded theory of conscientious individualism: in the conduct of, and deliberation over, civil affairs, no preference is to be given to the consciences of the orthodox, for in the civil sphere every conscience is equal.

There is no conclusive evidence that Williams applied the theory in the same radical way to gender relations as he did to politics, although there are some interesting hints. For one thing, Williams gave aid and comfort to Anne Hutchinson, a notorious dissenter in Massachusetts Bay, who reflected the new spirit of women's liberation rampant in the sectarian circles of the time, and who, like Williams, was eventually ejected from the colony.[27] For another, he appeared to consent to a majority judgment by the citizens of Providence to expel "from our civil freedom" one Joshua Verein because he violated his wife's "liberty of conscience" by severely punishing her for attending too many religious meetings and neglecting her duties to him.[28]

What the Hutchinson and Verein instances illustrate is the influence of "new thinking" concerning women's rights to conscience, and the possible sympathy Williams had for such thinking. A conservative Puritan reprimanded Anne Hutchinson for having stepped "out of your place," for being rather "a husband than wife," "a preacher than a hearer," "a magistrate than a subject," and thereby for having tried "to carry all things in Church and Commonwealth as you would."[29] But Anne Hutchinson and Mrs. Verein were having none of it. Like other women of the period, they were emboldened to reject the conventional wisdom according to which women were thought to be incapable of being as conscientious as men. They denied categorically the idea that women were afflicted with "mentall and sex-deficiency," producing a "greater susceptibility to error," and because of which they were expected to submit to their male betters.[30]

Women like Hutchinson and Verein drastically challenged the authority of the husband as "lord over [a wife's] conscience" and, in the bargain, the father's authority as well. In the "family, as in the commonwealth, it was religion which had kept the subject in obedience." But to remove the religious sanction, as sectarians like Hutchinson and Williams were doing, and to advocate opportunities for reorganizing social and political life in accord with an expanded notion of conscientious individualism, were to threaten "the very foundations of the old patriarchal family," along with the established hierarchy in church and civil order.[31]

Clearly, Roger Williams, drawing and dilating upon the idea of conscience embedded in the Christian tradition, contributed enormously to the spread of diversity. He advocated and began, well ahead of his time, to implement religious pluralism of both a descriptive and a normative kind. So far as religion goes, his position exemplifies a weak theory of pluralism. He is a monist who found reasons to welcome and tolerate a wide diversity of religious views. But, generally speaking, he also implemented political and social pluralism, which had strong ethical overtones in regard to accommodating new, more inclusive, patterns of citizenship, interreligious and intergender behavior, and so on. Under Williams's "leveling" influence in Rhode Island, the institutions of government, church, and family encouraged and became susceptible to a variety of new and divergent opinions and influences.

For our purposes, however, the important question is, Precisely what sort of impact did Williams's doctrine of conscientious individualism have upon ethical pluralism, understood as a normative theory? We know, roughly, how he went about accommodating a diversity of religious opinions. How far did he go in explicitly accommodating a diversity of opinions concerning social and civil behavior?

The short answer is that his tolerance for ethical diversity was more limited than it was for religious diversity, although there are some clues in his thought (and in the tradition he inherited) for liberalizing his approach. Williams has some interesting things to say about "social regulation," and "citizenship," which call now for comment. Although he did not directly discuss "life-and-death decisions," or questions of "human sexuality," it is possible to apply his method constructively, if conjecturally, to those matters.

Social Regulation

Williams would have agreed with Locke's dictum concerning the over-lapping relationship between religion and morality:

> A good life, in which consists not the least part of religion and true piety, concerns also the civil government; and in it lies the safety both of men's souls and of the commonwealth. Moral actions belong therefore to the jurisdiction both of the outward and the inward court, both of the civil and domestic governor; I mean both of the magistrate and the conscience. Here, therefore is great danger, lest one of these jurisdictions entrench upon the other and discord arise between the keeper of the public peace and the overseers of souls.[32]

Points of tension might well arise between "the outward and the inward court" because their jurisdictions converge, and may possibly conflict, in regard to certain kinds of outward action, namely those that impinge on "public safety, order, health, or morals," to borrow the language of the international human rights instruments.[33] But, rather surprisingly, Williams didn't worry too much about such points of conflict, because he seems to have shared Locke's rather complacent attitude that "all difficulty in this matter" can be "easily removed," if only "the limits of both these governments" are duly attended to.[34]

To be sure, Williams's core convictions in this matter, like Locke's and those of all their predecessors in the tradition of conscientious individualism, are tied to a belief in natural law (the second cognitive standard) that is in certain formulations (in my opinion) significant and defensible.[35] That belief implied, straightfowardly, that there are some common, basic moral norms that are "given" and that conjointly ought to govern the outward and the inward forums. Anyone, anywhere, who acted so as systematically to violate such norms could not, according to Williams, Locke, and the whole tradition, be said to be "conscientious." No matter who they were, they would have, as St. Thomas had put it, an "evil," or thoroughly corrupted, conscience. Williams summarized his thinking here in a characteristically prophetic way:

> Adulteries, murders, robberies, thefts,
>   Wild Indians punish these!
> And hold the scales of justice so,
>   That no man farthing less.
> When Indians hear the horrid filths,
>   Of Irish, English men,
> The horrid oaths and murders late,
>   Thus say these Indians then.
> We wear no clothes, have many gods,
>   And yet our sins are less:

You are barbarians, pagans wild,
Your land's the wilderness.[36]

Accordingly, Williams held that it was "the duty of the civil magistrate to punish anyone whose conscience led [that person] to undertake actions against public safety and welfare," as defined by the natural law. That would include the prohibition, by coercive means if necessary, of such things as human sacrifice, even though practiced for conscience's sake, as was the case, Williams pointed out, in Mexico and Peru.[37]

The problem was (and this is a problem for the entire tradition of natural law) that the list of "nonderogable" (unabridgeable) offenses was imperceptibly expanded from self-evidently punishable actions to ones that were less clearly so. Williams had no doubt that just as instances of gross arbitrary injury, such as were performed by his countrymen against native Americans, ought to be forcibly restrained and punished, so governments had every right to impose tight regulations upon other forms of activity, as, for example, reading licentious material, or practicing offensive patterns of dress and speech found among certain religious groups, "as the monstrous haire of women, up[on] the heads of some men," or the use by Quakers of the familiar, and, to Williams, contemptuous, "thou" in addressing superiors. Beyond that, Williams believed magistrates might properly regulate public speech that demeaned civil or other authorities.[38]

It is one thing for the state to protect against violence and extreme forms of arbitrary injury, and another for it to restrict behavior that is offensive but otherwise harmless, or to shield public officials from rude or contemptuous criticism. Though the line is not always easy to draw, Williams undoubtedly obscured it from time to time. A consistent theory of conscientious individualism would appear to favor more tolerance and greater pluralism than Williams himself displayed in regard to the preceding examples, as well as on one other occasion, to be taken up next.

Responsibilities of Citizenship

As "president" of Rhode Island ("an office with no defined powers, of little dignity and no salary"),[39] Williams was faced with the need to organize a militia to provide defense for the colony. A number of the citizens of Providence, mostly Baptists, invoked Williams's avowed principles against him, claiming the right of conscientious objection to military service on grounds of religious scruple.

Surprisingly, Williams rejected the claim.[40] He likened the predicament of the citizens of Rhode Island to the situation of passengers on a ship at sea called upon to protect, when needed, "their common peace or preservation." While Williams denied (as would be expected) that the captain of the ship might force "Papists, Protestants, Jews, or Turks" among the passengers "to come to ship's prayers or worship," or compel them "from their own particular prayers or worship, if they practice any," the captain nevertheless "may judge, resist, compel, and punish" "if any refuse to help, in person or purse, towards the common charges or defense."

There is some uncertainty as to whether Williams here means simply to counter the claims of conscientious objection to military service or whether he is attempting to answer a broader and more ominous challenge to the very principle of civil government itself.[41] In any case, what is, for our purposes, most noteworthy about Williams's letter is that he never even entertains (here or anywhere else) the possibility of selective exemption from civil law or obligation on grounds of conscience. It would therefore seem fair to conclude that he, like Locke, did not perceive any serious conflict of duties between the internal and external forums, primarily because he possessed excessive confidence that these two jurisdictions are easy to compartmentalize.

Constructive Suggestions

We may conclude by gathering up and applying to the four problem areas of ethical pluralism certain suggestions that, for the proponent of a Christian theory of conscientious individualism, would seem to follow from our analysis.

Social Regulation

On the composite theory sketched out here, "conscientiousness" presupposes devotion to "a fundamental universal moral law that underlies all consciences" (the second cognitive standard). That law, typically called "natural law" in the tradition, applies to both the internal and the external forum. Accordingly, there are understood to be certain sorts of violation that are intolerable, and thus are properly restrained and punished—coercively, if necessary—by the state.

Because anyone who, even in the name of conscience, culpably violated the "natural" prohibition against arbitrary injury, might be said to have "no conscience," or at least to have one that is severely deficient, *appeals to conscience do not apply*, and such action is rightfully restrained and punished by the civil order. It follows that in justifying social regulation of this sort, a (weak) normative theory of ethical pluralism that is consistent with conscientious individualism could not accommodate positions that advocated arbitrary injury (such as fascist justifications for genocide or ultranationalist justifications for "ethnic cleansing").

But while theoretically important to establish, this prescription does not carry us very far. What about harder cases, like justifications for policies of female genital alteration? Here a more comprehensive consideration of the standards of conscientiousness is required.[42] The second cognitive standard—concern (among other things) for the fundamental moral prohibition against arbitrary injury—is certainly relevant. Indeed, its relevance its underscored by the initial *suspicion* outsiders inevitably have, in hearing descriptions of practices of female genital alteration, that the prohibition against arbitrary injury is in fact being violated by such practices. But this standard is not the only one that is pertinent. In such cases, it will be necessary to consult some of the other cognitive standards of conscientiousness in order to determine whether such practices, however dubious or "erroneous" they may appear to the outsider, are nevertheless tolerable.

One such standard that needs to be (and is often) applied is the first cognitive standard—reviewing and consistently accounting for basic commitments as they relate to the case at hand. It is frequently pointed out, in assessing justifications for policies of female genital alteration, that appeals to Islam, which are widespread among proponents, are, in fact, not well founded. If there is reason to conclude that such appeals are irrational, as many Muslim scholars argue,[43] then one important supporting reason for the practice collapses.

The third cognitive standard (pursuing, evaluating, and applying all relevant factual data pertinent to the case) and the fourth (clarifying all motives, flattering and unflattering, that might influence the verdict or its implementation) must also be considered in assessing the "conscientiousness" (and thus the "tolerability") of the policy in question. As to the relevant factual claims, there would appear to be serious errors. Assertions about the need to restrain female promiscuity (in comparison with male promiscuity) by imposing such a procedure, as well as about the alleged harmless or even beneficial effects of the procedure, appear to be profoundly flawed.

All of this brings us to the last cognitive standard, to the matter of "clarifying motives." On inspection, there appears good reason to think that there are very important *undisclosed* motives driving the practice of female genital alteration, which are fairly described, in general, as "patriarchal" in character. (Shades of the complaints of the radical Puritans!) If that is true, then a proper assessment of the justifications for the practice would be inclined to conclude that the consciences of those advocating the practice are not only "erroneous" but "culpably" (rather than "inculpably") erroneous. It follows that the assessment would be disposed *against* tolerating practices of this kind and in favor of their "social regulation." In short, the assessment would appear to rule *against* tolerating such policies under a theory of ethical pluralism.

A final word on the subject: in undertaking this kind of assessment of "conscientiousness," the second cognitive standard is pivotal. If there is strong suspicion that a fundamental moral principle (like the prohibition against arbitrary injury) is being violated by a given policy, then the bar for "reasonableness" represented by the other three cognitive standards would appear to be raised all the higher and become all the more demanding. In a word, *reasons justifying policies that impinge closely on concerns protected by fundamental moral prohibitions have a much-reduced margin for error*.

Citizenship

In regard to the "dissenting views on the civil status of women,"[44] the low assessment of the conscientiousness of their opponents presented by the radical Puritans of the seventeenth century seems to me worthy of emulation. In brief, the feminists of the period called into question the factual beliefs about the inferiority of women, as well as the motives for supporting policies of male domination. On the strength of the principle just enunciated—that reasons justifying policies that impinge closely on concerns protected by fundamental moral prohibitions have a much-reduced margin for error—seventeenth-century feminists and their supporters would appear to have made a convincing case against the discriminatory conventions of the time. Therefore, their conclusions in favor of equal citizenship (and social regulation toward that end) seem valid.

On the question of the responsibilities of citizenship, raised by the exchange between Roger Williams and the citizens of Providence as to whether "conscientious objection" to certain common civil obligations is permissible, Williams, as I hinted already, took too restrictive a position.

Certainly, Williams is right that on a proper understanding of the tradition, appeals to conscience cannot automatically trump just and duly authorized civil laws and policies. The constitutive assumption of the conscience, which assumes two relatively independent authorities—the internal and the external forum—excludes that. The question is whether there exist *any* areas of action, normally under the authority of the civil order, where it is reasonable to permit conscientious exemptions. When, in Locke's terms, "the jurisdiction" of "the outward" or "the inward court" "entrench[es] upon the other and discord arise[s] between [them]," may "the inward court" ever prevail?

It is interesting that James Madison, writing more than a century later, proposes just such an exemption regarding conscientious objection to military service. He suggests the following wording (not adopted) for what was to become the Second Amendment of the United States Constitution: "The right of people to keep and bear arms shall not be infringed; a well regulated militia being the best security of a free country: *but no person religiously scrupulous of bearing arms shall be compelled to render military service in person.*"[45] It is also interesting, in a contemporary setting, that the Human Rights Committee, which provides authoritative interpretation of the International Covenant on Civil and Political Rights, has ruled that a right to conscientious objection, on grounds broader than simply religious ones, can properly be inferred from Article 18 of the covenant, the article that guarantees freedom of thought, conscience, religion, or belief.[46] Incidentally, Madison's original proposal for the language of the First Amendment would have opened the door to the more inclusive interpretation of the Human Rights Committee, since he specified protection of "the equal rights of conscience," in his words, which could by implication include religious or nonreligious appeals.

The reason for proposing special exemption for conscientious objection to military service may well be one that is actually close to Williams's own convictions: mixing conscience and force is highly problematic. Because force is such a profoundly inappropriate instrument in the domain of conscience, and accordingly must have very restricted access thereto, it is understandable that people reflecting in the name of conscience would find perplexing, if not self-contradictory, the prospect of being forced to use force. In any case, Madison and the Human Rights Committee surely assume some such argument in order to single out and give special consideration to conscientious objection to military service over a much broader array of imaginable appeals for conscientious exemption. The pluralism they recommend in this regard is a strictly limited one.

It should be noted, also, that even if such exemption were permitted (which appears to have growing support in international human rights circles), it will still be necessary to "test" the conscientiousness of the objector, as typically happens, under conditions of conscription. That process involves examining for "sincerity" (a synonym for conscientiousness), which of course is determined by testing the objector according to the various cognitive and volitional standards we have employed throughout this essay.

Human Sexuality

Claims against extending civil rights to homosexuals would, on the theory of conscientious individualism, also be tested according to the standards of conscientiousness that have been invoked throughout the essay.[47] Moreover, there appear to be some suggestive parallels between the arguments of the radical seventeenth-century Puritans favoring women's rights and the arguments of advocates of gay rights in our time.

The argument against granting gay rights has been put forward by people like the Reverend Jerry Falwell.[48] On the basis of his reading of scripture, homosexuality is profoundly offensive to Falwell's conscience, and he strongly believes homosexuals ought not be treated as a "legitimate minority." His primary argument against legislation favoring gay rights is close to the position developed by Lord Devlin in his famous lectures, *The Enforcement of Morals*.[49] When it comes to determining the standards of public order and decency, and to protecting citizens from what is offensive, injurious, exploitative, and corrupting, the majority of citizens gets to decide. If, as Lord Devlin says, the "vast bulk" of the community is agreed on an answer, even though a minority resolutely disagrees, a legislator must act on the consensus of the "moral majority." "The community must take the moral responsibility, and it must therefore act on its own lights—that is, on the moral faith of its members."[50]

The major problem with this position, as Ronald Dworkin has argued,[51] is that it vastly oversimplifies the role of the legislator. "A conscientious legislator who is told a moral consensus exists must test the credentials of that consensus."[52] Interestingly enough, Lord Devlin, confessing second thoughts, admitted that he might have placed "too much emphasis on feeling and too little on reason." He proceeds, à la Dworkin, to agree that a legislator "is entitled to disregard 'irrational' beliefs," such as the conviction—however widespread—that homosexuality causes earthquakes.[53]

Dworkin takes the point from there. To assess the rationality of a moral consensus, rather than simply supporting it uncritically, implies that considerations of coherence and consistency of argument, along with respect for the rules of factual evidence, are therefore applicable to a legislator's decision. Indeed, in cases in which basic civil rights are at stake, such as the issue of gay rights, our previously stated principle—reasons justifying policies that impinge closely on concerns protected by fundamental moral prohibitions have a much-reduced margin of error—raises the demand for applying the standards of conscientiousness.

For example, Falwell states that a person "is not born with preference to the same sex, but . . . is introduced to the homosexual experience and cultivates the homosexual urge. It is innocent children and many young people who are victimized and who become addicts to sexual perversion."[54] But this is not an argument but an assertion that is, in fact, empirically highly controversial. In the absence of evidence, Falwell's claims do not qualify as a "reason" for anything.

Moreover, Falwell writes: "If homosexuality is deemed normal, how long will it be before rape, adultery, alcoholism, drug addiction, and incest are labeled as normal?"[55] But this implied argument begs the question and assumes what it must prove. Whether and why homosexuality is in a class with the other acts is what must be demonstrated. Until that is shown, our conscientious legislator must ignore unsupported assertions like these.

Of course, this is not to say that majority opinion can be ignored altogether in legislating in accord with "public order, security, health, and morals." But it is to say that any such legislation must be *conscientiously* evaluated, and if proposals fail the tests, they must be discarded.

Life-and-Death Issues

We suggested earlier that Williams may have been insufficiently pluralistic by failing to make room for conscientious objection within the Rhode Island community.[56] Questions were also raised as to whether it was consistent with a doctrine of conscientious individualism to punish, as Williams allowed, patterns of speech and dress displayed by Quakers and others that were found offensive but otherwise harmless.[57] However, despite these inconsistencies and shortcomings, there can be no doubt that the overall effect of Williams's notion of freedom of conscience revolutionized the idea of civil punishment, thereby affecting some "life-and-death" issues in a critical way.

There is no evidence that Williams opposed the death penalty as such, though it is of interest that "he never listed precisely what crimes he thought were worthy of death."[58] What is clear is that, in reaction to the conventions of his time, he substantially reduced the number of crimes that might legitimately be punished by "the civil sword" and concomitantly provided a new frame of reference for thinking about the subject.

> [T]he laws, rewards and punishments of several nations vastly differ from those of Israel, which doubtless were unlawful for God's people to submit to, except Christ Jesus had (at least in general) approved such humane ordinances and creations of men for their common peace and welfare. . . . Mr. Cotton, and such as literally stick to the punishment of adultery, witchcraft, etc. by death, must either deny the several governments of the world to be lawful . . . and that the nature and constitutions of peoples and nations are not to be respected, but all forced to one common law, or else they must see cause to moderate this their tenent in civil affairs, as persecution in affairs religious.[59]

Such sentiments are consonant with Williams's fundamental belief that "now under Christ, when all nations are merely civil," the earthly government, "being of a material[,] civil nature, [only] for the defense of persons, estates, families, liberties of a city or civil state, and the suppressing of uncivil or injurious persons or actions by such civil punishments," "cannot . . . extend to spiritual and soul causes, spiritual and soul punishment, which belongs to that spiritual sword with two edges, the soul piercing . . . Word of God."[60]

If civil governments no longer have any direct authority over the conscience, over private matters of spirit and soul, and the function of punishment is severely restricted to questions of "a material[,] civil nature," and is to be applied only in accord with the common or natural "civil-moral" law, then civil punishment must be reconceived as primarily *defensive* in regard to protecting the "outward" welfare of citizens against "uncivil or injurious persons or actions." Administering punishment in the name of God by executing people for "adultery, witchcraft, etc.," which Williams's New England neighbors characteristically assumed they had a right to do, was in Williams's mind forever prohibited in the light of the rights of conscience. The implication of Williams's point of view is that systems of civil punishment that go beyond what might be called this minimalist theory of "civil defense" are guilty of "cruel, inhuman or degrading treatment or punishment," to use contemporary human rights language.[61]

Consequently, the familiar objections to the death penalty under present-day conditions acquire special salience. As is often claimed, to take the life of an unarmed prisoner safely in captivity who no longer represents a direct threat to the community, when a significantly less severe alternative (extended imprisonment) exists that is capable both of neutralizing the threat and of imposing a significant penalty, seems a clear example of excessive government action, according to Williams's standards. Moreover, if the standard complaints about the administration of capital punishment in the United States are valid, there is an additional reason for rejecting the practice, namely, that it is manifestly inconsistent with the demands of equal justice entailed in the "common or natural 'civil-moral' law," as Williams understood it.

Since at least 1967, the death penalty has been inflicted only rarely, erratically, and often upon the least odious killers, while many of the most heinous criminals have escaped execution. Moreover, it has been employed almost exclusively in a few formerly slave-holding states, and there it has been used almost exclusively against killers of whites, not blacks, and never against white killers of blacks. This is the American system of capital punishment. It is this system, not some idealized one, that must be defended in any national debate on the death penalty.[62]

These considerations suggest that the administration of capital punishment itself becomes an example of the very thing that, on Williams's account, civil punishment is supposed to defend against, namely, arbitrary injury. That no doubt explains the beginning, these days, of movement in international human rights discussion toward significantly restricting the death penalty, if not abolishing it altogether. On 2 April 1983 the "Sixth Protocol" to the European Human Rights Convention was adopted by the members states of the Council of Europe, declaring that the "death penalty shall be abolished. No one shall be condemned to such penalty or executed."[63] The only exception permitted in the document applies during time of war or the threat of war.[64] The issue remains highly contentious, though a certain amount of momentum appears to be gathering in support of the Sixth Protocol to the European Convention.

A word about two other "life-and-death" issues of considerable present-day salience—abortion and physician-assisted suicide—are in order. There is no evidence that Williams's himself took a stand for or against abortion or self-regarding "mercy killing," and we are therefore left to apply for ourselves the approach to conscientious reflection we have been developing. In regard to both questions, we shall briefly attempt to open some space, within limits, for "conscientious individualism."

In its most elemental terms, the issue of abortion is posed because, arguably, two human lives stand in profound conflict with each other. In one setting, a mother is found to carry a prenatal life that, if allowed naturally to proceed "to term," would threaten death for the mother. Such circumstances entail a stark choice between allowing the prenatal life to live and the mother to die, or acting deliberately so as to protect the mother by aborting the prenatal life. In another setting, an act of sexual violation (rape or incest) results in an unwanted pregnancy with severe psychic consequences for the mother. Again, a choice results between requiring the mother to bear the "moral costs" of seeing the pregnancy through, or permitting a termination of the pregnancy. In the first case, the physical health of the mother is at stake; in the second, her psychic and "moral" health.

A critical point of contention in the issue of abortion is the status of the prenatal life. If, as some hold, the prenatal life is, from the point of conception, a "full human being," then it would appear to have a right to the same protection normally due any postnatal person. The idea that persons after birth might involuntarily be sacrificed for the good of others would be a flagrant violation of the principle against arbitrary injury. If, as we say, the prenatal life is equivalent in all pertinent respects, there would seem to be no grounds for an exception in its matter.

If, on the other hand, the prenatal life, as others hold, is at best "incipient life," physically interconnected with and dependent upon the
mother, especially in the early stages of pregnancy, then the status of
the prenatal life is exceptional in a variety of ways, including, it is claimed, the applicability of the principle against arbitrary injury. On this
reading, some latitude for discretion, some "freedom of choice," in
favor of the mother's physical and/or psychic health would be permitted, given the special intimacy of the relationship of mother and prenatal life, together with the morally objectionable prospect of legally
prohibiting an opportunity for the mother to protect her life against
a direct physical threat, or to escape the psychically destructive
consequences of an extreme violation of her dignity and integrity.

But even if this second position is affirmed (as it is by me), and the
door is thereby opened for tolerating ethically a "right to abortion,"
there are some remaining concerns. For one thing, there is the question
of how extensive that right is, of how many "indications" for permissible
abortion are to be allowed.

We have already claimed (in respect to the second option) that, given
the special intimacy of the relationship between mother and prenatal
life, the mother's physical and psychic health are allowable indications
for abortion. On further reflection, there would seem to be no good reason to limit too narrowly the range of indications to the mother's imminent death or to her right to escape the destructive consequences of
sexual violation. Questions of physical and psychic health are to an important degree matters of subjective conscientious determination. Is it
reasonable to demand that a woman accept her pregnancy if the consequence is not loss of life, but loss of a leg or kidney, or is some form of
severe psychic distress? Does it seem suitable that judges or legislators
be authorized to make these highly personal decisions regarding what
constitutes the physical or psychic health of an individual? Are there
not, at least within some limits, grounds for extending to the mother
considerable discretion, or as we might otherwise put it, for respecting
the exercise of individual conscience in these questions?

At the same time, even "incipient life" is potential human life, and
thus in need, it would seem, of appropriate protection against arbitrary
injury. There is reason, therefore, for a certain degree of social regulation of abortion. The legal provisions afforded by *Roe v. Wade*, according
to which the range of permissibility for abortion narrows as the prenatal life develops and comes increasingly to approximate postnatal
human beings, is an acceptable compromise. It affords extensive latitude
for material discretion in the early stages of pregnancy, and progres-
sively reduces that latitude as the prenatal life matures and approaches
the critical postnatal status in which equal protection against arbitrary
injury is guaranteed.

Physician-assisted suicide poses similar problems, requiring a similar kind of compromise in regard to social regulation. The fundamental issue is whether competent and consensually informed individuals should be granted conscientious control over their own life or death under conditions of terminal illness, irreversibly associated with severe forms of degeneracy and/or suffering, that are certified by an authorized physician. Incidentally, those circumstances are narrowly restricted to rule out an unlimited "right to suicide," on the assumption, among other things, that individuals are members of communities and thus morally obligated to live up to the responsibilities of their membership, despite temptations to the contrary. In that sense, the principle against arbitrary injury applies to the way individuals treat themselves, as well as to the way they treat others.

The worry in this matter, and therefore the concern over social regulation, is the possibility for abuse in regard to the taking of human life, voluntarily or not. For one thing, the individual, driven to distraction by the circumstances of illness, might rush irrationally and prematurely to arrange to die. For another, relatives motivated by financial or other ulterior interests might bring pressure on the patient to acquiesce in a decision to die. There is the additional concern that a physician, professionally committed to the preservation of life, might be charged with violating that fundamental commitment by engaging in assisted suicide.

So long as the procedures of authorization and patient protection, as well as the medical indications (severe and irreversible degeneracy and/or suffering) permitting a voluntary and informed decision to terminate life, are clearly defined and enforced, there would appear to be good reason to allow conscientious discretion on the part of the patient. As in the matter of abortion, it appears humane and compassionate to permit the person concerned to decide what degree of suffering and distress ought, under specified circumstances, to be borne. Nor, in the case of physician-assisted suicide, does such a conclusion necessarily conflict with the basic obligations of the physician. It is not morally self-evident that, when the choice is between death and suffering, suffering must automatically be preferred.

Conclusions

We have described and explicated a theory of conscientious individualism, as it has emerged from the Christian tradition, and especially as it was developed by Roger Williams, the seventeenth-century Puritan and founder of the Rhode Island colony. We have suggested this theory as one response to the challenge of "ethical pluralism." The theory was then applied to four areas of contemporary concern: social regulation, the duties of citizenship, human sexuality, and life-and-death issues. Williams's own responses to some of these concerns, where relevant, provided a background for our reflections. The proposal is that the theory is richly applicable to present-day problems, even where it modifies or revises some of Williams's own positions. Given Williams's commitment to "search and trial," without which no one "attains . . . right persuasion,"[65] the arguments with him, such as we have had these pages, would, one suspects, have received his full approval.

Notes

1. *Webster's New International Dictionary of the English Language* (Spring-field, Mass.: G. & C. Merriam, 1928), 1659. See John Kelsay, "Plurality, Pluralism, and Comparative Ethics: A Review Essay," *Journal of Religious Ethics* 24, no. 2 (1996): 405–28, for an illuminating discussion of the distinction between the descriptive and normative use of the term.

2. Michael Ignatieff, *Isaiah Berlin*: A Life (New York: Henry Holt, 1998), esp. 248–50, 284–86. "[Berlin] never claimed to have been the first to think about pluralism. But [he] had reason to believe that he was the first to argue that plu-ralism *entailed* liberalism—that is, if human beings disagreed about ultimate ends, the political system that best enabled them to adjudicate these conflicts was one which privileged their liberty, for only conditions of liberty could en-able them to make the compromises between values necessary to maintain a free social life. Beyond the obvious circularity of the argument, the real diffi-culty, as John Gray has argued, is that a pluralist logically cannot put liberty first. Liberty is simply one of the values that must be reconciled with others; it is not a trump card. If so, why should a free society be valued above all? Berlin's later work opened up these questions, even though it failed to supply adequate answers" (286). Moreover: "What Isaiah could affirm was that the century's ex-perience of infamy had brought the European conscience back to its senses. . . . The Second World War there had been a return to 'the ancient notion of natural law'—sustained this time not by faith *in, but fear of*, mankind. . . . He hoped that Europe had learned from its journey into the abyss; he deeply believed that the concentration camps offered the most conclusive justification ever for the ne-cessity of a universal moral law. But towards even his own moderately hopeful propositions, he remained what he had always been: a wise, watchful and in-curably realist sceptic" (250). It is not clear what we are to make of these com-ments about Berlin's position on a "universal moral law," and whether such a position is or is not compatible with the strong theory of ethical pluralism Berlin often claimed he held.

3. There appears in some philosophical circles to be an astounding lack of knowledge about the origins and development of the concept of conscience. In the entry on "Conscience" in the *Encyclopedia of Philosophy* (New York: Macmillan

and Free Press, 1967), 2:189–91, the author, Charles A. Baylis, gives the impression that the idea did not arise until the eighteenth century, with the treatises of Francis Hutcheson, Samuel Clarke, Joseph Butler, Immanual Kant, and others. (The bibliographical references exclude any pre-eighteenth-century literature.) Such a description provides a truncated and distorted analysis of the tradition.

4. C. A. Pierce, *Conscience in the New Testament* (London: SCM Press, 1954), 76.

5. Ibid., 11–28. Cf. Eric D' Arcy, *Conscience and Its Right to Freedom* (London: Sheed and Ward, 1941), 5–8.

6. Romans 2:14–16.

7. Ibid.

8. See Paul's discussion of what to do in face of a potential "conflict of conscience" over eating food that has been offered to idols at I Cor. 10:23–33.

9. I Cor. 9:7, 10, 12.

10. In a fuller account, of course, the Lutheran and Anglican contributions to the subject of conscience, among others, would need to be consulted. The account here is rather skeletal but serves for our purposes.

11. *Summa Theologica*, I–II, q. 19, a. 5; quoted in D'Arcy, *Conscience and Its Right to Freedom*, 156.

12. See D'Arcy, *Conscience and Its Right to Freedom*, 133–41.

13. Ibid., pp. 153–54.

14. See Brian Tierney, "Religious Rights: An Historical Perspective," in John Witte, Jr. and Johan van der Vyver, eds., *Religious Human Rights in Global Perspective: Religious Perspectives* (The Hague: Nihjoff, 1996), 17–45. By "natural right" I understand a subjective claim, regarded as inborn and unearned, that is antecedent to and independent of governmental authority, and that ascribes to individuals a legitimately enforceable title or warrant to constrain (or demand constraint) regarding such things as the exercise of conscience, political participation, control of property, and resistance to arbitrary authority.

15. John Cotton, "Massachusetts Does Not Persecute," in Irwin H. Polishook, ed., *Roger Williams, John Cotton and Religious Freedom* (Englewood Cliffs, N.J.: Prentice-Hall, 1967), 72.

16. See David Little, "A Christian Interpretation of Human Rights," in Abdullahi An-Na'im and Francis Deng, eds., *Human Rights in Africa: Cross-Cultural Perspectives* (Washington, D.C.: Brookings Institution, 1990), 59–103, for a fuller account.

17. Edward Gaustad, *Liberty of Conscience: Roger Williams in America* (Grand Rapids, Mich.: Eerdmans, 1991), 90.

18. Edmund S. Morgan, *Roger Williams: The Church and the State* (New York: Harcourt Brace & World, 1967), 53.

19. Robert Bellah has written ("Flaws in the Protestant Cultural Code: Some Religious Sources of America's Problems," in *The Robert Bellah Reader* [Durham, N.C.: Duke University Press, 2006]) that "Williams was a moral genius but he was a sociological catastrophe. . . . Since [he] ignored secular society, money took over in Rhode Island to a degree that would not be true in Massachusetts or Connecticut for a long time. Rhode Island under Williams gives us an early

and local example of what happens when the sacredness of the individual is not balanced by any sense of the whole or concern for the common good."

20. Gaustad, *Liberty of Conscience*, 128–53.

21. Sydney E. Ahlstrom, *A Religious History of the American People* (New Haven: Yale University Press, 1972), 172.

22. *Complete Writings of Roger Williams*, 7 vols. (New York: Russell & Russell, 1963), 4:508.

23. Ibid., 3:148.

24. Ibid., 3:142.

25. Ibid., 4:365.

26. Ibid., 3:249. The statement about seeing "her do her duty, . . . etc." is applied to the church. However, in the context Williams interchanges comments about the state and church. What goes for one appears to go for the other.

27. See Keith Thomas, "Women and Civil War Sects," *Past and Present* 13 (April 1958): 42–62.

28. See Timothy L. Hall, "Order and 'Civility,'" in *Separating Church and State: Roger Williams and Religious Liberty* (Urbana: University of Illinois, 1998), 103–5.

29. Cited in Thomas, "Women and Civil War Sects," 49.

30. Ibid.

31. Ibid., 52, 54–55.

32. John Locke, *A Letter Concerning Toleration* (New York: Liberal Arts Press, 1950), 46. Locke undoubtedly stands in the tradition of conscientious individualism we have been outlining. In particular, as I and others have argued elsewhere, he was profoundly influenced by the radical Puritans of the seventeenth century in this and related matters. Incidentally, it is rather surprising to say the least, to observe that John Simmons, in what is in many respects a fine book on Locke's theory of rights, completely ignores the place of a right to conscience, and the background and role of such a right, in Locke's thinking. A. John Simmons, *The Lockean Theory of Rights* (Princeton: Princeton University Press, 1992).

33. For example, International Convention on Civil and Political Rights, article 18.3.

34. Locke, *A Letter*, 46.

35. Such a defense would have to be provided by a proponent of a Christian theory of conscientious individualism. (For my part, I have tried to do that elsewhere.) An assumption about a universal moral law is important to what follows in respect to constructive reflection about the problems of ethical pluralism.

36. *Complete Writings of Roger Williams*, 1:227.

37. Morgan, *Roger Williams*, 134.

38. Ibid., 134–35.

39. Perry Miller, *Roger Williams: His Contribution to the American Tradition* (New York: Atheneum, 1954), 224.

40. Williams, "A Letter to the Town of Providence, January 1655," in ibid., 225–26.

41. Timothy Hall makes such a suggestion ("Order and 'Civility,'" 109). Apparently, some objectors had circulated a paper contending "that it is

bloodguiltiness, and against the rule of the Gospel, to execute judgment upon transgressors against the private or public weal," which sounds like an anarchist argument. Also, in the letter, Williams explicitly criticizes those who "should preach or write that there ought to be no commanders and officers because all are equal in Christ, therefore . . . no laws nor orders, nor corrections nor punishments," which does seemed aimed at Christian anarchists, who were not uncommon in the seventeenth century.

42. I have spent considerable time on this problem, but because of the demands of time, I here only summarize my conclusions, without providing reference to all the details and relevant literature.

43. "[Female circumcision] may be out of place in a book on Islamic aspects [of gynecology and obstetrics], for the practice is neither Islamic nor ordained by Islam. . . . The procedure long antedates Islam, and its geographical distribution is different from the map of Islamic peoples." Hassan Hathout, *Islamic Perspectives in Obstetrics and Gynaecology* (Cairo: Alamal-Kutub, 1988), 102; cited in Stephen A. James, "Reconciling International Human Rights and Cultural Relativism: The Case of Female Circumcision," *Bioethics* 8, no. 1 (1994): 10 n. 24.

44. I am considering in this section the "tolerability" of certain kinds of overt action, not ideas about action. A distinction needs to be made between tolerating ethical ideas and tolerating actions performed in the name of those ideas. Obviously, the "freedom of thought, religion, conscience or belief" needs to be protected, however permissible it may be to restrict overt action in the name of principle.

45. "Proposals to the Congress for a Bill of Rights, 1789," in Lillian Schlissel, ed., *Conscience in America: A Documentary History of Conscientious Objection in America, 1757–1967* (New York: E. P. Dutton, 1968), 47 (emphasis added).

46. According to the committee, the "Covenant does not explicitly refer to a right of conscientious objection, but the Committee believes that such a right can be derived from article 18, inasmuch as the obligation to use lethal force may seriously conflict with the freedom of conscience and the right to manifest one's religion or belief." Tad Stahnke and J. Paul Martin, eds., *Religion and Human Rights: Basic Documents* (New York: Center for the Study of Human Rights, Columbia University, 1998), 94. The opinion of the committee is more inclusive than Madison's proposal, because it links a right to conscientious objection not only to religious convictions, but also to "conscience" or "belief" (explicitly understood to cover nonreligious or even antireligious belief, so long as it is "fundamental," or occupies in the life and behavior of the objector the same status religious belief occupies for religious people).

47. This section draws on an earlier essay of mine, "Legislating Morality: The Role of Religion," in Carol Friedley Griffith, ed., *Christianity and Politics: Catholic and Protestant Perspectives* (Washington, D.C.: Ethics and Public Policy Center, 1976), 39–53.

48. Jerry Falwell, *Listen, America!* (Garden City, N.Y.: Doubleday, 1980), 253ff.

49. Oxford: Oxford University Press, 1959; reprinted 1965.

50. A summary of Devlin's view by Ronald Dworkin is to be found in an excellent article, "Liberty and Moralism," in *Taking Rights Seriously* (Cambridge, Mass.: Harvard University Press, 1977), 240–58.

51. Ibid.

52. Ibid., 254.

53. Ibid., n. 3.

54. Falwell, *Listen, America!* 182.

55. Ibid., 184.

56. See the earlier section on "Citizenship" under "Constructive Suggestions."

57. See the earlier section on Williams's views of "Social Regulation."

58. Morgan, *Roger Williams*, 102.

59. *Complete Writings of Roger Williams*, 4:488.

60. Cited in Miller, *Roger Williams*, 133.

61. Universal Declaration of Human Rights, article 5.

62. Jack Greenberg, "Against the American System of Capital Punishment," *Harvard Law Review* 99 (1986): 1670.

63. Sixth Protocol to the Convention for the Protection of Human Rights and Fundamental Freedoms concerning the Abolition of the Death Penalty, in Albert P. Blaustein, Roger S. Clark, and Jay A. Sigler, eds., *Human Rights Source Book* (New York: Paragon House Publishers, 1987), 477–79.

64. Ibid., article 2.

65. *Complete Writings of Roger Williams*, 3:13.

7

Pluralism as a Matter of Principle

JAMES W. SKILLEN

DAVID LITTLE BUILDS his case for a "weak theory" of ethical pluralism largely on the basis of what he calls "conscientious individualism." In response, I would like to argue that something broader and deeper than conscientious individualism is needed to account for both the diversity of ethical responsibilities that humans bear and the diverse, often incompatible ways they exercise those responsibilities. By enlarging and strengthening the normative basis, I believe it is possible to develop a strong, principled argument for pluralism, which is not the same as a defense of ethical relativism.

By a weak theory of ethical pluralism Little means that normative grounds can be found for welcoming diverse ethical positions without thereby rejecting a monistic theory. In the abstract, however, this sounds equivocal. How strong does a weak theory have to be to remain standing? How warm a welcome can be extended to contradictory, even fully contrary positions? And who does what kind of welcoming to whom— in the academy, in the political order, in churches and other religious bodies, and in other spheres of life?

As a point of entry into Little's argument and my own, consider his discussion of religious liberty in the thought and practice of Roger Williams. Williams established a political order that sought to respect and make room for the free (even if erroneous) conscience of every person. Standing in a long Christian tradition, according to Little, Williams distinguished between the "inner forum" of spiritual conscience and the "outer forum" of civil authority. The practical outcome was a *religious* pluralism under government grounded in the universal right of free conscience.

What does "pluralism" mean in this case? On the one hand, Williams accepted and worked with a distinction between inner and outer forums, yet he was building on more than simply freedom of conscience. Whether intentionally or not, he was also developing further the already familiar distinction between ecclesiastical and civil authority. He was affirming a plural structure of society, namely, that different institutional authorities bear different kinds of limited authority. This is more than the distinction between inner and outer forums.

Moreover, within the political sphere he was actually arguing for the establishment of a universal, nonpluralistic principle of freedom of conscience. A person's conscience may be mistaken, as judged from several vantage points, but as a citizen he or she should, nonetheless, enjoy the same public-legal protection as everyone else. In other words, what looks like (and is) religious "pluralism" from the perspective of the churches and individual conscience is, from the perspective of the civil authority, a definite ethical monism: the political-ethical principle of freedom of conscience is made to displace entirely the principle of church establishment or, more accurately, the principle of a religious qualification for citizenship. Clarifying the difference between two institutional communities—church and state—meant for Williams accepting at least two different points of view on religious life. What might be ethically legitimate in one sphere would *not* be ethically legitimate in the other and vice versa.

The most important "pluralism" for Williams, at least by implication, appears to have been the recognition of (at least) two different kinds of institutional jurisdiction in the "outer forum"—a political community of citizens and an ecclesiastical community of believers. A political community, he concluded, could not be justly constituted if it based membership on a religious confession. Yet he also surely held that a Christian church could not be a church if it did not base membership on religious confession. It would be ethically legitimate for a church to exclude non-Christians from membership, but it would be ethically illegitimate for government to exclude non-Christians from citizenship. What we might call Williams's strong affirmation of *structural* pluralism is on display in his distinction between church and state. At the same time, *within* each of those spheres he was not at all an ethical pluralist and certainly not an ethical relativist. His principles for each do not contradict one another, however, as long as the distinct institutional identity of each is accepted. Religious pluralism within the state, along with a variety of other pluralisms flowing from freedom of conscience and freedom of association, is the consequence of an agreed-upon identity of the political community itself. To put it another way, Williams, as political leader and founder, disagreed in principle with those who believed that a particular ecclesiastical qualification for citizenship should be established by the state. Thus, he would never have agreed that the state can support both freedom of conscience and an established church at the same time. That would be internally contradictory as a political stance—a relativism that would have led to political-ethical suicide. Williams's political-ethical monism appears in his decision to affirm religious freedom and to reject church establishment. Thus, he stood directly opposed to those Bay Colony monists who believed that confession or church membership was an essential criterion for citizenship.

Williams's contrary political-ethical monism becomes even clearer when we notice, as Little points out, that Williams was willing to "expel 'from our civil freedom' one Joshua Verein because he violated his wife's 'liberty of conscience' by severely punishing her for attending too many religious meetings and neglecting her duties to him." Clearly, a criterion for civic exclusion did exist for Williams. A citizen who violated a civil protection of another citizen's free conscience should be expelled. And undoubtedly Williams believed that churches could expel from church membership those who violated that church's laws. Williams was neither an ecclesiastical nor a political relativist. His "welcoming" of citizens who held erroneous religious beliefs did not signal that, as a church leader, he welcomed their religious error. However, having accepted the distinction between types of institutions and deciding that a political community should not be a community of uniform faith, he stuck to his universal, ethical-political principle for membership in the civic community.

Insofar as we are all heirs of Williams when we agree that citizenship should not be based on a confessional criterion, we have opened the door to the need for ever-increasing clarity about the normative criteria for determining institutional and organizational identities. What precisely should be the limits of the state's jurisdiction? And how many other institutional and organizational jurisdictions should be recognized if we are to do justice to the real diversity of society? These questions, it seems to me, cannot be answered by referring to individual conscience alone.

The Origin of Criteria for Making Distinctions?

Conscientious individualism cannot, of itself, generate the criterion by which to distinguish church from state, or family from state, or business from state. There are some Christians and many Muslims and people of other faiths who conscientiously believe that citizenship should be based, at least in part, on confessional criteria. Likewise, there are many people in the world and some in the United States who believe that a husband has every right to demand that his wife attend to his needs even if that inhibits the exercise of her religious conscience. As we will see in dealing with other issues, the possibility of achieving clarity about what should be required and not required, allowed and not allowed, of citizens in a state depends on what we believe a state ought to be. The same can be said of church, family, education, corporate enterprise, and so on. Few, if any, ethical pluralists welcome all expressions of conscientious conviction in every sphere of life. Little, in fact, suggests that the historical emergence of "individual conscience as a seat of religious and moral authority" arose as a result of social disruption and change that caused the differentiation of society into a diversity of independent institutions. Yet, we must ask, what was the source of that societal differentiation process? Did it just happen? And if we now live in a highly differentiated society, is the only seat of moral authority the individual conscience?

Little addresses this problem, in part, by appealing to natural law, or at least indicates that Williams and other Christians have done so. The conscience, in other words, can function actively as "legislator" only because it is, in part, a passive receptor of and responder to "a prior objective 'natural' moral law." The conscience displays its passive nature by, among other things, feeling "pangs of conscience" when guilt or error are experienced. Such feelings "are mostly beyond the control of the individual." Little apparently agrees with those who argue that individuals are not and cannot be "autonomous" in the sense of being a law to themselves or originating all law from themselves. Individuals are somehow bound by something prior to conscience, a law that can elicit feelings of guilt from the conscience. This certainly sounds Christian in the biblical sense that God's commandments originate with God, not with the human beings whom God obligates by them. A strong Christian affirmation of conscience thus entails a simultaneous affirmation of the Creator's laws that bind conscience.

Yet this is precisely where the limits of conscientious individualism become most evident. In Christian terms, the individual conscience is not the ultimate seat of authority. The Creator and the Creator's moral law function as the authority and the normative standards for human beings. Yet, from a biblical point of view, God's moral law does not drop from the heavens to confront lone individuals or isolated individual consciences. God created humans with a diverse array of responsibilities, including institutional and communal responsibilities. Therefore, in order to know how "natural law" binds the conscience, we must make judgments about the different responsibilities appropriate to each distinct institution and relationship. Listing a few of the obligations of the moral law in the abstract, as Little does, such as "nonmaleficence, benevolence, fidelity, veracity, fairness, and the like," does not shed much light on the differentiated institutions and organizations of society or provide insight into the criteria for distinguishing between church and state, family and state, and so forth. This is, of course, not a peculiarly modern limitation. Even in the most primitive social order of

Israel's clan structure, the Ten Commandments presupposed the institutions of marriage, family, clan, and property ownership. And if Israel did not know the separation of church and state, it *did* know the distinctions among prophet, priest, king, and clan elders. Biblically speaking, the commandments were not addressed to individual consciences but to persons in community, including those who held institutional authority as parents, priests, elders, judges, kings, and prophets.

We may laud the emergence of greater individual freedom in the West, leading to limits on the authority of both government and church to compel conscience. Yet if we approve of that enlargement of the sphere of individual conscience, and if we approve of the differentiation and limitation of the jurisdictions of church and state, we do so as ones who give moral approval to the differentiation of society and the diversification of spheres of human authority. Such approval or affirmation leads back to the question about the basis for such differentiation and normative pluralism. Conscientious individualism does not by itself clarify the criteria for distinguishing the types and limits of different authorities.

Structural Pluralism and Ethical Legitimacy

There are two kinds of identification and distinction that we find ourselves making or needing to make. The first kind concerns the diversities that belong to the legitimate differentiation of human society in this world, created by God. These are the different cultures, languages, and types of institution and innovative human behavior. We do not say English is the right language and French a wrong language; we say that many different languages are legitimate expressions of creational diversity, but within each language we distinguish its correct and incorrect use.

The second kind of identification and distinction has to do with this matter of the correct and incorrect use of a language, or the ethical and unethical types of behavior in each differentiated sphere of life. What are the criteria for judging between ethically legitimate and ethically illegitimate behavior in each different kind of institution or relationship that we consider legitimate? On what grounds, for example, do we affirm that parents should love and not destroy their children; that marriage is good and prostitution is bad; that governments should uphold justice by (among other things) protecting religious freedom and not require confessional uniformity; that teachers should convey truth, not error; that friends should be faithful, not unfaithful. Relativistic subjectivism offers no means of distinguishing between just and unjust acts, between logical and illogical judgments, between economic and uneconomic behavior. Ethical pluralism cannot stand as an "ethic" if it has no criteria for making judgments between good and evil, truth and error. Yet this type of ethical distinction presupposes a plural structure of society in terms of which we can recognize jurisdictions, competencies, and responsibilities. To judge that a state's discrimination against a particular religious group is unethical (unjust) derives from a prior judgment about what a state ought to be. And that takes us back to the first set of identifications and distinctions.

Let's take this a step further. If the distinction between church and state is legitimate, does it follow that churches should be free of all political interference in their decision, for example, to elevate or not elevate women to the highest offices of ecclesiastical authority? Two people might believe that women have the religious right to ordination and therefore believe that the denial of ordination to women is illegitimate—unethical—on the part of any church. Yet one of those persons may also believe that it is ethically *improper* for the state to intervene in the internal affairs of churches to force them to treat women and men equally, while the other person might believe that such intervention on the part of government or the courts is exactly proper and called for. Thus, the unavoidable question: Is the ecclesiastical ordination or nonordination of women ultimately an ecclesiastical or a civil matter? This is the structural-pluralist question.

At every ethical juncture there are questions about multiple jurisdictions of authority in relation to multiple judgments of conscience. Or to put it another way, an individual's conscientious conviction that women should or should not have equal opportunity to hold any office of authority must go hand in hand with a conscientious conviction about who bears responsibility to act on this conviction in each of several different institutions. Those whom I call undifferentiated, political-ethical monists on this subject will ask the government to act in every way possible to require equality between men and women. They will seek political or legal action wherever possible to encourage or require egalitarian marriages, teaching of egalitarianism to children in all educational settings, and the imposition of egalitarianism in every business, church, and voluntary association. If the ethical principle of equality is right and true and universal, in other words, the political-ethical monist will argue that it ought to be enforced everywhere by the highest authority. Ethical universality leads to or requires political omnicompetence. Consequently, even in those churches where women are welcome to hold high office, the ultimate authority for such ordination would be the state's civil laws, not the church's laws.

On the other hand, another person who believes just as strongly in the equal treatment of women might believe, contra omnicompetence, that the diverse responsibilities of families, schools, churches, business enterprises, and governments ought to be respected and upheld by public law. No institution should be allowed to function with omni-competent authority, not even the democratic state or federal Supreme Court. The state—or, better, the constitution of the state—should, uni-versally, uphold societal or structural pluralism, a plurality of compe-tencies and jurisdictions. The social-ethical perspective of this person will be pluralistic, not monistic, in regard to the struggle for women's equal treatment. Equal treatment of women in church office will have to be "fought out" in churches. The teaching of egalitarianism to children will have to be struggled for in schools. The equal treatment of women as citizens will have to be won in the political arena through legislation and constitutional appeals.

Conscience in Creaturely Context

While I would affirm, with Little, the importance of individual con-science, I would not begin there but with the biblical witness to human identity as the image of God, created by and for the God who commis-sions us for a diverse range of services to one another and to all creation for the glory of God. Human respect for "erroneous conscience" is, from this perspective, grounded in God's own covenantal commitment to the creation and patience with sinners who continue to bear crea-turely responsibility before God. It is also grounded in God's judging and redeeming purpose for creation in Jesus Christ. The Creator-Redeemer is the one who sends rain and sunshine on the just and unjust alike, upholding creation's responsibilities for all who have been created in the divine image. Conscience, then, is situated in the context of both divine norms for a differentiating creation order (a richer con-cept than natural law) and God's call for humans to fulfill multiple tasks in developing their diverse range of talents and capabilities. The differentiation of society, and human discernment of proper institu-tional distinctions, is thus seen as part of the context of our call to ethi-cal responsibility. And in each sphere of life, we are called to obedience, to what is ethically right in contrast to what is disobedient and unethi-cal. Making *political* room for religious and ethical error would, from this point of view, be justified not on the basis of religious and ethical relativism but as a matter of monistic ethical obedience to the political principle that government has limited authority in a political community and does not possess omnicompetent ethical authority.

The contest over institutional jurisdictions and competencies as well as over the distinction between moral and immoral behavior within each sphere of responsibility will undoubtedly continue for as long as human life continues in this age, because no human institution or person stands in the place of God. Yet Christians should always engage in these contests with the conviction that ethical clarity and resolution is possible.

Further Illustration of the Commitment to Pluralist Principles

The best way to continue this argument is by way of concrete illustration. I have already done that to some extent with regard to the distinction between church and state. Women's rights require slightly more development. Given my Christian affirmation of the creational legitimacy of the differentiation of society, one of the consequences is the necessity of articulating the identity and obligations of the state and membership in it. Here I would contend for equal civil rights for all people under government. Women and men, adults and children, people of all faiths and colors should receive equal treatment as citizens. This reflects the universal ethical monism of nonexclusivity in any state. It also assumes (though there is not space to argue it here) that the political community exists to protect life and the common good of all, including all of the nongovernmental responsibilities that belong to people. Human beings, in other words, are always more than citizens, and thus equal civil rights entails government's equal, nondiscriminatory protection of every nongovernment sphere of life (friendship, family, church, education, and so forth), each of which has its own nonpolitical jurisdiction. Within the framework of government's protection of life, upholding of equal civil rights, and guarding the public trust—the common political good of all—humans should be free to exercise various kinds of responsibilities and authority. Consequently, I would stand on the side of those who say that the authority of women in diverse religious bodies should be decided by those bodies and not by the government.

What about the protection of children? When someone says that government has the authority to *interfere* in the internal affairs of the family in order to protect children, it seems to me that this is worded improperly. Government's responsibility is to protect the life of all citizens. If any person's life is threatened, regardless of whether that threat comes from parents or an employer or a church authority, the *danger to life is an internal political affair*—it belongs to the very responsibility of government. Thus, the state is not *interfering* in responsibilities that belong to family life when it acts to protect endangered children; it is simply fulfilling its own responsibility. This presupposes, of course, that the family's authority is not that of a mini-state. The same can be said for churches, businesses, and academic institutions. The authority to use force, even to take life as in war or capital punishment, belongs to the state's jurisdiction, not to families, churches, and other institutions. At the same time, by contrast, it is important to say that parental authority does not derive from state authority. It has its own direct creational integrity before God. Thus, the state has no legitimate authority— no right—to intervene to displace the exercise of legitimate parental responsibility and authority.

Governmental authority entails the monopoly of force and the right to use it to protect the innocent and to punish those who threaten the innocent. This is precisely what has become differentiated in the course of history and can be defended on Christian, creational grounds. No longer do we recognize parents, or church authorities, or feudal lords, or corporate authorities as having the right to take life. This is not a set-tled consensus, however. Some people will argue that their religious convictions or individual rights require recognition of personal, or parental, or ecclesiastical authority to make ultimate decisions about medical care or even the taking of life. Just as I would argue that the state does not have original jurisdiction over family life, education, sci-ence, human labor, and worship, I would argue with equal emphasis that government *ought* to have jurisdiction over all matters of life and death. That is why the just-war criteria have been developed by Chris-tians over the centuries, and it is why I believe that abortion and euthanasia are ultimately matters of governmental jurisdiction.

From this point of view, the abortion debate over when the fetus becomes viable or whether it is a person is beside the point. Sexual in-tercourse leads to the propagation of human life—generation upon generation. Laws regarding the responsibility of parents for children, of physicians for medical care, and so forth, have been developed, and should continue to be developed, precisely to make clear the ways in which nongovernmental authorities and institutions have competence to nurture and enhance life but never to take it. The presumption of almost all such laws is and should be on the side of life and the genera-tion of life. Government's responsibility is to protect human life and either to certify or to make the final judgment about death (through established public laws governing health, police forces, the judicial process, and the military). Every child born must be registered publicly; every death, even natural death, must be certified publicly. My point is that no authority other than government should be allowed, on its own authority, within its own jurisdiction, to take human life—at whatever stage of development.

This means that the presumption in favor of life protection, including the protection of life-generating human intercourse that leads to preg-nancy, is an ethically monistic responsibility of government that cannot be delegated to any other institution or person, and no authority other than government should be allowed to make decisions about taking human life or interrupting the life-generating process. On this basis, I would approach the legitimacy of abortion somewhat the way I approach the matter of a government's justified entrance into warfare. Are there any circumstances in which the threat to life requires decisions by government that might lead to the destruction of one life for the sake of another? And can some of these circumstances be codified so that a doctor, or team of doctors, can be held responsible as public health official(s) to make publicly authorized decisions about the taking of life, much as the rules of policing and of warfare are codified so that police and military officers may, under certain circumstances, be authorized to make decisions about the taking of life? Yes, I think there are such circumstances, such as the danger of a pregnancy to the life of the mother, and probably others, such as pregnancy due to rape or incest. But these circumstances merely validate the presumption in favor of life and that exceptions to that presumption should be determined by government, through public law.

This line of argument also holds for euthanasia. Life-taking, whether through suicide or the decision of a loving family member or doctor, must in principle be rejected because of government's responsibility to protect life. Although the wholly artificial prolongation of life is not required by this principle, I know of no circumstance in which government may legitimately relinquish its responsibility to protect life and say simply, in law, that private persons, doctors, or anyone else should be free to take their own life or someone else's life when they judge that the life is no longer worthwhile or cost-effective or desirable to another.

In keeping with this argument, I would agree that many aspects of the law that governs capital punishment should, indeed, be debated today. There are many grounds, including that of "arbitrary injury" (mentioned by Little), that should caution Christians against insisting on the death penalty. Another ground is that the very basis given for capital punishment in the Bible may not be recognized by people in our society, and Christians definitely may not defend the death penalty as an act of purely human retribution. Nevertheless, Little does not confront the question of the death penalty directly as a matter of Christian principle. What if our criminal justice system can be designed to avoid arbitrary injury? What if it can be made clear that such retribution is a divine commandment, not a merely human reaction? Isn't human life valuable precisely because we are made in the image of God? Isn't that why the willful destruction of another person requires just recompense—the divinely instituted act of retribution, which is capital punishment?

What about the identity of marriage, the family, and homosexual relationships? Let's enter this discussion by way of analogy from the distinction made earlier between church and state. The first challenge is to identify institutional and relational distinctions and then to determine accountability for moral and immoral behaviors within those institutions and relationships. If, for example, we agree that church and state should be distinguished from one another and separated, we thereby affirm that government holds no jurisdiction to determine correct faith, theology, or church governance for churches. However, in order for government to do justice to the independence of churches, it must have some criterion for recognizing a church (or equivalent religious body) and distinguishing it from a family or a business enterprise. Even settling on this criterion may prove politically contentious, but deciding how to identify a church or churchlike entity is different from deciding what should go on inside such bodies.

Now, if we return to the question of marriage and gay rights, the first public-legal question, it seems to me, is how to identify and distinguish different kinds of relationships. I would contend, on the basis of historical and contemporary experience, that there are several possible kinds of marriage relationship, including monogamous and polygamous forms, and that there are multiple kinds of friendship, including homosexual friendships. I do not see how, at the level of identification, a homosexual relationship can be called a marriage, chiefly because my biblically grounded, Christian-creational perspective identifies marriage with reproductive potential and responsibility, which a homosexual relationship can never have. Now, within the realm of marriage I am ethically pro-monogamy and believe that polygamy expresses "erroneous conscience," just as in the realm of ecclesiastical organization I am pro-Christian and believe that atheism and other religions reflect an "erroneous conscience." But politically speaking, I would argue that those determinations of marital bonds and religious association should be left in the hands of marriage partners and religious bodies.

Likewise, within the realm of friendship, I am pro-chastity in regard to both heterosexual and homosexual friendships, but in the political realm I believe that the state should neither give special recognition to nor criminalize any form of friendship. Thus, I would oppose granting the legal identification of marriage to gay relationships not because I want to use state power to deny the right of homosexual friendships. To the contrary, I believe the state should give equal treatment, including equal protection of life and the freedom of association, to all citizens. But whereas the logic of my position could allow for the legal recognition of polygamy as a form of marriage (even though I don't think it is an ethically obedient form), the logic of my position leads in the

political sphere to rejecting the identification of homosexual relationships as a form of marriage.

Conclusions

Contentious issues of abortion and euthanasia, of gay "marriage" and
the equal treatment of men and women, cannot be resolved, it seems to
me, with an abstract or institutionally undifferentiated ethical argument. Whether one argues for conscientious individualism or for the
priority of individual freedom, one must still confront the fact that any
appeal to governmental or constitutional protection or empowerment
presupposes the existence of a differentiated and limited state. Whatever the rights of majorities and minorities to "have their way" in the
political arena, the deeper and prior question concerns the very identity
and jurisdiction of the state. Most of us now believe the state's jurisdiction was mistakenly defined in Williams's time when a confessional
requirement for citizenship existed, or, until recently, when a black person could be both denied civil rights and owned as another's property.
Resolving today's disputes will require more than universal ethical
appeals and political-legal crusades in favor of certain "good" things
and against certain "evils." Jurisdictional distinctions among institutions and relationships must be made in order that, within each of
them, arguments over good and bad, right and wrong behavior can be
contended for. Clearly, one of my first principles is to recognize the plural structure of society and to oppose all individualistic or communal-
istic reductions of that plural structure. The basis for such argument is
the biblical confession that this is God's creation—in all of its human
and natural diversity—and that Jesus Christ is lord of all, the judge and
redeemer of the very reality that was created in, through, and for him in
the first place.

Part IV _____

INTERNATIONAL SOCIETY

8

Christianity and the Prospects for a New Global Order

MAX L. STACKHOUSE

IT IS NO ACCIDENT that the issue of reconstituting international society appears before us today, at a moment when the economic, medical, cultural, and communication structures that play such a critical role in modern society are changing rapidly. Although civil society in the past largely coincided with the boundaries of the state, it is now being reconstructed internationally in ways that strain the capacity of any government to order, guide, or control. In fact, some observers foresee little but chaos since societies are no longer confined within a single legal system and no one seems to be in control.[1] Even if agreement between states plays an increasingly important role in the future, as we expect, it may well be subject to frequent abuse or breakdown, for its moral and spiritual authority is fragile.

This monumental shift toward a global society and, perhaps, global anarchy has been well under way for more than a century, although many signs of the shift have been obscured by the radical statism of the twentieth century—most notably those of the antimodern national socialisms of the right and the hypermodern proletarian socialisms of the left, each fueled by the notion that there neither is nor could be any ontological, metaphysical, epistemological, or ethical principle to serve as a reliable basis for law across time or space or condition.

These trends were reinforced after the Second World War by the wave of decolonization movements that, while overthrowing exploitative metropolitan regimes, also joined the territorial and ethnic relativism of nationalism to the historicist and class-based relativism of socialist ideologies. These "liberation" movements repudiated the purported universalism of Western religious and philosophical thought, especially insofar as it legitimized constitutional democracy, human rights, and corporate capitalism.[2] Both Christianity and the Enlightenment were viewed as manifestations of Western hegemony, the by-products of material interests that had to be overcome so that competing interests could be acknowledged. That presumption obscured the growth of a wider global interdependence, invited antinomian efforts to debunk all culture-transcending thought, and prompted militant efforts to overthrow existing institutions.

Life, however, cannot be lived under that presumption. Such views can deconstruct, but they cannot reconstruct. They neither generate nor preserve the tissues of enduring commitment needed to sustain reliable human relations. Indeed, they evoke distrust of the structures of commonality on which we depend. Yet a new set of global interdependencies, which we are unsure how to conceive or assess, much less whether to nurture or resist, is appearing on the horizon.

Many are today unsure what could shape the fabric of a common life that is increasingly transnational, cross-cultural, multiethnic, and post-political. Though some argue that a common international legal system is already at hand, more skeptical observers suggest that we have no reliable theory of justice or other mode of authoritative legitimization on which to ground such a system. These skeptics suggest that such law as we possess is little more than a set of tools for those with means to manage the Global Cultural Bazaar, the Global Shopping Mall, the Global Workplace, and the Global Financial Network.[3] Such economistic images reveal something of the power of corporate and market forces today; but they do not convey how much the global economy is itself built on widely accepted values that support science, technology, democracy, human rights, a work ethic, professional standards, or capital investment. Nor do they give us any guidance as to how we ought to respond to the economic forces at work or the values on which they rest. Economistic analysis alone cannot account for the shape and character of international law.

It is also questionable whether we can rely on philosophy alone, as many sought to do in the past. Philosophy today is preoccupied with deconstructing itself, and its resources for rethinking our new situation are therefore thin. All sorts of postmodernists (and not a few anti-modern or premodernist traditionalists) are eager to tell us that Western thought is suffering fatal epistemological and moral disease. It is, they say, impossible, even totalizing and therefore immoral, to speak of anything as being categorical, general, or universal.[4]

Such voices were of little use to the new Russian or South African governments as they sought to write national constitutions.[5] Nor do they help us think in wider terms, for every effort to alter a political order must proceed on the assumption that, although things are contingently disorganized, we can know something about the "right order of things" or the "ultimate ends of life" so that we can improve the situation. It is true that every attempt to define justice has to be repeatedly renewed, because we do not know justice fully and because the concept must be continually reexamined in new situations. This clarification and recasting, however, presumes that the norms of justice are, in some sense, universally discernible.[6]

Many efforts to identify principles on which a universal normative order could be built draw little from, indeed scarcely mention, any of these challenges to the enterprise. They turn instead to contemporary heirs of Classical and Enlightenment modes of analysis, without noting that these heirs are under suspicion. But we cannot ignore these challenges, for they may well expose a weakness—namely, that these forms of thought cannot guarantee their own foundations. They may require theological treatment.[7]

This perception touches on a still inchoate recognition of the devastations brought about by the intentionally antireligious or postreligious ideologies of our century and a longstanding suspicion of religious concerns in international law.[8] Not only have the secular ideologies (sometimes using religion as weapon or cover) behind the Holocaust, the Gulag, and the modern killing fields of Cambodia, Bosnia, and Rwanda brought more vicious destruction than the Crusades or the Holy Wars of old, these secular ideologies are increasingly recognized as incapable of guiding the common life. And this recognition suggests that the engagement of theology with jurisprudence should be renewed, and even that the biblical heritage can make an indispensable contribution to it.

Christian Responses

The varieties of theology most promising in this area are those that remain alert to the contributions of cultures and philosophies beyond the sanctuary. Most forms of Christian theology do this. Orthodox, Catholic, Evangelical, Reformed, Liberal, and Ecumenical modes of thought have all attempted to show the pertinence of biblical themes to ethical and social concerns in ways that invite, and in some ways demand, the formation or reformation of just social and political institutions.

Not all Christians approve such efforts. Early in this century, the great social historian of the relationship of Christianity to the sustaining structures of civilization, Ernst Troeltsch, identified three interpretations of the faith that show a great suspicion of the structures of society. Some focus only on the inner self and its experiences of transcendence (so that social questions are ignored or left to those who deal with merely exterior things). Others try to avoid the evils of civil institutions by constructing alternative communities of holy fidelity distinct from the ways of the world (as in monastic orders and communitarian sects).

And still others attempt to defeat the evils of the world by militant action (to bring about an entirely new order, against the bulwarks of evil).[9] All left indelible traces in Christian thought, but only the third, as it found expression in the Crusades, the Inquisition, and the Peasant's Revolt, is thought to have discredited Christian political theology.

These interpretations have a point: the customary or enacted laws of society are not the same as the normative laws of God. A higher order, a greater purpose, a wider authority ultimately is the source and norm of all that is truly right and good, and it is this "other" level that puts every legal order as it appears in human history in perspective. Indeed, a gulf always exists between divine perfection and the necessities of governance in a fallen and divided world. In substantial measure, the whole of Christianity shares these themes not only with the minority traditions within itself but with its elder brother, the Jewish tradition; with its stepbrother, Islam; and even with its more distant theistic cousins in India and Africa.

For the most part, however, the main streams of Christianity do not hold that the church, the tradition, or its sacred texts are entirely opposed to human society and culture. Indeed, Christianity is driven into engagement with culture since it does not claim that its sources contain all that is necessary to form the laws of society. Christianity has never had anything quite like the Torah or *shari'a* (or even an *Arthashastra*) to propose as a constitution for civil society, however high its regard for them. In its selective adaptation of the laws of the Pentateuch, in its establishment of the internal laws of the church through canon law, and in its attempts to influence civil law in Europe and to found it under the American Puritans, Christian advocates of biblical insights always drew on ideas that derived from nonbiblical sources. This in turn evoked what some call a "Christian social philosophy" or "public theology"— an effort to address common issues, including those of jurisprudence, by employing theological concepts in public discourse. This effort is undertaken in the conviction that such concepts provide the firmest base for public policy.[10]

Christians gravitate to those forms of thought that honor human freedom, for Christians believe that humans are made in the image of God. Christians also hold that this freedom is to be exercised under moral mandates not of our own construction—the laws and purposes of God. We can claim to know these mandates only in part, for they are not fully present in human experience or holy scriptures and everywhere have to be interpreted and applied. We live nonetheless under a kind of cosmic moral constitution that serves as the basic framework for all concrete efforts to discern and establish justice. Further, the human soul, the biophysical world, and the events of history bear traces of this constitution, so that even the most horrendous betrayal and distortion cannot finally overcome it. Yet, precisely because it is obscured by various evils, if this morality is neglected or repudiated, bias, oppression, and dehumanization will corrode any society.

The majority traditions of Christianity have also held that one can be—indeed, ought to be—a member of at least two societies. We are born into a "natural society" with its "orders of creation" as members of a family, a civil polity, an economy, and a cultural-linguistic group. But baptism (and, for some, confirmation) is required for church membership, and brings with it the more universal, catholic, or ecumenical principles of justice. Christianity, in its central traditions, thus demands a separation of Christ and Caesar, *sacerdotium* and *imperium*, patriarch and czar, pope and emperor, minister and magistrate, and thus, church and state. This principle has been periodically violated in Christian history, but the deeper logic of the faith presses against such violations and claims that religious membership cannot be the basis for citizenship, and that participation in a political order is not a basis for religious identity. Each domain has its own laws, and one cannot say that one is right and good and the other necessarily wrong and evil. One can suggest, however, that the wider structures of civil society—those that define and regulate marriage, ownership, economic exchanges, race relations, and foreign policy—ought to respect the more general principles of justice pointed to by this second membership, and not only the interests or social consensus that exists within a particular familial, racial, national, class, or cultural tradition. Freedom of religion, in particular, is a decisive mark of justice in the human world.

To be sure, Christians are also taught to be "obedient to the rulers who are appointed by God" and who are "not a terror to good conduct, but to bad," as we learn from Paul, a disciple *and* a citizen, and these teachings imply that we can, in some measure, discern which regimes are constituted on a godly basis according to ethical criteria. But, as Peter taught, when and if it comes to a conflict, we are to "obey God and not humans," and it is Christ, not Caesar, who should guide the discernment of the one from the other.

Thus, while Christianity does not have within itself an intrinsic theory of international law, it does have a profound sense of the basis of the "right order of things," the "ultimate end of things," and the "grounding authority of all structures of society" that is, in some measure, knowable, and that therefore ought to influence all aspects of life. Christian theology tells us that a quite personal ubiquity, whom we call God, is the foundation of all knowledge and makes dialogue between the world religions and between believers and unbelievers possible. God provides the basis on which general laws can be discerned, debated, codified, and reformed under changing conditions. Their confidence in this proposition derives from the fact that Christians believe that something reliable about God, who alone is truly universal, has been disclosed in the very creation of the world, in the creation of humanity in the image of God, in biblical history, in the concrete particularities of the life, teachings, death, and resurrection of Jesus Christ, and in the ongoing presence of the Holy Spirit.

Christians do not deny that others can know something of the reality toward which believers point, nor do they assert that only believers have an exclusive grasp of truth. Indeed, when the faithful speak seriously about these matters, they assume that serious, nonbelieving listeners can understand what is being talked about and can teach believers things that they need to know. Nevertheless, Christians hold that the fullest comprehension of the universality that believers and nonbelievers share cannot be stated without a nuanced, differentiated understanding of God, best framed in trinitarian terms.

Most Christians hold that belief cannot be imposed, for that would lead to a lie in the soul, but also that every effort to deal with international or cross-cultural realities that is closed to theological possibilities will be tempted to cultural imperialism, or else remain unable to convince the world that its presuppositions are grounded in what is ultimately real. It will be tempted to imperialism because it has no higher principles than its own by which to guide its interactions with others or to critically evaluate its own historical convictions; and it will be unconvincing to others because it cannot point to a context-transcending reality that is universally present in being, culture, society, and a sense of the sacred. Moreover, without a monotheism understood in trinitarian terms, human beings will be tempted to one or another kind of monism, dualism, or polytheism, none of which can fully account for the rich complexities of life.

Much of what Christianity has to offer is shared with other traditions, but at least two other aspects of Christian theology are especially pertinent to the question of international society: a view that theology is necessary to a sustainable theory of international law, and a view of sin and salvation with regard to the limits of that law.

Theology and International Legal Theory

Christianity teaches that not every human problem can be solved by law; yet it also teaches that law is necessary to the common life. Christians have, over the centuries, honored the efforts of great lawgivers to constitute just societies. American Christians, for example, join other

Americans in honoring the images of Hammurabi, Solon, Lycurgus, Justinian, Confucius, Ashoka, Manu, and Muhammad flanking Moses above the desk where the justices sit in the United States Supreme Court. Not only does this frieze symbolize that American law stands under norms beyond those generated out of its own history and procedures, but these great figures are properly acknowledged as framers of legal systems that attempted to approximate justice and bring about peace in complex civilizations.

In addition, it is widely acknowledged that Gregory, Thomas, Calvin, Pufendorf, Althusius, Grotius, Locke, and the English religious dissidents developed many aspects of legal theory that made modern constitutionalism possible, and they did this because they held that, in the final analysis, the chief lawgiver for the whole world is God.[11] They pointed to transcultural principles of justice, provided intellectual resources for subjecting powerful rulers to the rule of law, recognized the necessity of associations outside the state, provided for councils, courts, and parliaments to correct and extend the law, and defined the patterns we consider basic to constitutional government. They echoed the ancient prophets and the early church: the world is governed by a moral order and undergirded by a providential care; life is most blessed when humans live by these realities. And they anticipated the recognition that if these truths are denied, the denial brings nihilism in all things.

For this reason, Christian theology has historically embraced those philosophers, social theorists, and scholars of jurisprudence—Christian or not—who attempt to identify and articulate features of human thought and practice that point toward the universal, ethical, and spiritual realities that make and keep human life human. Theology must make its case by the power of persuasion. And in that truth lie critical points of contact between a Christian theological perspective and careful nontheological outlooks.

We can illustrate this point by noting that theology has long recognized two dimensions of persuasion—intellectualist and voluntarist.[12] The former holds that humans can know something about the basic form of justice because God has written the moral law in every heart. Thus, a common reference point, which major strands of the theological tradition call the *iustitia originalis*, is accessible, in principle, to all. This provides the basis for constructing international law or assessing any international agreements and practices that exist. The exact content of this moral knowledge is not altogether clear, however, in part because there are two major theories as to how best to understand this common reference point. One is teleological and seeks to identify the good toward which all things tend, including the common good, and to direct all members of the body politic toward that end. The other is deontological and seeks to identify the first principles of right, and to establish the normative guidelines within which the many members of the body politic may then pursue their distinctive ends. The one tradition is more organic, hierarchical, and comprehending; the other is more associational, pluralistic, and confederative.[13]

Advocates of these "natural right" or "natural law" positions enjoy the prospect of convergence through intellectual persuasion, despite sometimes sharp intramural disputes. This is particularly clear in the case of those writing in the traditions of Aristotle and Kant. It also informs a modified version of the Kantian view represented by the "cosmopolitan" perspective, a version that, in its theory of *the good* and its definition of *the right*, recognizes the dignity of all persons around the globe.[14]

Theology shares with these views a key question as to what the law of nations *ought* to be, in contrast to the question of the "faculty of law" as to what the law *is*. From the perspective of the "faculty of theology," however, the philosophers face the difficulty of explaining why, if all human beings have a sufficient natural knowledge of the good or the right, a just and universal international law is not immediately at hand. How is it that unjust convention or arbitrary authority comes to dominance again and again, always managing to distort the natural inclinations, the moral law, and the rights of persons? It is, in other words, a suspicion of theology that the intellectualist impulse is not self-sustaining, although it may be a useful and necessary ally to a stronger foundation.[15]

It is for this reason that we must recognize that persuasion may be voluntarist as well as intellectualist. People make choices, select between loyalties, develop interests, form alliances, willfully ride emotions, and are swayed by symbols. Intellectualist claims about the justice of the law are inextricably mixed with desire and interpretation. People invent moral rules and goals and choose legal ideals ("values") that are in fact merely pragmatic adaptations for securing what they desire. They bend ethics, philosophy, and law to fit the preferred conditions of their lives.

For that reason, those who hold either a teleological or a deontological view of the nature and character of law will have to show how and why people would want to choose the good or the right taught by the mind or discovered in the heart. Even more, those who do not accept such "realist" positions, but hold to fully voluntarist theories of law, like positivism or contractualism, will have to show why any person or any group would choose to be obedient to the law so derived if they found doing so to be disadvantageous.

There are two basic answers to this question. The first is that it is in the practical interest of all concerned to yield to the rule of law, and that

we often call a "right" or "good" "value" (thereby choosing to acknowledge the authority of) that which meets our practical interests. Either
we do not want to pay the price of punishment by those who make and
enforce the law, or we gain more by obeying the law, or we are successful by taking advantage of it. Positivists and contractualists are probably
accurate in pointing out the enormous amount of human choice that
goes into the making of law in this mode, and correct in pointing to how
much of it is going on today. Their views remind us of Louis Henkin's
remark that "the process and politics of law-making in our time can be
studied (and nearly understood) as the most ambitious, most popu-
lous, most extended, most complex law-making effort in international
history."[16] But it is not clear that they understand the grounds on which
this is taking place, and they seem unaware how easily law-making
can support imperialism, colonialism, or hegemony—as their critics
suggest.

It may be well to consider again Max Weber's often-neglected argument that the formation of rational and legal institutions on what look
like positivist or contractual grounds is, in fact, an instance of the "rou-
tinization of charisma," and that if this charisma were of a different
sort, or if it were rationalized by ill-motivated special interests, it would
assume more ominous forms.[17] To put the matter another way, it is the
parenthetical "nearly" in Henkin's remark that needs attention, for
while the lawyer may wish, for certain purposes, simply to focus on the
fact that laws exist and that people obey them for practical reasons, the
understanding of law (and, even more, of justice) that can be expressed
in purely positivist or contractualist terms is limited.

We should note that many of the values that incline people to favor
one rather than another understanding of international law derive from
religious assumptions.[18] Many have forgotten where these values came
from, but if they are absent, or actively resisted, the laws so derived will
be subverted or exploited whenever people find it advantageous to do
so. Those who have a voluntarist view of human association rooted in
practical interests can have no recourse but to accept that prospect.

At this point, theology suggests that it is necessary to recognize the
influence of a realm beyond this one, one that shapes the deeper orientations and dispositions of our will by carving the deep channels of
social valuation, of which the positive and contracted law are derivative expressions. It may be necessary, as Weber suggests, for even the
religiously unmusical interpreter of modern law to acknowledge how
deeply religious impulses influence choice. This is voluntarism at
another level, on the brink of "the Will of God."

To be sure, such an acknowledgment is not yet fully theological, it is
only religious. To become so, this deepest voluntarist insight must be
joined to philosophy. This is the wisdom that discovers the level on

which theology and jurisprudence are interconnected. It is with this insight that earlier Islam and later Catholicism adopted the natural law traditions of the Greeks, Calvinism retrieved much of the thought of the Stoics, and Modern Protestantism and Judaism embraced the natural-rights traditions of the Enlightenment. In each case, the formation of a cosmopolitan morality lent authority to international law. All the great world religions point toward a transcending reality that connects the best knowledge of the right and the good to the deepest commitments of the will. Some do it better than others, and that is why jurisprudence cannot neglect theological issues.

Those who presume to shape the common life through law must worry about these connections between the moral and the theological. Their codes determine who shall have and who shall forfeit liberty, wealth, standing, or relationship, even who shall live and who shall die. They decide how coercive force shall be used to defend what society, guided by what morality, philosophy, and—ultimately—theology, have identified as right or good or holy. Those who define these criteria define what is to be considered just, and even if they cannot bring themselves to speak of what is godly, their contribution remains limited if they do not see what they do from the standpoint of ultimacy.

What Is Missing from This Picture?

Most contemporary discourse about international law is uninterested in the theological grounds of international law, perhaps out of fear that these grounds cannot have universal application.[19] What an odd argument! In no other area is this position held. Few doubt that German Jews can discover the laws of relativity in physics, Arabic Muslims the logic of mathematics, or Japanese Buddhists the arts of gardening or poetry, or that these discoveries are of universal interest. And all agree that when a particular tradition identifies a deep structure that is pertinent everywhere, the presuppositions that make that discovery possible are to be honored. Other traditions look deep within their own resources to find whether or not some analogous pattern exists. If so, it is to be cultivated; if not, a conversion or borrowing of some sort is often possible. Confronted with the argument that the authority of international law might have theological roots, however, many scholars ride off like Ichabod in all directions.

To be sure, the question of theology is awkward. Few want to convert and many fear being forced to do so. Besides, much that is called theology is simply the semirationalized assertion of a privileged perspective containing elements of magic, superstition, and ignorance. Furthermore, a religious perspective may bring violence if it is convinced that the ultimate forces of the universe need defending to the death. But we have long known that religion is high voltage, that it can electrocute as well as energize. That is less reason to neglect it than to pay it careful attention. Certainly twentieth-century attempts to construct societies on postreligious and antitheological grounds have brought disasters of their own.

But if God is the deep foundation of everything, as theology holds, and if we can know this in any significant way, why do we not already have a world order and, indeed, why do our current political and international structures not more nearly approximate a graceful social order? The answer lies in the unavoidably theological concept of sin. The will is joined perfectly to the right and the good only in God, and therefore always imperfectly in humans. Human beings are always inclined to crime and corruption. Thus, they need to have not only a personal relationship to God but a structured social ecology that constrains their worst inclinations. Law helps create that environment. It must wrestle with the problems of crime, control situations that allow corrupt interests to evolve into exploitation or erupt into war, and sustain a decent social order under conditions in which sin, corruption, and violence are never fully banished. Theology must wrestle with the question of what saving powers—in the face of sin—provide the best prospect for repentance, forgiveness, and renewal internally, and for responsible and reformed living externally, and thus construct a public argument about what law must defend.

Force is always necessary for law to be effective, but it is resisted when it is used by an unacknowledged authority. If the regulatory structures in civil society, domestic or international, are held to be without moral and spiritual legitimacy, law is systematically ignored, avoided, or subverted. It is not quite true, as has been claimed, that power corrupts; it is that human sinfulness seeks to accumulate power to exploit the existing corruption and to secure acknowledgment of its authority. In this way, the law itself becomes a source of crime and corruption. We need, then, checks not only on power but on legitimacy. There must be limits to law, in part because law is incapable of generating the moral authority that sustains it.

What generates moral authority and can limit crime, corruption, and the legitimized distortion of law? More than anything else, this depends on the formation of networks of mutuality, sacrifice, affection, and responsibility that create and sustain trust and trustworthiness. Where these networks are absent, law alone cannot hold relationships together. In personal life, we see relationships of friendship and love in, for example, parents who give years of their lives to nurture the next generation. In public life, we see some who are willing to assume responsibility for the general shape of things: philanthropists who donate their wealth to public works; public servants who suffer abuse from opponents yet still carry out their duties; voters who vote against their private interests for the common good; and soldiers who give their lives that others may live.

Above all, we see this in religious communities, where people not only face the difficulties of personal and interpersonal life, forming the networks of trust that are at the core of every civil order, but reflect on the most important questions. The portion of the population that does this, and the portion of our lives wherein we grasp the significance of this, are close to the soul of civilization. The patterns of life and the institutions sustained by these forms of giving and community are the means by which humans flourish and are preserved from their own worst tendencies.

The institutions, especially the churches, that do these things on a world scale are few, feeble, and frail. Most of the theological world is quite realistic about this, yet it has never believed that the world will be saved by governments. A viable civil society, global in scope, supporting a comprehensive vision of justice and developing a moral and spiritual network of trusting relationships, may, however, preserve us from some of the imperialism, ethnocentrism, and exploitation to which we are prone in our dealings with one another.

It is not clear that there is moral progress in history apart from this. Souls today are not notably more perfect than in other ages; Christian hearts are not noticeably more pure than in other religions. Among us, love is not more dedicated than among our forebears, beliefs are not more sincerely held than in other faiths, and habits are not obviously more virtuous than in other times or places. But the possibilities of a wider, more comprehensive cross-cultural order of justice, modulated and sustained by a concrete company of those committed to love, coupled with a quest for God's truth, and justice, may signal a real gain. Such an order would at once disperse power (because it recognizes that corruption constantly distorts us all), allow sufficient concentration of power to control crime, protect the human rights of all, evoke a vigorous participation in civil society, and especially, provide for the freedom of those communities of faith that remind us that we live under a moral order not of our own making and need resources and guidance we cannot ourselves supply.

At present, though the structures of legitimacy, the issues of an international civil society, and the moral and spiritual fabric of faith are not sufficiently universal to sustain a global order, they are sufficiently on the horizon that theology must join with leaders in other fields to establish the conditions under which these things can be made more actual. It is potentially a "calling" of our time to be engaged, under God's watchful eye, in cross-cultural research and teaching, in developing new forms of global communication, in struggling with the global implications of disease and poverty, and in seeking to improve international institutions, including the many nongovernmental associations that are building the networks of trust between peoples from the inside out.

Today the material foundations of a global civilization are closer to hand than at any time in human history, thanks in substantial measure to the influence of world-transforming religious impulses that in previous ages inspired trade, missions, and the founding of schools and universities. As a result, it is easier to demonstrate the interdependence of different modes of interaction and the need for wider agreement. Above all, the contention of theology that we live in a common universe created by a single, just, and loving God, and both do and should share a common destiny and therefore need a common ethic, is recognized, implicitly if not explicitly, by all those who are concerned about ecology, peace, and human rights. Theology contends that because of God, we can speak of taking responsibility for the world. Without God, we remain an aggregate of peoples, each with our own gods, cultures, and histories but without duties to one another or to the world as a whole.

The problem is this: we do not yet have a worldwide civil society, even if we recognize that something greater than what we now have is beginning to emerge. But the New Jerusalem, the Kingdom of God, is not present, and stands forever beyond history. The best we can do within history is to strive humbly for greater degrees of duty, virtue, and order in the depths of our will and in the delicate arrangements of common life, and to work toward wider networks of federated interdependence, establishing each provision as close as possible to the universal moral order we almost know.

In concert with a necessary theological vision, the quests for a new international order will have to become not only more substantively just and practically enforceable, but more orthodox, more catholic, more ecumenical, more reformed and reforming, and more attentive to the interfaith realities of our world. Efforts here to clarify the standards, arguments, and guidelines by which we can imagine what that kind of an order might look like are a blessing to humanity and may prove to be *ad maiorem gloriam dei*.

Notes

1. See Paul Kennedy, *Preparing for the Twenty-First Century* (New York: Random House, 1993).

2. See, for example, Frantz Fanon, *The Wretched of the Earth* (New York: Grove Press, 1968).

3. Richard J. Barnet and John Cavanagh, *Global Dreams: Imperial Corporations and the New World Order* (New York: Simon and Schuster, 1994).

4. See, for examples, Jean-François Lyotard, *The Postmodern Condition: A Report on Knowledge* (Minneapolis: University of Minnesota Press, 1984), and Alasdair MacIntyre, *Whose Justice? Which Rationality?* (Notre Dame, Ind.: University of Notre Dame Press, 1988).

5. See "The Future of Religious Liberty in Russia," *Emory International Law Review* 8, no. 1 (Spring 1994), entire issue, and Charles Ville-Vicencio, *A Theology of Reconstruction: Nation-building and Human Rights* (Cambridge: Cambridge University Press, 1992).

6. Current discussions about how we can reliably know these things can be found in A. W. Musschenga, et al., eds., *Morality, Worldview, and Law: The Idea of a Universal Morality and Its Critics* (Maastricht: Van Gorcum, 1992), and Arthur Dyck, *Rethinking Rights and Responsibilities* (Cleveland: Pilgrim Press, 1994).

7. See Max L. Stackhouse and Stephen Healey, "Religion and Human Rights: A Theological Apologetic," in J. Witte and J. van der Vyver, eds., *Religious Human Rights in Global Perspective* vol. 1 (The Hague: Martinus Nijhoff, 1996), 85–516.

8. See Mark W. Janis, ed., *The Influence of Religion on the Development of International Law* (The Hague: Martinus Nijhoff, 1991), especially 137–46.

9. Ernst Troeltsch, *The Social Teaching of the Christian Churches*, trans. O. Wyan (New York: Harper, 1934).

10. See my *Creeds, Society, and Human Rights: A Study in Three Cultures* (Grand Rapids: Eerdmans Publishers, 1985).

11. These are variously treated in John Witte, Jr., and Frank S. Alexander, eds., *The Weightier Matters of the Law: Essays on Law and Religion* (Atlanta: Scholars Press, 1988); Harold J. Berman, *Law and Revolution* (Cambridge, Mass.: Harvard University Press, 1983); Brian Tierney, *The Crisis of Church and State* (Englewood Cliffs, N.J.: Free Press, 1964); Jacques Ellul, *The Theological Foundation of Law* (New York: Seabury Press, 1960); James Hastings Nichols, *Democracy and the Churches* (Philadelphia: Westminster Press, 1961); and Georg Jellinek, *The Declaration of the Rights of Man and of Citizens*, reprint ed. (Westport, Conn.: Hyperion Press, 1979).

12. This is a main theme of Reinhold Niebuhr's monumental treatment of theological anthropology, *The Nature and Destiny of Man*, 2 vols. (New York: Scribner's, 1939–41). The history of theology is reviewed in terms of this distinction by James Luther Adams, *On Being Human Religiously* (Boston: Beacon Press, 1976), chap. 4.

13. The unsurpassed comparative study of these is F. W. Dillistone, *The Structure of the Divine Society* (Philadelphia: Westminster Press, 1951). A Catholic statement that bends toward certain Protestant themes in this same period is collected in Jacques Maritain, *The Social and Political Philosophy of Jacques Maritain* (New York: Charles Scribner's Sons, 1955); a Protestant view that does the reverse is Emil Brunner, *Christianity and Civilisation* (New York: Charles Scribner's Sons, 1949).

14. While the Aristotelian view is identified with Roman Catholic and the Kantian with Protestant thought, both touch the cosmopolitan perspective. See Richard Neuhaus and George Weigel, eds., *Being Christian Today* (Washington, D.C.: Ethics and Public Policy Center, 1992); David Hollenbach, *Claims in Conflict* (New York: Paulist Press, 1982); and my *Creeds, Society, and Human Rights*.

15. See Joshua Mitchell, *Not By Reason Alone: Religion, History and Identity in Early Modern Political Thought* (Chicago: University of Chicago Press, 1993).

16. Louis Henkin, *How Nations Behave: Law and Foreign Policy*, 2nd ed. (New York: Columbia University Press, 1979), 212.

17. Max Weber, *Economy and Society*, 3 vols., trans. by G. Roth and C. Wittich (New York: Bedminster Press, 1968), esp. vol. 2, chap. 8 and vol. 3, chap. 14. Weber's argument is best grasped in the context of his comments on law in his five volumes of studies of religion.

18. Max L. Stackhouse, D. McCann, et al., eds., *On Moral Business: Classical and Contemporary Sources on Ethics and Economic Life* (Grand Rapids, Mich.: Eerdmans Publishers, 1995). See also Max L. Stackhouse, *Public Theology and Political Economy* (Lanham, Md.: Scholars Press, 1991).

19. In some areas of engaged reconciliation, the increased role of religion is recognized, if not yet the theoretical importance of theological views. See, for instance, Douglas Johnston and Cynthia Sampson, eds., *Religion, the Missing Dimension of Statecraft* (New York: Oxford University Press, 1994).

9

Globalization and Catholic Social Thought

MUTUAL CHALLENGES

JOHN A. COLEMAN, S.J.

I CONFESS TO SOME trepidation in addressing the topic: Globalization as a challenge to Catholic social thought. Why not its inverse: Catholic social thought as a challenge to globalization? As we will see, they represent a mutual challenge to each other. Moreover, the title of this essay made me mindful of solemn advice earlier imparted to me: never try to explain the obscure by the even more obscure! Catholic social thought, notoriously, has been dubbed "our best kept secret."[1] Some of its key ideals and concepts, such as subsidiarity, justice as participation, solidarity, the option for the poor, and, especially, its cornerstone notion of the common good are not exactly coin of the land (or, for that matter, in the realm of Catholic pews).

Boston College ethicist David Hollenbach writes in his book *The Common Good and Christian Ethics* that "a central concept advanced by the Bishops' 1986 Letter on the economy—the common good—was nearly incomprehensible to most of the people the bishops sought to address."[2] Globalization itself is a highly contested process as to its definition, scope, components, and directionality. How can such a hugely abstract and elusive phenomenon illuminate the challenges and future directions for Catholic social thought?

Three realities, however, lead me to choose the topic. (1) I just finished editing a book entitled *Globalization and Catholic Social Thought: Promise or Peril?*[3] (2) I have always been convinced that the deepest meaning—the bite, really—of Catholic social thought is illumined less in philosophical/theological accounts of it than in its steady application to public policy and looming new social phenomena and problems. (3) Finally, I am intrigued by a throwaway line of the Boston priest and Harvard Professor of Social Ethics Bryan Hehir, who once provocatively asked, "Can Catholic social thought survive globalization?" Hehir pointed to the ways in which the classic statements of Catholic social teaching derive largely from nation-state systems and from civil society within national states, and lack any full assessment of the burgeoning new global phenomena such as intergovernmental organizations (hereafter IGOs), international nongovernmental organizations (hereafter NGOs), and the multinational corporation.

In global society, the remit of the state is, increasingly, being curtailed. Nothing quite like civil society can be found on a global scale. Moreover, for some interpreters, globalization reverts us back to the kind of savage capitalism and mistreatment of workers excoriated by Pope Leo XIII in the first of the modern encyclicals, *Rerum Novarum*. It was as if we were transported in a time warp back before the rise of modern Catholic social teaching—its nuanced teaching ignored and stricken from history—to the conditions of penury, insecurity about jobs, health care, and old age provisions; back to Satanic mills and factories and the marginalization of the poor that Dickens so well depicts in *Bleak House* and that the popes condemned in their social encyclicals as high and gross injustice.[4]

I want to cover three main topics in this essay. The first is how to define, or at least delineate and situate, what is meant by globalization. The second is how globalization affects Catholicism, and what resources in the social teaching Catholicism brings to this new, startling reality. Finally, I will signal three lacunae or gaps in the social teaching that will need a more careful address or expansion before Catholic social teaching can play a more commanding role in the debates and social movements around globalization.

Globalization Delineated and Situated

In his 1999 Director's Lectures on globalization at the London School of Economics, sociologist Anthony Giddens remarked, trenchantly, that no one could be a practicing social scientist even of any minimal sophistication, if she did not grasp or master the debates about globalization. For Giddens, this debate about globalization is, by far, the most significant controversy now occurring. It confronts us with a world not firmly under our control, says Giddens, but one that seems "to be an erratic, dislocated world, if you like—a runaway world."[5] Globalization, that much-vaunted if often quite ill and differently defined term, names, nevertheless, something real that is urgent, in many ways new and unsettling (as the Industrial Revolution was in its time). Catholic social thought, if it, too, is to serve as a resource of some sophistication and wisdom, must channel its rich intellectual tradition of root metaphors about human and social life and its ethical principles for society to position itself, effectively as well as humanely, in the debates and advocacy about the direction of globalization.

Yet it becomes exceedingly difficult to take any stance that is unambivalent about a "process" that is still quite *in* process, incomplete, contested in a world, in the words of Harvard International Relations expert Robert Keohane, that remains only "a partially globalized world."[6] I recently spent six months on sabbatical at the University of California, Santa Barbara, whose Center for Global Studies speaks easily about globalization(s)—in the plural. There are fiercely competing hopes and fears about our global risk society. Globalization seems to divide as much as it unites. It clearly has—at least in the short run (and, as John Maynard Keynes once pithily said, "In the long run we are all dead!")—both winners and losers. To be a loser in this global gamble can mean to lose security about the most basic human needs; to undergo identity dislocation; to suffer humiliation rather than dignity; to face uncompensated mass resettlement (as in India and China) to make way for mega-dams; or to find one's job, suddenly and irretrievably, "outsourced." Global climate changes due to excessive and growing greenhouse gases might force people to abandon their homelands or bring about the melting of all the glaciers. As one South Sea native of Tuvalo (which is sinking into the sea because of rising sea levels due to global warming) put it to Mark Lynas: "We are being made the victims of something that has nothing to do with us at all. The industrialized countries caused the problem but we are suffering the consequences."[7]

Sociologist Roland Robertson has always famously insisted that the essence of globalization lies precisely in its simultaneous compound effect of producing differentiation *and* homogenization, a trend that is universalizing but also attempts to reinvent and reassert the local. Robertson coins the inelegant word *glocal* to indicate that the advancing process of globalization will likely foment the resistance of more nationalistic and ethnic groups, as well as the repressive suppression (by governments, by IGOs, such as the International Monetary Fund or over-reaching multinational corporations such as Nike in Indonesia or Shell Oil in Nigeria) of vibrant varieties of localism.[8] So-called anti-globalization movements, such as we saw in Seattle in 2000 at the meetings of the World Trade Organization, may, paradoxically, eagerly anticipate an alternative, more humane, form of globalization. "Another world is possible" runs their slogan. Globalization involves perilous risks. Do we not now all live in an increasingly interdependent risk society where the spillover effects from weapons of mass destruction, the potential impact of genetically modified crops, terrorism and global crime syndicates, climate changes, new diseases such as SARS, the simply irresponsible and shocking loss of forests, water pollution, the depletion of the fishing stock in the global commons of the ocean, the Asian or Brazilian financial crises—all leave residues on and in our own terrain and portfolios? There are, to be sure, also immense opportunities ingredient in globalization: the vision of a global commons; a shared sense of the *humanum*; the world as global village; promises of economic and health betterment around the world.

Starkly differing projects of globalization contend. The neoliberal project is painted for us by David Korten in his book *When Corporations Rule the World* as an attempt "to integrate the world's national economies into a single borderless global economy in which the world's mega-corporations are free to move goods and money anywhere in the world that affords an opportunity for profit, without governmental interference. In the name of increased efficiency, the alliance seeks to privatize public services."[9] Indeed, as a potential trillion-dollar-a-year industry, the IMF, the World Bank, and many corporations have tried to privatize something as essential as water. In response to an enforced privatization of water, imposed as a condition for a World Bank loan, outraged citizens of Cochabamba, Bolivia, protesting skyrocketing costs for water supplied by the French multinational corporation *Suez Lyonnaise des Eux*, carried placards that read, "Water is God's gift and not a merchandise," "Water is life." As Vandana Shiva puts it: "When water disappears, there is no alternative. The water crisis has commercial causes but no market solutions. . . . More than any other resource, water needs to remain a common good and requires community management."[10] For his part, British sociologist Zygmunt Bauman echoes Korten's unmasking of some rhetorics about globalization: "Robbing whole nations of their resources is called promotion of 'free trade,' robbing whole families and communities of their livelihood is called 'downsizing' or just 'rationalization.'"[11]

Quite different and in explicit opposition to neoliberal economics is the project of the World Social Forum, which convenes popular movements and NGOs (including representatives from Brazilian Catholic agencies) around a hope of meeting basic human needs, reducing poverty, guaranteeing the rights of indigenous peoples, encouraging citizens' involvement in government, and championing a program of disclosure, transparency, and accountability for IGOs, such as the World Bank and WTO. *New York Times* columnist Thomas Friedman can exalt market liberalization as inherently benign and contend, in his whimsical "golden arch" theory, that "no two countries that both have a McDonald's have ever fought a war against each other since they each got their McDonald's."[12] Princeton political scientist Richard Falk, on the other hand, speaks forthrightly in his chosen book title of a kind of predatory globalization.[13]

Still others seek to contain the bad initial effects of globalization and bring in reforms around a strategy of containing negative globalization, promoting new forms of global governance and functional regulating regimes, expanding civil society's input and access to IGOs such as the IMF, linking globalization to democratization, and working for ethical codes for multinational corporations.

So, a precise definition of globalization—which remains an inherently contested process and project, involving, as it does, power and wealth rearrangements—seems inopportune at this time. Yet how, at least, to delineate and situate the phenomenon, and thus to enter the debates and contestations about globalization? Let me venture a few helpful descriptions of the phenomenon we confront together, whether we applaud or curse it. In an essay entitled "World Society: Structure and Trends," political scientist Dirk Messner describes it this way:

> Globalization denotes a process in the course of which the volume and intensity of trans-boundary transportation, communication and trade relations are rapidly increasing. It is undermining the divisive connotations of national boundaries and intensifying the impacts of border crossing economic, social and political activities for national societies. Many pressing problems cut across territorial boundaries. More and more events are simultaneously perceived throughout the world, making themselves felt with increasingly brief delays in more and more places.[14]

The empirical data seems to bear out that this process is occurring. Trade and travel between nations increased four times between 1980 and 2000. $400 billion in cross-border currency now passes hands every six hours (more money is now exchanged in just six hours than *ever* was dispersed by the World Bank in its fifty-year history). The number of migrants working in countries other than their own has grown exponentially. Refugees greatly inflate these numbers. Remittances from migrant workers to relatives back home have also increased dramatically: $3 billion a year pours back to India in this form, and an equal $3 billion yearly flows to Mexico just from Mexican migrants in California. In some countries, such remittances are their largest source of foreign investment. Indeed, in some countries (e.g., the Philippines), we can now speak of a globalized family system with siblings or nieces and nephews working in Saudi Arabia, Ireland, and the United States.

A boom in international nongovernmental organizations has occurred. There are some 50,000 NGOs active at the global level (a 90 percent increase since 1970). Increasingly, transboundary issues elude any single national solution: the drug and private arms trade, arms control, money laundering, pollution, refugees, common heritage issues concerning the ocean and its mineral and fish resources, the atmosphere, population pressures, and health and infectious disease.

Globalization has been driven both by a self-conscious project of the economic integration of a world market and by technology, especially information technology. The internet serves multinational corporations, scientists and scholars; crime syndicates (e.g., the increasingly international forms of Russian, Colombian, and East Asian drug, smuggling, and sex-trade cartels), and human rights and environmental moral reformers. Globalization, like God's sun, seems to shine on the good and the bad alike. Without the internet, there would never have been an international anti-personnel land-mine treaty, nor a World Commission on Dams, nor the boycott of Nestle's unhealthy baby formulas in the Third World. New global financial rules and the internet are a money launderer's or a porn and drug addict's dream! Globalization has involved every bit as much a communications revolution as an economic one. Roland Robertson speaks of globalization as entailing "a rapidly increasing global connectivity on the one hand and fast expanding and intensifying reflexive global consciousness, on the other."[15] Increasingly, we have become a community of common fate and responsibility—if not a global village, then a spaceship earth. We may not be seeing Francis Fukayama's end of history but, instead, a kind of end to geography.

There are both positive and negative effects of globalization. Positively, we have become more conscious of being one world. Information flows are now more democratically available. Human-rights language increasingly permeates a wider global consciousness. Among the alleged negative effects of globalization is its gross insensitivity to human suffering. A second negative effect involves the inattention (by multinational corporations in extractive industries) to ecological sustainability. A third negative effect entails polarization (political and economic and in terms of life chances and life expectancies) between and within nations. The gap between the poorest and richest nations has been steadily growing, not declining, under globalization. The inequalities within the sectors or classes of the developed world itself have also been growing. There is an immense internet gap between the rich and the poor.

The facts, once again, are glaring: fewer than one percent of Africans have ever used the internet, and there are more telephones in Tokyo than in all of Africa. Forty percent of Latin Americans still cannot read or write. As the Canadian social scientist Pierre Hamel puts it: "Uneven development trails globalization like a shadow. The buzzword is globalization but we inhabit a divided world."[16] A strong fear is that the poorest countries of the world (and in the case of Africa, entire world regions) will become marginalized to the process, so that there will be both greater world integration and loser societies almost completely left out, in a kind of globalization apartheid.

Finally, people fear the erosion of the ability of governments to provide the societal goods traditionally expected of the state: physical security (especially in the growing number of failed states), economic welfare and opportunities for human betterment, a social safety net, distributive justice—in sum, what Catholic social teaching enunciates as the common good. To be sure, states remain indispensable actors if globalization is to be civilized, humanized, something other than "savage capitalism" and what George Soros has called "casino financial markets." Yet the ability of states to deliver on social goods or counter the negative faces of globalization has eroded. Change in our social and economic realities has far outpaced change in the political institutions and processes that once firmly embedded them. So, a last working definition of globalization, taken from a book by David Held and Anthony McGrew, *Globalization/Anti-Globalization*, might help us here:

> Globalization, simply put, denotes the expanding scale, growing magnitude, speeding up and deepening impact of trans-continental flows and patterns of social interaction. It refers to a shift or transformation in the scale of human organization that links distant communities and expands the reach of power relations across the world's regions and continents. But it should not be read as pre-figuring the emergence of a harmonious world society or as a universal process of global integration in which there is a growing convergence of cultures and civilizations. For not only does the awareness of growing interconnectedness create new animosities and conflicts, it can fuel reactionary politics and deep-seated xenophobia. Since a substantial proportion of the world's population is largely excluded from the benefits of globalization, it is a deeply divisive and, consequently, vigorously contested process. The unevenness of globalization ensures it is far from a universal process experienced uniformly across the entire planet.[17]

We may not be able to agree on any precise definition of globalization, but few can doubt that globalization is, empirically, a real phenomenon. Individuals, corporations, NGOs, and nation-states seem to be able to reach around the world farther, faster, deeper, and cheaper than ever before. Few can also doubt that new global units or actors— IGOs such as the WTO, NGOs such as Doctors Without Borders, Greenpeace, Amnesty International, or Transparency International—have grown apace and change many of the received rules of the game for economics, geopolitics, ecology, and persons. The key issue becomes: How do we humanize globalization and make it serve our habitat and humanity and not just the Halliburton Corporation? How do we bring about an ethical and just world order? How do we integrate a world economy so it serves people? To the pressing question "Is the earth still governable?" the empirical facts of globalization—whatever one's varying definition or project for it—force the answer: clearly not by the old rules or with the old cast of characters. Multilateralism is the new game, since no one nation—not even the hegemon and would-be new empire, the United States—can, on its own, address and solve a host of transborder issues of poverty, illness, global security, crime, terrorism, financial stability, secure health, and ecological degradation. Yet as Yale ecologist James Spaeth puts it, in a stunning book on the global environmental crisis and the sheer arrogance of the world's largest polluter to face the issue, *Red Sky at Morning*: "Addressing the global environmental threat will require a global effort in a world where international cooperation on the scale that may be required is seldom achieved."[18]

Catholic Social Thought's Response to the Challenge of Globalization

Of course, given Catholicism's position as the world's largest transnational organization and as a purveyor of a nuanced and thoughtful social ethic, in many ways the inverse proposition *is* equally true: Catholic social thought presents a decided challenge to some projects of globalization. Clearly, social Catholicism does not fit nicely with neoliberal theories of an entirely autonomous economy unrelated to legitimate regulation for the common good or with overly vigorous statist communitarian doctrines that deny, stringently restrict, or restrain justice as participation and subsidiarity. As the Welsh political scientist David Ryall has put it, "The church has been involved, as a primary agent and subject of globalization, for at least as long as any other body." Moreover, Ryall asserts, "In Catholic political culture qualified and pooled sovereignty, transnational structures, subsidiarity and devolution have long been familiar concepts."[19] Yet, paradoxically, Catholic voices—except on the issue of debt relief for poorer nations as found in the Jubilee 2000 initiative—seem fairly muted in the major NGO globalization campaigns concerning population explosion, the environment, transparency and anti-corruption programs for governments and multinational corporations, and the women's movement.[20] What are the peculiar strengths or shortcomings in Catholic social thought in its address to globalization?

In papal encyclicals and episcopal letters from countries ranging from Canada to the Philippines and Brazil, and in specialized transnational religious groups such as the Jesuits, the Community of San Egidio, and *Pax Christi*, Roman Catholicism has been an interested participant in debates about globalization. Long before the term "globalization" became fashionable about fifteen years ago, after all, social Catholicism had been continuously dealing with key issues of development within the poorer nations, immigration, the arms race and weapons of mass destruction, the addressing of basic human needs, the right to participation, and the need for new structures to guarantee a global common good. These issues all have now become uppermost in globalization debates. Especially since the 1980s, Catholicism has made human rights a decided center of its diplomatic and teaching strategies. Some secular international-relations specialists could even claim that the church has been at the vanguard of the global human-rights revolution.

Social network activists tend to emphasize six salient themes for building a more humane globalization: Working toward a global ethic; devising more just trade and economy; collaborating with the United Nations and other IGOs (such as, for example, the World Criminal Court, which the Vatican has endorsed) to improve global governance; developing interreligious dialogue in initiatives to avoid or overcome what Samuel Huntington ominously prophesizes as a coming "clash of civilizations"; building a new concern for the environment to protect biodiversity, the ozone layer, and global temperature; and supporting movements for the emancipation and education of women (women's education represents the greatest single predictor of population stability in Third World countries). Catholic voices have been active—but certainly, with the exception of human rights and interreligious dialogue, never dominant or truly salient in NGOs working on all six global arenas.[21]

The Commission of the European Catholic Bishops commissioned a 2001 document from a committee that included Michael Camdus, the former director of the International Monetary Fund, entitled Global Governance: Our Responsibility to Make Globalization an Opportunity for All.[22] This document endorses a need for a global ethic. It follows Swiss theologian Hans Kung's reasoning: no world order without a global ethic; no world peace without peace between the religions; no peace between the religions without dialogue between the world religions.[23] As Bryan Hehir once famously said, globalization may have a logic of its own, but it lacks any ethics of its own. Although Catholic social teaching on its own cannot, as such, provide the needed global ethic, it can contribute strongly to it.

Basically a reformist document, the European Bishops' document draws on strands of Catholic social teaching to underscore common values for a global world: human dignity, solidarity, responsibility, human rights, a care for the common environment, accountability, participation, and transparency. It calls for the creation of a United

Nations special agency—akin to the WTO and the International Labor Organization—devoted to global environmental issues. "Global Governance," to this point, is the most sophisticated and explicit Catholic social teaching source dealing with global governance.

Significantly there is, as yet, no truly rounded treatment of globalization in Catholic social teaching, although Pope John Paul II has addressed some aspects of it in his World Day of Peace speeches and in a special session of the Pontifical Academy of Social Science. Incipient Catholic discourse on globalization tends to see it as a complex, rapidly evolving, ambiguous phenomenon—in itself neither good nor bad. "It will be," in John Paul II's frequently reiterated throwaway line, "what people make of it."[24] Elsewhere he supplies the motto: "We need a globalization of solidarity." The papacy insists that globalization has great possibilities and potential risks: "For all its risks it offers exceptional and promising opportunities, precisely with a view to enabling humanity to become a single family, build on the values of justice, equity and solidarity," avers the pope.[25] As sociologist José Casanova has argued, "The Catholic Church has embraced globalization, welcoming its own liberation from the strait-jacket of the territorial sovereign nation-state which had restricted Catholic universal claims. But the embrace is not uncritical."[26]

The church's public voice insists that globalization must serve solidarity and the common good, be truly global, fully respect the human rights of all persons, and provide for participation according to appropriate responsibilities. Catholicism distances itself from neoliberal projects of globalization, although it fully accepts the role of markets and entrepreneurship. It notes, too, the deficits in current globalization, without joining with anti-globalization forces: threats to welfare and a decent floor to meet human needs; the inability of globalization—to this point—to reduce world poverty (indeed, world poverty has been exacerbated in the last decades); dangers of a homogenization of culture (making the world safe for McDonald's and MTV); the need for socially responsible investment; and a democratic deficit. In slogans much repeated, Catholics claim they want a globalization without marginalization, a globalization with a human face, a globalization that does not homogenize culture. Catholic voices endorse a notion of global civil society and embrace the concept of subsidiarity in any global governance regime.

Monsignor Frank Dewane, of the Pontifical Council for Justice and Peace, asserts:

There are different starting points [in debates about globalization] for churches as opposed to businesses. The churches' concern must be for the poor, those not able to benefit from the goods of creation and human inventions. Churches must be concerned very much with how wealth is distributed. Comments of churches on the complex questions like economic progress and growth and for that matter on all aspects of globalization should be critical; critical of received wisdom, critical of the current consensus and critical of new theories.[27]

Yet there may be also some severe limits to any role Catholicism might play in globalization debates and advocacy. It is very—indeed, extremely—striking how truly jejune are the treatments of Catholicism in the burgeoning literature on globalization, as I discovered recently when writing an essay on Catholicism as a global actor for a forthcoming *Encyclopedia of Globalization*. Indeed, given Catholicism's size, global reach, and armory of rich theoretical and institutional resources, what strikes one is how marginalized, in many ways, Catholicism remains in globalization campaigns and debates. Why might this be so?

Some of it may reflect a blindness of the secular enlightenment thinkers to what religion can bring to policy debates. In part, the church still hankers in many places for a religious hegemony, foreign to a cosmopolitan globalization. Like many religious groups, it frequently jealously keeps its own autonomy and is not, as a large institution, a very good or reliable networking partner. Catholicism remains, as a world organization, much too cumbersome a resource for "alternative information flows" and quick networking of a type that has been such an effective tool of NGOs working in global civil society.

In general, the global networking of successful NGOs (about landmines, sweatshops, child labor, sex trade of women, indigenous people's rights, the environment), as Margaret Keck and Kathryn Sikkink demonstrate in their study of advocacy networks in international politics, is nonhierarchical, involves wide partnerships, and remains truly flexible.[28] The church, moreover, remains distrusted by many international women's groups (a powerful global movement) and groups working on population questions, and it is seen itself to suffer from a democratic deficit. Paradoxically, this most potent global unit may lack the inner organizational flexibility for a rapid and networked response to global issues as they arise. Hence, it is much more likely that semiautonomous and more local Catholic subgroups will be the major Catholic actors in activist global networks. To the extent that the hierarchical church attempts to rein in or control such local Catholic NGOs (or, because of its stance on abortion, disallow partnerships with women's or other groups who hold for abortion, even on issues *totally unrelated* to abortion, as has happened in some places), their own flexibility for networking and initiative will be stifled. Emory sociologist

Frank Lechner has explicitly studied religious groups in globalization movements and debates. He argues that, with a few exceptions, such as the Jubilee 2000 campaign to relieve Third World debt, Catholic groups tend generally to play subaltern, supportive roles in someone else's network concerning globalization.[29]

We can take as an important index of the success of Catholic social teaching a remark of Pope John Paul II that social Catholicism is found not just in social doctrine but "in her concrete commitment and material assistance in the struggle against marginalization and suffering."[30] We still have a long way to go to build the kind of social teaching, from the bottom and not just the top, that Paul VI challenged us to in his *Octogesima Adveniens*: "Christian communities, with the help of the Holy Spirit, in communion with the bishops who hold responsibility, and in dialogue with other Christian people and all people of good will, need to discern the options and commitments which are called for in order to bring about social, political and economic changes seen in many cases to be urgently needed."[31]

Three Lacunae in Catholic Social Teaching about Globalization

I want to lift up briefly three lacunae in current versions of Catholic social teaching for its encounter with globalization: Global governance; the multinational corporation; and the environment. My treatment of each will be relatively jejune, more evocative than demonstrative, more indicating the issues than fleshing out the precise directionality of the response.

Global Governance

To be sure, as early as the 1960s, Pope John XXIII in *Pacem in Terris* signaled glaringly unfinished business in governance: "Under the present circumstances of human society, both the structure and form of governments as well as the power which public authority wields in all the nations of the world must be considered inadequate to promote the universal common good."[32] Although this shortcoming is signaled, no systematic thought has been given to the contours of what kind of institutions might yield a global governance that is not some world government (which would violate, presumably, subsidiarity and constitute a threat to the Catholic sense of limited government). To the extent that institutions are mentioned in the literature, they tend to be either states; IGOs such as the UN, the International Labor Organization, UNESCO, or the World Criminal Court; or some generic support for the expansion of the rule of international law.

For those who follow the globalization literature, this emphasis almost uniquely on states and IGOs seems old-fashioned and one-sided. In point of fact, much of the global governance that is incipient takes the form of somewhat amorphous governing units called "regimes" or "global policy networks." If what I am about to say about regimes and global policy networks seems a bit arcane, keep these following bromides in mind. *Governance* is not the same as *government*. It is possible that other units, besides states and intergovernmental organizations, can provide the needed coordination and governance. After all, Standard and Poors does an effective job in coordinating the bond market! When we look at effective global regimes (e.g., the International Civil Aviation Organization or the International Postal Union), we discover that some of them flow entirely from an IGO—for example, the World Health Organization of the UN; some, such as the Basle Committee on Banking Regulations and Supervisory Practices, involve public-private partnerships, for example, between IGOs and banks; some are purely private regimes in the public interest (the Internet Corporation for Assigned Agencies). In a similar way, there are now hundreds of what can be called global policy networks, such as the World Commission on Dams (which unites IGOs, such as the World Bank, corporations, governments, and environmental NGOs as co-stakeholders); the Coalition to Stop the Use of Child Soldiers; or Transparency International, which focuses on exposing and reforming corruption in governments and corporations. Global policy regimes more and more follow the logic of networks. Functionally specific and defined, such networks avoid bureaucratic inertias and bring together diverse sectors from society.

Often global policy networks have shown special ingenuity in their use of information technologies. They place new issues on the global agenda or raise issues that have been neglected (or treaties that are not being implemented). They help fashion a truly public discourse on such issues. They can facilitate the negotiation and setting of global standards (e.g., for regulations to catch and monitor money-laundering or for environmental management). Global policy networks are natural units for gathering and disseminating knowledge. They can serve, at times, as innovative mechanisms by which IGOs outsource pieces of the implementation of their policy. They also close the participatory gap in global governance. Too often we think of subsidiarity too single-mindedly as a kind of *vertical* subsidiarity (e.g., from local to regional to national governance). But there is also a kind of *horizontal* subsidiarity that looks to a leaner form of governance, one that bypasses top-heavy bureaucracy and coordinates the many stakeholders into governance units that respect both the local and the legitimate stakeholders. If a co-ordinating global network can do the job, why introduce a more cumbersome bureaucratic IGO bigger than necessary to get the global job done?

What one looks for in international regimes and policy networks is efficiency, accountability, transparency, participatory access to legitimate stakeholders, and the removal of corruption, both from governments and from multinational corporations. One seeks effective coordination and a kind of socialization of global actors to a quasi-constitution of rules about issues such as aviation, banking, the postal union, anti-personnel landmines, etc.[33] Note that many of these salient themes (transparency, corruption, regimes that are neither states nor IGOs) are rarely spoken about anywhere in current Catholic social teaching.

Two topmost issues in global governance (whether in IGOs, which are often run by bureaucratic elites, or in some policy regimes) are a democratic deficit at the global level—nothing quite analogous to democratic parliaments or truly global social movements exists on the ground—and the adequate financing of global organizations. Presently, financing for global regimes depends entirely on the goodwill of states and has absolutely no provision for dealing with the free-rider problem (i.e., those who gain from the global governance scheme but do not pay for it). Neither topic has received a systematic address in Catholic social teaching. Despite its vaunted call for an international common good, inasmuch as the common good intrinsically includes an institutional imagination, the Catholic social tradition has remained much too vague and moralistic when it comes to thinking through global governance.

The Multinational Corporation

In his encyclical *Centesimus Annus* in 1991, John Paul II treated the business corporation as creative entrepreneurship in a free-enterprise economy.[34] But he never really dealt with the new forms of the multinational corporation, as such. World Bank economist Wolfgang Reinecke, in his book *Global Public Policy*, demonstrates that the multinational corporation has a different organizational logic and form than its earlier national corporation type (the type dealt with in *Centesimus Annus*).[35] A journalist writing in the *Manchester Guardian* could claim that "corporations have never been more powerful, yet less regulated, never more pampered by government yet less questioned, never needed to take social responsibility, yet never more secretive. To whom will these fabulously self-motivated, self-interested supranational bodies be accountable?"[36]

Multinationals merge and acquire. Frequently, they enter into secure interfirm alliances to defray costs, or into outsourcing of intermediate inputs. Notoriously, parts of a Japanese automobile may have components made in France and the United States. International outsourcing and multiple affiliates help the multinationals insulate the company from risk, exchange-rate fluctuations, and unwanted regulations. Thus, if country X engages in an embargo of its products to country Y, the headquarters of a company in country X (making guns, pharmaceuticals, or cars) can simply transfer the contracts to an affiliate to avoid the regulation. The new multinational business corporation makes both regulation of industry or its taxation by any one country nearly impossible. Indeed, frequently profiting from governmental research and development money, and all too often eluding the payment of any taxes and benefiting from state policies of corporate welfare—free to treat the environment as some externality—many multinationals are the veritable prototypes of the free-rider.

To be sure, there will be no humane globalization without the cooperation of multinationals. And many multinationals, prodded by consumer boycotts and consumer education, have moved toward good global citizenship behaviors. Because many corporations have shown themselves to be good global citizens at times and have voluntarily subscribed to ethical principles—for example, the UN global compact based on principles of fair enterprise (including avoiding child labor, respecting the human rights of workers, guaranteeing labor safety, etc.)—we cannot simply demonize them. They provide jobs and create wealth. They find ways, through the market, to maximize efficiencies and bring forth new products. They will be indispensable actors in discovering and marketing more environmentally friendly energy sources. The Sullivan principles, applied to apartheid in South Africa by corporations, gave leverage to those resistant to a racist regime.

But we do need a vigorous address to the pervasive role of corporations in setting agendas in politics (both in domestic politics and in IGOs such as the World Bank) or dominating regulatory agencies. Perhaps David Korten goes too far, but he suggests that corporations, as such, be kept from *any* direct political lobbying or involvement.[37] By almost any standard, the disproportionate sway of corporations and moneyed interests over politics seems excessive and dangerous to democratic principles, the environment, and workers' rights.

If multinational corporations will, willy-nilly, play an indispensable role in any humane globalization, the lack of any systematic analysis by Catholic social thought (both sociological and ethical) of the multi-national form (its strengths and dangers, its limits and need for ethical monitoring, the necessity of a counterforce to check its enormous powers) limits its effectiveness in debates on globalization.

The Environment

Both John Paul II and the American bishops have said some humane, wise, forceful, and thoughtful things about the environment.[38] Yet their thought about the environment tends to tack it on to the original thrust of the social teaching around economy and politics. The model remains, at best, the model of stewardship. But many are rightly arguing that we need, at this time, two crucial paradigm shifts in thinking about the economy and the environment. The first is a shift from an overly anthropocentric understanding of life on planet Earth to a deeper sense of the cosmos (in all its varieties and speciations) as the mirror of the glory and wisdom of God. The human is not the only image and likeness of God. It may be, stretching the metaphor too much to speak of the cosmos as the body of God, but the cosmos is, in some real sense, an integral part of creation in its own right and not just some useful means for human flourishing.[39] Catholic social thought has been rooted almost entirely in theological anthropology and theological ethics. It needs a new situating in cosmology. The second paradigm shift—a massive one—would make the economy subordinate to ecology. The economy must increasingly be seen as a subset of ecology. Rather than being an externality to the economy, the ecological realm is the nesting niche for any true economy. We are coming to see that if life-support systems are destroyed irreparably, if water shortages increase, if food supplies decrease, if fisheries are depleted, if global warming remains unchecked, forests ravaged, and topsoil degraded, there will be no viable economy. Fully half of all jobs worldwide relate to nature: farming, fishing, and forestry. Catholic social thought needs to avoid tacking its environmental thought on as a kind of humane afterthought and instead needs to integrate it fully and from the outset into its teaching about the economy.

If, in places, I have critiqued Catholic social thought, it has been to strengthen a distinguished and distinctive body of thought. For in the end, religious voices will be essential for any humane globalization. Princeton political scientist Richard Falk contends that the prevailing bankruptcy of the regnant global schemes cries out for a religious voice: "The best of secular thinking falls short of providing either a plausible path to travel in pursuit of humane global governance or a sufficiently inspiring vision of its elements to mobilize a popular grass roots movement for drastic global reform."[40] For Falk, religions contribute the following key components for a humane globalization: They take suffering seriously and respond to real people who suffer; they tap into deep roots in popular culture; they anchor an ethos of solidarity; they provide normative horizons based on a transcendent ethic; they rely, in overcoming pessimism, on the transformative power of faith; they foster a sense of limits (and of human fallibility); they provide people with rooted identities in a runaway world; and they believe in both justice and the need for reconciliation. Thus, avers Falk, "It is in the end the possibility of a religiously grounded trans-national movement for a just world order that alone gives hope."[41]

Notes

1. Peter Henriot, Edward DuBerri, and Michael Schultheis, *Catholic Social Teaching: Our Best Kept Secret* (Maryknoll, New York: Orbis Press, 1988).

2. David Hollenbach, *The Common Good and Christian Ethics* (New York: Cambridge University Press, 2002), xiii.

3. John A. Coleman, S.J., and William Ryan, S.J., *Globalization and Catholic Social Thought: Promise or Peril?* (Ottawa: Novalis, 2005; Maryknoll, N.Y.: Orbis, 2005).

4. Charles Dickens, *Bleak House* (London: Penguin Books, 1996).

5. Anthony Giddens, "Runaway World: The Reith Lectures Revistited," lecture 1, Nov. 10, 1999, at www.lse.global.

6. Robert Keohane, "Governance in a Partially Globalized World," in David Held and Anthony McGrew, eds., *Governing Globalization: Power, Authority and Global Governance* (Malden, Mass.: Basil Blackwell, 2002).

7. Mark Lynas, *High Tide: The Truth about the Global Crisis* (New York: Praeger, 2004), 97.

8. Roland Robertson, *Globalization, Social Theory, and Global Culture* (London: Sage Publications, 1992).

9. David Korten, *When Corporations Rule the World* (San Francisco: Berret Koehler Publishers, Inc., 2001), 3.

10. Vandana Shiva, *Water Wars: Privatization, Pollution, and Profit* (Cambridge, Mass.: South End Press, 2002), 15, 19.

11. Zygmunt Bauman, *Globalization: The Human Consequences* (New York: Columbia University Press, 1998), 123.

12. Thomas Friedman, *The Lexus and the Olive Tree* (New York: Anchor Books, 1999), ix.

13. Richard Falk, *Predatory Globalization* (Malden, Mass.: Basil Blackwell, 1999).

14. Dirk Messner, "World Society: Structure and Trends," in Paul Kennedy, Dirk Messner, and Franz Nuscheler, eds., *Global Trends and Global Governance* (London: Pluto Press, 2002), 39.

15. Roland Robertson, "Anti-Global Religion," in Mark Juergensmeyer, ed., *Global Religions: An Introduction* (New York: Oxford University Press, 2003), 145.

16. Pierre Hamel, "Introduction," in Pierre Hamel et al., eds., *Globalization and Social Movements* (New York: Palgrave, 2001), 3–4.

17. David Held and Anthony McGrew, *Globalization/Anti-Globalization* (Malden, Mass.: Basil Blackwell, 2002), 1.

18. James G. Spaeth, *Red Sky at Morning: America and the Crisis of the Global Environment* (New Haven, Conn.: Yale University Press, 2004), 3.

19. David Ryall, "The Catholic Church as a Trans-national Actor," in Daphne Josselin and William Wallace, eds., *Non-State Actors in World Politics* (London, Palgrave, 2001), 46.

20. Frank Lechner, "Religious Rejections of Globalization and Their Directions," paper presented to the annual meeting of the Association for the Sociology of Religion, Anaheim, Calif., 2002.

21. For some of these themes on a humane globalization, cf. Patricia Mische and Melissa Merkling, eds., *Toward a Global Civilization: The Contribution of Religions* (New York: Peter Lang, 2001); Samuel Huntington, *The Clash of Civilizations and the Remaking of World Order* (New York: Simon and Schuster, 1997).

22. Commission of the Bishops' Conferences of the European Community, "Global Governance: Our Responsibility to Make Globalization an Opportunity for All," a report to the Bishops of COMECE, October 2001, available at www.comece.org.

23. Hans Kung, *A Global Ethics for Global Politics and Economics* (New York: Oxford University Press, 1998).

24. Address of John Paul II to the Pontifical Academy of Social Sciences, April 2001, on www.vatican.va.

25. John Paul II, "Message for the Celebration of the World Day of Peace," January 1, 2000, on www:vatican.va.

26. José Casanova, "Religion, the New Millennium, and Globalization," *Sociology of Religion*, 62, no. 4 (2001): 415–41 at 433.

27. Msgr. Frank Dewane, "Theological Response to Globalization and the Role of the Church," paper delivered on June 15, 2002, at a conference entitled "Economy in the Service of Life: Consultation on the Western European Church's Response to Globalization and the Financial System," Soesterberg, The Netherlands.

28. Margaret Keck and Kathryn Sikkink, *Activists beyond Borders: Advocacy Networks in International Politics* (Ithaca, N.Y.: Cornell University Press, 1998).

29. Lechner, "Religious Rejections of Globalization and Their Directions."

30. John Paul II, *Centesimus Annus*, no. 26, in David O'Brien and Thomas Shannon, eds., *Catholic Social Thought: The Documentary Heritage* (Maryknoll, N.Y.: Orbis Press, 1992), 458.

31. Paul VI, *Octogesima Adveniens*, no. 4, in O'Brien and Shannon, *Catholic Social Thought*, 266.

32. John XXIII, *Pacem in Terris*, no. 135, in O'Brien and Shannon, *Catholic Social Thought*, 152.

33. For policy networks, cf. Wolgang Reinecke et al., *Critical Choices: The United Nations, Networks, and the Future of Global Governance* (Ottawa: International Development Research Center, 2000).

34. For a papal treatment of the corporation (but not a truly multinational corporation), cf. John Paul II, *Centesimus Annus*, nos. 34–36, in O'Brien and Shannon, *Catholic Social Thought*, 464–67.

35. Wolfgang Reinecke, *Global Public Policy: Global Public Policy without Governing* (Washington, D.C.: The Brookings Institute, 1998), 11–51.

36. John Vidal, *Manchester Guardian*, April 23, 1999, p. 23.

37. Korten, *When Corporations Rule the World*, 290–97.

38. For Vatican documents on the environment, see Marjorie Keenan, ed., *From Stockholm to Johannesburg: A Historical Overview of the Concern of the Holy See for the Environment* (Vatican City: Pontifical Council for Justice and Peace, 2002); for the American bishops on the environment, see Drew Christensen, S.J., and Walter Grazer, eds., *And God Saw It Was Good: Catholic Theology and the Environment* (Washington, D.C.: United States Catholic Conference, 1996).

39. Sally McFague, *The Body of God: An Ecological Theology* (Minneapolis: Fortress Press, 1993).

40. Richard Falk, "The Religious Foundations of Global Governance," in Mische and Merkling, *Toward a Global Civilization*, 54.

41. Richard Falk, *Religion and Humane Global Governance* (New York: Palgrave, 2001), 30–32, treats of these benefits of religion for globalization. The citation is from his "The Religious Foundations of Global Governance," 54.

Part V ————————————————————————

WAR AND PEACE

10

The Ethics of War and Peace in the Catholic Natural Law Tradition

JOHN FINNIS

Peace and War

Law, and a legalistic morality and politics, can define peace and war by their mutual opposition. Any two communities are either at peace or at war with one another. If they are at war, each is seeking a relationship to the other ("victory over," "prevailing over") which that other seeks precisely to frustrate or overcome. If they are at peace, each pursues its own concerns in a state of indifference to, noninterference in, or collaboration with the concerns of the other.

But sound moral and political deliberation and reflection is not legalistic. Despite some tendencies towards legalism, the Catholic tradition of natural law theory very early articulated and has steadily maintained a richer and more subtle conception of peace and war. From the outset, the philosophers in the tradition have accepted that social theory (a theory of practice) should have a distinct method, appropriate to its uniquely complex subject matter. It should not seek to articulate univocal terms and concepts which, like the concepts a lawyer needs, extend in the same sense to every instance within a clearly bounded field. Rather, it should identify the central cases of the opportunities and realities with which it is concerned, and the focal meanings of the terms which pick out those opportunities and realities. What is central, primary, and focal, and what peripheral, secondary, and diluted, is a function of (that is, is settled by reference to) what is humanly important, which in turn is a function of what are the good reasons for choice and action. So there are central and secondary forms of community, of friendship, of constitution, of the rule of law, of citizenship—and of peace. The secondary forms are really instances. But a reflection which focuses on them will overlook much that is important both for conscientious deliberation (practice) and for a fully explanatory reflection (theory).

So: to describe or explain peace as the absence of war is to miss the important reasons why, as the tradition affirms, peace is the point of war. That affirmation is not to be taken in the diluted and ironical sense of the Tacitean *solitudinem faciunt pacem appellant*.[1] The tradition knows well enough that wars are sometimes, in fact, waged to annihilate, out of hatred or sheer delight in inflicting misery, destruction, and death, and that even such wars can be said to be "for the sake of peace," that is, for the inner peace of satiation of desire and the outward peace of an unchallenged mastery over one's domain.[2] But even the inner peace attainable by such means is partial, unstable, and unsatisfying, and the peace of an unfair and cruel mastery is deeply disordered and deficient. More adequately understood, peace is the "tranquillity of order," and "order is the arrangement of things equal and unequal in a pattern which assigns to each its proper position."[3]

But a definition of peace in terms of things resting tranquilly in their proper places still fails to articulate the peace which could be the point of war. It remains too passive. The account needs to be supplemented by, indeed recentered on, what Augustine had treated as primary in the two immediately preceding sentences: *concordia* and *societas*, concord and community. For concord is agreement and harmony in willing, that is, in deliberating, choosing, and acting, and community is fellowship and harmony in shared purposes and common or coordinated activities. Peace is not best captured with metaphors of rest. It is the fulfillment which is realized most fully in the active neighborliness of willing cooperation in purposes which are both good in themselves and harmonious with the good purposes and enterprises of others.

Peace, then, is diminished and undermined generically by every attitude, act, or omission damaging to a society's fair common good—specifically, by dispositions and choices which more or less directly damage a society's concord. Such dispositions and choices include a proud and selfish individualism, estranged from one's society's (or societies') concerns and common good;[4] contentiousness, obstinacy, or quarrelsomeness;[5] feuding with one's fellow citizens[6] and sedition against proper authority;[7] and, most radically, war.

To choose war is precisely to choose a relationship or interaction in which *we* seek by lethal physical force to block and shatter at least some of *their* undertakings and to seize or destroy at least some of the resources and means by which they could prosecute such undertakings or resist our use of force.[8] (Do not equate "lethal" with "intended to kill": see under "Attitudes toward War and Nonviolence" below.) In the paradigm case of war, the *we* and the *they* are both political communities, acting as such—what the tradition called "complete or self-sufficient (*perfectae*) communities." But there are only "material," not "formal" (essential, morally decisive), differences between that paradigm case ("war" strictly so called) and other cases:[9] the war of a political community against pirates; the revolt of part of a political community against their rulers, or the campaign of the rulers against some part of their community, or some other form of civil war; the armed struggle of a group or individual against gangsters, bandits, or pirates; the duel of one person against another. In each case, the relationship and interactions between *us* and *them* which we bring into being in choosing to go to war replace, for the war's duration, the neighborliness and cooperation which might otherwise have subsisted between us and them. But the tradition teaches that a choice of means which involves such a negation of peace (of concord, neighborliness, and collaboration) cannot be justified unless one's purpose (end) in choosing such means includes the restoration, and if possible the enhancement, of peace (concord, neighborliness, and collaboration) as constitutive of the *common* good of the imperfect community constituted by any two interacting human societies.[10]

This requirement of a pacific intention is, for the tradition, an inescapable implication of morality; it is entailed by the truly justifying point of any and every human choice and action. For peace, in its rich central sense and reality, is materially synonymous with the ideal condition of integral human fulfillment—the flourishing of all human persons and communities.[11] And openness to that ideal, and the consistency of all one's choices with such openness, is the first condition of moral reasonableness.[12]

In the classic sources of the tradition, that primary moral principle is articulated not as I have just stated it, but as the principle that one is to love one's neighbor as oneself, a principle proposed as fundamental not only to the Gospel law but also to the natural law, to practical reasonableness itself.[13] Accordingly, the tradition's classic treatments of war are found in the treatises on *caritas*, precisely on love of neighbor.[14] Justice removes obstacles to peace, and is intrinsic to it, but the direct source of peace is love of neighbor.[15] And war is to be for peace.[16]

For true peace, not a false or seeming peace. War might often be averted by surrender. But the peace thus won would often be a false peace, corrupted and diluted by injustices, slavery, and fear. Preserving, regaining, or attaining true peace can require war (though war will never of itself suffice to achieve that peace[17]).

Motive or Intention

An act, a deed, is essentially what the person who chooses to do it intends it to be. Intention looks always to the point, the end, rather than to means precisely as such; intention corresponds to the question, "Why are you doing this?" But any complex activity is a nested order of ends which are also means to further ends: I get up *to* walk to the cupboard *to* get herbs *to* make a potion *to* drink *to* purge myself *to* get slim *to* restore my health *to* prepare for battle *to*. . . .[18] So, though intention is of ends, it is also of all the actions which are means.

English lawyers try to mark the distinction between one's more immediate intentions and one's further intentions by reserving the word "motive" for the latter. The spirit in which one acts, the emotions which support one's choice and exertions, can be called one's motives, too, but become the moralist's direct concern only if and insofar as they make a difference to *what* is intended and chosen. If the proposal one shapes in deliberation and adopts by choice is partly molded by one's emotional motivations (more precisely, by one's intelligence in the service of those emotions), then those motivations are to be counted among one's intentions (and motives), help make one's act what it is, and fall directly under moral scrutiny.

A war is just if and only if it is right to choose to engage in it. A choice is right if and only if it satisfies all the requirements of practical reasonableness, that is, *all* relevant moral requirements. If one's purpose (motive, further intention) is good but one's chosen means is vicious, the whole choice and action is wrong. Conversely, if one's means is upright (say, giving alms to the poor) but one's motive—one's reason for choosing it—is corrupt (say, deceiving voters about one's character and purposes), the whole choice and action is wrong. The scholastics had an untranslatable maxim to make this simple point: *bonum ex integra causa, malum ex quocumque defectu*, an act will be morally good (right) if what goes into it is entirely good, but will be morally bad (wrong) if it is defective in *any* morally relevant respect (bad end, or bad means, or inappropriate circumstances). Treatises on just war are discussions of the conditions which must *all* be satisfied if the war is to be just.

The preceding three paragraphs enable us to see that, in the tradition, no clear or clearly relevant distinction can be drawn between "grounds for" war and "motive or intention" in going to war. The proper questions are always: What are good reasons for going to war? What reasons must not be allowed to shape the proposal(s) about which I deliberate, or motivate my adoption of a proposal?

In the first major treatise on war by a philosophical theologian (as opposed to a canonist), Alexander of Hales (c. 1240) identifies six preconditions for a just war. The person declaring war must have (1) the right *affectus* (state of mind) and (2) authority to do so; the persons engaging in war must (3) not be clerics, and must have (4) the right *intentio*; the persons warred upon must (5) deserve it (the war must have *meritum*); and there must be (6) *causa*, in that the war must be waged for the support of the good, the coercion of the bad, and peace for all.[19] Here the word *causa* is less generic than in the maxim *bonum ex integra causa*, but less specific than in Aquinas's discussion of just war, about thirty years later. Aquinas (c. 1270) cuts the preconditions down to three: authority, *causa iusta*, and *intentio recta*. Aquinas's *causa* is essentially what Alexander of Hales had called *meritum*. There is a just *causa*, says Aquinas, when those whom one attacks deserve (*mereantur*) the attack on account of their culpability; just wars are wars for righting wrongs, in particular a nation's wrong in neglecting to punish crimes committed by its people or to restore what has been unjustly taken away.[20]

Thus it is clear that, in Aquinas, the term *causa* is not equivalent to "a justifying ground." Rather, it points to something more like the English lawyer's "cause of action," a wrong cognizable by the law as giving basis for a complaint, a wrong meriting legal redress. As Francisco Suarez notes, 350 years later, a discussion of such *iustae causae* for war is primarily a discussion of the justifying grounds for war *other than* self-defense:[21] to act in self-defense really needs no *causa*. (Throughout I shall follow Article 51 of the UN Charter in using the term "self-defense" to include all cases of justifiable defense, *légitime défense*.) So there is an important difference between a present-day inquiry into the justifying grounds for war and a medieval inquiry into *iusta causa*. Aquinas had more reason to distinguish (as he firmly does[22]) between *causa* (in his sense) and *intentio* than we now have to distinguish between "ground" and "motive or intention."

Is there nonetheless some room, in considering the rightness of initiating or participating in a war or act of war, for an inquiry into the spirit or sentiment in which a people, an official, or a citizen acts? Perhaps there is. We might draw a distinction between "grounds" and "spirit" by recalling that war is paradigmatically a social and *public* act. Now, just as an individual's act or deed is essentially what the person who chooses to do it intends it to be, so the acts of a society are essentially what they are defined to be in the public policy which members of the society are invited or required to participate in carrying out. That defining policy, which organizes the *actions* of individual participants in a war (thus constituting their acts a social act),[23] and does so by more or less explicit reference to war aims and strategy, can often be distinguished both from any accompanying propaganda and from the emotions and dispositions of the leaders who shaped and adopted it. Thus individual citizens can, in principle, assess the public policy, the announced reasons for going to war, the announced war aims, and the adopted strategy (so far as they know it) and assess the justice of the war (taking into account the facts about the enemy's deeds, operations, and plans so far as they can discover them). Such an assessment can set aside the moral deficiencies of the society's leaders, except insofar as those deficiencies—manifest bellicosity, vengefulness, chauvinism, and the like—should be taken into account in judging the truth of the leaders' claims about facts and about the absence of suitable alternatives to war.

Notice that this does not carry us very far. Individual citizens have (in varying measure) some duty to consider the justice of the war, even if there is a weighty presumption in favor of accepting the public policy; in carrying out that duty, they must not allow themselves to be swayed by exciting but evil motivations: "the craving to hurt people, the cruel thirst for revenge, a bellicose and unappeasable spirit, ferocity in hitting back, lust for mastery, and anything else of this sort."[24] The same goes for the leaders: the shaping and adoption of their choice to go to war, of their war aims, and of their strategy will be wrongful if *affected* by any such seductive emotions.

Yet that malign influence might (and perhaps not infrequently does) remain undetectable by those who are called upon to participate in the war. To these citizens, the grounds for war, and the war aims and strategy which provide the grounds for particular operations, may reasonably seem morally acceptable. Indeed, those grounds may sometimes *be* morally acceptable even when the leaders of the society would in fact not have acted on them but for their own immoralities of disposition ("spirit") and motivation ("intention").

Grounds for War

It is primarily by harnessing reason to devise rationalizations that emotions create temptations to injustice (and to other immoralities). Rationalizations are plausible grounds which make proposals for choice and action attractive to reason and will but which, in truth (as indeed the deliberating or reflecting agent could discern), fail to satisfy all the requirements of practical reasonableness. As we have seen, the first such requirement is openness to integral human fulfillment, articulated in the tradition as love of neighbor as oneself. (The tradition—even, tentatively, in its purely philosophical articulations[25]—adds, "Out of love of God, source of the very being and life of self and neighbor alike.") All other moral principles are specifications, more and less general, of this primary moral principle. One of the most immediate specifications is the Golden Rule of fairness, in each of its forms, positive and negative: do to/for others as you would have them do to/for you; do not do to others what you would not be willing to have them do to you. This in turn is specified in the presumptive obligations to keep promises, to respect the domain and goods of others, to compensate for wrongful harm, and so forth. And these obligations in turn rule out a good many alleged grounds for war.

Sifting the types of reason put forward to justify or explain a decision to fight, the tradition became clear that only two could justify such a decision: self-defense, and the rectification (punitive or compensatory / restitutionary) of a wrong done.

Aquinas runs the two grounds together in a single, foundational proposition: "Just as rulers rightly use the sword in lawful *defense* against those who disturb the peace within the realm, when they *punish* criminals . . . so too they rightly use the sword of war to *protect* their polity from external enemies."[26] Later scholastics, such as Vitoria (c. 1535) and Suarez (c. 1610), while not repudiating Aquinas's resort to arguments which assimilate defense to punishment, do distinguish between defensive and offensive wars: war is self-defensive if waged to avert an injustice still about to take place; it is offensive if the injustice has already occurred and what is sought is redress.[27] And while they consider self-defense a ground so obviously just that it scarcely needs argument,[28] they consider offensive wars to be justified basically by the justice of retribution (*vindicatio*).[29] An offensive war is like the action of the police in tracking down and forcing the surrender of criminals within the jurisdiction, action assimilated (in this line of thought) with the action of the judge and the jailer or executioner.

As so often, Suarez's care brings nearer to the surface of the discussion an issue which seems to me to present the tradition with a notable difficulty. Private persons may forcibly defend themselves,[30] but "a punishment inflicted by one's own private authority is intrinsically evil," that is, it is wrong in all circumstances, even when one cannot get retributive or compensatory justice from a judge.[31] (For punishment is essentially the restoration of a fair balance between the offender and the law-abiding, a balance which the commission of an offense disturbs by enacting the offender's willingness to take the advantage of doing as one pleases when the law requires a common restraint; and persons who are not responsible for upholding the balance of fairness in distribution of advantages and disadvantages in a community *cannot* by "punitively" repressing wrongdoers accomplish that restoration of fairness which their act, by purporting to be punishment, pretends to accomplish.) It is because private punishment is always immoral that the tradition, following Cicero,[32] insisted on public authority as one of the essential preconditions for just war (meaning just offensive war). But in a world without any world government, are not states and their rulers in precisely the position of private persons? How can they punish if they are not world rulers, or even international rulers, and so lack the type of responsibility that grounds acts of punishment—responsibility for maintaining and restoring a balance of justice between wrongdoers and the law-abiding, or between wrongdoers and their victims? This difficulty is often raised in a slightly different form: how can a state or government rightly act as both judge and party? That is a fair question, which Suarez identifies and tries to answer,[33] but I think the form in which I have framed the difficulty is the more fundamental.

The issue is complicated, above all by the flexible extension of "defense" and "punishment" and their convergence or even overlap in a range of situations. Note first that a war, or a military operation, is not taken out of the class of *defensive* acts by the mere fact that it is initiated to forestall a reasonably anticipated and imminent unjust attack.[34] More importantly, defense is of rights and does not become inapplicable on the first success of a violation of them. If it is self-defense to resist forcibly the entry of squatters into my family house, is it not self-defense to eject them forcibly when I discover them on returning home in the evening? Defensive measures seem to extend to self-help reclamation of what one has just lost.[35] And why should the mere temporal immediacy, or delay, of one's measures make an essential difference? Again, Vitoria, without seeking to justify the Spanish appropriation or colonization of the Americas on this ground, upheld the right of the Spanish to make war on the Amerindians *in defense of* the many likely innocent Amerindian victims of Amerindian cannibalism, human sacrifice, and euthanasia of the senile.[36] "For the defense of our neighbors is the rightful concern of each of us, even for private persons and even if it involves shedding blood."[37]

Moreover, much of what the tradition says about the *punitive* function of war between polities relates not to the punishment's primary, retributive rationale but to punishment's function as a deterrent, general or special. "Without the fear of punishment to deter them from wrongdoing (*iniuria*), the enemy would simply grow more bold about invading a second time."[38] May not the same thought play a legitimate part in one's deliberation as a private person deciding whether or not to expel squatters from some part of one's domain? Note how Vitoria not only moves back and forth between defense and punishment, but also treats each as an aspect of the other:

> The license and authority to wage war may be conferred by necessity. If, for example, a city attacks another city in the same kingdom, . . . and the king fails, through negligence or timidity, to avenge [impose retribution for] the damage done (*vindicare iniurias illatas*), then the injured . . . city . . . may not only defend itself but may also carry the war into its attacker's territory and teach its enemy a lesson (*animadvertere in hostes*), even killing the wrongdoers. Otherwise the injured party would have no adequate self-defense; enemies would not abstain from harming others, if their victims were content only to defend themselves. By the same argument, even a

private individual may attack his enemy if there is no other way open to him of defending himself from harm.[39]

Thus the conceptual boundaries between defense and punishment are somewhat blurred. Still, the distinction remains, and with it the question: Why is punishment morally allowable in the state and its government, but not in the individual whose rights are not and perhaps cannot be vindicated by the state? Suarez gives the technical answer:

> Just as the sovereign prince may punish his own subjects when they offend others, so he may exact retribution [*se vindicare*] on another prince or *state which by reason of some offense becomes subject to him*; and this retribution cannot be sought at the hands of another judge, because the prince of whom we are speaking has no superior in temporal affairs.[40]

But the proposition I have italicized smuggles the conclusion into the premises. If this wronged state or government has no rightful human superior in secular matters, the same will be true of the offending state or government, and the proposition[41] that the offense puts the offending state (morally speaking) into a state of subjection is question-begging or a fiction.

A number of recent writers have surmised that the issue was obscured from the tradition's classical writers by the notion that all Christendom was one realm, so that the wars of a state or government within that quasi- universal realm could the more readily be supposed to be analogous to the use of police power to bring to justice wrongdoers within a realm.[42] But this hypothesis, though not altogether groundless, is scarcely satisfying; the emperor's sovereignty over Christendom was manifestly a fiction, and the existence of states outside the empire was all too well known. Moreover, the traditional position that punitive war is justified survived after the replacement of Christendom by states which everyone accepted were wholly independent sovereignties.

Without, I think, the benefit of much clear discussion among the tradition's representatives, recent witnesses to the tradition—notably Pius XII, John XXIII, and the Second Vatican Council—have spoken as if the only justifying ground for war were defense.[43] Several moralists who uphold the main lines of the Catholic natural law tradition argue that this is a legitimate development of the tradition, that it renders the tradition more consistent with its own principles.[44] Inasmuch as they rely on a supposed change in the nature of warfare by virtue of technological developments, their argument is unpersuasive. Many present-day wars are fought in traditional ways at more or less traditional levels of limited destructiveness. Moreover, although a world government can now be envisaged as in some sense a practical possibility (again by virtue of technological development), and although leaders and people ought to do what (if anything) they responsibly can to bring such a world government into being,[45] these considerations do not justify the conclusion that, in the meantime, states must behave precisely as if they already had a common superior, effectively responsible for maintaining the worldwide common good, on whom exclusively they must treat the police power (of bringing wrongdoers to justice) as having been devolved. If self-defense (*légitime défense*) is to be held to be the only just ground for war, it must be on the ground that the tradition (1) rightly judged that private individuals as such have no right to punish those who have wronged them, but (2) erred in supposing that independent states purporting to punish states which have wronged them are in an essentially different moral position from private persons purporting to punish people who have wronged them. Vitoria and Suarez uneasily ascribed the supposed moral difference between the positions of private persons and independent states to "the consent of the world" and the customary positive law (*ius gentium*), not to natural law.[46] The same consent and custom grounded slavery.[47] As the customary institution of slavery came to be discerned by the tradition itself as contrary rather than supplementary to natural law, so the tradition has come (or is coming) to discern the true moral character of the custom ascribing to states the authority to levy punitive war.

Other Distinguishing Criteria

Having a good ground is not the only prerequisite for justly going to war (and fighting it). *Bonum ex integra causa, malum ex quocumque defectu*; there are other conditions which must all be satisfied if one's warring is to be justifiable. All of these further conditions are, I think, implications of the Golden Rule (principle) of fairness, rather than of the principle that one must never choose to harm the innocent. The most important of these implications is that it is unfair not only to the enemy but also to one's own people (1) to initiate or continue a war which has no reasonable hope of success, or (2) to initiate a war which could be avoided by alternatives short of war, such as negotiation and nonviolent action.

The condition that the foreseeable side effects of going to war be not excessive ("disproportionate") was usually stated by the tradition in connection with the justification-conditions of punitive wars. A government's initiation of a war for the sake of retributively restoring an order disturbed by a wrong done to its own country could not be justified if the war were likely to expose that country unfairly to loss and risk of loss (for example, great risk of substantial loss, or significant risk of great loss). Indeed, it seems to be only such wars that the tradition explicitly declares to be subject to this condition.[48] But there can be little doubt that even the decision to put up a defense must be subject to the same sort of precondition. Modern restatements of the tradition which make defense the only just ground for war do treat *probability of success* and *proportionality* (of anticipated damage and costs to expected good results) as preconditions.[49]

That is not to say that a military unit faced with overwhelming odds must, in fairness, surrender. Everyone knows that one unit's willingness to fight to the last man can sometimes inflict such losses that the enemy's overall operation and strategy is weakened or delayed and so can be defeated—its victory over the unit destroyed was Pyrrhic. And everyone knows that an isolated unit, in the dust of conflict, can rarely discern with confidence how its resistance would affect the overall outcome of the war. Military discipline is therefore not unfair in imposing a strong presumption in favor of fighting on. But, when standing alone against the enemy, those in command of the whole nation or its armed forces as a whole must very seriously ask whether it is consistent with the Golden Rule to undertake a hopeless resistance which will impose immense losses on the combatants of both sides, on noncombatants of both nations (especially the nation attacked), and perhaps on the citizens of neutral states lying (say) in the path of the fallout.

The same sort of fairness-based considerations underlie the requirement that war be considered a *last resort* after the exhaustion of peaceful alternatives.[50] The losses accepted in a negotiated settlement, however unpalatable, must be compared with the losses that would be borne by all those likely to be destroyed or injured by the alternative option, war.

How are such comparisons and judgments of (dis)proportion to be made? Not by the simply aggregative methods taken for granted by utilitarian, consequentialist, or proportionalist ethics, which blandly but absurdly ignore the incommensurability of the goods and bads at stake in human options.[51] It is a matter, rather, of adhering to the *rational* requirement of impartiality by an intuitive awareness of one's own *feelings* as one imaginatively puts oneself in the place of those who will suffer from the effects of the alternative options (not forgetting the different status of the various classes of potential sufferers, some of whom would have willed and initiated the war and thus accepted the risk). As the U.S. Catholic bishops indicate, to identify proportionality one must "tak[e] into account" both the expected advantages and the expected harms, but with the purpose (not of measuring incommensurables but rather) of "assess[ing] the justice of accepting the harms," an assessment in which "it is of utmost importance . . . to think about the poor and the helpless, for they are usually the ones who have the least to gain and the most to lose when war's violence touches their lives" (not forgetting, however, their fate in an unjust peace).[52] As we shall see when we consider unfairness ("disproportion") in the conduct of military operations, the deliberations and conduct of a party to the conflict will provide a referent against which to assess the requirements of impartiality as they bear on other conduct of that same party.

The Conduct of War

All the moral requirements which bear on the decision to go to war apply also to the willingness to carry on fighting and to the conduct of the war in particular military operations. Indeed, they apply also to the adoption of a deterrent strategy in the hope that war will thereby be averted.[53] The distinction between *ius ad bellum* and *ius in bello* is scarcely part of the Catholic natural law tradition. Nor is it a helpful distinction. True, it teaches that the rightness of a decision to fight does not entail the rightness of everything done in fighting; but that is more fundamentally taught by the more general principle, applicable to all decisions and actions, *bonum ex integra causa, malum ex quocumque defectu*: *every* choice must satisfy all moral requirements.

So it must be clear at the outset that, in the Catholic natural law tradition, there can be no question of different moral constraints pulling against one another. Each of the constraints is a necessary condition of justifiability, and compliance with one or some of them is never a sufficient condition. The combatants, like the leaders who opted for war, must have upright intentions: their motivations must be free from unfair bias and cruelty, they must intend to fight on some just ground, they must not be willing to impose unfair devastation. And, just as their leaders in deliberating about whether to go to war must not intend the death of innocents (noncombatants), either as an end (malice and revenge) or as a means (of breaking the enemy's will to fight, for example, or of bringing neutrals into the war), so, too, those who plan and carry out military operations are subject to precisely the same constraint, the same exceptionless requirement of respect for (innocent) human life. So too, indeed, are those who participate in the public policy and act of maintaining a strategy of deterrence involving threats which they hope will never (but could and, as far as the policy is concerned, would) be carried out.[54]

Curiously, Aquinas's little treatise *de bello* makes no reference to the exceptionless moral norm that innocents must not be deliberately killed. But there is no doubt that he held that norm to be applicable to war. For the norm itself is one which, a little later in the same part of the *Summa Theologiae*, he clearly affirms and defends as exceptionless.[55] And, as we shall see in the next section, he explicitly affirms (with the whole tradition) that such norms remain requirements of reason and thus of morality whatever the circumstances. As if to make the point economically, his treatment *de bello* affirms the exceptionless applicability to war of another moral norm which many people violate in war, indeed violate perhaps even more freely and with even fewer qualms of conscience: the moral norm excluding all lying (as distinct from subterfuges which do not involve affirming as true what one knows to be untrue).[56] And the whole tradition after him peacefully accepts the absolute immunity of noncombatants from deliberate attack, that is, attack intended to harm them either as an end or as a means to some other end.[57]

Combatants are all those whose behavior is part of a society's use of force; if we are engaged in just defense, enemy combatants are those whose behavior contributes to their society's wrongful use of force. Anyone whose behavior during warfare could not be used to verify the proposition, "That society is at war with us," is clearly a noncombatant. But some of those people whose wartime behavior could be used to verify that proposition (little old ladies knitting khaki socks, for example) nevertheless contribute so little, and so merely symbolically, to the acts of war whose violation of just order is ground for war that they are reasonably considered noncombatants. The principle of discrimination—that one must not make noncombatants the object of attack as one makes combatants—requires one to respect the distinction between combatants and noncombatants, but does not presuppose that drawing the distinction is easy. There are in fact many borderline cases: farmers, workers in public utilities, members of fire brigades, and the like, who engage in certain performances specified by war and essential to it, yet very little different from their peacetime occupations and essential to the survival and well-being of all who are certainly noncombatants. Some theorists in the tradition have called them combatants, others in the tradition have called them noncombatants. But, on any view, the population of a political community includes many people who are certainly noncombatants; their behavior would in no way help to verify that the society is engaged in operations of war against another society. They include in particular those who cannot take care of themselves, together with those whose full-time occupation is caring for the helpless. The behavior of people of these sorts contributes nothing to a society's war effort, but actually diverts resources which might otherwise be used in that effort.

Noncombatants, then, are innocent; that is, they are not *nocentes*, not engaged in the operations which most of the tradition assimilated to capital crimes and which the newer conception proposed by (say) Grisez treats as activities warranting forcible resistance in self-defense. Noncombatants may not be directly harmed or killed; "directly" here means "as a means or as an end."[58] (Does it follow that combatants may be directly killed? See the last section below.) But, without intending any harm to noncombatants, one may choose to plan and carry out military operations which one knows will in fact cause noncombatants injury or death; and such a nonhomicidal choice can be justified provided that the choice is otherwise fair and well motivated (*malum ex quocumque defectu*). The proviso just mentioned is often expressed as "provided that the death-dealing or other harmful effects on noncombatants are not disproportionate." Here "proportionate" can have a rational meaning which it could not have if it referred simply to sheer magnitude; its rational meaning is *unfair*, imposed by a biased and partial, not an impartial, measure and judgment. The standard is the Golden Rule, and I have sketched in the preceding section the ways in which it gains content. The basic measure is: what people do, or are unwilling to do, to themselves and their friends. For example: In 1944, Allied air forces followed a policy of precision bombing when attacking German targets in France, and a policy of blind or other imprecise bombing when attacking German military targets in Germany.[59] Thus they showed themselves willing to impose on German noncombatants a level of incidental harm and death which they were not willing to impose on French civilians. This was unfair; the collateral damage to German civilians was, therefore, disproportionate.

Are there prudential as well as moral constraints on the conduct of war once it has begun? Here I take "prudential" in its modern meaning: in my/our own interests. Doubtless sane leaders will regulate their decisions with an eye to the consequences for themselves and their community. But the tradition is quite clear that there is no coherent and nonarbitrary prudence apart from a morally regulated, indeed morally directive, prudence which respects *all* the requirements of reasonableness, including fairness and respect for the humanity of *all* persons in every community. So, in the final analysis, it is futile and misleading to investigate a prudence distinct from morality. Machiavellianism, for all its impressive rules of practice and its attractions to the emotions of self-preference and the aesthetics of technique, is a mere rationalization which cannot withstand rational critique. For it cannot justify its horizon, its presupposed demarcation of a range of persons or communities whose well-being it will then take as the measure of prudentially "right" action. The so-called paradoxes of nuclear deterrence are merely one exemplary sign of the unreasonableness of every prudence which falls short of the requirements of morality's first principle.

Morality in Extremity

The remarks in the preceding paragraph indicate the tradition's fundamental response to the question of morality in extremity. For "extremity" denotes the grave and imminent danger that *we* will be overwhelmed or destroyed (unless we take certain measures). The tradition does not suggest that the requirements of morally decent deliberation take no account of such a danger. On the contrary, all the requirements of the Golden Rule are liable to be profoundly affected by the presence and degree of such risks.

The so-called rules of war include many norms which are valid and binding because they have been *adopted* (posited) by custom or agreement or enactment by some body empowered by custom or agreement to make such enactments. This is true not only of modern international conventions, but also of much in the tradition's moral treatises on war, where such norms are described as *de iure gentium* (as distinct from *de iure naturali*).[60] Now, the moral force of positive law, including the *ius gentium* inasmuch as it is positive law, rests on the Golden Rule (taken together with the rational requirement that one be concerned for the well-being of others and thus of the communities to which one belongs). Having taken the benefits of others' compliance with the rules, I cannot fairly renege on one of those rules when it requires compliance from me. But the principle articulated in the preceding sentence, though reasonable and usually decisive, is not absolute. That is to say, it does not apply exceptionlessly. For if the situation now is such that, had it obtained when compliance with some rule by others was in issue, I would not have wanted and expected (demanded) those others to comply, it can be fair for me to withhold my compliance; I can fairly do as I truly would have been willing for others to do in a like case.

So, in principle, those rules of war which depend on custom, agreement, or enactment are liable to be set aside in extremity. On the other hand, the tradition holds that where a rule, though positive (*de iure gentium*, not *de iure naturali*), has been adopted precisely *for* and *with a view to* regulating conduct in situations of extremity, it cannot rightly be set aside. Thus, since the rules of fair trial for a capital crime are designed precisely for the extremity in which persons on trial for such crimes find themselves, those who are convicted on perjured testimony must patiently endure death,[61] and judges who know the truth but after every effort can find no legal way of proving it (or of excluding the false evidence) must follow the rules of evidence and sentence to death someone whom they know to be innocent.[62] So there may well be rules of war which, though positive, are not subject to dispensation in emergency, since they were adopted precisely for that type of extremity.

Moreover, not all "rules of war" are merely positive. Some are true implications of the basic requirements of practical reasonableness, which are morality's (natural law's) foundational principles. And some of those basic requirements entail exceptionless moral norms. What Kant identified as the requirement that one treat human persons always as ends in themselves and never as mere means is a bundling together of the requirement that one never meet injury with injury (even when one could do so fairly), which excludes all acts of mere revenge, and the requirement that one not do evil (such as intentionally to destroy, damage, or impede a basic human good) for the sake of good—each requirement being, in turn, an implication of the first moral principle of openness to integral human fulfillment (love of neighbor as oneself). One of the exceptionless moral norms entailed by the requirement that evil not be done for the sake of good is the norm which excludes intending to kill, and intentionally killing, any (innocent) human being.

But, at least in situations of extremity, would it not be the lesser evil to kill a few innocents (say, hostage children) to prevent the extermination of thousands and the utter ruin of a decent community? The whole tradition, while very attentive to the need to prevent bad consequences and to the bearing of likely bad consequences on duties of fairness, denies the claim that reason can identify such a killing of the innocent as the lesser evil.[63] It accepts the Socratic, Platonic, and Catholic maxim that it is better (a lesser evil) to suffer wrong than to do wrong,[64] and rejects as an understandable but ultimately unreasonable temptation the thought[65] that it is better for one innocent man to be framed and put to death than for the whole people to perish. It accepts that self-defense is a situation of necessity,[66] but rejects as unreasonable and morally false[67] the Roman and Cromwellian maxim that necessity knows no law. Or rather, the maxim is given its proper, subordinate role: necessity (that is, great danger) can entitle one to make an exception to rules adopted for human convenience, or concerning human goods which are not basic; thus rules about fasting and sabbath observance, or about rights of property, can be overridden "by necessity," as fairness suggests and permits.[68] But the basic goods of the human person must be respected unconditionally.

One can find in the tradition occasional statements which clearly face up to the gravity of the matter:

> In such a situation, the law of God, which is also the rule of reason, makes exceptionally high demands. . . . The principles the Church proclaims are not

for some ideal or theoretical world or for humanity in the abstract. They speak directly to the consciences of men and women in this world. They are principles that can on occasion demand heroic self-sacrifice of individuals and nations. For there are situations, for example in war, in which self-defense could not be effective without the commission of acts which must never be done, whatever the consequences. Innocent hostages, for example, must never be killed.[69]

But such statements are less frequent than one would think needful to prepare people to live up to the taxing responsibilities of suffering wrong rather than doing it in situations where everything is or seems to be at stake.

To be sure, the tradition's adherence to exceptionless moral norms is reinforced by faith in God's providence, redemption, and promise of eternal salvation. But it is not logically dependent upon that faith. Nor is it, ultimately, a legalism, in which exceptionless rules might be promoted for fear that allowing exceptions would have bad consequences (for example, by abusive extensions of the permission). It understands itself, rather, as an unconditional adherence to the truth about what reason requires. An understanding and defense of the tradition thus depends upon a critique of claims that reason does not warrant these (or any) exceptionless specific norms.[70]

Resistance to Political Authority

The tradition is not content with so cloudy, euphemistic, and characteristically modern a term as "resistance." The Resistance was trying to overthrow German rule in France, and in conscientious deliberations such a venture deserves to be known for what it is, and distinguished from disobedience, "civil" or otherwise.

The tradition's reflections on the forcible overthrow of governments proceed in the same dialectic of private right and public authority, of defense and punishment, as its reflections on war between nations. For such overthrow is truly a warlike venture. There are two main sorts of unjust government which might rightly be overthrown: (1) governments which seized power unjustly and by force and have not been legitimized by effluxion of time and absence of alternatives, and (2) governments which came to power lawfully but govern with manifest gross injustice (looting, murdering, framing, etc.).[71] If a government of either type pursues certain private citizens in an attempt to kill or mutilate them, they can rightly use force in the exercise of their rights of self-defense, and doing so is not necessarily made unacceptable by the fact that it will have the side effect of killing even the supreme ruler.[72]

But no private citizen, as such, can rightly undertake to kill any or all of the rulers, as punishment (or revenge) for their wrongdoing, however wicked, any more than private citizens can rightly kill a well-known murderer on the score that they are administering capital punishment (or vengeance).[73]

Still, might not such a citizen claim to be defending the community against the future crimes of the government? In the case where the government had come to power justly or acquired a moral entitlement to govern, the answer given by the tradition was: yes, if the wrongs such a citizen seeks to prevent are violent, but not otherwise; for in any other case, the attempt amounts to levying offensive war, which is never within private authority, any more than a private citizen can rightly resort to personal violence to incapacitate a forger. In the case where the government came to power illegitimately and remains illegitimate, the tradition is willing to treat the government's acts of ruling, however peaceful in themselves, as amounting to a continuing act of violent injustice against the community (banditry). Accordingly, unless the community by some communal act makes it clear that it wishes no such deliverance, any private individual has the tacit and assumed public authority and constructive consent needed to seek an illegitimate government's violent overthrow, not as an act of punishment but as defense of self, country, and every innocent member of the community.[74] Such an act must, of course, satisfy all the other relevant requirements of proper motivation, exhaustion of alternatives, prospect of success, and fairness in accepting the foreseeable bad side effects.[75]

The risk that any attempt to overthrow a government by force will have very bad side effects is often great. The tradition, for the most part, inculcates caution and emphasizes the general desirability of preferring nonviolent or "passive" forms of resistance, always within the context of a wider teaching that government and positive law create moral obligations which, though by no means absolute or indefeasible or invariably strong, are significant and prevail over the contrary inclinations and desires of subjects in all cases save where the exercise of governmental power in question is certainly unjust. The tradition also recognizes other cases of justifiable disobedience, short of revolutionary violence intended to overthrow—that is, acts of war against—an unjust regime.

First, there is the important class of cases where administrative or legal requirements demand the performance of immoral acts (to surrender Jews to the Nazi authorities, for example). Violation of such requirements is both permissible and obligatory.

Second, government property may be specifically dedicated to wicked activities: concentration camps, slave ships, abortoria, human-embryo experimentation equipment, nuclear weaponry deployed for deterrence by a strategy involving city-swapping and final counter-value retaliation, etc. In circumstances where destroying the property and impeding the evil activities would be likely to save some persons from serious injustice, those actions would be justified.

Third, there is civil disobedience strictly so called. This involves essentially (1) overt violation of a law (2) to express one's protest against that law, or against something public closely connected with some application of that law, together with (3) ready submission to the law's sanctions (a submission not morally required in the other classes of justifiable disobedience). The violation must not involve doing anything otherwise immoral, and its manner and circumstances must make it clear to observers not only that it *symbolizes* opposition to some important and clearly identified matter of law or policy, but also that this opposition seeks justice, not advantage. Since civil disobedience must not involve doing anything otherwise immoral, its justification does not cover use of force against any person. Nor does it cover the destruction of property which is at all closely connected with the well-being of individual persons who would be damaged by its destruction, removal, or temporary or permanent inaccessibility. Above all, it shuns the maxim "Evil may be done that [greater] good may come of it"; indeed, that is the maxim which underpins most (though not all) attempted justifications of the laws or policies or proposals which are the objects of the civilly disobedient protest. So-called civil disobedience will be corrupted and corrupting if the campaigners subscribe to that maxim and so are willing to do real harm, not in self-defense but to advance their cause. The "harms" one does in justifiable civil disobedience must be actions which, in their full context (as set out in the definition just given), are of a type accepted by one's upright fellow citizens as essentially no more than vivid expressions of authentic moral-political concerns, and thus as not truly harms. The essential analogy here is with the blows given and received on the football field, or the touchings and jostlings in a rush- hour crowd; in their full context these are not harms, even though in other contexts they would constitute assaults.[76]

The most fundamental point and justification of civil disobedience is to *show* that the wickedness of the laws or policies in question takes them outside the ordinary web of politics and law, and undermines the very legitimacy of the state or government itself—a legitimacy founded on justice, not on calculations of advantage in which the lives of innocents might be directly sacrificed in the interests of others.

Attitudes toward War and Nonviolence

The tradition emerged and flourished in coexistence with a body of customary laws (*ius gentium*) which it in part reformed but in part
accepted with a complacency which now seems disconcerting. But at
no time was the tradition an apologia for war. Rather, its thrust has
been, and ever more clearly is, to teach that wars are *certainly unjustified*
unless a number of conditions are satisfied. It involves no belief that
many wars are just, or that the conduct of any war is in fact free from
wicked injustice. Even in teaching (as it used to do but now scarcely
does) that offensive war could be justified to punish guilty rulers and
their agents, the tradition required that war be the last resort, initiated
only after communications, negotiations, and where practicable a
ceding of rights for the sake of peace.

The tradition is still developing, on the basis of its own fundamentals. Those fundamentals entail, I think, that war can be justified only as
defense. In the absence of a world government, no state or political
community or ruler can rightly claim the authority to punish; the custom on which that authority was formerly rested[77] should now be
regarded as immoral and ineffective. To purport to exercise such authority, in these circumstances, is to do no more than to reproduce the
practice of feuding, writ large. And if there were a worldwide government, its rulers' justifiable powers against communities would be
police powers: to take steps to bring offending individuals to justice,
and to defend themselves and overcome resistance in the course of taking those steps, but not to administer punishment to whole communities, or to punish individuals otherwise than by impartial judicial trial
and public sentence.

As it reaches this point in its development, one can discern that the
tradition's fundamentals implicitly entail the rejection of a belief which
is explicit not only in the tradition but also in both classic pacifism and
"political realism"—the belief that war must involve *intending to kill*.
The act- analysis involved in Aquinas's discussion of private self-defense entails, as Aquinas makes clear, that defensive acts foreseen to be
likely or even certain to kill can nonetheless be done without any intent
to kill. One's choice in choosing such an act of defense need only be to
stop the attack, accepting as a side effect the attacker's death, unavoidably caused by the only available effective defensive measure. Such
choices do not violate the exceptionless moral norm excluding every
choice to destroy a basic human good. They will be justifiable choices
only if they also involve no violation of any other requirement, especially the requirement of fairness: a deadly deed cannot be fairly chosen

to fend off a harmless blow; those who are themselves acting unjustly cannot fairly resort to deadly force to resist someone reasonably trying to apprehend them.

And the structure of the action of political societies can be the same as that of individuals' acts of self-defense. Deadly deeds can be chosen, not with the precise object of killing those (other societies and their members) who are using force to back their challenge to just order, but simply to thwart that challenge. If the social act is limited to the use of only that force necessary to accomplish its appropriate purpose, the side effect of the death of those challenging the society's just order can rightly be accepted.[78] The distinction between innocents (combatants) and noninnocents (noncombatants) remains: lethal force may rightly be used against persons whose behavior is part of the enemy society's wrongful use of force (against combatants), but not against others. The innocent (noncombatants, those not participating in the use of force against just order) cannot rightly be made the objects of lethal force.

The tradition, even as substantially developed and refined by the exclusion of punitive justifications for war and of intent to kill in war, wholly excludes pacifism—that is, the claim that lethal force can never be rightly used. Pacifism is not to be found in the New Testament[79] (in which the Catholic understanding of natural law already emerges), read as an integrated whole. What does there emerge is the vocation of some individuals and groups to nonviolence (unconditional abstention from such use of force) in witness to the truths that peace, like all true goods, is a gift from above—of divine grace working in a privileged way by healing mercy and reconciliation—and that war, though its point is peace, can never be the efficient cause of peace.

Notes

1. Tacitus *Agricola* 30, imagining a speech by a British chieftain: "They [the Romans] make a wilderness and call it peace."

2. Cf. Augustine *De Civitate Dei* 19.12.

3. Ibid. 19.13: "Pax omnium rerum, tranquillitas ordinis. Ordo est parium disapariumque rerum sua cuique loca tribuens dispositio."

4. Aquinas *Summa Theologiae* II-II q. 37 aa. 1 & 2 (*discordia in corde*).

5. Ibid. II-II q. 38 aa. 1 & 2 (*contentio in ore*).

6. Ibid. II-II q. 41 aa. 1 & 2 (*rixa*).

7. Ibid. II-II q. 42 aa. 1 & 2 (*seditio*).

8. The tradition is scarcely concerned with formulating a definition of war more satisfying than Cicero's *decertare per vim*, "contending by force" (*De officiis* 1.11.34).

9. On the many forms of war in a general sense, see Francisco Suarez *De bello* prol., in Gwladys L. Williams et al., trans., Suarez, *Selections from Three Works* (Oxford: Oxford University Press, 1944), 800.

10. "We wage war to gain peace. Be peaceful, therefore, even while you are at war, so that in overcoming those whom you are fighting you may bring them to the benefits of peace." Augustine *Epist. 189 ad Bonifacium* 6, cited in Aquinas *Summa Theologiae* II-II q. 40 a. 1 ad 3. See also II-II q. 29 a. 2 ad 2.

11. "Perfect peace consists in the perfect enjoyment of the supreme good, . . . the rational creature's last end." *Summa Theologiae* II-II q. 29 a. 2 ad 4.

12. See, for example, Germain Grisez, Joseph Boyle, and John Finnis, "Practical Principles, Moral Truth, and Ultimate Ends," *American Journal of Jurisprudence* 32 (1987): 99–151 at 125–31.

13. See Aquinas *Summa Theologiae* I-II q. 100 a. 3 ad 1.

14. In ibid. II-II q. 41 (*de bello*), and embedded in qq. 34–43 (vices opposed to *caritas*); see prol. to q. 43. Suarez *De Bello* disp. 13 in tract. 3 (*De Caritate*) in his *De Triplice Virtute Theologica* (1621).

15. Aquinas *Summa Theologiae* II-II q. 29 a. 3 ad 3.

16. See note 10 above; also Plato *Laws* 1.628d–e; 7.803c–d; Aristotle *Nicomachean Ethics* 10.7.1177b5.

17. Leo XIII, Apostolic Letter *Nostis Errorem*, in *Acta Leonis XIII*, vol. 9 (Rome, 1890), 48: "There should be sought for peace foundations both firmer and more in keeping with nature: because, while it is allowed consistently with nature to defend one's right by force and arms, *nature does not allow that force be an efficient cause of right*. For peace consists in the tranquillity of order, and so, like the concord of private persons, that of rulers is grounded above all in justice and charity" (my trans.; emphasis added).

18. The example, aside from the military purpose, is from Aristotle and Aquinas: Aquinas *In II Phys.* lect. 8 (no. 214); *In VII Meta.* lect. 6 (no. 1382); *In XI Meta.* lect. 8 (nos. 2269, 2284).

19. Alexander of Hales *Summa Theologica* 3.466, carefully analyzed in Jonathan Barnes, "The Just War," in Norman Kretzmann, Anthony Kenny, and Jan Pinborg, eds., *The Cambridge History of Later Medieval Philosophy* (Cambridge: Cambridge University Press, 1982), 773–82.

20. Aquinas *Summa Theologiae* II-II q. 40 a. 1c, quoting (in a slightly garbled form) Augustine *Quaestiones in Heptateuchum* 6.10; and see Barnes, "The Just War," 778.

21. Suarez *De Bello* 4.1 (Williams, trans., p. 816).

22. "Even when a legitimate authority declares war, and there is *causa iusta*, it can be the case that the war is made immoral/illicit by wrongful *intentio*." Aquinas *Summa Theologiae* II-II q. 40 a. 1c.

23. See John Finnis, Joseph Boyle, and Germain Grisez, *Nuclear Deterrence, Morality and Realism* (Oxford: Oxford University Press, 1987), 120–23, 131, 288, 343– 44; John Finnis, "Persons and Their Associations," *Proceedings of the Aristotelian Society*, supp. vol. 63 (1989): 267–74.

24. "Nocendi cupiditas, ulciscendi crudelitas, impacatus et implacabilis animus, feritas rebellandi, libido dominandi, et si qua similia, haec sunt quae

in bellis iure culpantur." Augustine *Contra Faustum* 22.74; Aquinas *Summa Theologiae* II-II q. 40 a. 1c.

25. See, for example, Plato *Laws* 4.715e–716d; cf. Plato *Republic* 6.500c.

26. Aquinas *Summa Theologiae* II-II q. 40 a. 1c: "Sicut licite defendunt eam [rempublicam] materiali gladio contra interiores quidem perturbatores, dum malefactores puniunt, secundum illud Apostoli, `Non sine causa gladium portat: minister enim Dei est, vindex in iram ei qui male agit,' ita etiam gladio bellico ad eos pertinet rempublicam tueri ab exterioribus hostibus."

27. Suarez *De Bello* 1.6 (Williams, trans., p. 804); cf. Vitoria *De Iure Belli* (1539) sec. 13; trans. in Vitoria, *Political Writings*, ed. A. Pagden and A. Lawrance (Cambridge: Cambridge University Press, 1991), 303.

28. Vitoria *De Iure Belli* sec. 1 (Pagden and Lawrance, eds., p. 297); Suarez *De Bello* 1.4, 6 (Williams, trans., pp. 803, 804).

29. Vitoria *De Iure Belli* secs. 1, 44 (Pagden and Lawrance, eds., pp. 297, 319; but note that the editors often mistranslate *vindicatio* and its cognates as "revenge"; even "vengeance" is, in modern English, misleading as a translation of *vindicatio*); Suarez *De Bello* 1.5 (Williams, trans., pp. 803–4).

30. Thus Vitoria *De Iure Belli* sec. 3 (Pagden and Lawrance, eds., p. 299): "Any person, even a private citizen, may declare and wage defensive war."

31. Suarez *De Bello* 2.2 (Williams, trans., p. 807) and 4.7 (p. 820); cf. Vitoria *De Iure Belli* sec. 5 (Pagden and Lawrance, eds., p. 300). Behind them, Augustine *De Civitate Dei* 1.17, 21. Contrast the non-Catholic tradition following Grotius *De Iure Belli ac Pacis* (1625) 2.20.8.2, in Grotius, *The Law of War and Peace*, trans. Francis W. Kelsey (Oxford: Oxford University Press, 1925), 472, and thence Locke, *Two Treatises of Civil Government* (1689–90), 2.2.7.

32. Cicero *De officiis* 1.11.36–37.

33. Suarez *De Bello* 4.6, 7 (Williams, trans., p. 819).

34. This is denied by some; for example, A. Ottaviani, *Compendium iuris publici ecclesiastici*, 4th ed. (Vatican Polyglot Press, 1954), 88.

35. Vitoria *De iure belli* sec. 3 (Pagden and Lawrance, eds., p. 299); contrast, however, sec. 5 (p. 300) and Vitoria *De Bello: On St. Thomas Aquinas, Summa Theologica, Secunda Secundae, Question 40*, in James Brown Scott, ed., *Francisco de Vitoria and His Law of Nations* (Oxford: Oxford University Press, 1934), cxvi: "It is impermissible for a private person to avenge himself *or to reclaim his own property* save through the judge."

36. Vitoria "Lecture on the Evangelization of Unbelievers" (1534–35) para. 3, in *Political Writings*, 347; "On Dietary Laws, or Self-Restraint" (1538), in *Political Writings*, 225–26; *De Indis* (1539) para. 15, in *Political Writings*, 288–89.

37. Vitoria "Lecture on the Evangelization of Unbelievers," in *Political Writings*, 347.

38. Vitoria *De Iure Belli* sec. 1 (Pagden and Lawrance, eds., p. 298); see also sec. 5 (p. 300).

39. Ibid. sec. 9 (Pagden and Lawrance, eds., p. 302).

40. Suarez *De Bello* 2.1 (Williams, trans., p. 806, emphasis added).

41. For example, Suarez *De Bello* 2.3 (Williams, trans., p. 807).

42. Barnes, "The Just War," 776–77 and 775 n. 23; Anthony Regan, *Thou Shalt Not Kill* (Dublin: Mercier, 1979), 77–79; Finnis, Boyle, and Grisez, *Nuclear Deterrence, Morality and Realism,* 315 n. 3; Germain Grisez, *Living a Christian Life* (Quincy, Ill.: Franciscan Press, 1993), ch. 11.E.3.b.

43. Pius XII, Christmas Message (24 Dec. 1944), *Acta Apostolicae Sedis* 37 (1945): 18, teaches that there is a duty to ban "wars of aggression as legitimate solutions of international disputes and as a means toward realizing national aspirations." Pius XII, Christmas Message (24 Dec. 1948), *Acta Apostolicae Sedis* 41 (1949): 12–13, teaches: "Every war of aggression against those goods which the Divine plan for peace obliges men unconditionally to respect and guarantee, and accordingly to protect and defend, is a sin, a crime, and an outrage against the majesty of God, the Creator and Ordainer of the world." John XXIII, *Pacem in Terris, Acta Apostolicae Sedis* 55 (1963): 291, teaches: "In this age which boasts of its atomic power, it no longer makes sense to maintain that war is a fit instrument with which to repair the violation of justice." Noting Pope John's point, Vatican II explains how "the horror and perversity of war are immensely magnified by the multiplication of scientific weapons," and draws the conclusion: "All these considerations compel us to undertake an evaluation of war with an entirely new attitude." *Gaudium et Spes* (1965), para. 80, with note 2 (note 258 in the Abbott ed.). In para. 79, the Council states: "As long as the danger of war remains and there is no competent and sufficiently powerful authority at the international level, governments cannot be denied the right *to legitimate defense* once every means of peaceful settlement has been exhausted. Therefore, government authorities and others who share public responsibility have the duty to protect the welfare of the people entrusted to their care and to conduct such grave matters soberly. But it is one thing to undertake military action for the *just defense of the people,* and something else again to seek the subjugation of other nations" (emphasis added). None of these statements unambiguously repudiates the tradition's constant teaching that punitive and, in that sense, offensive war can be justified.

44. Grisez, *Living a Christian Life,* ch. 11.E.3.b; Augustine Regan, "The Worth of Human Life," *Studia moralia* 6 (1968): 241–43; Ottaviani, *Compendium Iuris,* 88.

45. John XXIII, *Pacem in Terris,* paras. 43–46, in *Acta Apostolicae Sedis* 55 (1963): 291–94.

46. Vitoria *De Iure Belli* sec. 19 (Pagden and Lawrance, eds., p. 305) and sec. 46 (p. 320); but cf. sec. 5 (p. 300), seeking to derive the punitive authority of states from their self-sufficiency; Suarez *De Legibus* (1612) 2.19.8 (Williams, trans., p. 348):

> The law of war—in so far as that law rests upon the power possessed by a given state . . . for the punishment, avenging (*vindicandam*), or reparation of an injury inflicted upon it by another state—would seem to pertain properly to the *ius gentium.* For it was not indispensable by virtue of natural reason alone that the power in question should exist within an injured state, since men could have established some other mode of inflicting punishment, or entrusted that power to some prince and quasi-arbitrator with coercive

power. Nevertheless, since the mode in question, which is at present in practice, is easier and more in conformity with nature, it has been adopted by custom (*usu*) and is just to the extent that it may not rightfully be resisted. In the same class I place slavery.

47. Suarez *De Legibus* 2.19.8 (Williams, trans., p. 348).

48. See, for example, Suarez *De Bello* 3.8 (Williams, trans., p. 821).

49. Pius XII, Address to Military Doctors (19 Oct. 1953), in *Acta Apostolicae Sedis* 45 (1953): 748–49; United States National Conference of Catholic Bishops, *The Challenge of Peace*, Pastoral Letter of 3 May 1983 (Washington D.C.: U.S. Catholic Conference, 1983), paras. 98–99.

50. Ibid., para. 96 (exhaustion of peaceful alternatives).

51. See Finnis, Boyle, and Grisez, *Nuclear Deterrence, Morality and Realism*, chap. 9.

52. *The Challenge of Peace*, para. 105.

53. Finnis, Boyle, and Grisez, *Nuclear Deterrence, Morality and Realism*, esp. chap. 4.

54. See Finnis, Boyle, and Grisez, *Nuclear Deterrence, Morality and Realism*, chap. 5, on the impossibility of bluff in a complex society.

55. Aquinas *Summa Theologiae* II-II q. 64 a. 6.

56. Ibid. II-II q. 40 a. 3; see also q. 110 a. 3. Likewise Suarez *De Bello* 7.23 (Williams, trans., p. 852).

57. Vitoria *De Iure Belli* secs. 34–37 (Pagden and Lawrance, eds., pp. 314–17); Suarez *De Bello* 7.6, 15 (Williams, trans., pp. 840, 845); *The Challenge of Peace* (n. 49 above), paras. 104–5.

58. Thus "direct" killing of the innocent is explained as killing either as an end or as a means by Pius XII (12 Nov. 1944, in *Discoursi e radiomessaggi* 6:191–92); by Paul VI (*Humanae Vitae* [1968], n. 14); and by the Congregation for the Doctrine of the Faith (*De Abortu Procurato*, 18 Nov. 1974, para. 7; *Donum Vitae*, 22 Feb. 1987, n. 20). For similar explanations of "direct" in terms of "as an end or as a means," see Pius XII, *Acta Apostolicae Sedis* 43 (1951): 838 (killing) and 843–44 (sterilization), and *Acta Apostolicae Sedis* 49 (1957): 146 (euthanasia).

59. Finnis, Boyle, and Grisez, *Nuclear Deterrence, Morality and Realism*, 39–40, 264–65, 271–72. The attacks to which I am here referring are, of course, not the regular British obliteration or "area" bombing raids of 1942–45, directed at cities and their inhabitants as such, but attacks on railway yards or on the submarines congregated at Kiel, etc.

60. For example, Vitoria *De Iure Belli* sec. 19 (Pagden and Lawrance, eds., p. 305); Suarez *De Bello* 7.7 (Williams, trans., pp. 820–41) and, very clearly and fundamentally, *De Legibus* 2.19.8 (quoted above, n. 46).

61. Suarez *De Bello* 9.5 (Williams, trans., p. 859).

62. Aquinas *Summa Theologiae* II-II q. 64 a. 6 ad 3; q. 67 a. 2.

63. On the killing of innocent hostages, see Vitoria *De Iure Belli* sec. 43 (Pagden and Lawrance, eds., p. 319).

64. Plato *Gorgias* 508e–509d; Vatican II, *Gaudium et Spes*, para. 27; see John Finnis, *Fundamentals of Ethics* (Oxford: Oxford University Press and Washington,

D.C.: Georgetown University Press, 1983), 112–20; Finnis, *Moral Absolutes* (Washington, D.C.: Catholic University of America Press, 1991), 47–51.

65. Articulated for the tradition in John 1:50; 18:14.

66. Vitoria *De Iure Belli* secs. 1 (Pagden and Lawrance, eds., p. 298), 19 (p. 305); Suarez *De Bello* 1.4 (Williams, trans., p. 803); 4.10 (p. 823).

67. See Finnis, *Moral Absolutes*, 51–55; Finnis, Boyle, and Grisez, *Nuclear Deterrence, Morality and Realism*, chap. 9.

68. Grotius, though not Catholic, states the tradition accurately enough: "'Necessity,' says Seneca, . . . 'the great resource of human weakness, breaks every law,' meaning, of course, every human law, or law constituted after the fashion of human law." *De Iure Belli ac Pacis* 2.2.6.4 (Kelsey, trans., pp. 193–94). In 1.4.7.1 (pp. 148– 49), he exemplifies the latter category by pointing to the divine law of sabbath rest, subject to a tacit exception in cases of extreme necessity. See also 3.1.2.1 (p. 599). In Aquinas, the maxim *necessitas non subditur legi*, necessity is not subject to the law, is used just to make the point that, in an emergency so sudden that there is no time to consult authorized interpreters, it is permissible for the subjects to give to the law an interpretation that they think would have been approved by the lawmaker (assumed to be a morally upright lawmaker). "Keep the city gates shut," for example, can be regarded as subject to an interpretative exception "except to admit your own army in flight from the battlefield." *Summa Theologiae* I-II q. 96 a. 6c & ad 1.

69. Archbishops of Great Britain, "Abortion and the Right to Live," 24 Jan. 1980, para. 24.

70. Such a critique is available in, for example, Finnis, *Moral Absolutes*.

71. Suarez *De Iuramento Fidelitatis Regis Angliae* (1613) 4.1 (Williams, trans., p. 705).

72. Ibid. 4.5 (Williams, trans., p. 709). As always, the side effects of the ruler's death or overthrow remain to be assessed for the fairness or unfairness of incurring them.

73. Ibid. 4.4 (Williams, trans., p. 708).

74. Ibid. 4.11–13 (Williams, trans., p. 714). Aquinas, in his youthful *Commentum in Libros Sententiarum Petri Lombardi* II d. 44 q. 2 a. 2c, treats the killing of Julius Caesar as justifiable on this basis.

75. Aquinas *Commentum in Libros Sententiarum Petri Lombardi* 4.7–9. "The Church's Magisterium admits [recourse to armed struggle] as a last resort to put an end to an obvious and prolonged tyranny which is gravely damaging the fundamental rights of individuals and the common good." Congregation for the Doctrine of the Faith, *Libertatis Conscientiae*, Instruction on Christian Freedom and Liberation, 22 Mar. 1986, para. 79.

76. See further Finnis, Boyle, and Grisez, *Nuclear Deterrence, Morality and Realism*, 354–57.

77. Vitoria *De Iure Belli* sec. 19 (Pagden and Lawrance, eds., p. 305); see the quote from Suarez above, n. 46.

78. See further Finnis, Boyle, and Grisez, *Nuclear Deterrence, Morality and Realism*, 309–19.

79. See Grotius *De Iure Belli ac Pacis* 1.2.6–8 (Kelsey, trans., pp. 61–81).

11

Just War Thinking in Catholic Natural Law

JOSEPH BOYLE

I AM IN SUBSTANTIAL AGREEMENT with the analysis in John Finnis's chapter. Indeed, it is as good a short statement of just war theory within the Catholic natural law tradition as I know of. Given this, I think the most useful contributions I can make are to underline certain points that seem to me to be important, to develop some of the distinctions Finnis makes, and to draw out some of the implications of his analysis. I will also say something more than Finnis does about conscientious objection and the duty of citizens to support their nation's war efforts.

Peace and War

Finnis portrays the natural law tradition as not having been greatly concerned with the definition of war; it appears satisfied with Cicero's unsatisfying "contending by force." Part of the reason is that, although there is a paradigm case of war—a relationship between polities in which one seeks by physical force to thwart some of the other's undertakings and to seize or destroy some of the other's resources—there are variations on the paradigm that raise the same or similar moral questions and are governed by the same principles and many of the same norms. So, the tradition proceeds on the assumption that the effort to develop a general definition is not of much help and may in fact mislead.

Furthermore, within the tradition there is a recognition that among the activities that are called "wars," either in ordinary language or according to any definition that is not purely stipulative, there are activities of differing moral character. The idea is that the moral significance of bellicose actions, like that of actions generally, emerges not from a definition of the ordinary usage of terms like war or violence, but from a determination of how actions, considered not as mere behavior but as voluntary undertakings in which people choose to do certain things for the sake of certain benefits, are related to the standard of right reason. By reference to this moral standard, two behaviorally similar or even identical actions, which can both correctly be called wars, can be essentially different from the moral point of view, if done for different purposes or under different circumstances.[1] So, from the perspective of natural law, justified and unjustified wars are not two species of the same genus; they are essentially different kinds of action.

According to Finnis, the relationship of wars to the good of peace is central to the distinction between just and unjust wars. This good is inevitably at stake when warfare is contemplated or undertaken. Other goods are also surely affected, but these are reasonably incorporated into this relational notion. For the norms of justice regulate the harms that may be inflicted on people, their holdings, and their institutions, and justice is a part of the wider social good of peace as understood within the tradition.

Now, the idea of peace that the tradition develops from Augustine is plainly the idea of a basic good, a reason for which action can be undertaken without any further benefit in view.[2] As social animals, human beings have reason to want to form a community with others, to cooperate with them, and to live in harmony with them. Unjustified wars are evil because of the harm they cause to this good and its component parts; even justifiable wars need special justification because of their at least apparent conflict with this good.

But why should this good, rather than some others, be the *point* of war, as Finnis holds the logic of the tradition to require?

To answer this, it is first necessary to underline Finnis's point that there is a kind of peace that is not the real thing, but only an appearance of peace that includes enough of the elements of true peace to provide a reason for acting, organized in such a way as to block the realization of genuine peace. Thus, the harmony one seeks when one undertakes to dominate or enslave others or to satisfy one's desire for vengeance is not peace; these actions may aim at a kind of order and at a form of tranquility, but they block the harmony of wills and the genuine community that peace includes. Perhaps morally unjustified wars inevitably aim at this inadequate kind of peace, but plainly that is not what Finnis is referring to when he claims that peace is the point of war.

His claim plainly is normative: morally justified warfare should aim at peace, should be for the sake of peace. And it is not the fact that peace is a basic human good, an ultimate reason for action, that underlies this claim. For peace has an especially intimate relationship with basic moral principles as understood within natural law. The practical reasonableness prescribed by natural law requires action compatible with a will open to an ideal human community in which all the goods of all people are realized in interpersonal harmony.[3] This is the ideal prescribed by the commandment to love one's neighbors as oneself. It is, among other things, a peaceful community of human beings. Since all upright choice and action must be ordered toward this ideal, all upright choices to engage in warfare must also be so ordered.

In short, within the natural law tradition, wars can be morally justified only if they are morally good actions, that is, justified by basic moral principles; and those principles can be usefully formulated in terms of peace. Both these points are important for situating the natural law approach to warfare in relation to other normative approaches.

First, the dependence of the moral evaluation of any war on moral first principles clarifies both the character and the purpose of natural law reasoning about warfare. This reasoning is an application of the basic principles of morality to the special conditions of warfare and to the particular circumstances of individual wars. Thus, according to the tradition, the precepts governing warfare are neither the result of a generalization from considered judgments about what is acceptable and unacceptable in warfare, nor the result of casuistical reasoning from certain paradigm cases of wars that are plainly wrong and of wars that are plainly justified. The considerable casuistry within the tradition's analyses of war is part of the effort to clarify the character of various bellicose actions to allow a precise application of moral principles to the case at hand.

There is a recognition within the tradition of the complexity of the process of applying moral principles and general moral norms to individual actions.[4] Although the structure of this reasoning is deductive, the clarification of the kind of action to be evaluated is achieved by informal conceptual analysis.[5] Moreover, this deductive and analytical procedure can result only in the evaluation of an action as described, that is, in the evaluation of an action insofar as it is an action of a certain kind. Since further redescription of the individual action being evaluated can in many cases turn up features that might cause a change in the action's moral evaluation, and since there is no rationally determined limit to the possibility for redescribing an action, there remains an aspect of moral evaluation not reducible to rational analysis.[6]

Nevertheless, the application of moral principles to individual actions is at the heart of moral analysis according to natural law. For the correct application of moral principles to individual actions is necessary for the determination that those actions are in accord with moral truth. And the determination of the truth of concrete moral judgments, including those about warfare, is the purpose of moral analysis on the natural law conception.

Thus, on the natural law conception, the judgment that a given war meets the standards for a just war is in fact the judgment that the choice to undertake the war is in accord with moral truth. This means that the communal choice of a nation to undertake a war that is just is a morally good choice, and that the choices of soldiers and other citizens to support that communal choice are to that extent morally good. These choices are not necessary compromises with evil, nor are they immoral choices constrained from even greater evil by conventional rules; rather, they are choices completely in accord with moral truth. The determination of the moral truth as applied to given wars is the purpose of normative analysis on the natural law conception, and no war that fails to meet the standards of moral truth can be justified by these standards.

Second, the formulation of moral principles in terms of peace is useful for situating the natural law tradition's approach to war in relation to pacifism, especially Christian pacifism. For this formulation makes clear that any war that is morally justified must be at a deep level compatible with and in the service of peace. This suggests that disagreements between pacifists and natural law theorists are not located at the level of fundamental moral principle, but emerge within the reasoning from principles to concrete moral evaluation.

This suggestion is underlined by the following implication of Finnis's analysis. The pacific character of the principles governing war, together with the *bonum ex integra causa* principle, which, as Finnis explains, requires that a morally good act be in every aspect in accord with reason,[7] implies that a justified war is one that involves no choice or intention incompatible with the reality of peace.

This looks paradoxical: taking up arms against others seems to involve choosing something contrary to peace with them, even if for the sake of future peace with them. No doubt, many, perhaps most, wars are fought with such intentions, and pacifists are correct in objecting that those wars are immoral—instances of doing evil so that good might come of it. But not all wars need involve such intentions: if peace does not exist or must be protected, and if one's bellicose actions are necessary to bring it about or to protect it, then those actions need involve no choice or intention contrary to peace. Moral principles do not appear to exclude war in these conditions.

Pacifists deny this conclusion. But the fact that pacifists and natural law theorists agree in rejecting, for reasons that appear similar, a considerable class of wars suggests that the disagreement here is not over moral principles, but over concerns whether the conditions ever obtain that allow war to be fought compatibly with moral principles. In particular, it would seem that pacifists reject the natural law conclusion because they believe that the dispositions of nations and of individual soldiers are such that when they fight, they must inevitably turn their hearts against peace, even when defending or protecting it. If warriors necessarily willed to harm their enemies when fighting them, then the pacifist claim to inevitability would be justified. But as Finnis indicates, the natural law tradition's view of justified killing in warfare can be understood as excluding the intent to kill,[8] and this can be generalized to apply to other harms inflicted on one's enemies.

If this analysis is correct, a pacifist claim that choosing to engage in warfare inevitably involves turning one's heart against peace cannot be grounded in the essential intentional structures of the choices and acts of belligerents. Thus, one crucial point of disagreement between pacifists and natural law theorists is the truth of the pacifist claim that warfare inevitably involves choices incompatible with the good of peace. The truth of this claim is not evident, but neither is its falsity.

Motive or Intention

Finnis plainly holds that intentions are intrinsic to actions as voluntary undertakings. He also assumes that voluntary undertakings are the subject of moral evaluation. The intention essential to a human action as voluntary is one's active interest in some benefit for the sake of which one chooses to do something. So what one intends, strictly speaking, is a benefit, what the reason for which one acts promises as a desirable outcome.[9] This nonbehavioristic conception of human action often makes it difficult to determine from a third-person perspective what action a person, or a group of persons acting jointly, is performing. But these difficulties do not render impossible third-person identification of actions, and they surely do not preclude the possibility that individuals and groups, aware of their own practical reasoning and choices, can accurately identify their acts as voluntary undertakings. So, the conception of human action accepted by many within the natural law tradition is not incoherent.

Moreover, the tradition's judgment that actions so characterized are the subject of moral evaluation is not arbitrary, but is a function of a coherent, if controversial, understanding of the purpose of moral evaluation. As noted above, according to the natural law conception, the purpose of moral evaluation is to determine the truth of concrete moral judgments, and this purpose is realized when the morally relevant features of actions are correctly related to the principles of right reason. Why is it important that human actions be guided by moral truth, and so be determined to accord with right reason? The tradition's answer, more often left tacit than explicitly articulated, is that providing this kind of direction for human action is the only way human action as voluntary, as an exercise of the rationality and freedom in virtue of which humans are in God's image, can be rationally guided and genuinely fulfilling.[10]

In short, there are various conceptions of morality and its purposes, but the natural law conception is one according to which the point of morality is to allow one's practical reasoning and choices to be fully intelligent and good. Morality, on this conception, is not a constraining device to cause people to avoid the most socially destructive behavior of which they are capable or to get them to be as good as they can be without their own cooperation; rather, it serves to provide fully rational guidance for choices, for actions as voluntary undertakings.

It is perhaps worth noting that the doctrine of the double effect, an important component of the natural law casuistry of warfare, presupposes the tradition's conceptions of human action and of morality, but is neither equivalent to these conceptions nor implied by them. According to this doctrine, the difference between what a person intends and the side effects a person knowingly brings about in acting can have a decisive moral significance. For example, the just war requirement of noncombatant immunity is a prohibition of intentional attacks on noncombatants. The doctrine of double effect constrains the absolute prohibition to that of intentional attacks, and allows that, if certain other conditions are fulfilled, actions that predictably lead to the deaths of noncombatants may be undertaken.

Clearly, this doctrine is hardly intelligible without a conception of human action and morality like that held by the natural law tradition. Still, the attribution of decisive moral significance to the distinction between what is intended and what is knowingly brought about as a side effect is not a feature of these general ideas about action and morality. For it is clear that all the voluntary aspects of actions are governed by moral norms, not simply those included within one's intention. The significance of this distinction arises because there are absolute prohibitions, and those prohibitions cannot reasonably be extended to exclude bringing about harmful side effects.[11]

Given the natural law conception of human action and of the purpose of moral evaluation, it is not surprising that natural law statements of the conditions for just war include a requirement of right intention. But a puzzle emerges from standard statements of these conditions because of the addition of a condition requiring just cause. As Finnis notes, what one's reason for action promises and what one intends in acting are identical: why do Aquinas and the subsequent tradition treat right intention and just cause as two distinct conditions for the justifiability of a war? The assumption is that the just cause is the reason for action and that the benefit it promises is what one intends. Finnis's answer is that Aquinas had a technical, legal meaning for just cause according to which the just cause is not a justifying reason.[12] That seems plausible.

But I think there is a reason, compatible with the one Finnis proposes, for having two separate conditions here that would hold even if just cause were taken to be the justifying reason. Without the condition of right intention, the connection between one's action and the reason that justifies it remains contingent, and this allows for the possibility that just cause could be only a pretext or excuse for bellicose action aimed at some further goal beyond that which one's justifying reason supports, or at some completely independent goal that can be pursued using the justifying reason as a rationalization only. In other words, only to the extent that one acts for goals supported by the justifying reason, insofar as they are supported by it, and only for them, is one's bellicose action morally justified.

This does not mean that one cannot engage in war in anticipation of benefits that go beyond one's justified war aims. Those aims are goals that instantiate, often in a minimal way, the good of peace. Further goals that instantiate that good and that can be seen as possibilities if one's war aims are realized are thus justified if the war aims are. Thus, for example, the fact that in the 1991 Gulf War, the United States was motivated by the prospect of improved economic and political relations with some Gulf nations should its efforts to evict the Iraqis from Kuwait succeed does not seem to be the kind of further intention that violates the condition of right intention. That intention was for actions and benefits that became real prospects once the normal international relationships were restored by the successful achievement of the war aims. This kind of intention, which looks ahead to the future benefits of the peace created by achieving justified war aims, seems to me unavoidable and legitimate. The presence of such intentions has no tendency to suggest that the justifying reasons for war, and the specific goals they legitimize, are pretexts or rationalizations.

Acting with some intentions does, however, render one's justifying reason a mere pretext or rationalization. Suppose, for example, that the underlying motivation for the American involvement in the 1991 Gulf War were not the defense of Kuwait, but a desire to destroy Iraq's economic and industrial capacity to prevent future aggression, or to punish an erstwhile ally for insubordination. If one of these were the intention behind the war, then it would fail the condition of right intention, assuming (as I do) that intending these things is not justified. This would be so even though a just cause existed, and even if care were taken to carry out the war aims and to limit, for various reasons such as international opinion, military actions to those which carry out these aims. For in this scenario, the goals are pursued not as instantiating the justifying reason, but insofar as they instantiate the unjustified reasons. Indeed, when Elizabeth Anscombe in 1939 objected to the British decision to go to war with Germany, allegedly in behalf of Poland, her worry was not that there was no just cause available, but that it was not the reason for which Britain fought.[13]

Grounds for War

Finnis rejects the older tradition's belief that in addition to defensive grounds, the war of one nation against another can be justified on retributive grounds as a kind of punishment for wrongdoers. Representatives of the tradition in the last fifty years accept this judgment. But Finnis also rejects the reason commonly given, namely, that modern war is too destructive to be used except as a means of defense. His proposal is that the underlying rationale for retributive warfare is mistaken; the authority required to rightly punish other polities and those who act for them does not exist (although something similar to it would exist if there were a world government).

The rejection of retributive justice as a justifying ground for warfare seems to me to involve more than tinkering with the theoretical foundations of the natural law approach to war and peace. The idea is not that, although punishment is out as a justification, defense is a broader notion than we thought; with this approach, things would remain pretty much as they were at the practical level, except that the rationale of defense would now bear the justificatory weight that punishment used to bear. It is true that the notion of defense is broader than the older tradition assumed, but it is neither completely elastic nor coextensive with the notion of punishment.

One practically important respect in which the notions of defense and punishment differ is in the way they are related to past wrongs. A person cannot defend against a wrong already perpetrated, although he or she can defend against its continuing consequences. But a person can, and under the proper circumstances may, punish another for a wrong already perpetrated. Thus, if legitimate grounds for war are limited to defensive considerations, then just to the extent that standing grievances among polities are *past* wrongs, and not ongoing injustices, they are not legitimate grounds for war. There is no defending against them. (I am not suggesting that the casuistry needed to apply this distinction would be easy.)

Furthermore, and perhaps more importantly, defensive grounds limit the further goals one can adopt as a justified defensive war unfolds. The only deterrence one can legitimately seek is that which flows from successful defense, and the only punishment one can seek is that which is involved in successful defense. Thus, efforts to inflict punishment on the enemy beyond what defense justifies are immoral, as are efforts that go beyond what defense justifies to arrange the end of a war so as to put the enemy leaders on trial, or to destroy a polity or a regime. The desire to see war criminals punished is legitimate, and can be acted upon after the war, provided that an authority can be located that has the right to punish. But this desire cannot, if punishment is excluded as a legitimate ground for war, provide a justification for fighting, or for further fighting. I suspect that these limitations are widely ignored in modern warfare, as they were, for example, in the Second World War. They would be hard to maintain if punishment were a legitimate ground for war.

Resistance to Political Authority

In this section of his chapter, Finnis does not discuss the issue of conscientious objection. I will say something about this because it falls squarely in the middle of the natural law account of political authority and obedience. This account, at least according to some readings, has quite permissive implications concerning the responsibilities of individuals, especially soldiers, for their cooperation in war efforts, and in several ways seems to require a subordination of individual, conscientious judgment to the judgment of political leaders.

Alan Donagan has succinctly stated the norms that the natural law tradition regards as decisive in regulating the decisions of individuals in respect to their government's wars: "If it [a given war] is just, it is permissible to volunteer to serve in it, provided no other duty prevents it; and it is impermissible not to accept lawful conscription to serve. If it is unjust, it is impermissible to serve under any circumstances."[14]

These norms make sense only if the citizen is expected to make an independent moral evaluation of the justifiability of the war in which he or she cooperates. So natural law, along with the broader tradition Donagan calls "common morality," rejects the rationalization that Shakespeare puts in the mouth of one of Henry V's soldiers: "We know enough if we know that we are the King's men. Our obedience to the king wipes the crime of it out of us."[15]

The second of Donagan's three norms appears to exclude any interesting form of conscientious objection, that is, any refusal of lawful conscription based on any consideration other than the judgment that the war in question is immoral. Although the third of Donagan's norms states that this is a reason that requires one to refuse service, the second norm certainly suggests that there are no general grounds to which a citizen might appeal as a justification for refusing military service in his or her country's just war. This also has been the standard position of the Catholic tradition, at least up until about 1960.

The assumptions behind this view are worth noting: (1) that in a just war, political society may impose military service on its members; (2) that a citizen drafted for military service has a duty to obey and support the justified decisions of political authority; and (3) that this duty is very hard, if not impossible, to overturn. The first two of these assumptions are deeply embedded in the natural law conception of social life; but I doubt at the third can be justified, however deeply presumptions in favor of the prerogatives of political society may have permeated natural law thinking in the past. I do not see why this duty should be any less defeasible than any other structured and recognized social obligation.

Here are some reasons for being suspicious about this third assumption: the tradition includes an exception for a class of citizens—the clergy.[16] Their social role is such that they must not fight. So, this assumption cannot be accepted in its strongest version, namely, that the duty of citizens to fight in a just war when ordered is impossible to overturn. Moreover, one may also wonder whether reasons similar to those which exempt the clergy from the duty to fight do not also exempt others, either because of the special jobs they have or for other reasons having to do with special commitments they have undertaken. If the clergy is exempt, then why not also monks not in holy orders? If monks, then why not others like doctors or teachers or others whose work seems especially opposed to bloodshed? If these, then why not others who have adopted a particularly pacific or prophetic lifestyle? I doubt there is a good answer to questions like these. More generally, it is not clear why the duties people have as citizens should necessarily or generally trump the other duties they have within the other communities in which they live and work.

So, I think that the recent ecclesiastical statements that call for states to recognize a right of conscientious objection, a right that seems to go beyond protecting an individual who acts on the judgment that the war in question is immoral,[17] are a correct development of the tradition, and that this new teaching is justified by the tradition's growing wariness about excessive deference to the prerogatives of political society and perhaps of the clergy as well. If I am correct, this development does not imply an incipient willingness to accept the view that war is necessarily wrong, or that citizens do not have a real, though defeasible, obligation to fight in their country's just wars.[18] To recognize that a duty is defeasible is not to suggest that it might not exist.

Catholic teaching, then, does not endorse the position that pacifism—that is, the claim that war is always wrong—is a legitimate position. It does, however, appear to endorse the view that a conscientious refusal to fight in one's country's wars is easier to justify than earlier Catholic teaching or natural law theorizing have allowed.

So far, I have ignored the epistemic issues that complicate the efforts of citizens and potential soldiers to evaluate their nation's war. What should one do when one does not know that the war in which one is commanded to fight is unjust, but has doubts about the matter?

The standard answer seems to favor compliance with authority. Walzer quotes Vitoria: "A prince is not able . . . and ought not always to render reasons for the war to his subjects, and if the subjects cannot serve in the war except they are first satisfied of its justice, the state would fall into grave peril."[19] Walzer then goes on to look at the moral situation from the perspective of the draftee: under the circumstances he can hardly be blamed for going along with the authorities.

It is reasonable to refuse to blame those who out of fear of punishment, habits of law-abidingness and patriotism, or immaturity obey the commands of their political leaders. But considerations like these provide an excuse for those who comply, not a justification for the claim that even when in doubt about the justice of the war, they should comply.

Vitoria's brief argument addresses this question of justification, but inconclusively. He rightly notes that political leaders sometimes cannot and sometimes should not render reasons for waging a war to those they govern. But the inability of the leaders to explain the reasons for waging a war, even if this arises from their moral obligations as leaders, does not settle the responsibilities of potential soldiers in doubt about whether it is right to fight. Apparently to deal with this lacuna in his analysis, Vitoria adds that if subjects need to be satisfied of the justice of the war before they may serve, then the state will be in grave peril.[20]

Perhaps Vitoria means this to be a consequentialist argument: the peril of proceeding in this way provides a decisive reason for resolving doubts in favor of the decision of the political leaders. But this argument is problematic within a natural law context. First, it is not clear why, if consequentialist reasoning should be the tiebreaker in cases of doubt, it should not also be used more generally. But, plainly, consequentialist reasoning does not figure prominently in natural law analyses, and there is good reason to think it an alternative approach to moral thinking that is deeply alien to natural law.[21] Second, there is some reason to wonder whether a presumption for settling doubts in favor of the state will generally avoid the kinds of peril Vitoria is worried about, or whether avoiding such perils is generally a good thing.

A docile citizenry may make it easier for a country's leaders to engage in warfare, but that has its own dangers; and facilitating warfare is frequently not a good thing, whether from the perspective of a morally defined conception of the common good or from a consequentialist conception of the overall benefit and harm brought upon those affected by the war.

It remains, therefore, that the presumption that doubts should be settled in favor of the judgment of political leaders must be justified, if it can be, either by something specific to the situation of choice when there is doubt about its moral character, or by something specific to the way political authority figures in such situations. In general, one's responsibility in situations of doubt is to try to resolve the doubt, but in no case to do what one has reason to think might be wrong; for to do this would be to be willing to do what is wrong.

Given these norms for resolving doubts, the role of authority in the process is limited. It is often reasonable for a person to accept the authority of experts concerning judgments within the area of their expertise, even if the person cannot judge for himself or herself about the matter. Thus, the authority of moral advisors, scholars, and others with relevant experience can be important, and sometimes decisive, in settling doubts.

But it is hard to see how authority in areas other than those in which truth is discovered and moral reasoning correctly carried out could be relevant to settling doubts. In particular, it is hard to see how a presumption in favor of the judgment of political authority would figure significantly in a procedure for settling doubts governed by these norms. For political authority is based on the need of a community to act in concert, and so those who have political authority do not have it because of any special expertise in determining the facts or in moral reasoning.

Still, political authority is real, and citizens have a real, though defeasible, obligation to obey the lawful commands of political leaders. This obligation is often relevant to the deliberations of a potential soldier in doubt about the justice of the war in which he is commanded to fight. His obligation to obey this command can be overridden only if a reason is present for thinking that obedience would be immoral. Mere feelings of distaste, worries, or a feeling that what is commanded might be wrong are not sufficient to override the duty to obey. They are not doubts that generate moral dilemmas. Similarly, a conviction that one's political leaders are untrustworthy, that they lie to the country, or that they act with bad will, is not a reason justifying a refusal to obey, unless it is based on evidence. Without evidence, such convictions may be no more than an expression of unwillingness to accept the moral legitimacy of political authority.

Consequently, the authority of political leaders can play a role in the deliberations of the potential soldier in doubt about the justice of the war in which he is commanded to fight. Besides providing part of the context for setting aside putative doubts that do not establish a reason for doubting that a war is just, the authority of political leaders sometimes provides a reason for taking their statements about the justice of the war at face value. When there is no evidence or specific ground for distrusting the statements of political leaders, cooperative citizens will accept them as true, and sometimes that is enough to settle the doubt.

However, if such considerations as these do not settle the doubt, that is, if, after considering fully the obligation to obey legitimate authority and the obligation to accept the authority's credible statements, there remains a reason to think that the war is unjust, then the potential soldier should refuse to participate. For in that situation, the authority of the political leaders would be used precisely to enjoin obedience to a command whose moral legitimacy is in question, and the potential soldier would be commanded to do what he had reason to think was seriously wrong. Since doing what one has reason to think is wrong is itself wrong, one cannot be obliged to obey commands to do such things. Indeed, one is obliged to disobey them.

In a word, the presumption in favor of obeying political authority in conditions of doubt about the justice of a war is a weaker one than Vitoria and many others in the tradition have allowed. The prince is obliged, at least in some circumstances, to "render reasons" to his subjects. As Donagan notes: "War is such a horrible evil that only a very clear and great cause can justify it; and when such a cause exists, it should not be difficult to show it."[22]

Moreover, whatever the prince's obligations, potential soldiers must satisfy themselves that there is no reason to believe that the war they are asked to fight is unjust. So, natural law implies, and natural law theorists should hold, that individual moral judgment, if not "individual volition,"[23] must be brought to bear on the decisions of citizens and potential soldiers about whether to participate in their country's war.

The restriction of individual moral judgment to what citizens can certainly *know* appears to make things easier for political leaders and for citizens. But the effect of this limitation has often been to render just war considerations a dead letter, at least as they figure in individual deliberation.[24] The laxism of this development is obvious, and has brought justified scorn on the just war theorists and religious leaders who defend it.

The central moral problem is that obedience has no tendency to excuse or justify individual action contrary to conscience. For obedience is a form of social cooperation in which one's choice to obey is intelligible only as a part of a social act in which the goals of the polity are pursued. Obedience is justified in this situation only when honest moral reflection reveals no reason to think that there is a crime, and obedience is not morally justified as long as one has a reason for thinking the war is criminal, or as long as one negligently fails to determine whether such a reason exists.

I am not suggesting that one cannot comply with the orders of those who have power over one's life without strictly obeying them, that is, without entering into a form of social cooperation in which one endorses and actively promotes the goals of the powerful party. What the natural law tradition calls "material cooperation" is possible in wartime; without endorsing their government's unjustified war, citizens can cooperate in various ways with the government, even if this cooperation furthers the war effort. This kind of cooperation can be morally justified, and often is for citizens whose support of a war they judge immoral is limited to paying tax and carrying on their lives in a law-abiding way.[25] But the decisions of citizens to fight or to actively support such a war, however reluctant, appear to be acts not of material cooperation but of formal cooperation and obedience.

Notes

1. St. Thomas Aquinas *Summa Theologiae* I-II q. 1 a. 3 ad 3; see also q. 18.

2. See Germain Grisez, Joseph Boyle, and John Finnis, "Practical Principles, Moral Truth, and Ultimate Ends," *American Journal of Jurisprudence* 32 (1987): 103–8.

3. Ibid., 128.

4. See Aquinas *Summa Theologiae* I-II q. 100 a. 3.

5. See Alan Donagan, *The Theory of Morality* (Chicago: University of Chicago Press, 1977), 66–74.

6. See Germain Grisez, *The Way of the Lord Jesus*, vol. 1, *Christian Moral Principles* (Chicago: Franciscan Herald Press, 1983), 259–63.

7. Finnis, previous chapter, under "Motive or Intention."

8. Finnis, previous chapter, under "Attitudes toward War and Non-violence."

9. See Grisez, Boyle, and Finnis, "Practical Principles," 104; Aquinas *Summa Theologiae* I-II qq. 12–13.

10. See Aquinas *Summa Theologiae* I-II prol.

11. See Joseph Boyle, "Who Is Entitled to Double Effect?" *Journal of Medicine and Philosophy* 16 (1991): 475–95.

12. Finnis, previous chapter, under "Motive or Intention."

13. G.E.M. Anscombe, "The Justice of the Present War Examined," in her *Ethics, Religion and Politics: Collected Philosophical Papers*, vol. 3 (Minneapolis: University of Minnesota Press, 1981), 74–75.

14. Donagan, *Theory of Morality*, 111.

15. Michael Walzer, *Just and Unjust Wars* (New York: Basic Books, 1977), 39.

16. Aquinas *Summa Theologiae* II-II q. 40 a. 2.

17. Vatican Council II, *Gaudium et Spes*, para. 79.

18. Cf. David Hollenbach, *Nuclear Ethics: A Christian Moral Argument* (New York: Paulist Press, 1983), 7–8.

19. Walzer, *Just and Unjust Wars*, 39.

20. Ibid.

21. See Donagan, *Theory of Morality*, 172–209.

22. Ibid., 111.

23. Walzer, *Just and Unjust Wars*, 39.

24. See Donagan, *Theory of Morality*, 15–17.

25. See John Finnis, Joseph Boyle, and Germain Grisez, *Nuclear Deterrence, Morality and Realism* (Oxford: Oxford University Press, 1987), 342–54.

Christian Nonviolence

AN INTERPRETATION

THEODORE J. KOONTZ

I HAVE FOUR AIMS in this chapter. The first is to describe briefly something of the range of views that may fit under the heading "Christian nonviolence." The second is to give an account of the context out of which it makes sense to be committed to a certain kind of Christian nonviolence ("pacifism"). The third is to note how, from this pacifist perspective, the questions posed to just war theorists and realists are not the central questions about peace and war, and how focusing on them in fact distorts our thinking. The fourth is to attempt, nevertheless, to deal with these questions from this pacifist perspective. Needless to say, a discussion that includes all of these issues will be rather sketchy.

Varieties of Christian Nonviolence

There are a number of ways to classify views that might be seen as belonging to the "family" of Christian nonviolence. John H. Yoder presents over twenty different "pacifist" views, and Peter Brock, the dean of historians of Christian pacifism, identifies six pacifist views, all of which are essentially subsets of the first tradition I outline below.[1] Each of these views has a somewhat different basis, rationale, and perspective, and each might approach the questions posed by just war theorists in a somewhat different way.

For our purposes, I note three versions of Christian nonviolence—pacifism, abolitionism, and nonviolent resistance. None of these is exclusively "Christian." Historically, however, the first view is more closely tied to Christian thought in the West than the other two views, whose advocates have been more diverse.[2]

A comment on terminology is in order. Language here is confusing. "Pacifism" originally meant something closer to what I am calling "abolitionism," and people who are what I am calling "pacifists" previously often called themselves "nonresistants" and sharply differentiated themselves from "pacifists," that is, abolitionists.[3] The term "pacifism" has evolved in ways parallel, perhaps, to the term "liberalism" in politics, with parallel confusions. I use the term the way I do because I think this is closer to common usage today. There is also no agreement on what to call what was formerly called "pacifism." Essentially, what was called "pacifism" is what I am calling "abolitionism." The same basic perspective has been described by other authors and given different labels: "pacific-ism" by Martin Ceadel and "utopian pacifism" by James Turner Johnson, for example.[4] The first form of nonviolence, pacifism, is also the oldest. It is—minimally—the view that it is *morally* wrong for *me* to participate *directly* in *killing* in *all war*. Each of the italicized terms is important in carving out a minimal definition of pacifism. Pacifists often make larger claims (it is morally wrong for *everyone*, *all* killing is wrong, etc.), and the definition includes persons making such larger claims also. The term "pacifism" is, however, sometimes used to refer to those who have a strong desire for peace or aversion to war, but who are not necessarily committed to personal nonparticipation in all wars. This view is not included in my usage.

Pacifism, as understood here, was the dominant (though by no means only) position of Christians for the first three centuries of the Christian movement, the position of the early Waldensians, the early Unity of the Czech Brethren, and the Anabaptists. It has been and is the predominant (and official) position of Mennonites (and the related Amish), Quakers (Friends), and the Church of the Brethren.[5] In recent centuries, especially, one also finds an increasing number of individuals and subgroups within nonpacifist denominations who are pacifists. I will focus here primarily on the historical pacifist groups.

In the West, pacifism typically has been rooted in specifically Christian theological claims. It focuses on the need for *Christians* to live and act on Christian standards, rather than on what often seem to representatives of this tradition like less-than-Christian standards. It focuses on creating a new society, made up of believers who are committed to governing their lives together by those standards. It does not necessarily claim to offer readily applicable policy advice to public officials on matters of war and peace. It typically stresses the need for conversion in order to enable persons and communities to live nonviolently, defenselessly, and is most often pessimistic about the prospects of peace in a world that does not know Christ. Although pacifists know that sometimes turning the other cheek is effective in transforming the enemy, they tend to stress readiness to accept suffering as an essential part of the disarmed life.

The second tradition I call "abolitionism." Within this tradition, there is a commitment to abolish the evil of war, in a way somewhat parallel

to the way in which there developed a commitment to abolish the evil
of slavery. War in this view is no more an inherent part of life or a necessary evil than slavery was. There is a moral mandate to set up a world
system that will make war obsolete. There is a great moral revulsion
against war, and a skepticism about its utility that is typically absent
from "realist" and just war writings. At the same time, there is an opti-
mism about getting rid of war that is typically absent from just war and
realist thought, and from much pacifist thought. And, in contrast to
pacifists, abolitionists do not *necessarily* (though some do) firmly refuse
to participate in all wars. There is a focus on transforming the whole
world (not on living a new life in an alternative society made up of
those who have voluntarily chosen to follow Christ's way), and there is
a confidence in human nature (apart from conversion) and in education—helping people see the evident follies and costs of war as a means
of settling conflicts—that is quite different from the most typical
expressions of Christian pacifism.

The abolitionist tradition goes back at least to Erasmus and is not as
exclusively Christian in its membership as the pacifist tradition. Nor is
it as necessarily Christian, meaning it depends less upon uniquely
Christian theological claims. Immanuel Kant's scheme for perpetual
peace, along with other world-peace plans propounded by figures such
as William Penn (among others), reflect this perspective.[6] Various peace
societies that emerged in the nineteenth century in England and the
United States came to have predominantly this coloring.[7] This was the
dominant mode of American and British "liberal pacifists" in the early
part of this century.[8] In a less nearly pacifist form, it also was behind the
internationalism and idealism that led to the formation of the League of
Nations and the United Nations. Throughout the last two or three
decades, this viewpoint finds embodiment in its more radical form in
much of the "peace movement," and in a less radical form in groups
like the World Policy Institute that press for a more effective international community, often including removal of military force from the
hands of independent states.

It is worth noting that although the tone and ethos of these first two
"types" of Christian nonviolence are quite different, they are not incompatible in a fundamental sense: one could be (many have been) a
pacifist— one personally refusing service in all wars—and an abolitionist. Thus, though it is helpful to differentiate them, they should not be
separated too sharply.

The third member of this "family" we might best call "nonviolent
resistance." Though the name stresses *resistance*, and though this perspective has been developed most fully in settings where the need for
resistance to unjust political power is a primary motivating factor, the

perspective also includes efforts to find ways of *defending* relatively just political systems from aggression (or, to make this compatible with our terminology, ways of *resisting* aggression).

This perspective is characterized, especially in relation to "pacifism" as portrayed here, by its insistence that there are normally (if not always) pragmatically effective nonviolent means of "fighting" that are viable alternatives to war and military conflict and that can achieve or protect crucial values. Although its chief practitioners can be, and often have been, pacifists in the sense of renouncing all use of arms on ethical grounds, this position does not necessarily rely on a theological/ethical argument, though such an argument is often part of the case made for this view. What distinguishes it from "pacifism" is its stress both on the effectiveness of nonviolent action and on the need for active involvement in the pursuit of justice. The Gandhian movement in India and the civil rights movement in the United States led by Martin Luther King, Jr. have been the chief inspirations for this viewpoint. The chief intellectual architect of this position in the contemporary secular Western world is Gene Sharp of the Albert Einstein Institution in Cambridge, Massachusetts, which is probably the major research center devoted specifically to "advancing the study and use of strategic nonviolent action in conflicts throughout the world." Central to this view is the claim that power depends upon the consent—or acquiescence—of the governed. This means that the tyranny of governments can be overcome through nonviolent resistance and that countries can be defended against aggression nonviolently. Adherents to this view do not necessarily hope that threats, including military threats, will disappear as better conflict-resolution mechanisms evolve and as people and groups become more internationalist in outlook (as abolitionists seem to hope). Instead they argue that there are effective nonviolent means for dealing with such threats—as the first view often does not assume.

As the mention of Martin Luther King, Jr. suggests, there are important bridges between "pacifist" commitment (as defined above), Christian theological understanding and commitment, and certain strands of nonviolent resistance to evil. King's own writings reflect these bridges, combining a theologically based commitment to nonviolence and an activist commitment to the pursuit of justice. Thus, as he shows, Christian "pacifism" and Christian "nonviolent resistance" belong together, even though intentionally moving to confront evil, as King did, often has not characterized pacifist groups. In its Christian versions, "nonviolent resistance" relies less on pragmatic claims about effectiveness, stressing especially both the need to identify with the poor and marginalized and the cost of doing so.[9] Nevertheless, those holding such views do generally seem to have a greater hope for the transformation of entire societies through effective nonviolent struggle than is typical of most pacifist groups historically.

The overthrow of communist regimes in Eastern Europe and the former Soviet Union is seen by advocates of nonviolent resistance as providing recent and dramatic evidence in favor of this perspective. From this vantage point, it is striking in light of recent events in Eastern Europe, the Philippines, and Iran (to mention only the places where "revolutions" have taken place essentially along lines advocated by persons like Sharp) that the power of nonviolence is not reflected more in essays on the topic. Surely it is the case that such power does not always "win," as Tiananmen Square shows. But the same is true of violence. Don't these events challenge some of the basic assumptions of realism and just war theory, or at least raise questions about when we have reached last resort? What would it mean to take these experiences seriously as we seek to rethink our views about ethics and war?

I hope this brief description is useful in showing that these pacifist views are different in significant ways. At the same time, it is important to note that they are not necessarily opposed to one another in important respects. In fact, they often overlap and intermingle. One could, for example, be a pacifist who promoted strengthening international institutions and who advocated nonviolent defense. These three members of the Christian nonviolence "family" share, in contrast to most realist or just war views, an understanding of power that is not easily correlated with the ability to coerce or force others to do one's bidding through military means. Even though pacifists stress the power of persuasion and example (rooted for Christian pacifists in the power of suffering love and God's overarching power or control), abolitionists emphasize the power of reason and common interests, and advocates of nonviolent resistance underscore the power of withdrawing consent through nonviolent actions, each group in its own way disputes the claim that power grows out of the barrel of the gun. Thus these viewpoints are less inclined to see the "necessity" of war than are most other views "outside the family."

Understanding Christian Pacifism

In this section, I am intentionally narrowing the focus to the first of the three views outlined in the previous section, and to one version of that view. Even so, the task is not an easy one. How does one make Christian pacifist commitment intelligible to the wise of the world? I frankly doubt that it can be done. But if it can, I believe the only possible way to proceed is by seeking to show how reality looks from within the world of those (or some of those—there is diversity) who hold this view, not by arguing for it.[10]

"Showing how reality looks" from this Christian pacifist perspective requires challenging some assumptions that we commonly make. One such assumption is that we come to know the truth primarily through intellectual argument and exchange, and, perhaps, that there is something like "neutral" ground on the basis of which to judge alternatives. A closely related assumption is that a conference or a classroom is the primary venue though which we come to know the truth. I do not intend to argue here that these assumptions are wrong. I do not know how to make such an argument. But I do want to claim that these are not the assumptions that Christian pacifists make, and that if one wants to understand why some people are Christian pacifists, one must suspend these assumptions and enter their (our) world on their (our) terms. In making this claim, I do not mean to say that such activities are illegitimate, or to claim that we Christian pacifists do not engage in them (I make my living, after all, standing in front of a class and attending conferences), or to put what I say beyond the reach of criticism. But I do mean to say that when we engage in intellectual arguments with those outside the Christian pacifist tradition, we are speaking, as it were, a "second language," and we are doing so in a context that is not our "home."

Worship, it seems to me, is where Christian pacifists are most deeply at home, where they (we) come to know the truth, where we speak our first, our deepest, language. It is in this context of worship, with its "language" of hymns, prayers, sermons, stories, testimonies, confession, praise, celebration, and communion, that Christians come to know God's will. One might well state it even more forcefully. It is worship that in fact constitutes and defines the community. It is worship that creates and sustains it. Worship is not mainly an activity the community undertakes, but its reason for being, that which makes it a community.[11]

Thus much of what gives power and vitality to the tradition of Christian pacifism cannot be perceived in a book like the one you are reading. Our "truth" is apt to be invisible here, or in an academic conference. Nevertheless, I can seek to open a small window onto the world of Christian pacifism by bringing a part of our "worship" before you. I have chosen to do so through an excerpt from a sermon I preached one Palm Sunday. There is nothing exceptional about the sermon. Indeed, that is the point. In important respects it is typical of the viewpoint that Christian pacifists hold and that shapes their (our) understandings of ethics, war, and peace. It was titled, "Blessed Is the King!"

I began the sermon by noting that in two important respects Palm Sunday is a Sunday of false hope: first, because it proclaimed a victory before it was won—Jesus, the one who was proclaimed messiah on Palm Sunday, was arrested and crucified within the week; and second, because Jesus was not the kind of messiah the people wanted. He did not break the power of Rome and restore the glory of the Davidic kingdom. Yet the Christian Gospel claims that he is king, messiah, that he is victorious, powerful. How can this be?

His is a strange victory, a strange power. Victory came, and can come, but in a radically different way than the Palm Sunday crowds expected. The victory of Jesus is not a popular, political, national liberation victory. It is a victory that is realized when it takes root in the hearts and minds of people who have eyes to see and ears to hear and who form communities to celebrate the victory they see and hear. It is a victory that the powers that rule in the capitals of the world can, if they choose, simply pretend is not real, at least for a very long time. It is a victory that conquers no one except as they open themselves to it. Yet it is a victory that is extremely hard to resist if one does open one's eyes to see, and does unstop one's ears to hear. And it is a victory that freed and empowered those frightened first disciples when they finally saw it, heard it, even while the structures of Roman power remained unshaken. While it is a victory that threatens, and ultimately overcomes, the resistance of the enemy, it is a victory that can be experienced, celebrated, lived, even while the enemy still sits smugly on his throne.

The victory of Jesus is also strange because it is not the work of a dedicated band of revolutionaries who seized the reins of power in order to remake human history. Rather, the victory of Jesus, confirmed in his resurrection, is one that comes by Another's hand. Whatever else Christian faith may mean, it surely has something to do with affirming this kind of surprising, powerful, renewing action by God. It means not finally resting our hopes on ourselves or on other humans, although we surely have our part.

If the shape of the victory of Jesus is strange, so too is the power that wins the victory. I think it is their failure to recognize this strange power as *true* power that causes Jesus to say of the people of Jerusalem as he overlooks the city, "If only you had recognized the things that make for peace" (Luke 19:42). One way to describe this power that makes for peace is to call it the power of vulnerability. It is the power that comes when defenses fall, when fear of being hurt or killed disappears, when one is no longer interested in defending oneself, but in doing God's will. When we no longer seek to protect or defend ourselves, when we make ourselves fully vulnerable, we are free. Of course we can be killed. But nothing can deter us from doing or saying what we believe is true. When we accept vulnerability, literally nothing has power over us.

For many years I had puzzled over what it might mean to say, as Paul does in Colossians 2:15, Jesus "disarmed the principalities and powers and made a public example of them, triumphing over them in it (the cross)."

How did Jesus disarm the powers, or make a public example of them through the cross? What is the nature of the power that this King Jesus exercises, the nature of the power that he offers to us?

I was helped to understand this by remembering the story of "The Emperor's New Clothes" by Hans Christian Andersen. . . . The emperor in the story is not that different from many modern "emperors," who won't admit to mistakes or sins for fear that doing so will undermine their authority. They would rather pretend they are not naked—stripped of the moral right to rule—and punish those who point out that they are, than change their ways.

More important, the people around Andersen's emperor are not that different from many modern people, who, fearing punishment or loss of position, go along with their emperor's pretensions. There is a powerful incentive for officials, and for ordinary citizens, to pretend they don't see the emperor's nakedness because emperors often torture and kill those who expose them.

But despite this, the power or authority of emperors is still dependent on the people being willing to go along with emperors' claims to "legitimacy" (the emperor's moral *right* to rule). If ever there has been a historical moment when the truth of this claim ought to be evident, it is now. Within the last fifteen years we have witnessed the fall of incredibly powerful regimes that could not withstand the power of people who were willing to say, "The emperor is naked!" From Iran, to the Philippines, to Eastern Europe, to the Soviet Union, change that was unimaginable, and that could not be brought about by force of arms, has taken place. As my colleague Walter Sawatsky and others have shown, central to the changes in the East was a commitment of a few to begin speaking and living the truth, a commitment to refuse participation in the lie, a commitment to begin living now "as if" honesty, freedom, and human decency were already the norms by which society ran.[12] It is simply true, to turn to another source of authority for Americans, the U.S. Declaration of Independence, that governments derive their "powers from the consent of the governed." When enough people, despite fear of repression, see and *say* of illegitimate regimes, with the child in Andersen's story, that the emperor is naked, then his power is gone, because his power is based on fear. What is most remarkable about governments is not their incredible capability to repress dissent but their fragility when their moral nakedness is exposed.

This, I think, is what Jesus showed us. Jesus had power over the powers that be because their power *is*, finally, dependent on the acquiescence of the people— and Jesus refused to acquiesce. Jesus stripped the emperor's power over him because he did not let fear of what the authorities could do to him force him to pretend the emperor was clothed. Since, when consent is absent, terror is the only kind of power left to emperors, Jesus did, in fact, "disarm" the powers that be, he "made a public example of them," showing not only their illegitimacy but also their literal "powerlessness" in the face of those who refuse to be terrorized. Thus he "triumphed over them," precisely "in the cross."

The key to this triumph, though, is overcoming fear, accepting vulnerability. So long as we are ruled by fear, we can be neither free nor powerful. How can we overcome fear, accept the possibility of the cross, live lives that are, paradoxically, both fully vulnerable, and wonderfully powerful? I believe that the key lies in really seeing, in really *believing*, that Jesus is King. Though we take for granted the Kingship of Jesus and, unlike the people of his time, understand that his Kingship is radically different from that of worldly kings, I wonder if we *really* understand, I wonder if we *really* believe.

I remember the power of Martin Luther King, Jr., and how that power required overcoming fear. He lived with constant threats, and survived a number of attacks aimed at him. Perhaps a small sense of the pressure under which he lived can be gained by recalling the story told by Joan Baez of a meeting with King in 1964, four years before he was killed. King, Baez, and another friend went to a restaurant at an odd hour for a quiet conversation. At a table nearby in the nearly empty restaurant there was a group of men sitting, watching them. Curious about what they were doing, she went over and asked them. Sheepishly, they answered that they were reporters who had been assigned to follow King wherever he went. Their purpose was to be there so that they would have the scoop when the inevitable happened and King was assassinated. Shaken, but seeking to act normal, Baez returned to King's table and sat down. Before she could say anything, King said quietly and matter-of-factly, "They are waiting for me to be killed, aren't they?"

Now King, like Jesus, is a heroic, larger-than-life figure. We may not be called to live with such radical vulnerability. Their examples may seem irrelevant to us. Yet I think we often fail to choose the power of vulnerability, even though we have a very small amount to lose by choosing *that* power instead of the power of self-protection, the power of hiding behind the emperor's clothes. If you are like me, you often have refused to speak to someone with whom you disagree and have allowed a barrier to grow between you, because of fear of confrontation. If you are like me, you have sometimes failed to speak to friends about things that trouble you concerning their behavior. If you are like me, you have sought to block potential criticism by issuing a quick and superficial "I'm sorry," or simply by avoiding one who may have reason to admonish you. If you are like me, you often do not speak of that which matters most to you, about your faith, about your fears, about your dreams, about your failures, yes, even about your sins. If you are like me, you often do not reach out deeply to those near you who face struggles, because entering deeply into their struggles may mean exposing and facing your own struggles. Behind all these failures to live freely, powerfully, vulnerably, lies fear, fear growing out of our desire to protect ourselves. And to the extent that our lives are shaped by fear, to that extent we testify that we, like the people of Jesus's time, do not understand, do not believe, that Jesus is really King. Have we, any more than the disciples, really seen the new thing that Jesus did?

In this regard, I was struck by the text, "Do not remember the former things, or consider the things of old. I am about to do a new thing; now it springs forth, do you not perceive it?" (Isa. 43:18–19). We all have been well trained to see the "old things," to understand, and use, the kind of power that the Kings of this world use, though, of course, on our own modest scale. It is a power that seeks to perpetuate and solidify our ability to make ourselves *invulnerable*. It is the kind of power that has dominated the writing of history. A challenge to this view of power, this view of how history moves, is at the center of Christian faith. It is an illusory power, as Jesus's defeat of the powers shows, yet it is an illusory power that has a tenacious grip on us. When we can open ourselves to the Kingly, yes, even the Godly power of Jesus, when we can say "Blessed is *this* King," when we can overcome fear with love because we know that God is love and that God is all-powerful, when we can see the new thing that the Kingship of Jesus teaches us—when we can do these things we will become strangely powerful, we will be blessed with the power of God. Of course, exercising this kind of power sometimes will be costly. But when we truly see the power of Jesus, we also will see that the risk is worth it, for it is through accepting the power of vulnerability that we find abundant life. It is, after all, our servant-King, Jesus, the one who reveals to us God's nature, who promised, "Those who find their life will lose it, and those who lose their life for my sake will find it" (Matt. 10:39). We have nothing essential to lose in choosing to live by relying on Jesus's sort of power. And we have authentic life itself to find.

If one enters into the world of a people shaped by this kind of sermon, one will note that some additional widely held assumptions come into question. These include the assumption that we have a "right" to violently defend ourselves from harm, the assumption that we have a responsibility to ensure that we and our neighbors are not harmed by enemies if it is within our physical ability to do so, the assumption that we have the responsibility to provide an ethic for rulers that they can use and still maintain their domineering power, and the assumption, which seems to lie behind the idea that war is sometimes "necessary," that the most powerful power is the ability to force others, by physical threat or force, to do what we want them to do. Of course, the cross symbolizes the fact that Jesus's sort of power is not without cost. But then, neither is the power of war.

Topics

The nature of the questions we raise is as important as the answers to our questions. Which questions guide our lives? Which

questions do we make our own? . . . Finding
the right questions is as crucial as finding the
right answers.[13]

Before addressing directly the questions raised by just war theorists
and realists, I want to reflect on them a bit more. A helpful place to
begin is with Henri Nouwen's devotional book, *Lifesigns*. He observes
the extraordinary degree to which fear drives us, controls us, and how
this fear is rooted in accepting fear-full questions as our own.

We are often seduced by the fearful questions the world presents to us. Without fully realizing it, we become anxious, nervous, worrying people caught
in the questions of survival. . . . Once these fearful survival questions become
the guiding questions of our lives, we tend to dismiss words spoken from the
house of love as unrealistic, romantic, sentimental, pious, or just useless.
When love is offered as an alternative to fear we say: "Yes, yes, that sounds
beautiful, but. . . . " The "but" reveals how much we live in the grip of
the world, a world which calls Christians naive and raises "realistic"
questions. . . .

When we raise these "realistic" questions we echo a cynical spirit which
says: "Words about peace, forgiveness, reconciliation, and new life are won-
derful but the real issues cannot be ignored. They require that we do not
allow others to play games with us, that we retaliate when we are offended,
that we are always ready for war. . . .

Once we accept these questions as our own, and are convinced that we
must find answers to them, we become more and more settled in the house of
fear. When we consider how much of our . . . lives are geared to finding
answers to questions born of fear, it is not hard to understand why a message
of love has little chance of being heard.

Fearful questions never lead to love-filled answers. . . . Fear engenders
fear. Fear never gives birth to love.[14]

I sense that the questions posed to us by just war theorists and realists are questions coming from "the house of fear." I am convinced that
"defensive" or "justifiable" war is one of the deepest expressions of fear
in human life, despite the undoubted courage of many who fight such
wars. The questions, and "good" wars, are expressions of fear because
they suggest that, unless we at least hold open the option of engaging
in the carnage that war brings, what we care about will be destroyed.

This is, of course, a "realistic" fear. Yet Nouwen suggests that when
we allow such a fear to dominate us, "we are back again in the house of
fear." And he holds the conviction that "love is stronger than fear,
though it may often seem that the opposite is true. `Perfect love casts
out all fear,' says St. John in his first letter." The question, he suggests,

is this: "Is it possible in the midst of this fear-provoking world to live in the house of love and listen there to the questions raised by the Lord of love? Or are we so accustomed to living in fear that we have become deaf to the voice that says: `Do not be afraid.'"[15]

What questions pertinent to our topic would we claim as our own if we lived in "the house of love," if we listened to the questions raised by the Lord of love? I do not have the answer to that. Some of my thinking on it, however, is reflected in the section below, "Morality in Extremity." Surely our questions would focus our attention much more on building peace than on asking when we may go to war. Generally, the key questions for Christian pacifists would be like these, I think: "How can we be conformed to the mind of Christ, enflesh his power? How can we incarnate God's radical, enemy-loving compassion, revealed in Jesus, in this case, in that situation? How can we break down the dividing walls of hostility?" More specifically, the questions may take these forms, as they have for particular friends and colleagues of mine in the last several months: "Should I leave my wife and two small children to return to Somalia for more peace-building talks, even though the last time I was there for that purpose I lost my leg and almost my life?" "Should I uproot my family with school-aged children so that I can work with other Christians to strengthen commitment to reconciliation in Serbia, Croatia, and Bosnia?" "Should we postpone or forego our plans for graduate school in order to volunteer for three years as teachers in an isolated West Bank village?" "Should we move our family to Mozambique so we can work with churches there in rebuilding, development, and reconciliation after more than a decade of war?" "Hearing" such questions surely requires us to hear the words of one who tells us, "Do not be afraid." Yet questions such as these seem to me to be the questions we will ask as we live in the house of love.

Nevertheless, even though the questions posed by just war theorists and realists seem to me to lead us into the house of fear, and thus to be the wrong questions, I am obliged to attempt a response. In what follows, I will speak to them primarily from the Christian nonviolence perspective I sketched in the previous section. Though at points I will suggest how other perspectives within the "family" might address an issue, I cannot be comprehensive or systematic.

Conceptions of War and Peace

For many Christian pacifists, war is understood as rooted most deeply in our "natural" (since the fall) sinful human impulses. Although the use of the term "war" is not limited, at least metaphorically, in this tradition to organized violence between large groups, our sinful human impulses spill over into group egoism, and into organized violence between groups—war. "What causes wars, and what causes fightings among you? Is it not your passions that are at war in your members? You desire and do not have; so you kill. And you covet and cannot obtain, so you fight and wage war" (James 4:1–2a, RSV). This description of war—war as the greedy grasping of selfish egos—sounds more realistic to many advocates of Christian nonviolence than do most moral justifications.

This perspective leads many Christian pacifists to a focus on the need for a voluntary, personal decision to accept the lordship of Christ and to allow God's power to begin transforming one so that it becomes possible to really love one's neighbor as oneself, so that it becomes possible even to love one's enemy, and thus, finally, so that it becomes possible to live nonviolently—without fear, in the house of love. This necessarily involves not only a personal experience, but participation in a community that undergirds and sustains such a commitment. The questions that are asked, the stories that are told, the conceptions of reality, including of God and God's power, that are communicated, have the effect of creating certain dispositions and orientations of persons within the community that foster a tendency to see things in a way that sustains nonviolent commitment and undergirds nonviolent living.

For Christian pacifists, then, peace would be understood broadly and positively (not simply as the absence of war), like the biblical term *shalom*, "a state of well-being, an all-rightness, an okayness."[16] This state refers to prosperity and security in the physical realm, to just and healthy relationships in the interpersonal or intergroup realm, and to honesty and integrity in the moral realm.[17] The tradition has been committed to finding ways to live in shalom concretely, here and now, within the community of faith and, as much as possible, in relation to the wider world. Though this has never been achieved fully even within the community, many ways of seeking to do so have evolved, including various kinds of mutual aid and sharing (barn-raisings are perhaps the most conspicuous example, though persons in a part of the tradition, Hutterites, have held all property in common, and many other kinds of mutual assistance have developed), and immigration when military service was demanded or when lack of land threatened to impoverish permanently some members of the community. Traditionally, elders within the many pacifist churches would visit members before communion to make certain that all serious hurts and conflicts were dealt with so that the body could be united in its celebration of the Lord's Supper. These practices, and many others, have been designed to foster shalom in a full sense, especially within the faith community.[18]

Though Quakers have long engaged in "positive peacemaking" in the wider world, in the twentieth century this shalom-building in the world (not withdrawal or passivity) has increasingly typified the orientation of other Christian pacifist groups as well.[19]

Yet although the vision of peace is broad, encompassing, positive, the tradition has also held that one can be "at peace" with one's enemies, in situations that are far from shalom. One will not always be treated rightly, justly, no matter how much one seeks to treat others that way. In such cases, this tradition has encouraged injured persons (and others knowing of the injury) to seek redress by confronting the party doing wrong (following the model of Matt. 18:15–17, for example, in cases involving other believers). Pacifism is not passive acceptance of abuse. Yet the tradition has also stressed the need to forgive repeated offenses (Matt. 18:21–22), to let go of hurt, anger, animosity, to forego retaliation.

> You have heard it said, an eye for an eye and a tooth for a tooth, but I say unto you, do not resist one who is evil. But if any one strikes you on the right cheek, turn to him the other also. . . . You have heard that it was said, "You shall love your neighbor and hate your enemy." But I say to you, Love your enemy and pray for those who persecute you. . . . For if you love those who love you, what reward have you? Do not even the tax collectors do the same? (Matt. 5:38–46)

With the enablement of God's transforming love, one need not either hate or return evil to one who does harm. Again, the tradition is full of stories that illustrate this, and that undergird commitment to live this way, the foremost being Jesus on the cross: "Father, forgive them, for they do not know what they are doing" (Luke 23:34). Another central story from the Anabaptist Mennonite tradition is that of Dirk Willems. Dirk's story is retold in *The Martyrs Mirror*, a book second in importance only to the Bible in Mennonite homes for generations. It is a bloody, 1,100-page account of Christians being martyred for their faith, often at the hands of other Christians. Dirk, the court record shows, was apprehended and confessed to his crimes: that

> he was rebaptized in Rotterdam . . . and that he, further, in Asperen, at his house, at divers hours, harbored and admitted secret conventicles and prohibited doctrines, and that he also has permitted several persons to be rebaptized in his aforesaid house; all of which is contrary to our holy Christian faith, and to the decrees of his royal majesty, and ought not to be tolerated, but severely punished, for an example to others.

Therefore, the judges condemned Dirk to be "executed with fire, until death ensues." Dirk escaped from prison and ran across some thin ice to get away from the "thief-catcher" who was sent after him.

The thief-catcher following him broke through, when Dirk Willems, perceiv-
ing that the former was in danger of his life, quickly returned and aided him
in getting out, and thus saved his life. The thief-catcher wanted to let him go,
but the burgomaster, very sternly called to him to consider his oath, and thus
he was again seized by the thief-catcher, and . . . put to death at the lingering
fire.[20]

Shalom living in the midst of a sinful world demands the ability to forgive and love even when an enemy continues to treat us as an enemy, to
continue to repay evil with good even in the face of injustice. "Heroes"
exemplifying this, like Dirk, shape character in rather different ways
than heroes like Rambo.

Attitudes toward War and Nonviolence

As is clear from what has been said previously, there is a very strong
presumption against war within the tradition of Christian nonviolence.
For most within this tradition, we might say that the presumption is absolute, allowing no exceptions. It may be worth reiterating, however,
that although Christian pacifism has generally been rooted in a theo-
logical/ethical framework that interprets Christian ethics as requiring
renunciation of violence in order to conform to the mind of Christ,
other grounds for a presumption against violence are present in other
strands of the tradition of Christian nonviolence.

These grounds include the claim that other structures can and should
be put into place that would provide alternative means for resolving
conflicts in more orderly and less destructive ways than war offers
(abolitionism), and the claim that there are other more effective means
for overthrowing unjust regimes or for defending against aggression
that are less costly and thus are to be preferred on pragmatic grounds to
war (nonviolent resistance). There is nothing logically inconsistent
about holding all three arguments for the presumption against war, and
many standing within this tradition do so. It might also be worth noting
that although the arguments in favor of abolitionism and nonviolent
resistance are often made on the grounds of pragmatic considerations
(perhaps at least in part in order to appeal to others who seem to base
decisions on pragmatic considerations), those who have advanced such
arguments or have found them most compelling are frequently committed to nonviolence as an ethical principle. Whether this is a matter of
wishful thinking, wanting to "have one's cake and eat it too," or
whether it is a case where commitment to an ethical principle enables
one to "see" viable alternatives that are not visible from perspectives that
typically dominate ethical thought in the West cannot be resolved here.

One further note. Persons standing within the tradition of Christian nonviolence generally respond to wars with a deep feeling of sadness. War represents for Christian pacifists an ultimate symbol of human fallenness. This sense of war's sinfulness sometimes leads to angry denunciations of it or to a sinful smugness ("we" are not sinful like "they" are), but more deeply and authentically it leads to soul-searching for both the roots of war and conflict within oneself and one's community, for ways to act concretely to relieve the suffering that wars bring, and increasingly, in modern times, for ways to facilitate the avoidance of and/or ending of wars. I have in mind here, of course, the various abolitionist projects one associates with the figures described in the section on abolitionism, but also particularly Quaker (though not exclusively Quaker) efforts to foster dialogues between conflicting groups in contexts where options for settling differences can be explored informally and off the record.[21]

The Grounds for War

Though the tradition of Christian nonviolence recognizes many *reasons* for war, often running along the lines noted above under "Conceptions of War and Peace," all those within the tradition would claim that there are virtually never "legitimate grounds" for war, and most would hold that there are never such grounds. As noted earlier, some abolitionists are not opposed to personal participation in all wars. Historically, the willingness of abolitionists to sanction war has come mainly when a war is seen as necessary in order to end war. The First World War as the war to end war is the prime example.[22] In a somewhat related way, abolitionists have sometimes been willing to approve of wars that are deemed necessary in order to create a situation of "justice" that is seen as a prerequisite for peace in a positive (shalom-like) sense. Thus some whom I have called "abolitionist" (in relation to abolishing war) sanctioned the American civil war as a necessity to abolish the injustice of slavery.[23] Also, in recent times, some abolitionists have sanctioned, or at least have been unwilling to criticize, wars of "national liberation" or wars against "oppressive" regimes.[24] In addition, there have been apocalyptic groups who were committed to pacifism in the present age, but who were also ready to pick up the sword to help usher in the kingdom of God upon Christ's return. Some of these groups have decided that the time to fight has arrived, and have therefore abandoned their pacifism in favor of a righteous war.[25]

It is also the case that a certain "particularism" in a "typical" Christian pacifist perspective (this particularism has been less true of Quakers than of most other pacifist groups) that expects those committed to the way of Christ to live in ways that are different from what can be expected in the world has left open the possibility of persons from this perspective providing a certain "quasi-legitimate ground" for wars, not by "Christians," but by the state. It has been clear from within the tradition of Christian pacifism that *Christians* are called to live by the standards outlined, for example, in Romans 12:

> Bless those who persecute you; bless and do not curse them. . . . Do not repay anyone evil for evil. . . . No, "if your enemies are hungry, feed them; if they are thirsty, give them something to drink; for by doing this you will heap burning coals on their heads." Do not be overcome by evil, but overcome evil with good.

But the central text for the state for many Christian pacifists has been Romans 13:1–7, in which Christians are told to "be subject to the governing authorities," to "do what is good" because "rulers are not a terror to good conduct, but to bad." Although it has not been worked out systematically, since the focus has been on ethics for the Christian community, sometimes there has been a reluctance to condemn for the state certain wars of the state. This reluctance has its roots in an understanding of the state as given by God to maintain order, to protect the good, and to punish the wicked.

A classical formulation of this view for the Mennonite tradition is stated in the Schleitheim Confession dating from the beginning of the movement in 1527: "The sword is an ordering of God outside the perfection of Christ. It punishes and kills the wicked, and guards and protects the good."[26] This view recognizes the state's ordering function, its calling to protect the good and restrain the evil; sometimes it even tacitly admits that the state's ordering function may entail the use of violence, perhaps even war. This recognition perhaps accounts for the fact that although pacifists have opposed participation in wars, some of them have not condemned a government's waging of certain of those wars (for example, American participation in the Second World War). This position seems to rest, at least in part, on a differentiation between the "vocation" or "calling" of Christ's disciples and that of the state. This differentiation has not necessarily been seen as meaning that Christians must reject all "governing," but it has meant that "governing," as well as everything else, must be done in ways compatible with Christ's teaching and example—and it has often meant much skepticism about the possibility of governing nations in a Christian manner.[27]

Having said all this, however, it must also be said that there has been no developed theory that seeks to argue exactly when wars might be "justified" for the state. In fact, "justified" must be in quotation marks, because war and violence are never finally, ultimately, "justified," from a Christian pacifist perspective. God's ultimate, final will for everyone is nonviolence. At best, war and violence are penultimately "justified" for persons who do not follow Jesus (as pacifists understand the meaning of that) and who are mandated to carry the ordering function of the state in a fallen world where "ordering" may require war or violence. If pressed on when wars might be "justified" for the state, pacifists within this tradition would perhaps utilize something like just war criteria. More generally, they might be inclined to argue that the appropriate standard for the state in international conflict, as well as in domestic law enforcement, could be derived from the concerns outlined in Romans 13, focusing especially on the state's responsibility to "protect the good." Such pacifists would also want to insist that this be done with the least possible degree of violence or coercion.[28] It is worth noting that the particularistic perspective reflected in this discussion, although it has deep roots in the Christian pacifist tradition, has increasingly been questioned by those who emphasize that the "lordship of Christ" extends not only over the church (where it is recognized) but over the world (even though it is not recognized there), and that there can therefore be no difference in ethical norm for the state as compared to the church. Persons holding this perspective would be more ready to condemn forthrightly all wars by the state, as well as all Christian participation in wars, while at the same time often being more ready to accept for Christians some "coercion" and "police" functioning than many more "particularistic" pacifists would be. Duane Friesen's work would be an example of this.[29]

Resistance to Political Authority

Christian pacifists have been quite ready to resist political authorities on points where they feel obeying political authorities would mean compromising obedience to God. The central text has been, "We must obey God rather than any human authority" (Acts 5:29). This resistance has taken various forms among those within the pacifist tradition, including, obviously, refusal of military service, but also sometimes including refusal to pay taxes used for military purposes, refusal to swear oaths, and refusal to engage in other practices that appear idolatrous. Sometimes pacifists have also seen nationalism, and the human sacrifices made in wars to the "gods" of the nations, as a kind of idolatry to be resisted.[30] In recent decades, resistance has also taken the form of pacifist agencies working against government restrictions that prevent them from carrying out their humanitarian programs. A case would be shipping medical supplies to North Vietnam in the early 1970s, thereby violating or circumventing the U.S. policy outlawing "trading with the enemy." Resistance to authority within the Christian pacifist tradition has normally taken the form of "civil disobedience" rather than revolutionary attempts (either violent or nonviolent) to overthrow regimes. Christian pacifists have generally seen Jesus's approach either as nonpolitical or as following a different model of "politics" than that adopted by the revolutionaries of his time, the Zealots.[31] Often citing a text like Romans 13, they typically have had a rather high regard for the legitimate authority of government (even when it must be disobeyed because of a higher loyalty to God), and also typically have had a low view of what one might hope for from governments. Thus, generally, they have not been inclined to revolutionary activity. The Quakers, however, often have been more hopeful of changing governments than most other pacifist groups have been, and they have thus been more politically active, though still not revolutionary.[32]

The "nonviolent resistance" perspective has often been supportive of efforts toward "nonviolent revolution" in oppressive situations and has sought to provide mechanisms for overthrowing oppressive regimes that do not represent the will of the people. A kind of "democratic" standard seems to operate from within this perspective: governments are legitimate when they have the support of the population, and are legitimately overthrown (nonviolently) when they lack such support.

In earlier centuries, Christian pacifists faced with military service generally just sought some way to avoid that service, since it violated their convictions. As more democratic notions about government and citizenship (that is, the notion of being citizens rather than simply subjects) have become more widely prevalent among pacifist groups, pacifists have become active in advocating the "rights" of conscientious objectors, including the rights of objectors to particular wars. Some pacifists have seen conscientious objection as a means to resist the government and its warmaking machinery, and have therefore sought to upset that machinery by refusing to cooperate with a conscription system. Other pacifists have accepted conscription as a "legitimate" part of a state system of which they do not necessarily approve and in which they do not exercise power, but to which they are subject. Such pacifists have typically not resisted conscription when alternatives to military service are provided, but rather have been grateful that the government has shown respect for their religious convictions. Despite the variations, it is probably fair to say that most Christian pacifist groups have had an underlying attitude of some suspicion or mistrust of governments.

Motive or Intention

The Christian pacifist tradition does focus on motivation or intention when it stresses love of neighbor and love of enemy. Love is certainly a motive and an intention, a desire to seek the best for the other out of compassion. At the same time, pacifists are typically deeply skeptical of views that emphasize that actions should be judged on the basis of motives or intentions when the actions themselves seem to belie the stated motive or intention, or that do not attend to the destructiveness of the actions themselves. Augustine, for example, sometimes focuses on the effects of war on the person waging it in a way that seems to downplay excessively what it means in itself or to its victims:

> What is the evil in war? Is it the death of someone who will soon die in any case, that others may live in peaceful subjection? This is mere cowardly dislike, not any religious feeling. The real evils of war are love of violence, revengeful cruelty, fierce and implacable enmity, wild resistance, and the lust of power, and such like.[33]

Specifically, pacifists have found it difficult to take very seriously views that, in the case of war, stress that one can really "love" a person and at the same time kill him or her. The point is not that no one could ever kill and still feel compassion for the one being killed, but that this is a mistaken understanding of what Christian love is. Love is not mainly a sentiment or a feeling (though proper motivation is surely a part of it), but an action that concretely seeks the best for the one being loved. In this sense, pacifists have wanted to focus on the inherent quality of actions, as well as intentions or motives. Just as the Book of James argues that "faith by itself, if it has no works, is dead" (James 2:17), pacifists tend to hold that motivations or intentions that do not take the form of *action* understandable by those *receiving* the action as reflective of the motive or intention are dead. It is as important to focus on the meaning of the action for its recipient as on the meaning of the action for its giver, for our actions are a central part of one of our most fundamental tasks, that of witnessing to, *communicating*, God's love.

All of this does not mean that pacifists have absolutely no interest in differentiating various motives or intentions related to warfare. But pacifists are deeply aware of the human heart's ability to deceive itself and, as a rule, tend to trust actions that are "inherently right" more than motives or intentions that are said to be "good"—even though the actions resulting from these motives or intentions violate normally accepted standards. It also means that pacifists often put more weight on not harming, and less weight on righting the evils of the world through the use of armed force, than many nonpacifists. This issue of self-deception, and of justifying actions that may be harmful to others on the basis of good intentions or good motives, is a central part of pacifists' problems with just war. From a pacifist standpoint, it seems that just war serves almost always to justify or legitimize *our* nation's war (rather than to call it seriously into a "court" where it must bear the burden of proof in showing that the normal presumption against war should be overridden), and to condemn *their* nation's war. And, of course, for "them," it works the same way in reverse.

The story of Dirk Willems calls to mind an additional reason for a typical pacifist skepticism about appeals to motives or intentions that then justify killing others out of love for them. Many of the torturers and killers of Anabaptist and other Christian martyrs claimed (I suspect sincerely) to be acting in love for them—and for other innocent souls who might be misled by them—as they cut off their fingers or put them on the pyre to burn them alive. I am struck by the fact that representatives of some groups that have been relatively powerless (Jews and pacifists) argue for a focus on actions, and that some of those who have been powerful (Catholic advocates of natural law) argue for a focus on intentions and motives. Is such a focus on intentions and motives a luxury of the powerful—or even a way of rationalizing to themselves their hurtful behavior—that the weak cannot afford?[34]

The Conduct of War

I noted earlier that some abolitionists give up their opposition to war when war seems especially necessary to achieve some crucial end. This can also result in an uncritical attitude regarding the conduct of war. The same has sometimes been true of apocalyptic groups.

Christian pacifists generally have been skeptical of the possibility of moral restraint in warfare once it has begun. In this sense many pacifists have been "realists." The violence of warfare has seemed to have its own, escalating, often senseless, logic. It is partly for this reason that pacifists have insisted that the line should be drawn between "war" and "no war" instead of between "just" and "unjust" war.

This does not mean that pacifists are committed to the view that war *ought* not be limited by moral constraints. Pacifists would typically side with just war theorists in hoping that wars can be so restrained, though they would be skeptical of the realism of that happening. Some pacifists have in fact tried to take just war seriously and engage it on its own terms in an attempt to strengthen the moral constraints on war.

These attempts to take just war seriously have often been disappointing because of being disqualified before the discussion starts (as Paul Ramsey does[35]), or because it seems very difficult to get many within the just war tradition to define the tradition in such a way that it is even theoretically possible for it to yield a *clear* negative judgment about a specific war, or because so many seem unable to apply a theoretically possible negative judgment to one's own country's wars.[36]

Morality in Extremity

From a Christian pacifist perspective, it is vitally important to begin doing ethics from the "center." It is always a temptation in ethics to become fixated on "the hard cases," and in doing so to lose sight of the central affirmations that make the cases hard. From a pacifist perspective, this frequently happens in discussion about war, and just war theory is part of the problem. Just war theory can be viewed (when it is not dismissed as a rationalization for wars, as some pacifists tend to do) as an elaborate system for controlling exceptional resort to war and as thus recognizing the norm of nonviolence that regulates everyday human life. So far so good. Yet the structure of the theory focuses our attention wrongly, on the periphery instead of on the center, on the hard case instead of on the normal case. From the pacifist perspective, the central question relative to international conflict would be something like, "How can we live together without killing each other?" not, as it is in just war thought, "When can war be legitimately waged, and how?" From a pacifist perspective, in other words, this elaborate theory too often has the effect of making war look "normal," rather than like an exception, and therefore has the effect of almost automatically justifying a nation's wars, and distracting us from what is most important— finding ways to hold to our key convictions rather than figuring out when we have to make exceptions to them. From a pacifist perspective, just war theory is a case of the tail wagging the dog. If the accuracy of this assessment is doubted, consider the following questions. Why is it that we have an enormously elaborated and nuanced moral theory about "just war," but no similarly elaborated and nuanced moral theory of "just diplomacy" or "just international relations" or "just peace"? Why is it that in debates on ethics of war and peace, the great bulk of our time is spent focusing on *war*—if, when, and how to engage in it— rather than on *peace*—how to build and maintain it? Even more concretely (if more removed from just war theory and this book), why do we spend, in the United States, more than $250 billion annually on our military, and a tiny fraction of that on diplomacy, economic aid, support for the United Nations, etc.? The point is that if we attended to the central question (from a pacifist perspective) and put both our theoretical and our financial resources into addressing it, we might well have far fewer situations where we need to address the "exception" that just war is designed to address.

Thus pacifists are skeptical of approaching ethics through the extreme cases rather than through the ordinary cases, where, often enough, we do not act ethically anyway. From this viewpoint, the most basic problem of ethical living is failing to do what we know we should do because it may be costly to do so, not deciding when to make exceptions to the normal rules that govern our lives.

All of this is not to deny that pacifists face awkward questions when asked things like, "How can you just stand by and let Muslim women be raped and murdered in Bosnia?" There are things for pacifists to say in response to such questions. These include noting that pacifist prescriptions for policy have normally been ignored in the years leading up to the crisis and then, suddenly, we are asked for a solution to a problem caused by someone else's policies. They include observing that often pacifists are not just "standing by" but are deeply involved in working to solve such problems in ways compatible with their convictions, often at considerable cost or risk to themselves. They include pointing to other options that may not have been attempted. And they include simply confessing that we have often not done what we could have done. Other responses could be added. But I grant that they are hard questions. And I grant that perhaps, in theory, just war theory may have more satisfying answers (from many perspectives) to them. But even if one is convinced that something like just war theory can yield a theoretically more satisfactory answer to a hard question about a hard case like Bosnia, are we really farther ahead morally by building an elaborate moral system to deal with the hard case? Might we not be farther ahead if we learned to say simply, "Killing is wrong," and refused to systematize war morally (and therefore legitimize it morally)? After all, it must be the case, simply on statistical grounds, that less than half of the world's wars can be objectively just according to just war criteria themselves. From the just war perspective, no war can be just objectively on both sides, and many wars (colonial wars where countries fight each other to take over someone else's territory, wars waged out of desire to satisfy the vanity of rulers, etc.) are just on neither side. In this light, and in light of the consistent tendency of persons in opposing countries to justify their own country's wars, pacifism seems a safer moral wager than trying to guess the rightness of wars.

This does not mean that pacifists can avoid the question of extremity. But, as should by now be evident, for pacifists, indeed for all within the tradition of Christian nonviolence, the issue of "extremity" arises at a different point (in one sense) than it does for those within the tradition of just war thinking. From the pacifist perspective, the question of extremity is not whether the normal rules of warfare can in certain extreme cases be overridden, but whether the presumption against any and all war can ever be overridden in an extreme case. Despite this difference, however, it is worth noting that it is not only the pacifist who is faced with the uncomfortable choice of holding to his or her moral principles or abandoning them in the face of what seems to be an overriding necessity. Like pacifists, just war theorists, if they hold to a "strict constructionist" view of just war theory, sometimes will need to choose between their moral principles and seeming "effectiveness" in reaching their (ostensibly just) goals. Indeed, any moral view that does not yield finally to a purely consequentialist perspective faces the same apparent collision between morality and necessity.

It is crucial to note, however, that from a Christian pacifist perspective, there is no such thing as "absolute necessity." There is only "necessity" in relationship to achieving certain ends that are deemed more important than holding to one's ethical commitments. Near the very root of Christian pacifist commitment is the freedom from the "necessity" to value my life, or the lives of my friends, above the lives of others, since my life, and the lives of my friends, are "safe" in God's hands. In like manner, Christian pacifists are also freed from the burden of "making history come out right."[37] Such pacifists insist that history is finally in God's control, and that it is our responsibility to act as Jesus teaches us to act, and that as we do so, God will bring about the outcome of history that God intends. We are simply not smart enough to know what the outcomes of our various actions will be. (In a certain way, a realistic appraisal of our limitations in forecasting outcomes itself is a strong argument for pacifism). We have no "responsibility" to violate standards revealed to us in order to help God out. This does not mean, of course, that we do not calculate consequences or that we ought not use our human intelligence to achieve good instead of evil. Yet the conviction that we do not bear the burden of history's outcome alone frees us from a compulsiveness about stopping what we perceive as evil or achieving what we perceive as good that, in the final analysis from a Christian pacifist perspective, reflects a kind of functional atheism. There are, after all, many evils that we simply, physically, *cannot* prevent, many goods we *cannot* bring about—because we are not God. Why should we feel compelled to try (with varying and unknown probabilities of success) to prevent those evils or bring about those goods if the only way we can do so involves violating our moral commitments? From this perspective, our responsibility for "making history come out right" is limited not only by our power to influence history's outcome (which pacifists often feel is much more modest than that of those who are used to ruling the world), but also by our higher responsibility to live in ways consonant with God's revelation to us in Jesus Christ.

There is one more approach to the issue of "extremity." In contrast to most politicians and many moralists, Michael Walzer argues for a stringent criterion to govern "extremity," what he calls (following Churchill) "supreme emergency." He says, in effect, that we should not be like Chicken Little, always contending that the sky is falling, thus rationalizing immoral action on the basis of "necessity." Unlike Chicken Little, we should only violate the rules of war when "the heavens are (really) about to fall."[38]

One way for a Christian pacifist to respond to Walzer's view is to ask, "Will the heavens fall? Can the heavens fall?" Another way is to ask, "Have the heavens fallen?" when nations have lost wars. In responding to these questions, much, obviously, depends on what one means by the "heavens." Walzer's way of putting the issue makes it evident that, for him, the "heavens" means something like, "my nation, or some political community with important moral commitments, good political institutions, etc." If this falls, the heavens fall. A view like this seems implicit in all views that defend the rightness of violating normal norms in war in the face of extremity, if only because wars are fought to defend political communities, nations.

A Christian pacifist response to these questions might go like this. On the one hand, the heavens surely *will* fall, no matter what we do to hold them up—we are not God—if we identify the heavens with our political community or ideology. No political community will last forever, whatever we do to preserve it. There is simply no way to hold the heavens up in the long run. If that time frame seems too grand, note also that it is the very thing that makes a political community most worth defending that is destroyed first when that community violates its own standards of right under the pressure of "necessity." Are the "heavens" the physical continuity of a certain nation or of its moral commitments?

On the other hand, I would insist that the heavens *cannot* fall. The heavens did not fall when Athens fell, when Rome fell, when . . . fell. They will not fall when the United States falls. They will not even fall when, in one way or another, the earth is destroyed. These are claims, I take it, that Christians make when we speak of God's providence, power, goodness, eternity, and of our ultimate destiny as being somehow with God. And they are claims that deny that any nation or political ideology or system amounts to "the heavens."

These observations about extremity get us back to the central claims of the pacifist position that I represent, a position that is finally dependent upon a conviction about God and God's action in the world (and its implications for our action) that is known to us in Jesus Christ. In the absence of faith in the God of Jesus Christ, this sort of pacifism is certainly foolishness. But, "to those who are called, both Jews and Greeks, Christ [is] the power of God and the wisdom of God. For God's foolishness is wiser than human wisdom, and God's weakness is stronger than human strength" (I Cor. 1:24–25).

Epilogue

Earlier in this chapter, I told the story of Dirk Willems. His death was part of a "debate" over religious truth. In sixteenth-century Europe it was believed, functionally at least, that questions of truth could be settled by torture and killing. I am personally grateful that today we generally don't settle questions of truth in this way, but rather through "argument." In a way, this rightly can be interpreted as a triumph of toleration. But we might also interpret this in a slightly different way. Someone has said, "We are all Marxists now," in the sense of recognizing that material interests are important shapers of action. I believe it is fair to say that in a similar way, in relation to questions of religious and philosophical truth claims, "We are all pacifists now." This is to say that Christian pacifists are committed to the propositions that our only "weapons" are words (and the way we live), that the most powerful power is finally the power of truth, and that one can only convince someone of something by . . . well, by *convincing* them, not by forcing them. Most intellectuals are now committed to this same proposition when it comes to understanding the truth. This "triumph" of pacifism is a cause for rejoicing—at least for those of us who are pacifists!

It is ironic—no, sad—however, that we in late twentieth-century Western culture do not believe that the "right" thing in relationships between peoples and nations must also be determined by using nothing other than words as "weapons," by relying on nothing other than the power of truth, the power of moral appeal. In settling questions of right between nations, we are still in the equivalent of the sixteenth century—we still use the methods used in that century to settle questions of religious truth. Is this because we simply have not "seen" in relation to political conflicts what we have "seen" in relation to the quest for philosophical or religious truth? Or is it because what matters to us now is not "true" religion, but our own and our nation's ideologies and interests? I frankly think it is probably mainly the latter. If this is true, there is less reason for rejoicing from a Christian pacifist perspective. If this is true, it means that we no longer take God seriously enough to fight over religion, but now as much or more than ever, we bow before idols of our own making—nations, and political ideologies and interests—and we make sacrifices on their altars, human sacrifices by the millions in the form of wars' victims. One of the hard theoretical questions put to me is whether I would not act violently to prevent the takeover of a civilized country by "barbarians," barbarians who even went so far as to practice human sacrifice. A good question. But I fear that the barbarians are not out there. We are the barbarians, complete with human sacrifice.

As long as we believe that the power that "wins" by dominating others, by cowing others into submission—the kind of power symbolized best by military force—is the strongest power, we will remain barbarians. As long as we believe that, we will be doomed to wars and more wars. But when we come to see that the power of truth, spoken and lived, is finally more powerful—when we come to see and accept the power of the cross through which Jesus disarmed the principalities and powers—then we will be free. The truth will set us free. Free from the need to compel others to conform to our visions of the right. Free from the fear that makes us submit to injustice. Free from the fear of death. And free from war.

Notes

1. See John H. Yoder, *Nevertheless: Varieties of Religious Pacifism*, rev. ed. (Scottdale, Pa.: Herald Press, 1992), and Peter Brock, *Pacifism in Europe to 1914* (Princeton: Princeton University Press, 1972), 472–76.

2. Brock has suggested essentially the same three viewpoints, in embryonic form, in the preface to *Freedom from War: Nonsectarian Pacifism, 1814–1914* (Toronto: University of Toronto Press, 1991), vii–viii.

3. John H. Yoder, *Christian Attitudes to War, Peace, and Revolution* (Elkhart, Ind.: Associated Mennonite Biblical Seminaries, 1983), 372–401.

4. Martin Ceadel, *Thinking about Peace and War* (New York: Oxford University Press, 1987), and James Turner Johnson, *The Quest for Peace: Three Moral Traditions in Western Cultural History* (Princeton: Princeton University Press, 1987).

5. This is by no means an inclusive list. Similar pacifist movements have appeared in many other times and places, though the pacifism of such movements has often been short-lived. This happened, for example, in nineteenth-century America. See Yoder, *Christian Attitudes*, 299–317, for a brief description. Also see *Proclaim Peace: Voices of Christian Pacifism in America Outside the Historic Peace Churches*, edited by Richard Hughes and Theron F. Schlabach (Champaign: University of Illinois Press, 1997). For additional examples, see both 1991 volumes by Brock: *Freedom from Violence: Sectarian Nonresistance from the Middle Ages to the Great War* and *Freedom from War* (both Toronto: University of Toronto Press).

6. Roland H. Bainton, *Christian Attitudes toward War and Peace* (Nashville, Tenn.: Abingdon Press, 1960), 178–84.

7. Brock, *Freedom from War*.

8. Cf. Yoder, *Christian Attitudes*, 319–40.

9. For additional expressions of Christian nonviolent resistance perspectives, see Philip McManus and Gerald Schlabach, eds., *Relentless Persistence: Nonviolent Action in Latin America* (Philadelphia, Pa.: New Society Publishers, 1991), and Dominque Barbé, *Grace and Power: Base Communities and Nonviolence in Brazil* (Maryknoll, N.Y.: Orbis, 1987).

10. As I understand it, this is one central point of Stanley Hauerwas's essay, "Can a Pacifist Think about War?" (in Hauerwas, *Dispatches from the Front* [Durham, N.C.: Duke University Press, 1994]), a point I wish to illustrate here and to make concrete.

11. There is literature exploring the connection between worship and ethics of which I became aware after drafting this chapter. See, for example, Vigen Guroian, "Seeing Worship as Ethics: An Orthodox Perspective," *Journal of Religious Ethics* 13 (1985): 332–39.

12. Walter Sawatsky, "Truth Telling in Eastern Europe: The Liberation and the Burden," *Journal of Church and State* 33 (1991): 701–29, and Timothy Garton Ash, *The Magic Lantern: The Revolution of '89 Witnessed in Warsaw, Budapest, Berlin and Prague* (New York: Random House, 1990).

13. Henri J. M. Nouwen, *Lifesigns: Intimacy, Fecundity, and Ecstasy in Christian Perspective* (Garden City, N.Y.: Doubleday, 1986), 18.

14. Ibid., 17–20.

15. Ibid., 20–21.

16. Perry B. Yoder, *Shalom: The Bible's Word for Salvation, Justice, and Peace* (Newton, Kans.: Faith and Life Press, 1987), 12.

17. The term "positive peace," used frequently in the modern peace studies movement, has a similar meaning. See, for example, the introductory text by David P. Barash, *Introduction to Peace Studies* (Belmont, Calif.: Wadsworth Publishing Company, 1991), 9–11.

18. Although it speaks to a somewhat different time and setting, for a fleshing out of what this has meant concretely from within this tradition, see Guy F. Hershberger, *The Way of the Cross in Human Relationships* (Scottdale, Pa.: Herald Press, 1958).

19. For an overview of what one Christian pacifist organization is doing to make the peace commitment an active and positive movement, rather than simply a passive refusal to participate in war, see the annual "Workbook" of the Mennonite Central Committee, Akron, Pa. 17501.

20. Thieleman J. van Braght, *The Bloody Theater or Martyrs Mirror of the Defenseless Christians* (Scottdale, Pa.: Herald Press, 1968 [original in Dutch, 1660]), 741–42.

21. See the book on Quaker conciliation efforts by C. H. Mike Yarrow, *Quaker Experiences in International Conciliation* (New Haven, Conn.: Yale University Press, 1978). There is also growing involvement of Mennonites in conciliation efforts, both locally and internationally. See the newsletter *Conciliation Quarterly*,

published by the Mennonite Central Committee, Akron, Pa. 17501, for regular reporting of Mennonite and related activity in this area.

22. Cf. Ray H. Abrams, *Preachers Present Arms* (Scottdale, Pa.: Herald Press, 1969 [original 1933]), esp. 161ff.

23. Cf. Peter Brock, *Freedom from War*, 117ff.

24. At least, this is a key criticism of some who are called "pacifists." Cf. Guenter Lewy, *Peace and Revolution: The Moral Crisis of American Pacifism* (Grand Rapids, Mich.: Eerdmans, 1988), but also various objections to Lewy's interpretation in Michael Cromartie, ed., *Peace Betrayed? Essays on Pacifism and Politics* (Washington, D.C.: Ethics and Public Policy Center, 1990).

25. Cf. James M. Stayer, *Anabaptists and the Sword*, 2d ed. (Lawrence, Kans.: Coronado Press, 1976), chaps. 4 and 11–12.

26. *The Schleitheim Confession*, trans. and ed. John Howard Yoder (Scottdale, Pa.: Herald Press, 1973), 14. "Sword" here refers to the coercive, order-maintaining function of the government. It does not refer specifically to warmaking (28 n. 44).

27. For a sampling of sixteenth-century Anabaptist views, see Walter Klaassen, ed., *Anabaptism in Outline: Selected Primary Sources* (Scottdale, Pa.: Herald Press, 1981), 244–64.

28. Cf. Ted Koontz, "Mennonites and the State: Preliminary Reflections," *Essays on Peace Theology and Witness: Occasional Papers*, no. 12 (Elkhart, Ind.: Institute of Mennonite Studies, 1988), 35–60.

29. Duane K. Friesen, *Christian Peacemaking and International Conflict* (Scottdale, Pa.: Herald Press, 1986).

30. Cf. Dale Aukerman, *Darkening Valley: A Biblical Perspective on Nuclear War* (Scottdale, Pa.: Herald Press, 1989). The activities of people like the Berrigans provide an example.

31. Cf. John Howard Yoder, *The Politics of Jesus* (Grand Rapids, Mich.: Eerdmans, 1972), esp. chap. 2.

32. Peter Brock, *The Quaker Peace Testimony: 1660–1914* (York: Sessions Book Trust [distributed in the U.S. by Syracuse University Press], 1990), is the best recent overview of Quaker pacifism.

33. Quoted in Arthur F. Holmes, ed., *War and Christian Ethics* (Grand Rapids, Mich.: Baker Book House, 1975), 64.

34. For a perceptive discussion of some roots of Christian religious "coercion" of other Christians, see Peter Brown, *Religion and Society in the Age of St. Augustine* (New York: Harper and Row, 1972), 260–78, 301–31.

35. Paul Ramsey, *The Just War: Force and Political Responsibility* (New York: Scribner, 1968), 259ff.

36. John Howard Yoder's book, *When War Is Unjust* (Minneapolis: Augsburg, 1984), is one example of a pacifist attempt to engage just war theory on its own terms. On the Gulf War, see also Yoder, "Just War Tradition: Is It Credible?" *Christian Century* (13 Mar. 1991): 295–98.

37. Yoder, *Politics of Jesus*, 233–50.

38. Michael Walzer, *Just and Unjust Wars* (New York: Basic Books, 1977), 231.

13

Conflicting Interpretations of Christian Pacifism

MICHAEL G. CARTWRIGHT

THOUGH HE DISCUSSES Christian nonviolence with scholarly care, Ted Koontz remains a passionately committed Christian. By insisting that the questions nonviolent Christians ask about the ethics of war and peace are different from the questions asked by those who approach the topic from other directions, he reminds us of the importance of religious convictions, or the absence of such convictions, in shaping how we understand war/peace ethics.[1] Moreover, his forthrightness in articulating the conceptions of truth and power that arise from the tradition of Christian pacifism, and especially from the practices of Christian worship, opens the way for a fuller assessment of the possibilities and limits of conversation between ethical traditions.

Koontz's chapter also evokes a number of critical questions, however. How adequate is the typology of Christian nonviolence he presents? Which conceptions of war and peace are omitted from his discussion? Given the differences he identifies between the "house of fear" and the "house of love," has Koontz exaggerated the contrast between Christian nonviolence and just war thinking? And if so, what are the implications of this exaggeration for assessing the particular understanding of truth and power he wishes to defend? Finally, might not his portrayal of the conversation between Christian pacifists and others distort, and thereby impede, this conversation?

No matter how we answer questions like these, Koontz has brought into view a set of concerns that, though not often examined in comparative ethics, are essential to understanding the moral logic of Christian nonviolence.

Interpreting Typologies of War/Peace Ethics

Koontz acknowledges that his chapter offers no more than "an interpretation" of Christian nonviolence. There are good reasons for such hermeneutical modesty. Christian ethicists—pacifist and nonpacifist—have struggled for many years with a broad array of hermeneutical issues,[2] and there remain significant and unresolved disagreements between the various forms of pacifism, abolitionism, and nonviolent resistance, as well as opposition to arguments outside the family of Christian nonviolence. Christian pacifists today have no choice but to take seriously the fact that "peacemaking" has become a kind of linguistic umbrella under which a diversity of theological approaches now collect. Nor can they ignore the fact that many nonpacifists regard their views as at best quaint and at worst dangerous.

Calling attention to the hermeneutic self-consciousness of Koontz's chapter opens the way toward assessing the other, more significant, interpretive issues he raises. To begin with, we need to examine the typology on which he relies. Some typologies are designed to characterize precisely each identified position,[3] others to identify "family resemblances" linking an unresolved diversity of positions. Koontz's typology is of the latter sort, though he is concerned to avoid misrepresenting the different positions that cluster under the label "Christian nonviolence." Nevertheless, how we define alternative types of ethical thinking about war and peace can significantly structure the ensuing conversation. Different typologies of pacifism project different conversations about war and peace.

If the conversation is framed as one between just war thinking and Christian pacifism, it is likely to proceed with advocates for just war focusing attention on Christian pacifists—as if *they* were the problem— while neglecting the challenge posed by other kinds of thinking about war and peace, such as "holy war" thinking, political realism, and Rambo-style militarism. But one can also frame the war/peace conversation in terms of a quite different typology, one designed to clarify the areas of theological agreement and disagreement that exist within a given tradition of Christian nonviolence.[4] In the former case, the conversation will be one that is focused on the responsibilities of citizen-leaders in relation to the state. In the latter, the typology points toward a conversation in which the identification of different types of peace theology is preliminary to developing a theological consensus (within the religious tradition) that can, in turn, lead to more articulate ways of representing Christian pacifism in ecumenical and political contexts.

In short, the usefulness of a typology of the ethics of war and peace depends upon which conversation is in view and which kind of conflict of interpretations is being assessed. It is a mistake to assume that there is one principle of classification that will sort everything out for us. The interpretive conflicts internal to particular traditions of moral thinking generate one kind of moral argumentation and disputation; conflicts between ethical traditions generate another. For this reason, Koontz's discussion, which seeks to represent Christian nonviolence in a dialogue between different perspectives, is less nuanced, theologically speaking, than were he to address the topic in the context of a debate about Mennonite peace theologies. But the conversation with other viewpoints implicit in Koontz's chapter has its own coherence insofar as it allows for honest disagreements over how to characterize the similarities and differences between perspectives.

Given his assignment, it is hardly an accident that Koontz has structured the conversation as he has. The threefold typology of Christian nonviolent perspectives—pacifism, abolitionism, and nonviolent resistance—serves several purposes in his argument. First, he uses it to describe an array of approaches, some explicitly grounded in theological conceptions and others more pragmatically or politically grounded. He does not attempt to identify conceptual differences within an array of historical categories. Instead, the typology merely describes a number of positions that have taken shape in relation to one another. In doing so, it hides important differences. In the case of abolitionism, for example, Koontz's formulation mixes two conceptually distinct approaches, one represented by what might be called "world order visionaries" like Erasmus, the other by the isolationist abolitionism of many liberal Protestant pacifists during the 1920s and 1930s. The moral arguments relied upon in each case are logically separable, however much these approaches may resemble each other in other ways.

Second, Koontz explicates the theological context of a single position within this typology—what he calls "Christian pacifism." But the typology permits him to include all three types of Christian nonviolence in answering the topic-related questions—questions that are particularly awkward to address from within the theologically grounded perspective of Christian pacifism.

It is important to be clear about what Koontz is and is not doing with his typology of Christian nonviolence in relation to his larger argumentative strategy. He does not use it to present certain categories as universally applicable and thus to delegitimize all forms of pacifism as "irresponsible." What he is doing is more nearly the opposite of such a strategy. Implicit in his chapter, however, and coinciding with his use of the typology, is a bid for respect from various interlocutors whom he identifies in relation to questions posed by just war theorists and realists. By arguing that if one wants to understand why some people are Christian pacifists, one must enter their world and on their own terms, Koontz appeals to his audience to set aside their assumption that pacifists are irrelevant or dangerous characters. Here we see him engaging in a subtle form of apologetic argument. In effect, Koontz is saying to his readers: "I want you to understand why it is that you cannot understand what I am talking about."

Must One Be a Pacifist to Understand Pacifist Arguments?

Had the conversation in which Koontz finds himself been structured by a different set of questions, he might not have felt the need to employ this kind of indirect apologetic. But the questions he critiques do not lend themselves to providing a "thick description" of his own theologically based pacifism. Accordingly, Koontz prefaces his discussion of these questions with a brief commentary on the significance of the kinds of question we permit to guide our thinking about the issues of war and peace. And he is right to do so, because, too often, the discussion of war and peace is conducted without awareness of how the questions we ask provide an overriding authority for some modes of ethical inquiry while they reject others. There is, for example, a tendency to assume that "consequentialist" questions are somehow definitive, and that moral viewpoints that reject consequentialist reasoning are, for that reason, defective.

But it is one thing to contest the adequacy of the questions being asked, and quite another to present the case for Christian nonviolence in a way that implies that one must be a pacifist to understand pacifist arguments. In this respect, Koontz appears to have overstated the incommensurability, philosophically speaking, of pacifist and nonpacifist conceptions of peace. It is unfortunate that he largely ignores the historical character of those conceptions of war and peace that are part of the wider family of Christian nonviolence, because the very shape of the conversation in which these conceptions have emerged has changed. To be precise, several changes have occurred during the past century in the way moral arguments about war and peace are engaged—changes in moral thinking and social analysis that also inform Koontz's own argument. Though no single factor has determined these changes, there is a sense in which Christian pacifists have repeatedly had to face interpretations of their stance that are unfavorable, even if not always tendentious. Nowhere is this more true than in the North American context, where Christian nonviolence is frequently seen as irresponsible unless its advocates assent to the interpretation of their conception of peace as apolitical.

Let us consider an example. On the eve of the Second World War, Reinhold Niebuhr provided an influential argument for "Why the Christian Church Is Not Pacifist."[5] As John Howard Yoder has noted, the impact of Niebuhr's argument that nonviolence is morally and politically irresponsible can be illustrated in the ways that Christian pacifists began to articulate their position at mid-century. Many Christian pacifists simply accepted the Niebuhrian distinctions between nonresistance and nonviolence without raising questions about the theoretical basis of such classifications. Although Niebuhr's conception of politics and its corollary dichotomy between "moral man and immoral society" have been criticized, theologically as well as politically, his "Christian realism" remains potent enough to inform a number of recent attacks upon Christian pacifists.[6]

Those Christian pacifists who have contested Niebuhrian-style polemics have shifted the burden of proof back to those in the just war and realist camps who characterize Christian nonviolence as irresponsible. Yoder, for example, has avoided conceding the authority of just war reasoning, and instead has used particular wars to test the adequacy of the idea of the "justifiability" of warmaking.[7] Others have adopted what might be called a "contrarian" approach, one that presumes that just war arguments mask ends other than that of restoring peace and that such arguments reflect an unannounced political agenda. This approach is contrarian, not only because of the combative way it rejects the legitimacy of just war arguments, but also because it questions the very framework within which the discussion of war and peace proceeds.

This contrarian tendency has been particularly noticeable in the wake of the 1991 Persian Gulf War. Stanley Hauerwas's "Whose Justice? Which Peace?" is illustrative.[8] Dissenting from the just war premises of the other essays on the morality of the Gulf War in the collection in which his appears, Hauerwas argues that "there is much more to the question of the moral evaluation of war than the question of whether a war conforms to just war criteria" and calls attention to assumptions that have dictated what are "widely regarded as the relevant questions for assessing the morality of the Gulf War." Having raised the issue of meta-ethical criteria, he goes on to argue that

> it makes all the difference who is asking questions about the "justice" of war and for what reasons. When questions of who and why are ignored, the history that has shaped just war reflection as well as the conflicting histories of the Gulf War are assumed irrelevant.

The Gulf War was fought by those for whom it was actually a kind of holy war, but who "found it useful to justify it on just war grounds."[9]

Though Koontz avoids Hauerwas's combative tone, he, too, adopts a contrarian strategy. Both argue that Christian identity is not only important for grasping the moral significance of Christian nonviolence, but further, that it is necessary for understanding. At their best, these arguments invite nonpacifist readers to consider the possibility that "the emperor has no clothes," but they also say, "I want you to understand why you cannot understand me." Though provocative, this stance does not invite further conversation—unless the nonpacifist reader is already disposed to convert to this position! Arguably, then, the contrarian style of argument can be taken to suggest that there is no reason for nonpacifists to engage in conversation with Christian nonviolence. By assuming antipathy on the part of the conversational partner, the contrarian overstates the incommensurability of moral arguments and thereby (prematurely) suggests that various kinds of dialogue, which may or may not develop, will *not* occur.

Oddly enough, Koontz's rhetoric stresses incommensurability while it appears to offer his readers a hermeneutical key to unlock the mystery that lies at the heart of Christian pacifism. Though he invites conversation to explore its disagreements with other viewpoints, Koontz severely limits that conversation by offering an account of Christian pacifism that itself presumes an ethical dualism based upon a "two kingdoms" political ethic. His argument differs from Hauerwas's inasmuch as Koontz identifies with the reader's incredulity instead of indicting the opponent's integrity. At the same time, Koontz goes beyond inviting the reader to consider the possibility that "the emperor has no clothes" to offer a theological assessment of the difference between those who inhabit the "house of love" (Christian pacifists) and those who dwell in the "house of fear" (realists and just warriors).

Nowhere is this tension between inviting conversation and rejecting it more prominent than in his sermon, "Blessed Be the King." The sermon provides outsiders with a glimpse of the theological conceptions underlying Christian pacifist discourse by illuminating the difference between what (from a Christian point of view) is the "false hope" that sees political and social progress narrowly in terms of the application of the power of the state, and what is an authentically *Christian* hope that condemns as false and even idolatrous conceptions of power that presume to eliminate the necessity of suffering.

When Koontz turns to the questions whose relevance he disputes, it is clear that the sermon not only has served the purpose of elucidating the theological warrants that underlie Christian pacifist claims about war and peace, but also has revealed the ideological conflicts that make it difficult for these claims to be registered as politically significant. For, he argues, the claim of "necessity" makes sense only in relation to ends that are deemed more important than keeping one's moral commitments. Unlike the political realist—or indeed, anyone else holding a consequentialist ethic—the Christian pacifist is free of the necessity of worrying about what is in God's hands, free from the burden of making history come out right. We can have no duty to "help God out" by violating God's moral standards.

In this context, Koontz's use of Henri Nouwen's image of inhabitants of the "house of fear" versus those of the "house of love" provocatively juxtaposes alternative worldviews. But it is not obvious that the contrast between the "house of love" and the "house of fear" is as sharp as this would imply. It may be true that "fearful questions never lead to love-filled answers," but there are many kinds of "fearful questions," and not all such questions are necessarily prompted by the same kinds of fear. To refine the image of the two houses, then, we might agree that not all rooms in the house of fear are equally well-furnished, morally speaking. Whatever may be said about the differences between just war and pacifism, for example, in contrast to *realpolitik* or "the blank check," just warriors and pacifists agree that the burden of proof is upon those who choose war. Both reject the primacy of consequentialist reasoning in making political as well as personal decisions. By putting political realism and just war thinking in the same house, Koontz exaggerates the moral differences that separate natural law and Christian pacifism while he neglects the differences between natural law and political realism. Because Koontz's image of the two houses exaggerates the contrast between pacifist and anticonsequentialist moral outlooks, it arbitrarily limits the possibilities for conversation between their adherents.

Conflicting Interpretations of Christian Nonviolence

The bold contrast that Koontz draws between those who have converted to the Christian position and those who have not reflects a broader conception of dualist ethics, one that sharply distinguishes the moral obligations of the Church from those of the (unconverted) world. According to the dualist conception, Koontz argues, those "committed to the way of Christ" are expected to live differently from those in "the world." The dualist conception therefore leaves open the possibility of a certain "quasi-legitimate" justification for war, provided it is chosen and waged not by Christians but by the state. This view of the "higher responsibility" of Christians has its origins in another ongoing conflict of interpretations within a number of Protestant traditions. As Koontz observes, the conflict arises out of two closely related scriptural passages, St. Paul's Letter to the Romans 12:9–21 and 13:1–7, and is dramatically evident in the 1527 Schleitheim Confession: "The sword is an ordering of God outside the perfection of Christ. It punishes and kills the wicked and protects the Good."

According to some historians of Christianity, the idea that there are different expectations for those who are part of the covenant of Christianity and those "outside the perfection of Christ" crystallized only at Schleitheim in 1527; others hold that the idea emerged long before this time. But even the "Schleitheim interpretation" has not always been

articulated with the same political assumptions in mind, either by
Christian pacifists in the Anabaptist-Mennonite tradition or by those in
the broader tradition of Protestant Christianity. Just as not all American
Mennonites have articulated their peace witness within the rhetoric of
"nonresistance"—some nineteenth-century Mennonites preferred the
older vocabulary of "defenseless" (*wehrlos*) witness, for example—not
all Christian pacifists have felt it necessary to adopt ethical dualism as
part of the rationale for their Christian pacifist stance.

Christian pacifists both inside and outside the Anabaptist tradition
who have adopted some version of ethical dualism with respect to the
state often cite the Schleitheim formulation as if it were applicable to
every situation of pacifist engagement with the state. But Yoder has
cautioned Christian pacifists about the conceptual error of "solidifying
the dualism" of the Schleitheim statement, arguing that the Schleitheim
formulation should not be treated as if it were a "systematic or comprehensive political ethic."[10] On the contrary, the Schleitheim formulation
represents a "tense missionary dualism" that became necessary in a situation marked by a refusal to tolerate the witness of Anabaptists in the
world in which they found themselves at the time. And, as Yoder goes
on to argue elsewhere, this particular response needs to be seen in light
of the "variety of logically possible positions which could be taken on
the question of the sword in the context of the Reformation debates."[11]

When this kind of historical analysis is performed, it becomes clear
that the "two kingdoms" dualism later generations have articulated in
relation to the Schleitheim Confession is not the only kind of response
consistent with the Christian Bible. The dualistic interpretation also
overlooks some of the most salient features of the political situation the
Anabaptists who gathered at Schleitheim were facing. An excessive
focus on Schleitheim can distort the conversation that Christian pacifists have with nonpacifists precisely to the degree that it assumes that
the Christian witness to the state always takes shape within one kind of
conversation. But this is not the case, as the existence of other kinds of
Christian nonviolence demonstrates.

The writings of James Douglass, a Catholic lay theologian and anti-
nuclear peace activist, offer a version of Christian nonviolence that is
not structured by ethical dualism and that therefore illustrates wider
possibilities for conversation between Christian nonviolence and the
nonpacifist traditions. Douglass's reflections on peace grow out of his
training in natural law and his subsequent conviction that the prospect
of nuclear war has made warfare pointless as a mode of settling differences. Douglass therefore bases his argument in *The Non-Violent Cross*
in part on just war grounds. But he also anchors it in the more elastic
conception of peace found in the papal encyclical *Pacem in Terris* of John
XXIII, which Douglass admires for its pervasive, though admittedly

undefined, conception of nonviolence. As he notes, though the encyclical is addressed to the Church, it is also "addressed far beyond the visible church," that is, to the larger world it may eventually help to transform.[12] Douglass acknowledges the many criticisms of *Pacem in Terris*, including those of Protestant moralists like Reinhold Niebuhr, but he resists Niebuhr's complaint that the encyclical lacks realism, and he even provides natural law arguments for what he sees as a coming "revolution of peace" through Gandhian nonviolence.

In retrospect, Douglass's arguments for the "transformation of man" and the "revolution of peace" seem careless and overstated. They do, however, provide an interesting specimen of a conception of Christian nonviolence that is not determined by the kind of ethical dualism to which Koontz is committed. For though Douglass's chapter on "Christians and the State" discusses the issues presented by Romans 13:1–7, it is clear that his conception of peace is not determined by the interpretation of this passage. There are two reasons why this is the case. First, Douglass sharply distinguishes between applying such a passage in Paul's time and the various "two kingdoms" interpretations of the passage articulated by Protestants like Martin Luther. Second, following Karl Rahner, he contends that the Church can be both catholic and in diaspora at the same time. Therefore, the Church's sphere of peacemaking is not confined to the community of belief, but takes the form of a "decisive confrontation" with the world in which the Church embodies the "cross of suffering redemptive love." In the end, then,

> there can be no ethical justification even for the governing authorities bearing the sword, because the only valid ethic is that revealed by Christ in the Gospel, a love that does no wrong to a neighbor.[13]

Thus, though tension between the peace of the Christian community and the so-called peace of the world continues, it is a mistake to attribute to St. Paul a "responsibility ethic" based on Romans 13:1–7.

Most observers would agree that Douglass's conception of peacemaking is not representative of contemporary Catholic thinking on war and peace. This may be more true of American Catholicism than of the Vatican itself, however. According to a 1992 editorial in *La civiltà Cattolica*, the Jesuit magazine published in Rome, the transformation of warfare in the modern era "obliges us to consider arguments for war from a completely new perspective." The editorial argues that Roman Catholic thinking on the ethics of war and peace has shifted significantly during the course of the century. The Catholic Church has formally condemned war in four important documents between 1920 and 1991. More and more, the Church "has absolutely condemned war and moved beyond the old arguments for the `just war' or `holy war' in defense of the faith," and "this attitude indicates an advance in Christian

conscience regarding the absolute immunity of war." The editorial discusses the 1991 Persian Gulf War as the principal example of the way an
"ideology of war" has co-opted just war theory in the midst of the
transformation of modern warfare. The author concludes:

> The theory of the just war is indefensible and has been abandoned. In
> reality—with the sole exception of a purely defensive war against acts of
> aggression—we can say that there are no "just wars" and there is no "right"
> to wage war.

Accordingly, Roman Catholics are called upon to "unmask" warmaking, even as they engage in positive efforts to make peace between individuals and nations.[14]

Like Douglass's argument in *The Non-Violent Cross*, that put forward
in *La civiltà Cattolica* posits no ethical dualism. The Church's pastoral
concern is addressed not only to its own members but also to non-
Christian citizens and governments, for whom it is presented as normative, on natural law grounds. In this respect, the editorial remains
squarely within the mainstream of Roman Catholic moral theology. But
by historicizing the debate about the justifiability of war and thereby
going beyond secular interpretations of just war thinking, the editorial
reasserts a broadly and distinctively Christian way of thinking about
the ethics of war and peace. Clearly, both these examples of Catholic
revisionism converge with the concerns of Christian pacifism, even
though they are argued from within a version of natural law ethics.
Both share Koontz's wish to articulate an ethic of peace that does not
rest on worldly conceptions of truth and power, but they do not share
Koontz's ethical dualism. This dualism disallows the possibility, yet to
be fully explored, of a convergence between pacifism and natural law.

Kingship and Martyrdom

These disputes about ethical dualism raise further questions about the
alternative conceptions of truth and power implicit in Koontz's treatment of the "kingship" of Christ in his Palm Sunday sermon. Recall
that, in this sermon, Koontz poses a question to his congregation: "How
can we overcome fear, accept the possibility of the cross, live lives
which are, paradoxically, both fully vulnerable, and wonderfully powerful?" The answer he offers is specified in terms of discovering the
reality of the kingship of Christ:

> I believe that the key lies in really seeing, in really *believing*, that Jesus is
> King. Though we take for granted the Kingship of Jesus and, unlike the

people of his time, understand that his Kingship is radically different from that of worldly kings, I wonder if we *really* understand, I wonder if we *really* believe.

As we have already noted, Koontz here attempts to identify the heart of the mystery of Christian pacifism for his readers while he also stresses the ultimate difference between those who "really believe" and those who do not.

The Acts of the Apostles suggest that the earliest Christian communities really did believe that Jesus Christ was their king (Hebrew "messiah"). Christians were characterized by the officials of the Roman empire as those "who have turned the world upside down . . . acting against the decrees of Caesar, saying there is another king, King Jesus" (Acts 17:6, 7). The early Christians were viewed with suspicion precisely because their witness (Greek *martyria*) called into question the political conceptions of truth and power upon which the Roman empire was built. Christian witness was often mistaken for atheism by those who did not recognize the King to whom they bore witness.

The example of Dirk Willems, the Dutch martyr, which Koontz discusses at two points in his chapter, also illustrates the alternative conceptions of truth and power toward which Koontz gestures. From the perspective of natural law, Willems's martyrdom seems unnecessarily heroic, an act of supererogation, and therefore not the kind of thing that should be regarded as a duty for everyone.[15] But his act becomes morally significant when placed in the context of a Christian understanding of the conduct required of those who bear witness to "King Jesus"—an understanding that places the meaning of history *not* in the progression of political actions, narrowly understood, but in the acts of God in the world in behalf of God's people, the Church.

But even more important than the striking difference in assessments evoked by this particular example of martyrdom is the overriding question of the relationship between conceptions of war and peace and conceptions of truth. As Koontz notes at the end of his essay, Dirk Willems's martyrdom cannot be detached from the broader framework of sixteenth-century theological disputes, as these disputes were handled in the political sphere. As he pointedly observes, Willems's death "was part of a `debate' over religious truth" in a society in which people believed that truth could be discovered through torture. Pushing his point even further, Koontz asserts that with regard to how we go about settling questions of right between nations, we have hardly progressed beyond this level.

Koontz also calls attention to the presumptions about power in the conflict of truth claims between the "defenders of civilization" and "barbarians." His eloquent homiletic conclusion demonstrates the difference that is made when one's analysis of human conflict is framed by the theological and historical vision of "the power of the cross through which Jesus disarmed the principalities and the powers." But when Koontz concludes dramatically that the barbarians are not "out there," that "we are the barbarians," he seems to have lost sight of the difference he previously posited between those who really believe and those who do not. If we are all barbarians, it would appear that even those who inhabit the "house of love" are possessed by fear.

This point brings us back to nonpacifist suspicions about the legitimacy of conceptions of truth and power embedded in the claims of Christian nonviolence. The presence of such suspicions cannot help but have implications for conversations between Christian pacifists and those whose thinking about war and peace is shaped by other ethical traditions. Yet, as different as Koontz's conceptions of truth and power are from those implicitly or explicitly present elsewhere in this volume, there is no reason to believe that the other contributors (or the readers of this book) cannot grasp the point Koontz is making in his sermon. Whether they will be persuaded to convert to Christianity (or to Christian pacifism) is another question! The point, however, is not to suggest that such an illustration must persuade. It is enough merely to show that the moral action embodied in Dirk Willems's martyrdom can be made intelligible. In this as in other matters, advocates of Christian nonviolence have little choice but to be patient as well as persistent in offering their nonviolent witness to the state.

Conversation Despite Interpretive Conflict

It is characteristic of the Christian pacifist understanding of itself that it should seek conversation with "the world" for the purpose of converting the world to the way of Christ. Once this purpose is understood, we are in a better position to assess the claim that pacifist and nonpacifist arguments are incommensurable.

As we have already observed, one of the conceptual tensions at the heart of Koontz's chapter is the relationship between the ideas of truth and power as these are understood within the "house of love" and the "house of fear." Here it may help to call attention to the practical and theological importance of the relationship between the *evangelical* practice of "speaking truth to power" as a way of engaging the world nonviolently, and the *ecclesial* practice of peacemaking between Christians, a practice identified in the writings of sixteenth-century radical reformation as the "Rule of Christ." Explicating these practices in relation to one another will help us see how the conversation between Christian pacifists and others might be structured in a way that escapes Koontz's overly hermeneutical contrast.

Most adherents to the tradition of Christian nonviolence agree that "speaking truth to power" is an integral part of Christian witness to the state. But there is disagreement about whether Christians can ever legitimize particular instances of violence by the state. Christians, it sometimes is urged, should focus their efforts on "living at peace with all people" insofar as this is possible (and here, as in so many things, we have to confront the limits of our moral imaginations), leaving vengeance as well as "making history come out right" in the hands of God (Rom. 12:9–21). In this respect, I would agree with Yoder's rather sparse, untheorized account of Christian witness to the state, which assumes that there is no such thing as "the state" per se.[16] There are simply states as we encounter them in particular historical situations. Just as we do not have to regard the Church's situation before the world to be, in all cases, like that presumed by the Schleitheim Confession, so we are not stuck with the "worldly authorities" described in Romans 13:1–7 or, for that matter, with "the beast" of Revelation 13:1–18.

Christian engagement with political authority must allow for other possibilities, including the possibility (however unlikely it may be in most instances) that the principalities and powers might join in acknowledging the Lordship of Jesus Christ and alter their practices accordingly. After all, according to the vision of the end of history described in Revelation 5:1–14, the procession of Christian worship will ultimately include every creature on earth. Christian pacifists should therefore not underestimate the political power of celebrating the Lordship of Christ. After all, this is the truth to which a story like that of Dirk Willems's attests.

Meanwhile, Christian pacifists have more than enough to do making a different kind of peace, one structured by a different set of questions, than the kind of peace sought by most governments most of the time. Here, too, I would join with Yoder in arguing that it is possible to "translate" or render intelligible "before the eyes of the watching world" specifically Christian conceptions of peace by focusing on particular practices.

Space permits only one illustration of how this works. The early Anabaptists received their name because they rebaptized people as an act of resistance to the Constantinian alliance between Church and State. But it is arguably the practice of the "Rule of Christ" that was more provocative politically because it located the source of authority in God's will as manifested in the practices of the community of Christian believers rather than in those of the "tax collector." The "Rule of Christ" is also known as "binding and loosing," after Matthew 18:15–20:

> If another member of the church sins against you, go and point out the fault when the two of you are alone. If the member listens to you, you have regained that one. But if you are not listened to, take one or two others along with you, so that every word may be confirmed by the evidence of two or three witnesses. If the member refuses to listen to them, tell it to the church; and if the offender refuses to listen even to the church, let such a one be to you as a Gentile and a tax collector. Truly I tell you, whatever you bind on earth will be bound in heaven, and whatever you loose on earth will be loosed in heaven. Again, truly I tell you, if two of you agree on earth about anything you ask, it will be done for you by my Father in heaven. For where two or three are gathered in my name, I am there among them.

These practices concretely embodied a different kind of political power and a different kind of truth-telling, both of which were intelligible only in relation to the life, ministry, death, and resurrection of Jesus.

The confidence of Christian pacifists in the face of religious repression, including the implied or actual threat of martyrdom, is perhaps best summed up in the sixteenth-century epigram "Truth is unkillable."[17] The immediate context of at least one famous use of this provocative declaration was an explication in the 1520s by Balthasar Hubmaier of "binding and loosing" as a practice of dialogue and discipline, centered in a congregation of Christians, that includes the possibility both of forgiveness and absolution (where repentance is present) and of excommunication (where there is no repentance).[18] This practice, which over time has taken several different shapes, is central to the tradition of Christian discipleship identified with the Anabaptists and with the Mennonite Church in particular.

More recently, Stanley Hauerwas has called attention to the moral significance of the ecclesial virtue of "peacemaking" described in Matthew 18:15–22. As the following passage suggests, this practice of peacemaking projects conceptions of truth and power that differ dramatically from those presupposed by nonpacifists:

> If peacemaking as a virtue is intrinsic to the nature of the church, what are we to say of those outside the church? First, I think we must say that it is the task of the church to confront and challenge the false peace of the world which is too often built on power more than truth. To challenge the world's sense of peace may well be dangerous, because often when sham peace is exposed it threatens to become more violent. The church, however, cannot be less truthful with the world than it is expected to be with itself. If we are less truthful we have no peace to offer to the world.

Secondly, Christians are prohibited from ever despairing of the peace possible in the world. We know that as God's creatures we are not naturally violent nor are our institutions unavoidably violent. As God's people we have been created for peace. Rather, what we must do is to help the world find the habits of peace whose absence so often makes violence seem like the only alternative. Peacemaking as a virtue is an act of imagination built on long habits of the resolution of differences. The great problem in the world is that our imagination has been stilled, since it has not made a practice of confronting wrongs so that violence might be avoided. In truth, we must say that the church has too often failed the world by its failure to witness in our own life the kind of conflict necessary to be a community of peace. Without an example of a peacemaking community, the world has no alternative but to use violence as a means to settle disputes.[19]

Hauerwas's way of making the point is useful for spelling out another set of conceptual problems embedded in Koontz's ethical dualism. First, whatever we may make of various attempts to provide empirical assessments of human disorder, theologically speaking, Christians have a stake in arguing that human beings are not naturally violent. Accordingly, while we recognize the "fallenness" of the world, we must nevertheless call the world to be that which God has created it to be, and part of what it means to communicate this more positive assessment of "the world as it was created to be" is to avoid resigning ourselves to the "fallenness" of the world.

Second, had Koontz paid even more attention than he does to the *practices* of peacemaking, he would not have overstated the hermeneutical contrast between Christian pacifism and other ethical perspectives. For political practices like "the Rule of Christ" ("binding and loosing") can provide, as Yoder puts it, "analogies for conflict resolution, alternatives to litigation, and alternative perspectives on `corrections.'"[20] In other words, the kind of ecclesial practice described in Matthew 18:15–20 can "function as a paradigm for ways in which other social groups may operate. . . . People who do not share the faith or join the community can learn from them."[21]

Finally, as Hauerwas suggests, the absence of alternative forms of peacemaking helps to explain why many people "in the world" find the Christian pacifist understanding of war/peace ethics implausible. In the end, conceptions of war and peace can only be fully explicated in relation to the practices that embody these conceptions. From a Christian pacifist perspective, the resolution of interpretive conflicts is ultimately subject to the persuasion that may or may not occur when Christian pacifists encounter those who understand the ethics of war and peace differently. Following Hauerwas's argument about the political significance of the practice of peacemaking, the best way to begin the conversation with the adherents of nonpacifist traditions as they encounter Christian pacifists may be to point to practices like "the Rule of Christ." If in the process these other traditions are able to understand the connection between this practice and the theological claim that the Lordship of Jesus Christ applies not only over the Church but over "the principalities and powers," and over history itself, then we will have succeeded in starting a conversation about Christian peacemaking in the midst of Christian pacifism's ongoing conflict of interpretations.[22]

Notes

1. The best discussion of the ethical significance of religious convictions is James William McClendon, Jr. and James M. Smith, *Convictions: Defusing Religious Relativism*, rev. ed. (Valley Forge, Pa.: Trinity Press International, 1994).

2. Awareness of the importance of interpretive issues occurs as early as Reinhold Niebuhr's *An Interpretation of Christians Ethics* (New York: Harper and Brothers, 1935). For discussion of the many ways in which the question of hermeneutics haunts contemporary Christian ethics, see William B. Schweiker's essay, "Interpretation, Teaching and American Theological Ethics," *Annual of the Society of Christian Ethics 1990* (Washington, D.C.: Georgetown University Press, 1990), 284.

3. See, for example, John Howard Yoder, *Nevertheless: Varieties of Religious Pacifism* (Scottdale, Pa.: Herald Press, 1971; rev. ed. 1992).

4. See, for example, the collection of articles in *Mennonite Peace Theology: A Panorama of Types*, edited by John Richard Burkholder and Barbara Nelson Gingrich and available from the Mennonite Central Committee Peace Office in Washington, D.C.

5. See the first essay in Reinhold Niebuhr's *Christianity and Power Politics* (New York: Charles Scribner's Sons, 1940), 1–32.

6. The most recent of these Niebuhrian attacks on Christian pacifism is Guenter Lewy's *Peace and Revolution: The Moral Crisis of American Pacifism* (Grand Rapids, Mich.: Eerdmans, 1988).

7. See, for example, Yoder's *When War Is Unjust: Being Honest in Just War Thinking* (Minneapolis: Augsburg, 1984), and his "Just War Tradition: Is It Credible?" in *Christian Century* 108 (13 Mar. 1991): 295.

8. Stanley Hauerwas, "Whose Justice? Which Peace?" in David DeCosse, ed., *But Was It Just?* (New York: Bantam Doubleday Dell, 1992), 83–105.

9. Hauerwas, "Whose Justice? Which Peace?" 83, 84, 88.

10. John Howard Yoder, *Christian Attitudes to War, Peace and Revolution: A Companion to Bainton* (Elkhart, Ind.: Associated Mennonite Biblical Seminaries, 1983), 193.

11. See Yoder's "Anabaptism and the Sword Revisited: Systematic Historiography and Undogmatic Nonresistance," *Zeitschrift für Kirchengeschichte* 85

(1974): 270–83. I am indebted to John Richard Burkholder for calling this comment to my attention. See Burkholder's "Mennonite Peace Theology: Reconnaissance and Exploration," *Conrad Grebel Review* 10 (1992): 264, esp. n. 13.

12. James W. Douglass, *The Non-Violent Cross: A Theology of Revolution and Peace* (London: Macmillan, 1966), 83.

13. Douglass, *Non-Violent Cross*, 205, 207.

14. An English translation of "Modern War and the Christian Conscience," originally published in *La civiltà Cattolica*, has been published in DeCosse, *But Was It Just?* The quoted passages are from pp. 118, 121, and 123 of this edition. Although the editorials published in *La civiltà Cattolica* are not official statements of the Vatican, they are reviewed by the Vatican Secretariat of State. According to the Rev. GianPaolo Salvini, editorial director of this journal, the article is "not contrary to the mind of the Vatican."

15. Although realists usually regard religious martyrdom as politically irrelevant, on occasion the martyr may be seen as dangerous. In 1993, for example, an exhibit of martyrs' stories scheduled to open at the Smithsonian Institution in Washington, D.C., was abruptly cancelled. The reason? According to museum officials, the public display "threatened national security." The proposed exhibit was to have included life-size illustrations made from surviving copperplate etchings from the 1685 edition of *The Martyrs Mirror of the Defenseless Christians*, among them a picture of Dirk Willems. For an account of the controversy, see Tom Price, "Mennonites Off the Wall," *Christian Century* (14–21 Jul. 1993): 200.

16. John H. Yoder, *The Christian Witness to the State* (Newton, Kans.: Faith and Life Press, 1964), 78, esp. n. 5.

17. For a discussion of the background of this epigram (*Die Warheit ist untödlicht*) and a justification of the way it has been translated, see John H. Yoder and Wayne Pipkin, *Balthasar Hubmaier, Theologian of Anabaptism* (Scottdale, Pa.: Herald Press, 1989), 76–77 n. 10.

18. Balthasar Hubmaier was one of the most articulate sixteenth-century Anabaptists. A theologian whose learned efforts to refute the charges lodged against the Anabaptists led to his own martyrdom on 10 March 1528, Hubmaier argued that Christians should forego violence "for the present," but he also appears to have expected the saints to wield the righteous sword of judgment on their behalf. Yoder and Pipkin, *Balthasar Hubmaier*, 18.

19. Stanley Hauerwas, *Christian Existence Today* (Durham, N.C.: Labyrinth Press, 1988), 95.

20. See John H. Yoder's "Sacrament as Social Process: Christ the Transformer of Culture," *Theology Today* 48, no. 3 (Apr. 1991): 33, 41.

21. Ibid., 41.

22. I am grateful to Ted Koontz, Richard Miller, and Terry Nardin for conversations related to this essay that helped to clarify several conceptual issues. I am also grateful to John Richard Burkholder, Stanley Hauerwas, and John H. Yoder, each of whom supplied me with materials used in this chapter.

Contributors

MICHAEL BANNER is a dean and fellow of Trinity College, Cambridge. He was previously professor in the medical school in the University of Edinburgh, and for ten years F. D. Maurice Professor of moral and social theology at King's College, University of London. His books include *The Justification of Science and the Rationality of Religious Belief.* He has written on the nature of Christian ethics and its relevance to a number of contemporary issues. Some of these essays appear in *Christian Ethics and Contemporary Moral Problems.* With Alan Torrance, he is editor of *The Doctrine of God and Theological Ethics.*

NIGEL BIGGAR is professor of theology and ethics at Trinity College, Dublin, and a recent president of the Society for the Study of Christian Ethics (U.K.). He is the author of *Aiming to Kill: The Ethics of Suicide and Euthanasia; Good Life: Reflections on What We Value Today; The Hastening That Waits: Karl Barth's Ethics;* and *Theological Politics.* He is also editor of *Burying the Past: Making Peace and Doing Justice after Civil Conflict; The Revival of Natural Law: Philosophical, Theological, and Ethical Responses to the Finnis-Grisez School;* and *Reckoning with Barth.*

JOSEPH BOYLE is professor of philosophy at St. Michael's College at the University of Toronto. He has published extensively on applied ethics and moral theory and is co-author with John Finnis and Germain Grisez of *Nuclear Deterrence, Morality and Realism.* A past president of the American Catholic Philosophical Association, much of his work is part of the contemporary effort to understand and develop Catholic natural law theory.

MICHAEL G. CARTWRIGHT is dean for ecumenical and interfaith programs at the University of Indianapolis. He is the author of the book *Practices, Politics, and Performance: Toward a Communal Hermaneutic for Christian Ethics,* and of several articles on biblical hermaneutics and the use of Scripture in Christian ethics. He has also co-edited books on the thought of John Howard Yoder and Stanley Hauerwas.

JOHN A. COLEMAN, S.J., is the Charles Casassa Professor of Social Values at Loyola Marymount University and formerly professor of religion and society at the Graduate Theological Union. His many books include *An American Strategic Theology; One Hundred Years of Catholic Social Teaching; Religion and Nationalism;* and *Globalization and Catholic Social Thought: Promise or Peril?*

JOHN FINNIS is professor of law and legal philosophy at Oxford University, Biolchini Family Professor of Law at the University of Notre Dame, and a fellow of the British Academy. He is the author of *Natural Law and Natural Rights; Aquinas: Moral Political, and Legal Theory; Fundamentals of Ethics; Moral Absolutes;* and (with Joseph Boyle and Germain Grisez) *Nuclear Deterrence, Morality and Realism.*

THEODORE J. KOONTZ is professor of ethics and peace studies at the Associated Mennonite Biblical Seminary. He has served with the Mennonite Central Committee as executive secretary of the peace section and as visiting professor at Silliman University in the Philippines. His publications include articles on Mennonite political thought and conscientious objection.

DAVID LITTLE is Dunphy Professor of the Practice in Religion, Ethnicity, and International Conflict at the Harvard Divinity School. He has also been a senior scholar at the United States Institute of Peace and a member of the U.S. State Department Advisory Committee on Religious Freedom Abroad. His books include *Human Rights and the Conflict of Cultures: Freedom of Religion and Conscience in the West and Islam* (with John Kelsay and Abdulaziz Sachedina); *Religion, Order, and the Law: A Study in Pre-Revolutionary England*; and *Comparative Religious Ethics* (with S. W. Twiss).

RICHARD B. MILLER is the director of the Poynter Center for the Study of Ethics and American Institutions and professor of religious studies at Indiana University. He is the author of *Interpretations of Conflict: Ethics, Pacifism, and the Just War Tradition; Casuistry and Modern Ethics: A Poetics of Practical Reasoning*; and *Children, Ethics, and Modern Medicine*. He has edited *War in the Twentieth Century: Sources in Theological Ethics* and published articles on humanitarian intervention, civic virtue, multiculturalism, medical ethics, and religion and public intellectuals.

JAMES W. SKILLEN, Ph.D. is president of the Center for Public Justice and has directed the Center since 1982. He also edits its quarterly *Public Justice Report*. He is the author most recently of *Pursuit of Justice: Christian-Democratic Explorations* and *With or Against the World? America's Role among the Nations*. The author or editor or more than a dozen books, he regularly writes essays, book reviews, and commentaries for popular magazines and academic journals.

MAX L. STACKHOUSE is the Rimmer and Ruth de Vries Professor of Reformed Theology and Public Life, Princeton Theological Seminary. He is the author or editor of some twenty-two books, including the four-volume *God and Globalization; Covenants and Commitments: Faith, Family, and Economic Life; On Moral Business; Christian Social Ethics in a Global Era; Creeds, Society and Human Rights*; and *Public Theology and Political Economy*.

Index